D1144816

AT THE GOING DOWN OF THE SUN

Love, loss and sacrifice in Afghanistan

GRAHAM BOUND

MONDAY BOOKS

A CIP catalogue record for this title is available from the British Library.

ISBN: 978-1-906308-62-9

Typeset by Elaine Sharples
Printed and bound by CPI Group (UK) Ltd, Croydon, CR0 4YY

www.mondaybooks.com
http://mondaybooks.wordpress.com/
info@mondaybooks.com

Dedicated to the men and women of the British Army, the Royal Marines, the Royal Navy and the Royal Air Force who served in Afghanistan; to their comrades in the Afghan national forces and those of other nations; and, above all, to those who made the ultimate sacrifice.

They went with songs to the battle, they were young,
Straight of limb, true of eye, steady and aglow.
They were staunch to the end against odds uncounted;
They fell with their faces to the foe.

from *For The Fallen* (Robert Laurence Binyon, 1914)

CONTENTS

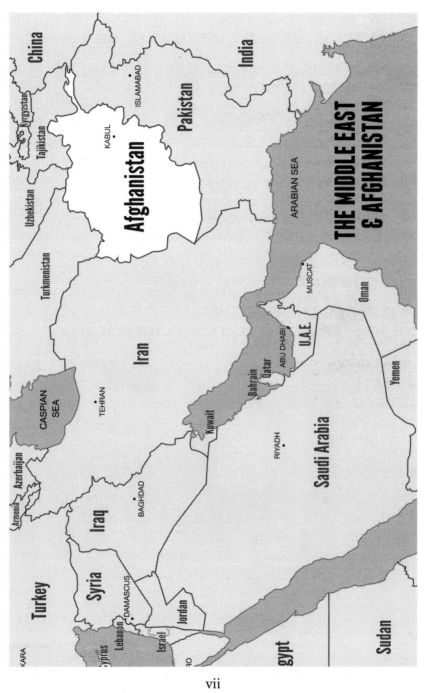

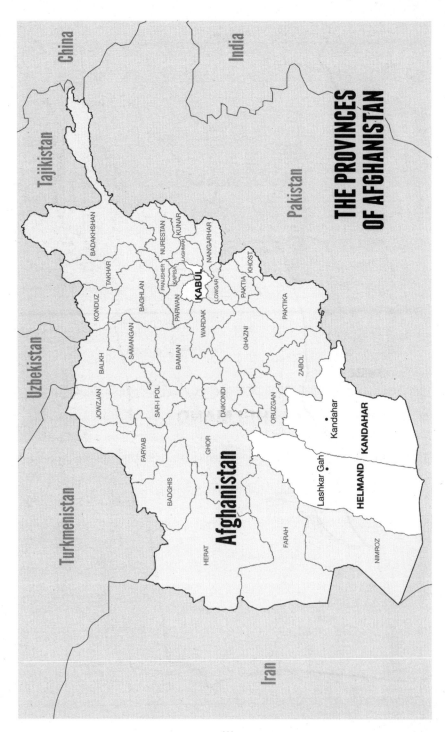

THE PROVINCES OF AFGHANISTAN

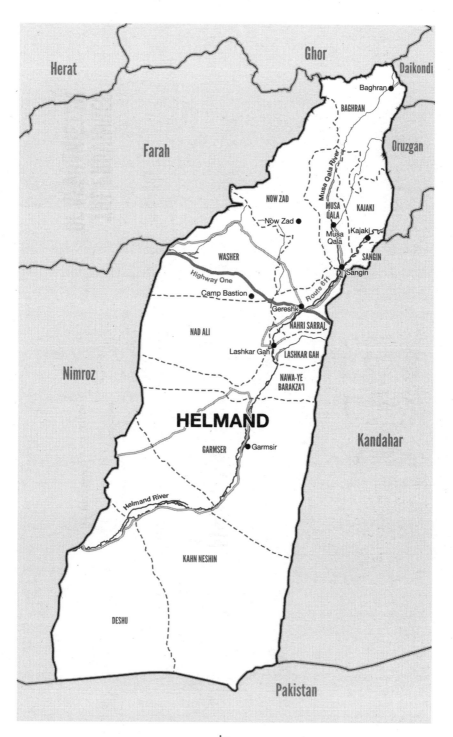

AUTHOR'S NOTE

Show me a hero and I'll write you a tragedy.
F. Scott Fitzgerald

AFGHANISTAN WAS BRITAIN'S longest war of modern times, and yet it was a curiously distant affair.

Since June 2006, when Capt Jim Philippson became the first man to die on 'Operation Herrick', a further 452 British men and women have lost their lives in that distant and benighted land.

How many of their names can we recall?

What do we know of them?

For most civilians, it has been entirely possible to live as though Afghanistan was not happening.

Thousands of miles away, in the scorching heat and swirling dust of a distant outpost, ordinary people from average homes in humdrum towns were fighting for their very lives.

Over here, a recession came and went, and an Olympic games, and a general election. We moaned about the weather, and went on holiday, and watched multiple series of *Big Brother* on the TV. We dreamed our nights away in comfort, while our brothers and sisters bedded down in the dirt and slept fitfully under mosquito nets, dreaming of the fresh horrors awaiting them in the IED-strewn poppy fields and tracks of Helmand.

Perhaps this was only to be expected. Not everyone accepted the premise for the war, much less that it was a matter of national survival.

As servicemen and women were killed, well-meaning official websites released their names, and those of their units, describing the IED attack or firefight in which they had died, and sharing some moving sentences that spoke of the love of comrades and families.

Newspapers, TV and radio reported the deaths, and the streets of Wootton Bassett, and hundreds of home towns and villages, were briefly full of those who wished to pay their respects.

But the conflict was not amenable to easy explanation, so coverage was sporadic; both the war and the media had to move on.

It would be outrageously cynical to suggest that the politicians and military strategists who took us to Afghanistan planned or hoped for this. But, as they tinkered with strategic objectives and fretted over 'mission creep', they may well have been grateful for it.

Had we, by some miracle, been able to know the men and women who died, to feel the grief of their loved ones, and to appreciate fully the tragedy of those lives and ambitions cut short, then those establishment figures might have had much more explaining to do.

The great majority of British forces have now left Afghanistan, and the campaign will soon be slipping into history.

But the stories of the fallen deserve to be known more widely.

They lived full and immensely valuable lives, even before their military careers began.

They were sons and daughters, husbands and wives, brothers, sisters and friends. They were loved and nurtured not just for who they were, and what they had done, but for the promise they held for the future.

In my quest to learn about twenty of these individuals, I interviewed more than seventy-five people who knew them intimately. The questions I put to mothers, fathers, brothers, sisters, husbands, wives, children, friends and comrades were often intrusive and sometimes distressing. I apologised often, but explained that it was necessary to explore such personal stories and delicate emotions. I was met with remarkable tolerance and courtesy. Not one interviewee pulled out of the project, and many endured my questioning with pride. I am immensely grateful to them and very admiring of their courage and dignity.

Various themes emerged, not least among these a sense of bravery and duty. For example, young soldiers – the average age of those killed in Afghanistan was twenty-two – often ensured their friends stayed back while they advanced to check out suspected IEDs (improvised explosive devices). And survivors put their own lives at serious risk to treat comrades and recover bodies. In the remarkable story of Mark Wright, who won a posthumous George Cross, no fewer than five other men were dreadfully injured as they tried to rescue a colleague who had lost a leg in a minefield.

Surprisingly, perhaps, some soldiers said they and their friends found 'kinetic' encounters – firefights – with the enemy to be exhilarating. When insurgents could be taken on in a gun battle, the

British soldiers' training invariably meant that they held the upper hand.

But the IED war was a different matter. In most areas of Helmand, crude bombs polluted the ground. Soldiers knew that death could come at any time. Those who survived an IED blast were sometimes maimed; those who were not often spent the next few hours searching for and bagging up the body parts of their friends.

The terror of IEDs undoubtedly contributed greatly to the disabling post-traumatic stress disorder that some interviewees described. We tell the utterly tragic story of one soldier, LSgt Dan Collins of the Welsh Guards, who was shot and saw friends die in Helmand. He came home physically well but mentally broken. The story of his life, his eventual suicide, and the devastation caused to his family, is heart-rending.

Living and fighting conditions were often appalling. Some military interviewees talked of spending weeks or even months at sweltering patrol bases without helicopter resupply. While ammunition was generally plentiful, food and water often was not.

And yet the sensitivity and humanity of these soldiers survived. In letters and messages home, they clearly tried to hide the grim reality of exhausting patrols, deadly threats, and miserable living conditions. Instead, they wrote of adopting and looking after local stray dogs, and helping Afghan farmers, or of their love for their families and their plans for R&R.

Bereaved families are sustained by the love that permeates these stories. They read and re-read letters and emails and texts sent to them from Helmand. They surround themselves with photos and set up memorial pages on Facebook. Some can talk freely about their lost loved ones, others cannot. Precious personal artefacts and memories are all they have left. For them, remembrance is not limited to one Sunday a year; it is constant and never-ending.

The book's title is borrowed from Robert Laurence Binyon's poem *For the Fallen*, one stanza of which has become the flawlessly beautiful and exquisitely sad articulation of national remembrance.

Every year, at services and ceremonies across the country, men and women listen in thoughtful silence as solitary voices – sometimes, and most movingly, those of men and women who themselves fought –

read the verse which ends with what must be the most evocative phrase in the English language:

> *At the going down of the sun and in the morning,*
> *We will remember them.*

Parents who face the memorials and murmur the last line in response instinctively grip their children's hands just a little tighter in a gesture of love and hope that they will be spared the need to go to war.

No-one can give that assurance. All we can expect – indeed demand – before British men and women are sent to fight overseas is that politicians and strategists carefully weigh up the likely costs in families destroyed and lives cuts short.

These stories are a reminder of how precious those lives are.

Graham Bound
November 11, 2014

CAPTAIN JAMES PHILIPPSON
F (SPHINX) PARACHUTE BATTERY
7th REGIMENT ROYAL HORSE ARTILLERY
JANUARY 13, 1977 – JUNE 11, 2006

JAMES PHILIPPSON WAS a brilliant soldier, a born leader, and the first man to die in action after British troops were sent to Helmand, in southern Afghanistan.

His death was a tragedy – not least because it was eminently avoidable. Capt Philippson was killed on a desperate rescue mission to help other British troops, who had been ambushed by the Taliban and had taken serious casualties. In the pitch dark, and sorely lacking firepower and night vision goggles, he and his colleagues stumbled blind into another enemy position, and found themselves outgunned.

James – Jim to his friends – was shot in the head, and died instantly.

He was in Afghanistan as part of one of the first 'omelettes' – the Operational Mentoring and Liaison Teams (OMLTs) made up of experienced men from various regiments and corps, and whose job it was to train Afghan National Army recruits to the point where they could take control of their country's security. It was a role he was made for. Indeed, he was made for the Army.

'I think it began at the age of five, when James had his first set of camouflage pyjamas,' said his mother, Tricia Quinlan. 'After that, he was always playing soldiers. He loved Action Man. We had strings all over the garden, and he would have his Action Man sliding and abseiling through the bushes and the flowerbeds. I always had to help him get his Action Man into its wetsuit, because it was too fiddly for

1

a small boy. When you look back, his play echoed the things he did for real later.'

'James' nickname *was* Action Man,' said his father, Tony Philippson.

'The first Army he joined was his own. I didn't know it then, but when he was about twelve he and his little band of friends, all dressed in camouflage, would pinch my air rifle and head off for the naturist camps in Bricket Wood. They'd load the gun with some hard little berries, sneak up on the nudists, fire these berries at their bottoms, and then escape on their bikes. So those were his first military exercises. He and his band were straight out of the *Just William* books.'

James Philippson and his brother David, younger by two years, had an idyllic childhood in St Albans, Herts. There were skiing holidays in the winter and lazy summers in Devon in the family's caravan. Every year they would go down to Beer, and Tony would speed around the sea in his little Zodiac boat, towing his giggling sons behind him in an inflatable donut.

'I have such happy memories of those times,' said Tricia. 'The kids were totally free to run and roam. They loved exploring rock pools – I remember James asking me if they had "come up yet", rather than, "Has the tide gone out?" which always struck me as funny. Even when we weren't on holiday, we spent as much time as possible outdoors. I'd pick the boys up from school, and we'd go down to the park for a picnic with Marmite sandwiches. We even went out in the snow, with hot tomato soup.

'He and David were very close, especially as they grew older, though of course they argued and fought sometimes, as young brothers do. I used to say to James, "You want to be careful! David might be bigger than you one day." And David did actually grow to be taller than James, who was always quite a slight child. He was born long and skinny, and he stayed that way. He bulked out a bit in his older years, but he was always very sinewy, even when he was in the Army. Sometimes you see soldiers that are built like brick you-know-whats, but James wasn't like them at all.'

'As a youngster, James really looked after his little brother,' said Tony. 'David didn't learn to walk until after he was two, because James did everything for him. He was very sweet with him, though that changed when they were older. They were like chalk and cheese. David is very mellow and slow to anger, but there was so much aggression in James. I used to be pulling them apart. David had a cutting way with words, James couldn't do that and he would get frustrated. James was about six foot tall and very fit, and his little brother took some time to catch up. Of course, David grew up, and one day I came home to find they'd been fighting in the garden and had wrecked all my flowerbeds. But, from then on, there was peace. They grew closer and closer as they got older, and David was devastated by his brother's death.'

Tony and Tricia divorced just as James was sitting his A levels, but he did well and went to Plymouth University. He had been planning to take a gap year, but his mother talked him out of that as she 'didn't like the idea of him wandering about Thailand and Cambodia aged eighteen'.

'He got a 2:1 in Psychology and Applied Economics,' she said. 'That always sounded like a peculiar degree to me, but then in the Army he ended up managing men, so it probably helped him. Mind you, he was captain of his school rugby team from the lower sixth, so he was leading boys older than himself even then.

'Rugby and running were his favourite sports. When I left Tony, I moved into a three-bedroomed house, intending that the boys would come with me. But, due to circumstances, they stayed with their father. I saw them as much as was humanly possible. I'd pick them up from school on a regular basis and take them back to my house. After about six months of difficult times, they began to accept the new situation and, while I can't say that it was all happy families at first, ultimately it was okay. James was particularly into running when he was building up his fitness to pass the Marines' recruitment tests. I remember him ringing me one Sunday morning and saying, "I'm going to run round and see you later." I thought he meant he was going to run round in the car, but he appeared on the doorstep an hour and a bit later, having *literally* run round with forty pounds of bricks on his back in a rucksack.'

James' plan had indeed been to join the Royal Marines after graduation, but he went travelling and found on his return that he had missed the recruitment deadline for that year. He was despondent for a while, but then he learned of the existence of 29 Commando Regiment Royal Artillery, the gunners who support the Royal Marines. He duly went to Sandhurst, commissioned into the Royal Artillery and then passed the All Arms Commando Course, earning the right to wear the famous green beret.

'At the time, Britain wasn't involved in any wars,' said Tricia, 'and it just sounded like a terrifically exciting option. James was very bright, but I couldn't imagine him sitting in an office. His physical side dominated his persona. I saw him change quite quickly at Sandhurst. I remember him showing me how quickly he could get from one end of the house to the other if he marched and swung his arms, and how he suddenly started speaking really loudly. We found that funny, and James himself didn't take anything dreadfully seriously.

'When he passed out, Tony and I hosted a big dinner in a Thai restaurant for him and his friends. There must have been thirty people there. Tony and I had bought him a ceremonial sword as a passing out gift, and I've got a picture of him being handed this and trying hard not to cry. He was really tough, but he could also be emotional.'

James took to military life like the proverbial duck to water. He made many new friends, played a lot of rugby, went skiing, surfing and scuba diving, and was notoriously full of fun. He would regularly gate-crash parties in the guise of Fat Elvis or a pirate; on one such expedition, while dressed as Spiderman, he called in to an off-licence with friends to stock up on provisions, only to find that the shop was being robbed. With help from his mates, James quickly subdued the men. When the local police arrived and took custody of the robbers from 'Spiderman', they were not quite sure whether the whole thing was some sort of practical joke.

His first operational deployment was to Iraq, in preparation for the 2003 invasion. He began his journey to war aboard the flagship HMS *Ark Royal*, but after a few beers one evening he somehow found himself commando-crawling into the Admiral's private cabin, on a top secret mission to capture some of the senior officer's prized toy soldiers. Instead, he was himself caught, red-handed and hiccupping – by the Admiral, no less – and unceremoniously transferred the following morning to the more lowly HMS *Ocean*. News of the escapade quickly travelled throughout 3 Commando Brigade and made James Philippson something of a legend.

The young officer's role in Iraq took him close to enemy lines, calling in artillery fire. He was 'thrilled to bits' with the opportunity, said his mother, by then living in Florida with her second husband, Steve.

'He kept in touch as well as he could,' she said, 'but this was 2003, and email and texting weren't so easy then. So I would get these brief calls: "I'm on the boss's satellite phone, so I haven't got long!" We had CNN on all hours of the day. It was a terrible time, though subsequent events overtook anything that I thought had been terrible in life. Everything paled into insignificance later.'

His parents had one nightmarish moment, when a helicopter carrying some British commandos was shot down, but James was not aboard. He was involved in at least one notable skirmish, when he and others from 29 Cdo, driving Land Rovers and armed with Milan anti-tank missiles, chased off a squadron of T72 tanks outside Basra. But he came home unscathed.

'The grub was so poor out there, and he looked emaciated,' said Tricia. 'But he was alive, and that was what mattered. He'd been promoted to captain, and he had about two thousand photographs, the most wonderful images of aircraft carriers, people, and football games with the locals. He didn't really talk a great deal about what he had experienced. I recall some philosophical chats about what you do if you see your friends killed or injured, but he didn't come back with any scars, mental or physical.'

After Iraq, James transferred from 29 Cdo to the elite 7 Parachute Regiment Royal Horse Artillery (7 RHA). Essentially, he was doing the same job but supporting the Paras instead of the Royal Marines. He had some leave due before he made the switch, so he hitched a lift to Florida on a Royal Navy warship to learn to skydive with the sun on his back.

'We went to meet him at Port Everglades,' said Tricia. 'This ship came sailing in with all the sailors on the deck. I was leaping around, waving like an idiot, thinking, *He'll be so embarrassed if he sees me.* Eventually, the ship docked and he appeared on one of the gangways and gave us this really cool wave. He came ashore and said, "I'm glad you're here, because I haven't got your phone number or your address." He always flew by the seat of his pants. A week later, he'd finished his free-fall course, and was off again.

'Not long afterward, he was posted to the Falklands. Immediately prior to that, he had met a very nice young woman. Typically, just as his heart was on his sleeve, he had to go so far away. That was a hideous piece of luck. Her name was Martha. They got on well, but I wouldn't like to say whether it had a future or not. That's too painful to think about.'[1]

On his return from the Falklands, James and Martha travelled to Portugal, where Tricia and Steve were now living.

'They were there for Mother's Day weekend,' said Tricia. 'We gave them four nights in a hotel right on the beach, near where we live. I remember they would race each other up the steps from the beach. I didn't know at the time that it was going to be his last holiday.'

Unfortunately, the war drum had started beating in earnest earlier that year, though in truth it had been sounding for much longer.

For centuries, Afghanistan had been wracked by internecine strife, and when its various warrior clans were not fighting each other they were banding together to take on foreign invaders. The British went to war there twice in the nineteenth century – largely to keep the Russian tsar's hands off an important gateway to India in the south, through what is now Pakistan – and it was never easy. In 1842, during the first of those campaigns, a 16,000-strong army under Major General Sir William Elphinstone was massacred almost in its entirety in the snowfields between Kabul and Jalalabad (one Englishman, Assistant Surgeon William Brydon, survived). In a harbinger of future actions, they were killed mostly by guerrilla fighters, who took advantage of Afghanistan's remote and difficult terrain to pick them off over many days.

In 1919, after a period of British rule, Afghan independence was declared. There followed a monarchy, which was overthrown by a military coup in 1973, which was itself overthrown by a further coup in 1978, this last carried out by pro-Soviet communists. The following year, the Soviet Union invaded, to prop up its ideological fellow-travellers.

The Soviet occupation lasted a decade, and was resisted by the *mujahideen*, a tribal alliance which was supported by the west (and whose members would in some cases later fight in the ranks of the Taliban). The occupation was characterised by extreme brutality on both sides – captured soldiers could expect to be skinned alive – and some 15,000 Soviet troops and a million or more Afghans died. It ended in 1989 when the USSR, in its own final death throes, pulled out of Afghanistan.

In the post-Soviet period, the country was torn even further asunder – if that were possible – by civil war, until 1996 when the Taliban seized control of Kabul and the majority of the country. An Islamic fundamentalist grouping, known for their strict interpretation of sharia law, they at least brought a semblance of stability for the next five years, though they were opposed by northern tribesmen under the banner of the Northern Alliance.

While the Taliban had little interest in affairs beyond their own borders, they were happy to host other Islamists with wider ambitions. Among these was Osama bin Laden, whose Al Qaeda organisation was allowed to set up training camps in Afghanistan's vast hinterlands. It was from there that the group planned and, in August 1998, carried out the truck bombings of the US embassies in Dar es Salaam, Tanzania, and Nairobi, Kenya. More than two hundred people died and thousands were injured, and then-President Bill Clinton responded by ordering missile strikes on suspected Al Qaeda sites in Afghanistan.

Bin Laden survived those strikes to plan and order his most infamous action, the passenger jet attacks on New York's World Trade Center and the Pentagon on September 11, 2001. That proved the final straw for the Americans. Within weeks of '9/11', US forces had overthrown the Taliban, and special forces troops, including members of the SAS and SBS, were in the mountains hunting bin Laden.

As history records, bin Laden escaped. Most of the Taliban leadership and rank-and-file escaped, too – either by discarding their trademark black garb and melting into the general Afghan civilian population in the south of the country, or by disappearing across the southern border, to Quetta, Pakistan, and its surrounding towns and villages.

More NATO soldiers – operating under ISAF, the International Security Assistance Force established by the United Nations Security Council in December 2001 – arrived over the next few years. They met with increasing resistance, as the Taliban regrouped and launched guerrilla attacks and suicide bombings from over the border. The logical entry point for the men and materiel needed for these attacks was through Helmand – it was far from Kabul, and so the official government writ hardly ran, and its many mountain passes and valleys made it very hard to patrol.

And so it was that, in January 2006, as Capt Jim Philippson was kicking his heels in the Falklands, the-then Defence Secretary, Labour's John Reid, made the fateful announcement that 3,300 British soldiers would be committed to Helmand province on Operation Herrick 4. At the time, Reid said that he would 'be perfectly happy' if British soldiers left 'without firing one shot'. It was a naïve hope, at best; in the year that followed, the troops would fire some four million rounds, and Britain's eight-year war against the insurgency would begin.

As Jim Philippson and his girlfriend enjoyed his final holiday in Portugal that spring, his mother Tricia several times found her son staring out to sea, pondering his future.

'He wasn't apprehensive,' she said. 'But he was clearly wondering what he was going to get into out there. We took them to the airport to fly back to England and there were big hugs goodbye. He was keen to go. And nothing very much had happened before then, so we weren't particularly worried.'

* * *

INITIALLY, AND TO his great disappointment, James Philippson was based in the safety of Camp Bastion[2], far from the roar of the guns and surrounded by miles of guard wire, sangars bristling with machine guns, and flat, featureless desert in every direction, which made any kind of enemy attack almost suicidal.

His enthusiasm for his OMLT task was soon tested. In one phone call home, he told his mother how 'ridiculous' it was that he was being asked to sit in safety instructing an Afghan colonel as to how to converse with his troops and allocate leave time, rather than getting out on the ground and teaching him the finer points of tactics and soldiering. This was not why he had joined the Army.

But Major Jonny Bristow of the Royal Scots, later to become Capt Philippson's immediate superior, *was* out on the ground, and he was not at all happy about it. Maj Bristow – a career infantryman, who had commissioned into the Army in 1992, and had served in Iraq and Northern Ireland – had been sent to FOB [*Forward*

Operating Base] Robinson, named after US special forces SSgt Chris Robinson who had been killed nearby.

'FOB Rob' was just south of the northern Helmand town of Sangin, in which many British servicemen would die. Sangin, a sprawling settlement of stone and mud-built houses, was home to some fourteen thousand souls, and of strategic importance as a gateway to the Helmand river dam at Kajaki[3], further north, which provided both hydro-electric power and irrigation to the valley below.

The locals were not all pleased to see the British. A naturally conservative and tribal people – whose often-longstanding mutual enmities had been deepened by the civil war which had followed the withdrawal of the Soviets in 1989 – they did not welcome interference from outsiders. And, while most were very poor, there were also substantial fortunes at risk. Much of the world's heroin came from the lush opium poppies growing in the fertile 'green zone' along the banks of both the Helmand and the Musa Qala rivers. Sangin stands at the confluence of the two, and was historically a major drugs market.

The Taliban were swimming in this toxic soup, using the town as something of an operations base. The decision had been taken – far too early, in Maj Bristow's view – to send the ANA and their OMLT teachers over there to help 'sort things out', as part of a wider effort involving 3 Para.

'We had thought our unit would just be involved in training and low-intensity activity,' he said. 'Our concept, from the start, was that the Afghans would not deploy on their own. But it never happened that way. There was huge pressure to get the ANA into the field before they were properly trained or equipped. That was morally bankrupt, as far as I was concerned.

'The change of mission came as a complete surprise to us. We told people up the chain of command that the Afghans weren't ready for operations, and that *we* were not equipped or ready for it, either. We lacked equipment across the board, particularly night vision kit. I think we had six sets between us. We had no Minimis or under-slung grenade launchers, which we'd requested. We had a few GPMGs and had scrounged a couple of .50cals, but those could only be used to defend the base because we didn't have the vehicle mounts needed to put them on the WMIKs.

'There is no ambiguity about this. We had flagged up red card issues, and said we were not fit for this mission. We were essentially told, "Tough! Just get on with it!" To a degree, we accepted that. It's how the British Army works: we're always under-resourced and historically we *have* just got on and made the best of it. But still, I was stunned at what we were being asked to do, and at the way people did not listen to us, and I thought it was very wrong.

'We all knew the dangers of this new scenario, as did the Afghans, who were concerned that they were going to be thrown into the fire. But in the end we had no choice. We had to get on with it without the equipment, without the manpower, and without the training.'

By the time they arrived, Sangin was already infamous.

'We had sent an advance party to FOB Robinson,' said Bristow, 'including my ops officer and one of the signallers. While they were there a number of Afghan soldiers were captured, along with two French special forces men[4]. They were mutilated and decapitated and their bodies were just dumped outside the camp. So we were under no illusions about how tough and hostile this place would be.

'Robinson was a large place, with a perimeter of perhaps a couple of kilometres, on some high ground, two to three kilometres from the centre of Sangin. The nearest buildings were probably about five hundred metres away. To the west was Route 611, and beyond that was the river Helmand. Conditions were quite mediaeval. There had been American and Canadian units there before, and they'd built up the defences a bit, but a lot of it was still mud structures. The Afghans slept in huts on the walls, guarding them. I spent the entire three-and-a-half months sleeping on a cam-cot out in the open, although some of the men had air-conditioned containers.

'Our greatest concern was being overrun. A Canadian had been killed during an attack on the base not long before, and it was very hard to defend because the perimeter was so large. The Americans had employed locals to provide security on the perimeter, but we weren't able to maintain that arrangement, because the budget wasn't there from UK PLC, and we had to let them go.

'We were near the bottom of the pecking order as far as the Helmand Task Force[5] was concerned, and the helicopter resupply was very poor. Fortunately, the Americans and Canadians had left a load of stuff, and a few Americans had stayed on at Robinson to sort of oversee the handover. There were three or four of them, working in a similar OMLT role to ours, except that they were training Afghan gunners, with some old Soviet-era artillery pieces. They were incredibly helpful. We pretty much survived on their rations. Somewhat gratuitously, there was also a troop of three [*Royal Artillery*] 105mm light guns with their crews at the FOB, and they had some supplies. We worked very closely with them.

'There were about 120 in the Afghan battalion, which should have been about 500 strong [*the rest had deserted on the way down from Kabul*], and the British force fluctuated between thirty and seventy, including the artillery guys. We were supposed to be training the Afghans – there was no possibility of that – *and* dominating the area through constant patrolling, *and* establishing a platoon house, *and* guarding the FOB. There was huge pressure to get a presence in central Sangin, and a degree of arrogance about it, I felt. It was about wanting the troops to be seen in soft hats, maintaining civil law and order. We thought that was ludicrous, and said so, but early on we did take over a building in the town, and we put four guys in it and a section of ANA. It was crazy, as the Paras later found out. You can't put four blokes in a house in a place like Sangin, and just assume everything will be okay. They were like tethered goats – I was convinced they were all going to be killed, and eventually I pulled them out. I disobeyed orders, basically.'

As Maj Bristow sees it, the whole mission was confused, badly planned, and under-resourced. He received few written orders, and the chain of command was labyrinthine.

'I thought then, and I still think, that much of what we were trying to do just made things worse,' he said. 'One of our first missions was to support the chief of police as he mounted an operation. We found out later that we'd just given him the freedom of movement to go into the centre of town, extort money, and rape some young boys. So all we'd done was upset the status quo.

'We were supposed to be trying to get some stability, but, as far as I could see, we were *de*-stabilising the place. We didn't really even know who the enemy were. We weren't given any intelligence from further up the line. We just knew there were different groups who were vying for power in the area. There was no single enemy, just often-changing groupings and constant unrest.

11

'My men were incredibly concerned, and so was I. We couldn't quite believe what was being expected of us, and we fully expected to end up like the French special forces chaps. Quite often, the Afghans would refuse to go out on patrol, and to be honest I completely understood that, because they had even more issues than we did about lack of equipment and lack of support. There was no planned leave structure for them, no planned rotation – in fact, no plans at all. They were just expected to sit in Sangin indefinitely.'

* * *

CAPT JAMES PHILIPPSON arrived into this somewhat chaotic situation as part of a resupply convoy, which was hit by at least one IED *en route*. The idea was that he would return to Bastion on the next helicopter that came in. But these were few and far between, so he was guaranteed at least some time at Sangin, and almost certainly some action.

'If anyone had wanted to get into the fight, it would have been Jim,' said Maj Bristow. 'He had been given a job he really didn't want to do back in Bastion, and he wanted to fight, although he was pretty amazed at what we were being asked to do. I liked him. He was an in-your-face, punchy guy; fit, strong, focused, and very intelligent. He was a bit prone to moaning, and a bit cynical, but in a good way. Because the unit at the FOB was based on 7 RHA, he knew a lot of the guys. You could see he was popular.'

The OMLT men and their ANA charges gradually settled into an uneasy routine of one or two patrols a day. They were contacted sporadically, and a number of ANA men died, but by the time Capt Philippson arrived there had been no British deaths.

Bristow's men were supported by the gunners at the FOB, who were using hand-launched unmanned aerial vehicles – small, remote controlled drones, equipped with cameras which could send back live images to their operators, and gave the British soldiers some idea of what was happening beyond the wire without having to put men on the ground. Not long after James Philippson's arrival, one of these UAVs crashed on the far side of the Helmand river, an area that was relatively unknown and inaccessible.

'We were patrolling every day, so I essentially reassigned a planned patrol to the area where the UAV had disappeared,' said Maj Bristow. 'It wasn't really about the UAV – they were a nice asset to have, and if the guys found it that was great, but they went down quite often and the loss of another one was not a major drama. Part of the point of the patrols was to go to areas we hadn't been to before – this was an area we hadn't been to before, so it seemed to make sense.'

That patrol was roughly platoon strength, and comprised some Gurkhas – who had recently been sent down in another attempt to establish a patrol house in Sangin itself – three or four OMLT men, and ten or so ANA. They left in the afternoon in a WMIK and a couple of Snatch Land Rovers, and headed across the river. They spent some time looking in vain for the UAV, and were eventually told by locals that the Taliban had taken it away. It was after they returned across the river, with darkness fast approaching, that they were contacted by a large group of enemy fighters. They were quickly pinned down, and a couple of the vehicles were immobilised. The 'scrounged' .50cals would have allowed them to return a decent weight of fire. But those were back at the FOB, because of the lack of vehicle mountings, so they could only reply with less powerful GPMGs and their personal weapons. One soldier – LBdr Tom Mason – was shot through the chest, and rounds were striking all around them and their vehicles.

A reasonably simple mission had suddenly turned into a matter of life-or-death.

'One of the guys, Sgt Castle from 7 RHA, requested assistance, and I began executing the QRF [*Quick Reaction Force*] plan, while at the same time trying to get the Task Force to send out a better-equipped force by helicopter,' said Bristow. 'They were twenty to thirty minutes' flying time away, and when the Chinook eventually deployed it only extracted Bdr Mason and buggered off. We'd been expecting them to land a much better-armed team and help drive off the Taliban, but they'd been tasked only to do the medevac.'

Worse, the patrol had also called for more ammunition, a message which Jonny Bristow had passed on to HQ, but the helicopter dropped no ammunition.

'Back at FOB Robinson,' said Bristow, 'we could hear and almost see what was happening. There was a heavy weight of fire going backwards and forwards, and we were very concerned. The patrol was calling in artillery from the three light guns that we had at the base, and they also were getting some air support from Apaches, but the Taliban were not being driven off. So I pulled together whatever resources I could from within the FOB to go out and help. This meant pretty much anyone I could free up, including Jim, some Royal Engineers who'd been working on the FOB's defences, and four American soldiers. The Americans were very good, and had far better weapons systems than we did. And the Afghan commander, who was a good chap who had experience from fighting with the Russians years earlier, mustered some men.'

The suddenness and drama of this decision was emblematic of the life of a soldier in Afghanistan. A few minutes earlier, James Philippson had been sitting on a compound roof in the late afternoon sun enjoying an iced tea and a chinwag with a couple of fellow OMLT officers, including Lt Tim Illingworth of The Rifles. It was 'a rare few moments of downtime,' Illingworth would later say[6]. 'One moment you're looking at the spectacular mountain scenery, the next you're dropping the iced tea and jumping off the roof to put together the QRF, and before you know it you're carrying Jim's body out of a firefight.'

It was rapidly becoming clear that the ambush was the worst engagement they'd had so far, said Bristow.

'Generally, the attacks had been shoot-and-scoot,' he said. 'But this time they knew that the patrol was vulnerable and had its back to the river. Still, a bit like the IRA had, they tended to disappear once you showed a bit of force and they realised the odds were against them. I was hoping that, as soon as we appeared, the enemy would fade away. We later found out that there had been intelligence about this grouping of insurgents, and had we known about them we probably would have avoided the area. But that hadn't been passed on to us.'

Acting on the advice of the men under fire, Maj Bristow's QRF approached from east to west on foot, dismounting from the vehicles where the ground became impassable. By that point, most of the ANA contingent had melted away, and those who had stayed the course were assigned to guard the vehicles. The cavalry therefore consisted of some fifteen to twenty British and American soldiers.

'It was pitch black by now,' said Bristow. 'We knew that either they'd bug out, or they wouldn't, and if they didn't then more than likely we were going to meet up. We were patrolling towards the area of the contact when we bumped into a group of them. It wasn't an ambush, it was a meeting engagement: we just came head-to-head with them. There was a full moon, but there was lots of vegetation and drainage ditches, and we were stopping quite often to try to see what was going on. I was at the front, and I heard something suspicious ahead of us, so I stopped and issued a warning so that our guys could take cover. Pretty simultaneously, they engaged us and we engaged them.'

Unfortunately, in that opening burst of fire, James Philippson was shot in the head and killed instantly.

'Jim was four men back, about ten metres from me,' said Bristow. 'I heard one of the other 7 RHA guys say, "Jim's been hit!", and I went back straight away to check on him. We called for the medic, though we knew straight away that Jim was dead. It was then that I took the decision that we had to get him back to the FOB, and then find another way in to help the first patrol. Of all the decisions I made that day, this is the one I have worried about, and ironically it was just about the only one for which I was not criticised. Of course, I was happy for Jim's family that we managed to recover his body, and things turned out okay, but I have often wondered whether it was the right thing to do. Certainly, it exposed us to much more risk – it needed four of us to carry him, and that was four fewer people to return fire – and it meant it was that much longer before we could get back to helping the original patrol.

'It was terribly difficult. We had to drag him through various culverts and ditches, and he was literally covered in shit… we all were, very quickly. So that made him slippery, and hard to hold on to. To make him lighter, we took off his body armour. I took care of his pistol, but we couldn't find his rifle. We were about a kilometre from the vehicles, so it was a matter of dragging and carrying him a little way, putting him down, returning fire – we could hear them talking to each other and trying to outflank us – and then picking him up and carrying on.

'We were fairly calm, I suppose because we had assumed we might suffer fatalities, but it was a testing time. Still, we managed to get Jim's body back to the vehicles in about thirty minutes, and then on to the

FOB. Then, because help from Task Force Helmand had still not materialised, we resumed our rescue mission. That was the last thing I wanted to do, but it occurred to me that, had he lived, Jim would have been the first to jump in and get involved again. He was a brave bloke and would not shy away from the action. In the early hours of the morning, we managed to link up with Sgt Castle's patrol. But by that time the attack was petering out, anyway. We'd heard that the Task Force were sending a company, so we waited for them to arrive and then we walked out with them.

Miraculously, there was only one other casualty, apart from James Philippson and LBdr Mason from the original patrol. Sgt Maj Andy Stockton, who was part of the QRF, had the lower half of his left arm taken off by a rocket-propelled grenade which smashed into him but, fortunately, failed to detonate. This failure was probably because the firer was too close – RPG rounds 'arm' themselves in flight – which shows how near the enemy were.

'Even now, I can't quite believe how lucky we were,' said Maj Jonny Bristow. 'The amount of rounds in the air was astonishing, but we were well-trained in finding cover and they were not very good shots. Jim was just terribly unlucky.'

* * *

JAMES PHILIPPSON'S mother was asleep at her home in Portugal when the phone rang.

'I always had my mobile on and near me in case James called,' she said. 'It was one or two o'clock in the morning, and it was David. He said, "I don't know how else to say this, other than there's two members of the Army here and… and James has been killed."

'It was just such a shock, straight out of the blue. I said, "James? How could anybody kill *James*?"

'It was in the middle of the night, so immediately I got onto the internet to book flights back to the UK the next day. At the airport, Steve went straight to the desk, explained what had happened, and asked if we could get on the plane first and sit on our own and, I suppose, be treated with kid gloves. easyJet were pretty remarkable, and did as much for us as they could.

'When the sun still came up, I just couldn't believe that the world was continuing as it had the day before.'

Tony Philippson was at a new holiday home he had recently bought in Nerja, Spain.

'A friend and I had just driven down there for the first time,' he said. 'It's a fourteen-hundred-mile journey, and quite exhausting, so I was asleep. The phone woke me up. It was David. My memories of it have faded a bit, because you don't like thinking about it. But I do know that it took a little while to sink in. It was overwhelming and terrible. I flew home the next day.'

James was given a full military funeral in St Albans, and was buried in the grounds of the cathedral.

'The roads were closed and all the traffic was stopped,' said Tony. 'And the turnout was amazing. The guard of honour was made up of men of 29 Commando and 7 RHA, and it seemed like half the Army was there. The bagpipes were so loud they were deafening. It's very difficult to think back over it. We organised a fabulous reception, and God, can soldiers drink! That's all I'd say.'

'The funeral was terrible,' said Tricia. 'But afterwards we met a lot of James' colleagues and friends at the local golf club where we'd laid on some food and drink. It was a real celebration of his life. So many men said to me what a great guy he was, and that there couldn't be a more honourable way to die. That didn't help me much as a mother, but it did give me something to think about. He was a great guy who'd worked so hard getting to where he was.

'Later, we went to a regimental service for James and others who'd been lost, and I met the chap who'd picked him up after he'd been killed. I don't know what his name is, unfortunately, but meeting him was quite heartening, because he said he didn't realise who he'd picked up until he laid him in the back of a jeep and looked at his dog tag. He said James' face was so peaceful. He'd lost all that driven, determined look he had. He said he looked relaxed, which is quite a nice thought.'

For Tony Philippson, a natural sense of pride in his son's service was soon added to by a mounting anger. An inquest into his son's death laid the blame squarely at the door of the Ministry of Defence. Oxford assistant coroner Andrew Walker, ruling that Capt Philippson was unlawfully killed, said, 'They [*the soldiers*] were defeated not by the terrorists but by the lack of basic equipment. To send soldiers into a combat zone without basic equipment is unforgivable, inexcusable and a breach of trust between the soldiers and those who govern them.'

An initial Army Board of Inquiry into the incident suggested that tactical errors by Maj Jonny Bristow were a factor. A second Board was later held, and this absolved Maj Bristow from any blame whatsoever. Indeed, it commended him for his 'tenacity and courage' on the night in question. But neither Board accepted the coroner's view that equipment shortages were a factor.

'Quite a long time passed between James' funeral and the first Board of Inquiry report,' said Tony. 'When I read it, I felt the whole thing stank. They were trying to move the blame for James' death to the man who was leading the patrol, and that was just not right. I met Major Bristow at the inquest, and I know he was very nervous because he thought I was going to be critical of him. But I assured him I wouldn't be. After that there was the second report, which told a truer story.

'Life has been difficult since James died. It doesn't go away, and every time someone dies I'm reminded about it. I'm not bitter about him being killed. It was his choice to join the Army, and he wanted to go where the action was. But I am bitter about the way the MOD treated them, and about their refusal to accept blame for not equipping them properly. If, for example, they had had sufficient night vision goggles, they would have seen the Taliban a lot earlier.

'The MOD maintains that, since James died in the first burst of fire, that would have happened regardless of how they were equipped, but you have to remember that they were going out to rescue another patrol that was pinned down, and they wouldn't have needed to do that if the first patrol had been more heavily armed. The WMIK Land Rovers should have been fitted with.50cal guns, but no-one had supplied the mounting kits.

'What matters to me more than anything else now is seeing that the Ministry of Defence will never again dare to send under-equipped troops overseas. That's my mission in life.'

Maj Jonny Bristow was shocked at the finding of the first Board of Inquiry.

'I didn't see the results until Jim's inquest,' he said, 'when someone from the MOD press office suggested that I might be heavily criticised. No-one had had the decency to show it to me before, and it came as a huge shock. To come back home and find that the finger was being pointed at us, that was a bit much. We didn't ask to be put into that predicament.

'Our weakness was that Brigade didn't see me and my team as part of the Brigade, so we were a convenient scapegoat. They said we were supposed to be there only to train the Afghan Army, we were not meant to be patrolling, and that we should have left that to the troops of Task Force Helmand. That was ludicrous. We made the point that even *after* Jim was killed we had to continue patrolling, because until 3 Para moved into Sangin later in the summer there was no-one else to do it.'

The second BOI in 2009 absolved Maj Bristow of all blame, but the whole affair left a bitter taste in his mouth. Although he returned to Afghanistan for a second tour in 2010, he left the Army not long afterwards.

'My career suffered greatly,' he said, 'and it has made my life pretty miserable. I would never have commanded the battalion, but I was ten years a major thereafter. I've done a number of non-jobs and my reputation suffered. It's given me a lot of sleepless nights and made me quite bitter against the Army.

'Obviously, that's as nothing when compared to the suffering of Jim's family. He was a great chap and the whole thing was a terrible tragedy.'

* * *

EIGHT YEARS ON, James Philippson's family are still mourning their lost son and brother. The pain will never go away; the most that they can hope for is that it softens with the passage of time.

'James's death enabled his mother and I to get a little closer,' said Tony Philippson. 'We work together on the charity that we set up in James' memory. I see Tricia now and again, and there is no problem. We generally keep in touch.

'I tried going back to the house in Spain on my own, but it didn't work so I sold it two years ago. I lost a lot of money doing so, actually, but the memories were in the walls.

19

'The loss of James has affected David even more than it affected me, I think. David won't come to anything that's related to the military, even though we're invited to some very special events from time to time. I have tickets from the Royal British Legion to attend a concert and reception at Windsor Castle, but he wouldn't come to that. It upsets him too much.

'I visit James' grave on his birthday and on June 11, the anniversary of the day he was killed. And I go there on Armistice Day. Someone has to put flowers there.'

Tricia still has difficulty in accepting that her oldest son is dead.

'Last year, somebody asked me how old James would be if he was still with us, and I really had to think about it,' she said. 'Because he's twenty-nine. That's when he ended. The old Remembrance Day thing, "They shall grow not old, as we that are left grow old… Age shall not weary them, nor the years condemn." That's true. He will always be twenty-nine in my mind.

'I don't give a great deal of thought to what he might have done, or whether he might have had children. But it'll be eight years next week since we lost our dear James. I still think he'll phone one day and say, "Hi mum, how's it going?"

'There's never a day goes by without him being in my thoughts somehow, whether it's because I'm walking up a hill, and it's tough, and I think of him encouraging me, or perhaps because I've just woken up, and it's a lovely day, and I think, *Oh, James would like this*. Sometimes a butterfly might fly past, and I'll think it might be his spirit.

'I dream about him quite a lot. Mostly they're nice dreams. In one, I was looking at a photo of him on the computer, and all of a sudden it became animated, and I said, "James! James! Is that you?"

He said, "It's alright, mum. Everything's okay. Don't worry. It's okay."

'And then I woke up, feeling quite a bit better. Once I saw a solitary poppy growing out of a kerbstone. I know it's daft, because I'm a perfectly rational woman, but I saw it as a sign. It was just one poppy growing there, and it seemed to tell me, "Go on! Get on with it. You can do it."

'I've got a great big rug he bought me in Afghanistan which was shipped back with his things. And, of course, I've got David, who is so similar to James in many ways. When James phoned he'd always say,

"Hiya! How's it going?" Sometimes now David rings and says the same thing, and it catches me out because their voices were so similar.

'People often say to him, "Gosh, you're so like your brother!" He had his arm tattooed with the words, "My brother lives on in me." David's felt the presence of his brother to spur him on, and not give up, and he's now a very successful businessman. They had this lovely admiration and respect for one another.

'I like looking at all our photographs. I've got millions of pictures of James, from when he was three hours old to when he was twenty-nine-and-a-bit. I can look at all those, and it's like seeing a different person; this little kid. But still, my overwhelming thought is that it was just such a waste. What a waste! All of his efforts, his abilities and his potential.

'I'm not optimistic about Afghanistan. I think the country will return to exactly the same state it was in before our intervention. I think all our lads and lasses that have been lost… It's a total waste. If we've managed to build some schools and educate some girls, then that's brilliant. But the Afghans will carry on killing each other.

'I don't have a very high opinion of politicians generally, I'm afraid. My impression is that they'll do whatever will get them into the history books. I've not heard of a single politician with a son or daughter who's gone to war. Not a single one.'

[*Tony Philippson sadly died in the summer of 2014.*]

CORPORAL MARK WRIGHT GC
MORTAR PLATOON 3rd BATTALION
THE PARACHUTE REGIMENT
APRIL 22, 1979 – SEPTEMBER 6, 2006

EVEN AS HE WAS about to be winched up into the Black Hawk rescue helicopter, with only a matter of minutes to live, Cpl Mark Wright's thoughts – as ever – were for others. The grievously wounded paratrooper shouted through the swirling dust to his comrades in the minefield, 'If I die, tell Gillian and my mum and dad that I love them.'

Gillian was his fiancée, and partner of seven years; they were to be married shortly after Mark's tour to Afghanistan ended.

The wedding never came. Despite the desperate efforts of the medics on the American chopper, the twenty-seven-year-old corporal bled out on the flight back.

He had spent the previous four hours or more lying, mortally wounded, in the dirt, waiting patiently for rescue. But he had stayed relentlessly positive and had constantly encouraged his fellow soldiers, many of whom had themselves lost limbs.

The dignity with which he behaved reflected a sobering conversation he'd had with his uncle on his R&R only two weeks earlier. Al Reid, himself a 3 Para veteran and a Military Cross winner in his own right, had discussed with Mark what it meant to die like a soldier, with courage and honour.

But the utterly selfless manner of Mark's passing was also entirely typical of the way he had lived his whole life.

When he was a little schoolboy in Edinburgh, his teacher had asked the class a question: What would you do if someone gave you a million pounds?

Most of his young pals had given the sort of answer one might expect – they would spend it on a new bike, lots of toys, boxes of sweets.

But Mark was different. 'I'd buy my Uncle Tom new eyes so that he could see,' he said.

Tom Reid – the twin brother of Mark's mother Jemima, and the older brother of Al – had been blind since birth.

Aged eleven, Mark had won a gleaming trophy for coming first in a ten-mile sponsored walk. At the end of the day, the judges presented it by accident to another youngster, a boy called Bobby. A couple of days later, Bobby's parents realised the mistake and telephoned Bob and Jem Wright to apologise.

Jem told her son that the judges were going to recover the trophy so that he could have it.

'He said, "No, the wee boy will be really disappointed, so tell him just to keep it,"' said Jem. 'So they compromised, and said they'd *both* won it. The other wee boy kept it for six months, and Mark got it for six months.'

At Mark's school was a young lad of Pakistani extraction called Raj. Raj was being bullied, so Mark took him under his wing, kept the bullies away, and the pair became close. Mark would often go to Raj's dad's restaurant for his lunch, and Raj to the Wright home for tea. Such was the bond between them that, after Mark was killed, Raj had Mark's date of birth tattooed on his arm, as a permanent reminder and a mark of respect to his lost friend.

There are countless further examples of Mark Wright's instinctive concern for others, and disregard for his own interests.

On September 6, 2006, those qualities were what led him, without hesitation, into an unmarked minefield to try to save his mates.

Three paratroopers, one of them a sniper, had left the relative safety of their observation post, in the blasted, lunar-like landscape around the Kajaki Dam, in order to take out two heavily-armed Taliban fighters who were clearly planning an attack. It was a risky manoeuvre, though well within the capabilities of the soldiers. But unfortunately, and unbeknown to them, the rocky terrain between the paras and their targets had been sown with anti-personnel mines by the Soviet occupiers twenty-five years earlier. Furthermore, over the intervening years, heavy winter rains had slowly washed the mines down the hillside until they were all grouped together. First one man trod on a device, then another. Before long, the ground was littered with bleeding soldiers. Several were missing legs, and even those who were so far unhurt were unable to move for fear of triggering yet more explosions. Into that hellish mess walked Cpl Mark Wright and several others.

What followed won Mark the George Cross – an award which ranks alongside the Victoria Cross, and is granted only for 'acts of the greatest heroism or of the most conspicuous courage in circumstances of extreme danger' – but it also cost him his life.

* * *

MARK WRIGHT WAS an only child, born in 1979. His parents had been married for more than nine years, and his mother had already lost an earlier baby at five months. It crossed their minds more than once that they might never have children, so Mark felt something like a miracle. His birth was, said Jem Wright, the happiest day of their lives. And their young son continued to give them nothing but joy.

'He was always a loving wee boy,' said Jem. 'Everybody says their kids are charming, but Mark really, really was. He was just a really nice lad. Just a normal boy. He liked playing with cars and doing the other things that boys do, but when he got to about three he said, "When I'm big I'm going to join the Army." He may have picked up his interest in the Army from my brother Al, who was a soldier and who would sometimes talk about it. In any case, Mark was often playing with his soldiers and guns, Action Men and so on. When he was older he joined the Army Cadets, and he really enjoyed that.

'He had plenty of other interests, too. He got on all right at school, he was in the cubs, and he did tae kwan do. He liked football, and he loved going fishing with my dad. I remember one day he told me how his granddad had led him astray. Apparently, they were sitting there fishing quietly when suddenly his granddad jumped up and said,

"Run, Mark! Run! I've not got a fishing permit, and here's the man coming!" He was an easy wee boy and, apart from near misses with his granddad, he was no trouble at all.

'He was shy – not awful shy, but shy. He was a great swimmer, and he could have been in the swimming team at school, but he hated to be on show so he refused a place on the team. He was the same with ice-skating and roller-skating; he'd rather stay at the back.

'And he was very kind and thoughtful. When he was about five, we went to one of his parents' evenings, and one of his teachers told us the story about the million pounds and his Uncle Tom's eyes. Mark was very close to Tom. If I was helping him with his homework but I didn't know the answer to a problem, he'd trot off and ring his uncle. "I'm phoning my Uncle Tom," he'd say, "because he knows everything!"'

Tom Reid remembers his nephew as a loving and gentle boy.

'I knew him as a kid and an adult,' he said, 'so when it was his funeral I gave one of the speeches, and I said that you had to think of him not just as a soldier, but as a child, too. What I remembered was a really relaxed child. It sometimes comes across to me that soldiers are brutal, hard, and violent. But that wasn't the case with Mark. He was pretty easy-going, and he had a pretty easy-going life at home. Though he was never going to sit behind a desk. I think at one point he thought about becoming a fireman, but whatever he did it would have been a physical job which involved a bit of risk-taking.

'He left school early. He didn't do badly, but he didn't find reading easy, especially when he was little. If I was visiting, or he and his mum were down on holiday with me in London where I live, I'd often say, "Read this for me, Mark, I cannae see it, so you read it." He'd whistle for his mum to come and read it instead. He couldn't get out of school fast enough... I think he just wanted to get out into the world and make some money.'

Mark worked for a couple of years alongside Bob in his small painting-and-decorating business. But although father and son got on together famously, the Army never left his thoughts for long, and he joined up at nineteen. Perhaps with his uncle Al's example in mind, it was the Parachute Regiment or nothing.

'He knew that the selection process for the Paras was very tough, but he said if he didn't get in he wouldn't stay in the Army,' said Jem. 'It had to be the Paras. I wasn't completely happy about it, but it was what he really wanted to do. I said to Bobby, "We can't tell him what to do. It's his life, not ours."'

Still, his parents made the offer – several times – to buy their son out if he decided it was not for him. But he took to life in uniform as to the manner born.

'When he left to begin training, I cried for three days,' said Jem. 'I couldn't even go to work. He'd grown up and was going away, and I just hoped nothing would happen to him. He loved training, he loved P Company [*the Parachute Regiment's extremely taxing entrance test*], and he loved being a soldier. He went to America to do his first free-fall jump, and I remember him telling us how, as they were getting ready to jump, his friend says to him, "What are we doing here?" Then they jumped, and when they got to the ground they looked at each other, and Mark said, "*Now* we know why we're here!"'

In Mark's early years, the Army was on a peacetime footing. Although he was based in Colchester, every weekend he would make the long, four hundred-mile drive back to Scotland.

'I asked him once why he came home every week,' said Jem. 'He said he just liked seeing everybody, and that it stopped him going out with the lads and spending all his money on drink. So he'd rather just come up the road. He used to turn up with all his washing, like any son. I remember he came home once with a really big bag, so I just spent the whole weekend washing and ironing. As I was ironing, I saw all these name tags. I said to Mark, "*Smith?* Whose washing *is* this?"

'He said, "Oh, the washing machine was broken, so I told the lads you'd do theirs!"'

Jem worked at a local nursery, and somewhere along the way Mark's eye was taken by a pretty schoolgirl who worked there part-time.

'I don't think they fell in love from day one,' said Jem. 'Gillian was still at school, after all. But it was a very nice relationship, and they did get together, and they were together for seven years. I always think it must be difficult to sustain a relationship when one of you is in the Army, but they bought a house together about two years before he was killed. They were engaged to be married, but of course what happened changed all that. We're not in touch with Gillian any more – she's moved on, which is only right. All she ever wanted was to have children, and she's married with a wee boy who's three now. So she's fulfilled her dream. That's great, and we're really happy for her.

'After Mark moved in with Gillian, he'd spend the weekend with her, of course, but even if he was arriving back in Edinburgh in the early hours of the morning he used to pop by our house first to say hello. They didn't live far away, so that was good.

'Then one day he just came home and said, "We're off to Afghanistan."

'I felt sick. I thought, *This is not good*. But I tried to put it in the back of my mind, and I just prayed that he would be safe and that everyone else would be safe, too. Although I was worried, I didn't think it was going to happen to us.'

Mark's father Bob recalls that sick feeling. 'We didn't know what lay ahead,' he said, 'but we were hearing about it on the news, and it wasn't looking very good. I think he was quite looking forward to going. And I know one thing, he wasn't afraid. Even as a kid, Mark used to say, "I'm not scared to die." I remember that someone had died, and we were talking about it. Mark said to Jem, "I don't want to live until I'm old." He said that a few times. He wasn't scared to die.'

'I do remember him saying one odd thing before he left,' said Jem. 'We'd been watching an interview on TV with the parents of a lad who'd been killed, and they were blaming the Army. Mark said to me, "If ever anything should happen to me, never say anything bad about it, because it was my choice. It's what I want to do, and it would be disrespectful to criticise anyone." So obviously he was thinking about what *could* happen.

'I remember saying to him, "Mark, please, *please* be careful." I told him if he saw anyone unfriendly to find a tree and hide behind it.

'He said, "Yeah, mum, there's trees all over the place out there!" But he said he'd be fine and not to worry, and we had a cuddle and a kiss, which was typical because he did show us how he felt about us. Whenever he phoned, he always finished by saying, "I love you."'

In 2006, the men of 3 Para – Mark Wright included – were deployed to Helmand Province in the south of the country, where it soon became clear that the-then government had been hopelessly optimistic – at best – about the likely course of the conflict. Capt Jim Philippson had been the first British soldier to die in action in Helmand on June

11. He was swiftly followed by many others, including the fourteen-strong crew of an RAF Nimrod who died when their aircraft crashed near Kandahar, three men who were killed when their Scimitar armoured vehicle was hit by an IED near Musa Qala, and two members of 3 Para – Pte Damien Jackson and Cpl Bryan Budd – who were both shot in Sangin during fierce fighting throughout July and August. [*Cpl Budd was posthumously awarded the Victoria Cross for his bravery on the day he died. The story of that action is told by Capt Hugo Farmer CGC in the Monday Books title* In Foreign Fields.]

As it happened, though, Mark seemed to have drawn a longer straw than some. After a time in Sangin, where the rounds and RPGs were bouncing around the streets, he and a small group of fellow paratroopers had been sent 30km north-east to protect the Kajaki Dam. Built by foreign firms in the peaceful 1950s, the one hundred metre-high dam – 320ft, in old money – supplied power and irrigation to the people below and, as such, was a target for Taliban sabotage attacks[7]. Nevertheless, it was a safer spot to be in than the urban 3 Para base to the south.

* * *

SNIPER STU HALE was one of Mark Wright's fellow paras at Kajaki. He remembers it as a difficult deployment.

'We didn't have the force density in 2006 that we had in 2008 through 2011,' said LCpl Hale. 'It was literally just the 3 Para Battle Group [*approximately 1,200 men*] trying to hold the whole of Helmand. We were very stretched. At Kajaki, we just didn't have the manpower to go out, dominate and hold ground – we were probably just under platoon strength, spread across two OPs and an occasional third one – so our orders were to stay firm and use our superior-range weapons and optics to look for the enemy.

'OP [*observation post*] Athens was furthest back, where the mortar barrels were located. CSgt Spud McMellon was in charge there, and in overall charge of the area. Mark was his 2IC and the No1 mortar fire control man. That was something he was incredibly good at. I'd heard of Mark getting a single round hit on a moving vehicle from quite a range. To do that you have to calculate speed, distance, and so on, and very few people could do that as accurately as him. As a sniper, I'd sometimes have to call for supporting fire, and every time I did that he'd have rounds away before I'd even finished talking. He was that slick; that good. He was also a great guy, by the way. A really nice chap, got on well with everyone, he wasn't in any particular clique, and he never had any fallings out.

'OP Normandy was closer to the valley. Cpl Stu Pearson was in charge there, with me as 2IC. I was the sniper at Normandy, and we also had three Fusiliers and four of our own anti-tank guys.

'Further on from that was Sparrowhawk, the occasional OP. I was always pushing to go out there to set up a twenty-four-hour OP, because beyond that was an area of dead ground and I wanted to know what was going on there. The Taliban knew that if they couldn't see you then you couldn't see them, so they would move around that area. But we simply didn't have the manpower to spread out across all three positions.

'Despite that, morale was generally good. We were high up on the hill with a clear view of the dam, maybe a kilometre or two away, and the village below, a place called Tangi that the locals had built along a runway laid by the Russians twenty-five years earlier.

'Those elevated positions did allow us to use our heavier weapons to greater effect. The range of the Javelin [*anti-tank weapon*] was greater because of the elevation, the mortars had better range, and so did sniper rifles. Personally, I'd had some good results because of that elevation, and we were at a major advantage over the Taliban. If they tried to take the dam in any real tactical sense, or tried to close in on us, we'd have the upper hand. That said, resupply was a massive issue. We kept requesting ammunition, and we got occasional food drops, but it got to the point that they just didn't have the ammunition, or they couldn't get it to us. We were warned off that the Taliban would have to be rolling up our positions before they'd get any more ammunition to us. In other words, it would have had to be virtually hand-to-hand fighting before they'd send a helicopter in. That, combined with the knowledge that everyone could see us, and knew exactly where we were, was very sobering.

'After what happened to the French special forces guys [*see Chapter One*], we were all well aware that, given the chance, a lot of the civilians would come out and do nasty things to us. The old Rudyard

Kipling poem kept coming to my mind, that was quite worrying for me.'

[*Kipling's* The Young British Soldier *finishes, 'When you're wounded and left on Afghanistan's plains, And the women come out to cut up what remains, Jest roll to your rifle and blow out your brains, An' go to your Gawd like a soldier.'*]

'To our south was an area of open ground leading up to the OP, and we felt exposed on that flank. We had surveillance systems that detect heat signatures, a very good piece of kit, but one guy sitting on top of a hill trying to cover three hundred and sixty degrees was not a guarantee that no-one could sneak up on you. I often woke up at night hearing Afghan voices within the OP. It was purely my imagination, but it's an indication of how worried I was. We were on edge all the time. One night, all our trip flares went off. It was just wild dogs, but it really spooked us.

'Of course, as it was there was actually never *any* danger of the Taliban coming at us from the south, because the whole place was strewn with landmines. But unfortunately we didn't know that at the time.

'We did come under Chinese rocket attack several times. They were fired from static positions, and often using a timer so that by the time we got eyes onto where they'd been fired from the Taliban were long gone. They used a system of tunnels in the area to move their kit around. The tunnels had been designed for irrigation, but in the summer fighting season it was very dry, so they could move along them.

'But we had a strategic advantage, and we felt reasonably safe. We were more worried about our guys who were based around Sangin and Musa Qala. They were fighting tooth-and-nail every night in Sangin. They were being attacked in waves there, a whole different intensity to what we were experiencing. We'd get reports through about casualties, but they wouldn't send us their names because the radios were insecure. So we'd have to wait a few days before their names were broadcast on the BBC World Service. It's your mates, so that was quite frustrating, and bad for morale.'

In his regular calls home to his parents and to Gillian, Mark Wright played down the dangers.

'He'd often phone in the mornings before I went to work,' said Jem. 'I'd pick up the phone, and he'd say, "Hiya, mum!"'

'I'd say, "What are you doing, Mark?"'

'He'd say, "I'm sitting on top of a hill... What are *you* up to?" That was about as much detail as he would ever give me. He'd never tell us much about the conditions and what they were doing. I don't know if it really was quiet, or if he just didn't want us to worry. But we did worry, of course. Every time you heard somebody had been killed, and they said the next of kin had been told, I'd think, *Oh, good. So that's not Mark.*'

Cpl Wright's R&R arrived in August. It was during that precious period of downtime that he took the opportunity to meet up with his uncle, Al Reid, himself a former member of The Parachute Regiment. They had a talk – 'one professional soldier to another', said Al.

'We were discussing Sangin, where he'd been based earlier in the tour, before he went to Kajaki. He and his colleagues had been among the first into Sangin, and it was a very hot place. The base's defences weren't much more than a few layers of sandbags, and at times the Taliban were almost over-running them. Mark was a mortar fire controller in Sangin, and he told me that sometimes he was having to drop rounds virtually on his own coordinates. That's how bad the situation was.

'What I said then was a serious message, although I didn't deliver it in a particularly serious way. We were both professional soldiers, even though there was fifteen years between us. I said, "If it's all going wrong, and you think you're going to die, it's better just to keep it to yourself. If you're really frightened, don't show it. Try to keep it inside, because showing it won't make any difference but at least people will remember that you had the courage to face death."'

Of course, there were lighter discussions, too. A lot of the talk was of the big wedding later that year, and it still loomed large after Mark's return to the battlefield.

'I remember talking about it on the phone to him,' said Jem. 'I told him I'd tried everywhere for something special to wear. He said, "Don't worry, just wear a pair of jeans and a T-shirt!" He didn't want a big fuss – they were getting married in a hotel rather than in a church. But Gillian was really excited, as we all were. I helped her buy her dress, and choose the flowers... I don't think Afghanistan had been forgotten, but the wedding was so close.'

* * *

AFTER ANOTHER BITTERLY cold night, the morning of September 6, 2006 dawned blue and clear over OPs Athens and Normandy on the rocky hillside above Kajaki.

After standing-to at first light, the weary paras made as hearty a breakfast as they could with the available rations, enjoyed a hot brew, and busied themselves with checking weapons and ammunition loads.

The temperature soon began to rise, and with it rose the spirits of the soldiers. Down below, in the village of Tangi on the old Russian runway, they could see Afghan locals milling around, going into and coming out of houses. This was usually a positive sign. An absence of villagers was a classic 'combat indicator' – the Taliban having warned them to leave the area before launching an attack – and the opposite also generally held true.

'We were quite upbeat,' said LCpl Stu Hale. 'Unfortunately, we soon realised that they were going back to get their belongings before moving away permanently, because the Taliban had told them it was about to kick off. That was a bit of a bummer.

'Later, when we looked out across the southern area, we saw that two men who were well-armed and obviously Taliban had set up a makeshift chicane. They were slowing down the traffic and talking to the drivers. They were also broadcasting over the Tannoy system that they used for the call to prayer. I'd done my basic language training and we had the interpreter there, so we knew they were putting out negative stuff. The interpreter said they were trying to rile up the locals. I started to get massively concerned by this. I thought, *What if they get a crowd together, and they get the lynch mob mentality, and they start to march up the hill?* Obviously, we had the whole thing of the French hanging over us from before. The last thing we wanted to do was start shooting civilians, even if they were trying to get into the OP to lynch us.'

By his own admission, Hale was 'flapping a bit', but he was determined to take the initiative.

'I decided to go down from Normandy to occupy a position, a small knoll overlooking the two enemy combatants,' he said. 'They'd be seven hundred metres away, if that, so I could eliminate them with two shots and then extract back up the hill.'

It was a fateful decision – and one taken in the best traditions of the British Army, for it would have been the work of moments for an excellent mortarman like Mark Wright to have dropped a bomb on the two Taliban, thus obviating the need for any of the paratroopers to leave the safety of the OPs. But, with innocent Afghans in the area, they could not be sure that no civilians would be hit, so they took the riskier option. And it *was* risky. Between LCpl Hale's OP and the Taliban fighters was the dead ground, with who-knew-what lurking in every dip, or behind every boulder. There was every chance that they might bump into a bigger gang of insurgents than a bolt-action sniper rifle is designed to handle, so Hale took with him a Fusilier, 'Faz' Farrell, armed with a light machine gun, and a paratrooper medic/radioman, 'Jarhead' Harvey.

Before setting out, of course, he cleared the mission with the man in charge at Normandy, Cpl Stu Pearson. Pearson was happy with the plan, but told Hale to further clear it with Spud McMellon higher up the hill at Athens. Unfortunately, the messages were slightly muddled: Hale thought Pearson had said that *he* (Pearson) would clear it with CSgt McMellon. As a result, said Hale, he and the other two men left OP Athens 'without HQ back in Bastion really knowing what was going on'.

'At the time,' he said, 'we didn't think it was a big deal. It was a fairly simple exercise. With Faz and his LMG, I had all my avenues covered. I thought we'd go down there, take the two shots, then extract back. I was completely focused on the insurgents. There was a chance that they would try to engage me. I might drop one, and have to work hard to pick the other off if he hid. And we might find an enemy position in the dead ground. There were loads of things going through my mind, but the possibility that we might be walking into a minefield was the last of them.

'We knew there were mines in other areas, but they were clearly marked. We were further reassured because a large boulder had been blocking one of the paths and it was rolled down into the area without setting anything off. We'd also seen locals walking around the minefield, so we were convinced there were no mines there.

'It was 10.30hrs. I did all my checks, gave Stu Pearson the thumbs-up, and we set off down the hill in seventy- to one hundred-metre tactical bounds. I went first. I should probably have put the LMG at point, because he would have a higher rate of fire if we bumped into anything. But I was the team leader, so you tend to take the risk yourself.'

Stu Hale headed down the hill in textbook fashion, at a slow and deliberate pace, continually scanning for movement or other signs of the enemy. His sniper rifle was heavy in his hands, and stones were skittering and tumbling after him. At the bottom, he came to a dry wadi bed which he leapt across.

'Normally, a good para would land with his feet and knees together,' said Hale, 'but I got a bit lazy and I led with my right foot. That's what hit the mine. It detonated and flipped me up in the air. I came-to thinking I'd slipped, and then I thought, *Oh, I dropped my rifle*. I rolled over to grab it, and that's when I saw blood on the stock and my finger hanging off. Then it dawned on me what had happened.

'My first thoughts were of that Rudyard Kipling poem again – Afghans cutting up injured soldiers. I knew I wasn't far from where the locals were, and that they would have heard the explosion, and I thought they'd be all over me very soon. I was absolutely convinced they would finish me off. I felt very alone for what felt like an eternity, although it could only have been seconds before Jarhead got to me.

'Out of bravery or stupidity – I suspect the former, because he knew I was in an open minefield – Jarhead came running straight to me. He started administering first aid, helping me to apply my first field dressing and a tourniquet. I told Faz to cover us, so that if and when the civvies came up the hill he'd be able to fire a warning shot. Or if the Taliban wanted to come out we'd have a bit of fire support.'

Up at OP Normandy, Cpl Stu Pearson had heard the explosion and the screams of his wounded comrade.

'I knew it was a mine,' he said, 'because I was used to the sound of rockets, and this was different. Up till then, we'd had no reason to believe it was mined. We'd never been through there before, but other guys had been down there setting up trip flares and we'd seen a local with his cattle in the area. They were probably only about three hundred metres away, between us and the ridgeline Stu was trying to get to. I radioed what I knew to Athens, and then three of us from Normandy went down to help.

'Because I knew it was a minefield, I told the guys to go from rock to rock. It only took us about five minutes to get there. We were concerned about the Taliban taking advantage of the situation and attacking, so I told the guys to keep their eyes open, looking out toward where a threat might come from. Jarhead was already treating Stu. Basically, I could see his right foot was gone from more or less at the ankle.'

He didn't let on, preferring to let LCpl Hale drift away on the morphine pumped into him by Jarhead Harvey.

'I was already starting to lose track of things,' said Hale. 'It's hard to gauge how long it took, but eventually Stu Pearson got to me and started to comfort me. I cracked a nervous joke about whether I'd be okay for SAS selection, because I was due for that. He said, "Yeah, you'll be fine." We had a bit of a chinwag, and things didn't seem to be so bad at this stage. I was the only one who was injured, and we'd managed to slow down my bleeding considerably. But I still had a broken femur, so my situation was complicated.'

'Complicated' is putting it mildly. It would have taken all day to get engineers to the scene to prove a way in and out of the minefield – by which time Stu Hale would long since have bled to death. Indeed, the injured soldier's stump pumped blood every time he moved, notwithstanding the tourniquet. A helicopter – one equipped with a winch – was urgently needed. That meant asking the British troops' American allies to send one of their rescue Black Hawks.

Not long after the small rescue party left Normandy, a second group came out from OP Athens. Among them was Cpl Mark Wright, and an RAMC medic, LCpl 'Tug' Hartley.

Now Cpl Wright entered the minefield with LCpl Hartley. As the medic got to work on Stu Hale, inserting an IV line to boost his fluids, Mark Wright began trying to get a chopper organised.

'Mark had a radio with him so he could talk directly to Spud at Athens,' said Stu Pearson. 'I shouted to him to get Bastion to get us a helicopter with a winch. That was denied.'

In fact the request was not so much denied, as impossible. None of the British helicopters operating in theatre at that time were equipped with winches, which were necessary to enable casualty extraction without landing, and all American winch-equipped Black Hawk helicopters were deployed on other missions. Lieutenant Colonel Stuart Tootal, 3 Para CO, would later blame NATO bureaucracy for this failure; angry at this and other perceived failures, Tootal would resign from the Army in 2008.

'I got on top of a small mound to get a better view,' said Cpl Pearson, 'and it was then that I saw some mounds made of red-painted pebbles. I knew that signified mines, although there was no indication where they were. But, essentially, I knew we were in the middle of a minefield. I asked Mark to ask Athens again to get us a helicopter with a winch. Again it was denied, so I looked for an area that I thought was far enough away that it was probably safe, and flat enough for a helicopter to land. I got the other guys to use bayonets and parts of rifle cleaning kits to clear a safe path to an area where I thought we might get a helicopter down, and then I got them to try to clear another area as a back-up.'

It was at that moment that an already bad situation turned catastrophic, as Stu Pearson's left foot slipped off the rock he was standing on and straight onto a second mine.

'I heard the bang and I felt myself getting blown up and turned around,' he said. 'I landed on my arse, and I knew straight away what I'd done. I was angry. I could see the top laces of my boot attached to my leg and nothing below that. I'd lost it about the height of my boot. I knew there was going to be blood, and so I threw a tourniquet to [*Fusilier*] Andy Barlow, and he started putting it on my left leg. I got morphine out and stabbed myself with it. I didn't have any pain at that point, but I knew it wasn't going to be long before I did.'

The blast had disheartened Stu Hale.

'I remember feeling wracked with guilt,' he said, 'because guys were now losing limbs because of me. Stu was in a bad way, initially. He'd only been hit by one mine at this stage, though he was injured again later on when another one went off.'

Hale also felt that his own chances of survival had taken a big hit.

'I didn't lose consciousness throughout the whole day,' he said, 'but

I did feel myself slipping later on. I wasn't falling asleep, but I sort of felt that I was fading – that's the best way to describe it. I just wanted to get stuff off my chest in case the worst happened, and my main concern was that my partner was due to give birth in December, which was three months away. I desperately wanted to see my baby, but if I couldn't see it at least I wanted people to know what name I wanted. So I kept on saying, over and over again, "Alexander for a boy, Sofia for a girl." That way, if I did go, then at least the guys would know what name I wanted, and they could pass that on. But I just got a slap from one of them, and was told to get a grip.

[*In the event, his partner gave birth to a daughter, Sofia.*]

'Gradually, I stabilised, and most of the bleeding had been stemmed. Stu Pearson was stable, too, and morale actually then got quite good, even though none of us could move. To be honest, we were laughing at the craziness of the situation. It was [*Pte*] Dave Prosser's birthday, and we were singing to him. It was all a bit surreal. At one stage we were in stitches we were laughing so much. I'm sure it was mainly from nervousness.'

By now, a helicopter had been dispatched to help the wounded men. Unfortunately, it was not an American Black Hawk, but an RAF Chinook. And since it was not equipped with a winch, the giant, twin-rotor aircraft was going to have to land among the mines. For the men on the ground, this raised an immediate fear – that the twenty-tonne machine, or its powerful downdraft, might somehow set off more explosions.

Stu Hale said, 'Chinooks make a very distinctive sound, and I remember it coming in. We were all dismayed to hear it, because we knew it was going to try to land. We had radios but no direct communications with the helicopter. We had to talk to the OP, and they would relay information to Bastion, and then on to the pilot. Some of the guys tried to wave it off, but they came in anyway. As it descended, everyone who could was covering Stu Pearson and me to try to stop dust getting into our wounds. Then the dust settled, the ramp was down and the loadmaster signalled to us to board. We looked at him as if he was insane. The guys just went like, "No! that's not going to happen." There was no way we could move from where we were.'

There is confusion as to what set off the third mine, but both Stu Pearson and Stu Hale believe the Chinook was somehow responsible

– though they do not in any way blame the crew, who were putting themselves in grave danger.

'Maybe the Chinook shouldn't have been sent,' said Hale, 'but the American helicopters were fully tied up supporting their own troops and we didn't have any serviceable helicopters with winches that could operate in a minefield, and they had to do something.'

'We were all screaming at it to fuck off,' said Cpl Pearson. 'But it landed, and initiated the third mine. Maybe a daysack or a rock was blown onto it, or perhaps the downdraft set it off. I guess we'll never know for sure.'

That third explosion, very close to Mark Wright, sent shrapnel and rock fragments flying through the air and into his chest, face, neck and arms. LCpl Alex Craig, another medic, was also hit, and Stu Pearson took damage to his right leg. Their terrible situation was worsening by the minute, and the paras were in danger of losing several men if a Black Hawk was not quickly found.

Realising that Cpl Wright was particularly gravely injured, RAMC medic LCpl Tug Hartley acted immediately.

'We were more or less divided into two separate groups maybe thirty metres apart,' said Stu Hale. 'I had Tug with me, and Mark and Stu were some little distance away with other men. Alex had a chest wound, and he managed to extract himself and get back up the hill, because he was no use to anyone like that. But Tug decided he had to treat Mark. So he stood up and started to throw his daysack down in front of himself to set off any mines that were there. If none went off, he'd jump to that spot. He moved across the minefield like that to get to Mark. That was the bravest thing I ever saw.[8] He got there safely and was able to treat Mark. He did his best.'

Cpl Wright's right arm had gone, and he had a hole in his neck. When Hartley gave him water, it dribbled out of the hole onto his chest. Despite this, once he was patched up as much as possible, Mark Wright continued to liaise with OP Athens, and to keep his comrades' spirits up.

'Mark was the senior guy in the minefield, and he knew that,' said LCpl Stu Hale. 'We needed to act quickly now, but there was nothing we could do but wait for another rescue attempt. Throughout it all, Mark kept it together. He was shouting encouragement to us and using the radio to keep in touch with the OPs, even though he was by far the worst injured. Mark saw it as his job to keep us going.'

Approximately an hour after the third mine was detonated, there was a fourth explosion.

'Somebody threw me a bottle of water,' said Stu Pearson, 'but I missed it. Andy Barlow was right next to me so he got up to get it and stood on a mine. So he lost his left leg, too. I'm pretty sure Tug Hartley got some of it, and Mark was also hit again, and injured more, although it didn't register with me just how badly injured he was. I said, "At least we've found the fourth fucking mine!" We knew that Russian doctrine was to lay them in groups of four.'

Pte Prosser was also hit by that explosion, taking a large piece of shrapnel to the chest – in Patrick Bishop's book *3 Para*, Prosser describes having 'blood pissing out of my chest and everywhere...' He lay on his side, his best lung uppermost, to try to keep fluid out of his lungs.

A few metres away across the blasted hillside, Stu Hale still heard Mark Wright's words of encouragement.

'He was shouting things like, "Remember, we're Para Reg!"' said Hale. 'He said to Stu that he was going to have to get a new set of number-twos [*formal dress uniform*] for his wedding because his arm was in tatters. It was just really bad, and it was so sad. The waiting went on for ages [*the whole episode lasted more than four hours*], and we all thought we were waiting to die.'

Despite the seriousness of his own condition, and the pain he was in, Mark Wright kept pressing for rescue helicopters. Eventually, he shouted out to his mates that a pair of Black Hawks were on their way.

'He said they would take an hour,' said Stu Pearson, 'but at least they were coming. I was just lying there, and I found myself drifting off to sleep. But Mark wouldn't let me. He kept me awake. We both knew that if I went to sleep I wouldn't wake up. It was a lovely, fantastic feeling, though. It was so peaceful. So blissful. No noise, no pain. By that time I had taken a lot of morphine – by the end of the day I'd taken about seven doses in the standard syrettes. Somehow we kept going.

'Eventually the two Black Hawks arrived. The medics took it in turns to fast-rope down with a basket. Each of us was placed in a basket and winched away. Stu Hale was the first to be recovered, then Mark went.

Before they lifted him away from me, he said, "Stu, if I die tell Gillian and my mum and dad that I love them."

'I said, "Shut up, Mark! This time next week we're going to be back in the pub." He then shouted the same thing to Tug Hartley.'

The Black Hawks ferried all seven injured men and their comrades to the RAF Chinook which had landed on the other side of the hill, and which contained a Medical Emergency Response Team. As soon as he was brought aboard, they set about trying to save Mark Wright's life.

Cpl Stu Pearson watched their efforts through his dreamy morphine haze.

'I remember lying there,' he said, 'and my first thought was, *Thank fuck we're out of there.* I looked over and saw Mark. Then I looked over to him again a little later, and the medics were giving him CPR. I hadn't realised how bad he was. And then I looked again, and he wasn't there. Clearly, he'd died and they had placed him in a body bag.'

LCpl Stu Hale remembers seeing the medics chest-pumping his friend, too.

'I'd had so much morphine that I was away with the fairies towards the end,' he said. 'The usual presumption is that casualties should be back in a hospital within what they called the golden hour, but our golden hour turned to two, then three, then four. Mark wouldn't let go until he knew we were all safe. Then I think he almost allowed himself to die. That was certainly the way it seemed to me.'

* * *

AS HER SON lay dying in that minefield thousands of miles from home, Jem Wright had been at work at the nursery. The first inkling she had that anything might be wrong was when she walked through the door just before 6pm that evening.

'Bobby said to me, "There's been an accident and a few people have been hurt,"' she said. 'There was nothing at that stage to indicate how serious it was or who was involved. Bobby was going out to see a decorating job, and I put the news on. They started talking about an accident in Helmand. Somebody had been killed, and so many had been injured. My gut feeling told me it was Mark. I just had a funny feeling, I don't know why. About ten minutes later, the doorbell went, and when I opened it there were two soldiers standing there. One chap said, "Mrs Wright?"

'I said, "Yes."

'"Can we come in please?"'

'I said, "No."

'They said, "Can we *please* come in? Is there anybody else here?"

'I said, "There's no-one else here. You can come if you're going to tell me he's been hurt. But you can't come in if you're going to tell me he's been killed."

'And then they did come in, and they did say he'd been killed. I just became hysterical. I called Bobby and said, "You've got to come home. You *have* to come home. Something's happened."'

Bob Wright said he 'just went blank'. Knowing in his heart of hearts that his only son was dead, he drove home. When he got there he didn't even notice the two men standing in his living room at first, much less that they were in uniform. They told him the terrible news.

'I think we just sat and cried for a while,' recalled Bob. 'Then someone went to get a neighbour and friend, Peter, who is a minister, and another friend, Janice. They came round to be with the family.'

In spite of the tragedy that was unfolding, Bob felt he had to contact a client.

'I was doing a job out near the airport, and I felt I had to go out there for some reason, perhaps to explain that I wouldn't be able to carry on working. I can't even remember driving along the by-pass. I got to the door and I thought, *Why am I here?* I just got back in the car again and went home. I was in a daze.'

Jem was in a similar state.

'I think I felt it was a dream,' she said. 'I thought it couldn't be happening to us, even when close family and friends started arriving. Then the press were at the door asking questions, but fortunately my brothers Al and Tom had arrived and were able to cope with them. Then Gordon Muirhead, the Army liaison officer, also arrived. He was a really nice guy. Bobby went to tell Gillian and bring her back to the house. I think she stayed with us for about the next three weeks. She was devastated. She'd lost the person she was going to marry, and everything they had planned could never happen.'

A few days later, their son's body was flown back to RAF Brize

Norton, along with those of four other soldiers, all aged under thirty – father-to-be Pte Craig O'Donnell, of the Argyll and Sutherland Highlanders, and LCpl Paul Muirhead, LCpl Luke McCulloch, and Rgr Anare Draiva of the Royal Irish Regiment.[9]

'Bobby and I went with Gillian to Mark's repatriation,' said Jem. 'Mark was the last one off the plane, and Bobby said, "They always keep the best until last." It was very harrowing. The coffins were taken away to Oxford for post mortems, and we just had to come home. Later, Mark's body was brought back to Edinburgh. Bobby, Gillian and myself went to the funeral parlour. Bobby was able to look at Mark, but Gillian and I just couldn't do that. So they brought him home, and he lay on the dining room table. A lot of the lads from the Paras came up the night before the funeral, and they spent time with him. It was very important to us that he was home for that last time.'

Mark's funeral was held in Edinburgh. More than six hundred people attended, including many comrades from the Parachute Regiment.

'The crematorium chapel was packed,' said Jem. 'Some representative of the Army spoke, and Al spoke about Mark and Gillian. But Tom spoke about when Mark was little, and he put some funny stories in it. He even had people laughing at some points. It was as good a day as these things can be.'

With poignant irony, the funeral reception was held in the hotel where Mark and Gillian had planned to hold their wedding.

The other seriously injured had also been flown back to the UK, and to Selly Oak hospital for treatment. It was from there that Fus Andy Barlow managed to get a message to Al Reid, Mark's uncle.

'The message was that Andy wanted to see me and had something to tell me,' said Al. 'So I went to visit him. I walked in and Andy said, "Are you Al Reid? I have a message to pass to you from Mark. But first I'd like to tell you about the situation we were in."

'He told me the whole story, and then told me what Mark had said to him. Andy had been lying next to Mark in the minefield, and near the end he'd said to Andy, "I'm going to die."

'Andy said, "No, you're not, Mark."

'But Mark was convinced, and he said, "No, I *am* going to die, and I want you to pass some messages on to my mum and dad, Gillian and to my uncle Al."

'The message for Bob, Jem and Gillian was that he loved them. But then he said this: "Tell my uncle Al that I died a good soldier."

'That was not easy for me to hear, because it had a lot to do with the conversation I'd had with Mark during his leave, about two weeks before he died. I know he was thinking of that conversation, and you can imagine the effect it had on me when I heard it. I pretty much turned around and walked out of the hospital.

'Some time later, I managed to speak to the American helicopter crewman who rescued Mark. He told me that, when he'd lifted Mark into the Black Hawk, Stu Pearson was already in it. This crewman could see that Mark's injuries were terrible. They only had one oxygen mask, so he went to place it over Mark's face. But Mark wouldn't take it. He pointed to Stu Pearson, making it clear that he wanted him to have it. The oxygen was passed to Stu.

'This helicopter crewman told me that he'd been involved in hundreds of rescues, but he'd never seen anything like Mark's courage. He was very keen that Mark's family knew about it.

'The George Cross and the Victoria Cross can only be awarded if a soldier has made a conscious decision that he knows will probably cost him his life. Mark made a conscious decision to do something, even though he knew it might well kill him. He was horrifically wounded but, in spite of that, he kept radio communications going, and he maintained morale in a terrible situation. He even refused oxygen so that another man could have it.'

In the December, Al Reid accompanied his sister Jem and brother-in-law Bob to Buckingham Palace, where they received Mark's posthumous GC – the official citation spoke of his 'complete disregard for his own safety' and 'gallantry of the highest order' – in a private meeting with the Queen. It was 'an amazing experience', said Jem, who 'didn't realise what a remarkable medal the George Cross is.'

'More people have received the Victoria Cross,' said Bob Wright. 'It's so rarely awarded that I didn't think Mark would be given it. Mark was a very caring lad, so what he did to help his friends would have been normal for him. There were other people getting awards at the event, including a few girls. I remember one girl in particular. [*Michelle Norris MC*] was under fire on top of an armoured vehicle while trying to treat a guy who'd been shot. It was unbelievable. It just showed the remarkable bravery of our troops. We were so proud of what Mark did. But we were proud of him anyway. Mark had a lovely nature.'

'Receiving it for Mark at Buckingham Palace was an amazing experience,' said Jem. 'Bob and I and Gillian and his uncle Al were lined up in a room, and the Queen came in. I remember being surprised at how small she was, and at the fact that she remembered Al from his own Military Cross ceremony. She shook hands with everybody, talked about Mark's bravery, and then apologised because she had to present other medals at the main ceremony. But she invited us to watch, so we followed her down the stairs and watched everybody receive their medals. Among them was Stuart Pearson, who was awarded the Queen's Gallantry Medal. And when the Queen was leaving, she came past us and she smiled. It was amazing, an absolutely wonderful occasion. The Queen was lovely, and the people who were with her were lovely. She spoke beautifully.

'We've loaned the medal to Edinburgh Castle, where they have it on show. These medals are very valuable, and we were worried about keeping it in the house, to be honest. But also it's good that it's there, because lots of schoolchildren visit the Castle and, if they see the medal, it may make them interested in Mark's story. He didn't put great value on medals. He had a few from Iraq and Northern Ireland, but he just threw them in the drawer, and never spoke about them. We've put them all together now and they're all on display in the Castle with a picture of him. We don't have any other family to pass it on to, so perhaps eventually we might leave it to the Castle.'

Because of the nature of the war, the spotlight soon moved on to another bereaved family, leaving Bob and Jem Wright to cope as best they could with the loss of their only child. It has not been easy, but the Parachute Regiment helped. Like all regiments, it is very keen to keep alive the memory of its fallen.

'Someone suggested an annual timed tab [*a speed march*],' said Jem, 'but the guys pointed out that Mark hated tabbing. He'd rather have run to the bookies than do a tab. The CO said to us, "I've had a chat with the chaps, I can't really have all my paras running up to the bookies, so what we've decided is to have a fun day in his memory."

'So now they have that annual day in Mark's name, and all the families come along and have a good time. Mark would have liked that. We used to visit the barracks in Colchester often, but it's eight years this year since we lost him and, as time's gone on, the people that served with him have moved on, so there are fewer people that we know.

'I think I've coped better than Bobby. During the day he'll be absolutely fine, because he's busy doing things. But when he goes to bed at night, that's when everything comes back. That's when it's really difficult. I've dreamed about Mark. I remember very soon after he was killed that I dreamt that he was in the back of our Jeep. He was sitting there in a white T-shirt, and he said, "I'm all right, mum."

'Sometimes I talk to him. Sometimes I do feel he's still around. This might sound bizarre, but Mark hated having photographs taken, and he didn't like having them on show, either. Of course, we had a lot of photos of Mark around the house after he died. But sometimes we'd come home at night and find all the pictures had been knocked flat, or were on the floor. I'd say to Mark, "Leave them alone!"'

Bob Wright has wound up his painting and decorating business.

'I thought, *What's the point in working?*' he said. 'Everything would have gone to Mark one day. But we set up a charity, The Mark Wright Project, to develop a drop-in centre in Dalkeith on the outskirts of Edinburgh. The Army recruits most of its Scottish soldiers from Dalkeith and the surrounding areas, so it's the right place for the centre. Soldiers who are suffering from PTSD, or need help in any way, can come and get a welcome and a cup of tea and a wee blether, or some good advice and practical help. It's been a real success. Some of the guys who come to us are looking for work, or are homeless. They often want help writing CVs. We even had one lad come to us recently looking for a dentist. We get them on courses, we get them driving lessons if that'll help them to get a job… It's been unbelievable. The charity just started off as a small drop-in centre, and it's just grown.

'We're open nine-to-five, and we have three people working there. The way we looked at it, Mark was kind and caring, so it was appropriate that he should give his name to a place that brought people in off the street and tried to look after them. The project keeps us busy and gives us a purpose.'

Winston Churchill said that every medal casts a shadow; the shadows cast by a day like Wednesday September 6, 2006 are longer still.

Stu Hale and Stu Pearson both left the Army, and now have prosthetic limbs. Hale will forever wonder: what if he had not decided to leave the OP to take out those two Taliban fighters?

'It's played on my mind a lot since that day,' he said, 'and it still upsets me. Sometimes I've thought it was my fault. Maybe it wasn't my mistake, but it was my fault, because the guys had to come and get me out of the minefield. They were never going to leave me. I don't blame myself, but it was ultimately my actions that led to it. I could have turned the other way, or not gone to engage those insurgents at all.'

Stu Pearson is upset at the way his career ended. 'I suppose I've recovered alright,' he said. 'The main worry wasn't my left leg that hit the mine, because I knew I'd lost that, but my right leg [*which was damaged in the later blast*] which I was hoping they could save. One of my friends was a nurse at Bastion and she asked the surgeon about me. He said that it was fifty-fifty for the right leg. But they did manage to save it, so now I walk with a prosthetic left leg.

'I stayed on for a while in the Army and got medically discharged two years short of my twenty-two years. I am a bit bitter about having to leave early, but I've not got any problem with the care I received. It was second to none.

'The George Cross was rightly given to Mark, because he knew he was dying that day. But he still maintained the radio, telling us what was going on and keeping them updated at Athens. He didn't have to do that. He clung on to the very end. He was a lovely lad. We were good mates, and I still miss him.'

You don't win a Military Cross, as Al Reid did, without being able to recognise courage. He believes Mark's actions were remarkable, even among the instances of bravery that he has himself seen in the field.

'I'm very proud of my nephew,' he said. 'I'd seen plenty of operations myself, and I'd been in some situations where I thought I might not survive. On one memorable occasion, I had destroyed everything which was personal and which might identify me as an individual, so that, if I was killed, the enemy would not have had the satisfaction of knowing that I was a man with dreams and aspirations. But Mark's bravery was a level of courage that was beyond my comprehension.

'The thing that upsets me the most is that he lay dying on a piece of earth in Afghanistan for nothing. He and I both knew that, as professional soldiers, you go where you're told to go. That is part of the contract. And, truth be told, you *do* want to see action. But we're leaving Afghanistan, just as we did Iraq, having lost all those lives – for what?

'My view is that we did the right thing by going into Afghanistan but – as was the case in Iraq, too – we didn't finish the job. There are a few politicians who I would have liked to have seen pick up a rifle and go to Helmand.'

LANCE CORPORAL JAKE ALDERTON
36 ENGINEER REGIMENT CORPS OF ROYAL ENGINEERS
AUGUST 16, 1985 – NOVEMBER 9, 2007

AS HIS FIRST operational tour of Afghanistan drew near, Jake Alderton's family threw a farewell party for him in the garden of their London home. He was a very popular young man, and a hundred or more people were there, laughing and dancing under a banner strung up by Jake's parents, Lesley and Keith.

'You can go,' it read, 'but be back soon.'

The words, from the hit show *Oliver!*, were appropriate in more ways than one. Perhaps unusually for a roughty-toughty soldier, Jake was a keen fan of West End musicals – *Wicked* was his favourite, and he'd recently taken his girlfriend Nicole to see *The Sound of Music*. His mum had bought the tickets as a pre-deployment present; if the twenty-two-year-old hadn't joined the Army, she said, he'd probably have ended up on the stage. Not that he looked like your average thespian. Jake was a weight-lifting boxer, and a man who had been specially selected for a perilous role in Sangin. The previous year, Mark Wright's 3 Para colleagues had been engaged in a hellish fight there, which had led to a score of medals being awarded, including Cpl Bryan Budd's posthumous VC.

Jake and his fellow Engineers were deploying as part of an OMLT with troops from 2nd Battalion The Yorkshire Regiment, and he had just finished months of training for the role. Daniel Salvage, a good friend of Jake's from the regiment, who would be flying out with him, said he was 'relishing' the challenge ahead.

'He took pride in being chosen,' said Salvage. 'It was the kind of thing that we'd joined up to do. We were looking forward to it, though it wasn't until we got to Afghan, and had a talk from some of the Engineers we were taking over from, that we really understood what we'd be facing. They told us how many deaths and injuries there'd been in the Sangin area since they arrived, and that this was one of the most dangerous areas in the whole country.'

But back at the party, on that August afternoon in Eltham, in the south-east of London, everything was right.

Jake's brother Joseph – older by almost three years – was there. The two of them were great mates, and were buying a house together. Later, Joseph would name his firstborn son 'Sid Joseph Jake' in honour of his beloved brother.

Their sister Sarah, the baby of the family and five years Jake's junior, was also there. She, too, would name her first son – Jake Joseph Keith – in her brother's honour.

The three of them were the best of friends, and both Joseph and Sarah would ensure that Uncle Jake's legend would be passed on to their boys, along with tales of how he inspired other young people.

Of course, like any siblings, they had had fallings-out when they were younger.

'Sometimes there'd be fisticuffs between the boys, like there is with brothers,' said Lesley Alderton. 'Jake would wind Joseph up with his banter, and then Joseph would get physical because he couldn't beat Jake on the banter. I could never be angry with him for long because he'd always make me laugh. But after he joined the Army, he and Joseph became much closer, and he was very close to his sister, too, and very protective of her. In her teenage years, I remember, he gave her a talk about how boys would respect a nice girl.'

Steve Daniels was at the party, too. Steve was one of Jake's closest civvie friends, and he felt he owed Jake almost everything.

'We first met when I was fourteen and he was a year older,' said Steve. 'When I was about sixteen, I got into a lot of bother with my family, and I had to move out. The two of us were sitting on a park bench one day and I was upset because I couldn't go home. I remember him saying, "I'm not going to leave you with nowhere to go, Steve. Come back to my place and my mum will put you up." Lesley and Keith didn't hesitate to take me in. I'm okay with my family now, but my life would have been completely different without him and them. They're an amazing family.

'You couldn't ask for a better friend than Jake. I couldn't fight my way out of a wet paper bag, but he'd stand in front me if someone was going to have a go, and say, "I know he's a wally, but you're not going to do anything to him." I remember the party that his mum and dad held before he left. It was a great day, but people were worried about him, and upset that he was going. Deep down, I worried about him, too, but he was so fearless. He didn't worry about anything, so I didn't think that would be the last time I saw him.'

Jake's parents felt the same. 'He left on September 16, 2007,' said Lesley. 'We drove him to the barracks, and I hugged him and kissed him goodbye. Not for one minute did I think that he wouldn't return. I was tearful, of course, and I went on to worry about him every night that he was there. I'd lie awake and pray for him and the others. But, yes, I suppose I thought he was invincible.'

The only inkling that Jake himself had any doubts about what lay ahead came in a conversation one day, not long before he deployed.

'He was at home listening to some music,' said Lesley. 'And one song really caught his imagination. He said, "Listen to this, mum!" and he played *Don't Stop Me Now* by Queen. He said, "Mum, if anything ever happens to me, I'd like this played at my funeral."'

* * *

LESLEY WAS ALMOST twenty-nine when Jake was born. 'His was the easiest birth out of the three,' she said. 'He just shot into the world and carried on from there. He was like the little thoroughbred of our family, very energetic and mischievous. He'd take his brother's toys apart to see how they worked, and we had to stop him taking the wallpaper off the walls when they'd just been decorated. Once, when he was about two, he escaped into the next-door neighbours' garden by making a hole in the fence. I was upstairs, and I happened to look out of the window. And there he was… Just walking through their garden as if he was in Wonderland.

'He loved being outdoors, and was a really active boy. Whenever we went out into the country for the day, Jake was always the first one to jump out of the car and run across the fields. He played a bit of football at school, but he really loved boxing, and he had a punch bag hanging up in the garden. And he learned to snowboard on the artificial slope not far from where we lived. He loved that.'

Jake's liveliness meant he caught the eye of his teachers.

'These days he'd probably be diagnosed with ADHD,' said Lesley. 'He found it hard to concentrate and sit still for long. He spent quite a lot of time in the naughty corner, but he'd make funny faces at the other children and make them laugh. I was often called in to see the teacher. Nevertheless, he went to school every day with a smile – even when he knew he was going to be in trouble for something he'd done the day before, he'd still walk through those gates with that big grin on his face.'

It was something his teachers remembered years later – along with his considerate and thoughtful nature.

'Jake was a very sensitive and kind person,' said Lesley. 'When he was six or seven, I remember him saying he'd like to give his toys to kids who had nothing. Another day, he was lying in the garden, flat on his back, looking up at the sky. I said, "Jake, what are you doing?" He said, "Oh, I'm just lying here, mum, imagining what it must be like to be homeless."

'Shortly after Jake's death, we got a phone call from the local pub, saying that one of their regulars wanted to meet us. So we went to the pub, and a Scottish man we'd never met before said, "I'm not a well man. I have motor neurone disease, and, when I came to the pub, Jake would be the first youngster to get off of his stool or chair and give it to me." He couldn't drink because of all the medication he was on, so Jake would put his pint to one side and go and get him an orange juice and drink it with him. He said, "I would have loved Jake to have been my son."'

The Army seeds were sown early, when the ten-year-old Jake went with his father to The Extravaganza at Earls Court. He successfully completed the mini assault course, and came home with shining eyes and a mug emblazoned with 'Army Be The Best'.

'He ran into the kitchen and said, "Mum, when I grow up, I'm going to be a soldier,"' said Lesley. 'From then on, that's all he wanted to do.'

School flew by. Jake was particularly good at drama and English, and always had his head in a book – often poetry, or a book of Shakespeare passages given to him by his mother, which he treasured and would carry around in his back pocket. His mischievous sense of humour often burst out.

'He was playing the part of a dog in one play,' said Lesley, 'and he cocked his leg up on stage as if he was doing a wee. He thought it was very funny, but the drama teacher wasn't amused.'

As a young teenager, he joined his local Army Cadets, and decided he wanted to be in the Royal Engineers. His GCSE results did not reflect his obvious intelligence, and he was concerned that they were not sufficient for him to pursue his dream.

'But we went along to the Army Careers Office and he did a test there,' said Lesley. 'He got top marks, and they told him he could do anything he wanted to. So he signed up, and he never looked back. He was just sixteen when he went to Arborfield [*Army training base*], but he loved every minute of it. It seemed like the moment he put on a uniform, his shoulders went back, the baseball cap came off, and he was a different person. The transformation was amazing. We were very proud of him. He liked Army life so much that when he was on leave he'd quite often say, "Mum, I can't wait to get back." I think it was the camaraderie and the banter. He was never politically correct and, in the Army, he could get away with his humour.

'He even loved the discipline. They got beasted a bit during training, but Jake used to say, "You can't take it personally, and I'd rather take it on the chin than have a bad report written about me. Anyway, all those who beast us have been beasted themselves. It's what makes us the great Army that we are."'

After competing his Combat Engineer course and passing out at Gibraltar Barracks, and after trade-training in building and structural finishing at Chatham, Jake was based in Germany. There, aged eighteen, he had a nasty fall from a thirty-five foot window which could have killed him and left him with serious back injuries. But, after spending time in a body cast, and recuperating at home, he recovered and went back to the Army.

That was the year of 9/11, and Lesley and Keith Alderton could see storm clouds gathering.

'I knew what was coming,' said Lesley. 'I thought, *My son is going to war because of that.* The world had been relatively peaceful when he joined up, but that suddenly changed, and it did trouble me. But he was having a lot of fun. He went snow-boarding in Austria, he was posted to Medicine Hat in Canada, and of course he made lots of great friends in the Army. And he wanted to go to Afghanistan. He'd passed the lance corporal cadre, which is really hard, but he said he didn't feel right wearing the stripe until he'd seen some action.'

Jake had met and fallen in love with Nicole Thangarajah, the girlfriend who would be with him until the end.

'They had a wonderful relationship,' said Lesley. 'Nic would often go down to Maidstone to stay with Jake at the barracks, and she stayed here with him when he was on leave. She wanted to study law and had started going to college, but then she took a break from education so that she could work and bring some money home.

'Jake didn't approve of that. He said to her, "You need to live your dream, Nic. You only get one life, so if you go back to college and study law I'll take you on a holiday to Portugal at my expense. If you don't agree to go back to studying, you can pay for it yourself!" He was laughing, as usual, but he really did want her to study. Although he was a joker, Jake was very intelligent and responsible. He took his job in the Army very seriously, and he was like that in other things. He never had a credit card or any debts. He'd say, "Mum, I can't afford it, so I can't have it." And he was buying a house with his brother at the time of his death, so he was a home-owner at a very young age. That was before he met Nic. Joseph lived in the house, and Jake would live at home with us when he was on leave.

'Anyway, Nic agreed to go back to college, and they did go to Portugal for a week. That was in the May and he deployed to Afghanistan in the September. When Jake died, we gave Nic some money from his will to help pay for her studies, and she went on to get her degree in law. We were so pleased, because that was what he wanted.'

* * *

DANIEL SALVAGE FIRST met Jake Alderton at the Royal Engineers' base at Maidstone. Fresh out of training, he wondered how easy it would be to slot into the regiment. Jake Alderton made it very easy.

'We both liked lifting weights, and I bumped into him in the gym,' said Salvage. 'He was really welcoming, and made me feel at home straight away. But we really became good friends in Canada on Op War Paint, preparing facilities for the following summer's training programme. After that, we were selected with two others in the squadron to be part of an OMLT, which was quite a privilege. You had to be able to fit in with a team you hadn't worked with before, and you needed to be level-headed and to be able to convey authority, because the ANA needed to see that.'

The team were deployed to Sangin, where they moved around between patrol bases, staying a week or so at each. When they weren't out on patrols in an infantry role, they were working hard to build up the bases' defensive walls and 'winterising' the accommodation.

'For the first half of the tour, we were out on patrol every day,' said Salvage. 'We wouldn't get the chance to do that normally, so we enjoyed it. But our living conditions were not good, at all. The toilets were just holes in the ground, and we didn't have any showers, just buckets of water. But at least we had camp beds, and every evening we'd split the rations up and cook it all up as a big hotpot over an open fire. We were a happy bunch of guys, which is easy in such a small team. Jake loved playing poker, and he was good at it. He wasn't the kind of gambler who would throw his money away, but often, when we'd finished work, you'd hear, "Right, who wants to play?" He was never far away from a pack of cards.'

Jake's parents would later present his favourite pack of cards, in an engraved box, to his old unit as a memento.

Despite the horror stories coming out of Sangin, the tour started quietly.

'There always seemed to be fighting going on nearby,' said Salvage, 'but we didn't engage with the Taliban much while Jake was with us. We had some contacts, and we were shot at, but usually by the time we could respond they'd gone. It was shoot-and-scoot stuff. When we were moving from place to place, I'd be Jake's driver and he'd be my top-cover. Standing up and manning the machine gun was relatively dangerous because you were exposed, but Jake wouldn't shy away from it.'

In the way that the fates can sometimes seem to conspire, Jake Alderton's death was the result of that bravery and a tragic combination of events.

First, he went down with the sort of diarrhoea and vomiting bug which hit many soldiers in Afghanistan, where raw sewage often ran through the streets they were patrolling. As a result, he was transferred to the main Sangin DC, where the medical facilities were better, for treatment.

Meanwhile, Daniel Salvage and the rest of the team pushed out to a new outpost, PB Waterloo.

'We'd been at Waterloo for two or three days when we learned there was going to be a deliberate operation to arrest or take out a Taliban leader,' said Salvage. 'Three of us had to go on that mission, and the rest of us would stay behind to protect the base. I was in the group that stayed behind. Because the patrol was leaving from Sangin DC, those who were involved went there to be briefed. Meanwhile, Jake had recovered and was waiting for the first available transport from the DC to Waterloo. As this special mission would be returning via Waterloo, he was included in the team. As far as I'm concerned, this was a bad happening. If he hadn't been ill and gone to the DC, he'd have been with me, and he'd probably still be alive today.'

The kill-or-capture mission left Sangin DC in the early hours of November 9, 2007. As he had on many previous occasions, Jake Alderton put himself in harm's way by taking on the dangerous Pinzgauer top-cover job.

The small convoy's route took it over a narrow bridge. At around 0400hrs, in the pitch black, and with headlights out to avoid drawing attention, the vehicle was accidentally driven off the bridge and into the water below. Everyone escaped unscathed – except for the vehicle commander, who suffered a serious arm injury, and Jake, who was pinned underneath it and crushed.

'I'd been over that bridge about thirty times,' said Salvage. 'So I knew it had a strange kink to it. If you didn't swerve at the right moment, you'd go over the edge. Of course, that's what happened. The driver of the Pinzgauer, a Gurkha, was driving over it for the first time, in the middle of the night. That hurts me, because if I'd been driving I don't think it would have happened.

'We got word of his death at 0600hrs. I was devastated. I knew that if Jake hadn't been ill, or if I'd been driving, it might have been so different. It was really horrible. Jake didn't even have to be up there, because he was a lance-corporal and someone more junior could have done it. But I can imagine Jake saying, "I'll do it!" because he knew he was good at it, and that's what he was like.

'A padre came from somewhere to have a chat with us. It was a couple of days before Remembrance Day, so we had a little service, and reflected on losing Jake. Just ten of us, in the middle of nowhere. And then it was back to normal. I believe they named the bridge after him, but I never saw it again because we avoided it. The guy who'd been driving the Pinzgauer came to our patrol base later. He was always quiet around us – he must have felt a tremendous sense of guilt. I think I was pretty annoyed with him at first, to be honest, but it wasn't long before I felt better about him. I'd never have said anything to him, anyway.'

* * *

IN LONDON, LESLEY Alderton was waiting for her son to make one of his regular cheerful phone calls home.

'I used to look forward to those calls so much,' she said. 'He always sounded happy. He usually rang on a Tuesday, but the last call I got was a Saturday, just before bonfire night. I remember it vividly. He spoke to me, then his dad, then his sister, and then he came back to me. He said "Mum, we're not getting as much support as the Americans."

'I said, "What do you mean, Jake? There's a charity just been launched called Help for Heroes. I'll ask Joseph to get some of the wristbands and I'll send you out some information. Everyone back home is thinking about you all."

'With hindsight, I think he may actually have been talking about the poor quality of the equipment they were issued with. Our soldiers have always been good at improvising, but just because they can improvise doesn't mean that they should have to.'

Indeed, an inquest into LCpl Alderton's death found that it was caused in part by failures in both training for driving at night with night vision goggles, and in the provision of effective night vision equipment. It was also found that there were no 'drop-down' bars fitted which might have helped Jake to get back inside the Pinzgauer before it fully turned over. Furthermore, it was established that lights on the dashboard would not extinguish; the contrast with the pre-dawn dark outside the vehicle made it almost impossible for the driver to see the road ahead.

'I remember the day very clearly,' said Lesley. 'We were going out, and I'd gone upstairs to get ready. The strange thing was, I'd put a black outfit on. I came downstairs, looked in the mirror and said to Keith, "I don't like this," and went back up to change. While I was upstairs, the doorbell rang. I looked down and saw two suited men. My first thought was that they were from the double-glazing company, because we'd had windows fitted that we weren't happy with. I think I heard Keith say, "My wife's not going to want to see you."

'I came down and said, "Who is it?"

'They, or Keith, said, "It's Jake. Jake has been killed."

'I collapsed to the floor and said, "No, no, it can't be! You must have made a mistake. It's not Jake." But they were shaking their heads. They said he'd been killed in a road traffic accident. I thought, *A road traffic accident? How could he be killed in a road traffic accident?* Then I remember sitting there with Keith, holding his hand, saying "What are we going to do? What are we going to do?" I had a complete feeling of helplessness. It was like the ground had opened up and sucked us all in, and there was no way out. It was absolutely the most awful day of my life.

'Joseph was at work, so Keith phoned him and said, "Joseph, we've lost Jake." Joseph's exact words were, "No, no, dad! I don't want to be hearing that." He came home in a cab and, as he walked in, I remember he looked at the two Army officers, and said, "No! Not my little brother! Not my little brother! We shared a room for sixteen years."

'Keith phoned my friend Kim, who's known me since childhood, and she came to stay with me, while he and the two Army officers went to find Sarah at college to tell her and bring her home.'

Sarah remembers being called to a room at the college, where she met Keith and the two Army representatives.

Her father said, 'I'm so sorry, Sarah, it's Jake. It's Jake.'

She fell to the ground, punching the floor, her screams of, 'No! Not Jake! Not my brother!' echoing round the building. Once she had recovered a little, she went home with her father. But, at just seventeen years of age, she found it hard to express her feelings with the rest of the family, and so she went to the stables to be with her horse, Bally.

Meanwhile, said Lesley, Joseph had thought of Nicole.

'I remember him picking the phone up,' she said, 'and I could actually hear Nic screaming from the other end of the phone. It was a scream like I'd never heard before, and I'd never wish to hear again.

'When my friend arrived I was in the bathroom, just crying and crying. I couldn't come out, so she sat on the stairs. Then Keith came back with Sarah, and she was also crying her eyes out. That night, all these youngsters, Jake's friends, turned up. There was a crowd of them, and they sat there sobbing. I was still numb, but holding on to each other like we did was a good feeling.

'My sister Jo-Anne spent that night with me on the sofa. She was hugging me as we both tried to sleep. Around five o'clock, I woke up and heard someone crying. I found Jo-Anne in the doorway, just looking out into the garden, sobbing.

'I don't know how we got through, but you have to, somehow. We had two other children who loved and needed us. But still, my whole world had just fallen apart, and it would never be the same again.'

The family were taken to RAF Lyneham to see Jake return home.

'It was just him in that huge aircraft,' said Lesley. 'He was taken to a little chapel. His coffin was draped in the flag, and it was nice to spend a little time with him before he was taken off. The hearse drove through Wootton Bassett and people were out on the streets to pay their respects. It was lovely to see that.'

Jake's body was taken to a chapel of rest near his home, and his family and friends were able to see him.

'I felt I had to see Jake before I could really believe it was him,' said Lesley, 'because he'd died so far away and so abruptly. When I saw him in the coffin I knew it was Jake, but at the same time it wasn't. It was as if the lights had gone out in him, because he was always so full of life and so bright.'

Jake's funeral was held at Holy Trinity Church in Eltham. It was full to overflowing, and beyond.

'There were so many soldiers, including the Gurkhas Jake had worked with, that they had to park their vehicles in the B&Q car park,' said Lesley. 'Among them was a Gurkha sergeant who had just lost his own five-year-old son. Keith asked him how he could attend Jake's funeral while suffering his own personal tragedy. The sergeant said, "I had to come, because Jake was one of my men."'

Lesley was deeply impressed by the number of people who came out of the shops to pay their respects as the cortege went down the High Street.

'I'll never forget seeing a van full of builders stop,' she said. 'They all got out and just stood there. At the funeral, Jeff, one of Keith's closest friends, supported him as he somehow found the strength to talk about Jake's life. The Padre spoke beautifully. He gave all Jake's friends a matchstick to put in their wallets to remind them of the light that shone from him. He'd saved a couple of his friends when they were in their deepest, darkest places, and the Padre knew that.'

Jake was buried at the military cemetery at Fort Pitt, Kent. Afterwards, his family faced the near-impossible task of getting on with their lives.

'I slept, surrounded by over 200 sympathy cards, on the sofa in the front room for months,' said Lesley. 'I don't know how I even opened the curtains some days, and if it wasn't for the dog I wouldn't have got up at all. I had to walk her. I remember my brother turning up one day and finding me lying there in complete darkness. He couldn't see me like that, and had to walk away.

'I wasn't eating, although people were coming around with food and friends were putting things in the oven and *making* the two of us sit down and eat. I think it's more difficult for men, in a way, because they have to try to be the strong ones and not to show their feelings as much as we do. Keith was very strong. I suppose we both were in a way. I should probably give myself some credit.

'We all grieve differently. My husband was desperate to get back the Lesley that I was, but I'm still not back, and our relationship has suffered greatly. Lots of marriages don't survive the loss of a child. We've been through so much together, but this was the heaviest blow we ever suffered. We're now going through a divorce, and the house will probably have to be sold. That will be painful, because this is where the children grew up. Jake was only two when we moved here.

'I'm still on medication, and I still have very bad days. I've been diagnosed with severe PTSD. I have these terrible flashbacks and nightmares about Jake's death, because I read the Coroner's witness statements and they were very vivid descriptions of what happened. I had a nightmare last night, and the night before. Sometimes I feel like I haven't slept at all. Sometimes my dreams are about Jake as a man, and sometimes he's a baby. I've dreamed that I'm in the shower, and the water is not going down the plughole. I put my hands down, thinking it's the sponge that's blocking it, but it's not – it's Jake as a baby, and I'm trying to save him.

'People say these are only dreams, but when I have them it's as if I'm living them. Usually they're horrible, but recently I dreamed of Jake just putting his arms around me and holding me. One of the counsellors I've seen said, "You always speak of Jake as if you've lost him, and you never say to me that he died or he's dead. But when you lose something you normally have a chance of finding it again. That tells me that you haven't come to terms with his death."

'At Jake's funeral, his corporal said to me, "Whenever we were at our lowest ebb, Jake would pop up with his big smiley face and say, 'Things could be worse!'"

'I think that, on that night he was killed, if Jake could have said anything, he would have said the same thing. "Things could be worse! We could *all* have perished. But we didn't. It was only me."

'I know he wouldn't want to see me the way I am now, still devastated and having trouble living my life. But I'm trying to get better, and I won't give up. I go to SSAFA [*Soldiers', Sailors' and Airmen's Families Association*] bereaved families events. We call ourselves the survivors, and I think that's what we really are.

'I walk Skye [*the family dog*] and I use the gym, because I think if I can get my body fit, my mind might follow. The gym does help me to switch off, but I still think of Jake every day. I've had loads of counselling and therapy.

'I feel anaesthetised. Since losing Jake, I've lost other people who are very dear to me, but I haven't been able to feel the grief of losing them. It's as if nothing else can hurt me like losing Jake did. A lot of people say, "You look really well, Lesley." But if only they knew. I've lost all my confidence and self-esteem. I really want to go back to work, but I can't face an interview. When I lost Jake, I was working with children with disabilities and behavioural problems, and I'd just gained my NVQ3 in Health and Social Care. I went back to work there three months after his death, but only stayed for four months, because it was very challenging work at the best of times and almost impossible for me then. My friend who worked there more or less carried me. She'd always make sure we were on the same shifts. But then she had to leave the job, and I felt I couldn't do it any more on my own, so I left. I've done some charity work since then for Help for Heroes, and I've given talks at events. It helps to keep Jake's memory alive and it helps his comrades who have been coming home with horrific injuries.'

It has been hard on all of the family, of course.

'Sarah said to me the other day, "I always feel my brother with me,"' said Lesley. 'I said, "He *is* always with us, Sarah." And I do believe that. Sometimes, when I'm coming home on a really cold, dark night, I suddenly feel as if someone has wrapped a quilt around me. How can you feel that warmth all of a sudden on a bitter cold night? And whenever we go to the cemetery, no matter what the weather, the sun always peeks through… Even if it's been pouring with rain, the sun peeks through and shines down. Sunflowers remind me of him, because they're so bright.

'Since losing Jake, I've gone to church quite often, and I try to lead my life in a Christian way. I'm not overly religious, but I do remember that Jake said to me once, "We're not soldiers, mum; we're guardian angels." Maybe he was right, because the Padre said to me after his death, "Jake has made a difference, you know. Women are coming out of their houses and children are playing on the streets in Helmand."

'But we've lost so many young lads, and, to be honest, I think that when we do finally withdraw from Afghanistan it's going to go back to the way it was before we went there. The Padre said to me that Jake and his friends made a difference, but I just fear for what may happen when we leave.

'I am very disappointed and angry that no-one has taken

61

responsibility for Jake's avoidable death. The MOD never apologised for not equipping the driver properly or training him properly. But they never do apologise, because if they do it's like accepting they were at fault. Even the head of the Army at the time, Sir Richard Dannatt, said that Jake's was one of the avoidable deaths.'

Daniel Salvage believes the war *was* worthwhile.

'I still believe we had to do it,' he said. 'I'd like to think that all those who died there gave their lives for a reason. What really makes me sick is what's going on in this country. I've seen nineteen-year-olds not able to get up in the mornings to get a job, so they're given Job Seekers' Allowance. But I was in Afghan at the age of nineteen, and I lost my best mate at that age.'

Jake's good friend from civvie street, Steve Daniels, also lost his best mate, 'the funniest bloke you could ever meet'.

'He was wise beyond his years,' said Steve. 'He taught me a lot. While I was living with Jake's family, I wasn't earning much money and I used to have a bit of a problem with the fruit machines. We were in the pub one night, and I put my last £20 into a machine. I was feeling a bit down, and asked him if he'd buy me a pint. Jake said, "I'm not being funny, mate, but you need to stop that. Yeah, I'll get you a pint." So he went to the bar and brought me back a pint of water. I got the point.

'I struggled a lot with his death. I knew it couldn't hurt anyone more than it hurt his family. Even so, they supported me a lot. A couple of weeks later, Jake's dad came to watch me playing football. I thought, *You shouldn't be doing this, you've got other things to worry about.* But that's just the way they are.

'Jake brightened up my day every time I saw him, and I miss him massively. But I've got memories and no-one can take them away from me. Seven years on, I don't feel any better, but Jake would want us all to live our lives as best we can. I'm getting married in three months' time, and I'm without my best man. Of course, my brother will take on the job, and – don't get me wrong – I'm really happy about that. But when I look around, I see that everyone has their best friend. I don't have one anymore.'

CORPORAL SARAH BRYANT
152 DELTA PSYCHOLOGICAL OPERATIONS EFFECTS TEAM
INTELLIGENCE CORPS
DECEMBER 17, 1981 – JUNE 17, 2008

IT WAS NUDGING forty degrees in the pitiless, sun-baked lands outside Lashkar Gah as the six-vehicle patrol edged forwards.

A number of those in the vehicles were Territorial Army [*now Army Reserve*] soldiers, drafted in to support the regulars who were already being stretched by the developing war.

The men had originally been involved in training members of the Afghan national police, but had now reached the end of their tour and were days away from going home. But then came news of a Taliban assault on a jail at Kandahar, a hundred kilometres to the west. Walls had been destroyed, guards murdered, and hundreds of prisoners freed – many of them insurgents.

The order had quickly come down: Intercept any escapees who might be heading west from the prison towards 'Lash'.

The plan took them into a zone that was particularly dangerous, even by Helmand's deadly standards.

A young female corporal from the Intelligence Corps, Sarah Bryant, was alongside four of the TA men in one Snatch Land Rover.

Not long before, she had contacted her mother and father back home in Cumbria with news that their 'little girl' was being promoted to sergeant, and with words of reassurance.

'Don't worry,' she had written, 'I have the best bodyguards a girl could have. I'll be home in a month and I can't wait to see you both.'

That pending promotion was evidence of the regard in which Cpl Bryant was held by her colleagues and superiors. She was a PSYOPs [*psychological operations*] expert, who had served on the staff of the Deputy Commander of Coalition Forces in Iraq. In Afghanistan, she worked at the HQ of 16 Air Assault Brigade as a Target Audience Analyst, collecting and analysing information about enemy deployments and plans, and briefing the patrols which were sent out to interdict the enemy. Often, she travelled with the soldiers, checking the accuracy of information she and colleagues had collated, and the reliability of their sources.

She had been marked out for further elevation, and was widely believed to have a sparkling future in the British Army.

At 3.40pm local time, the rear wheels of Sarah Bryant's Land Rover rolled over a pressure-plate linked to a massive IED hidden in the ditch alongside.

The resultant explosion flipped the five-tonne vehicle onto its roof like a twig and spread wreckage over a square mile.

Other soldiers who rushed to help could do nothing for half an hour, as the remains of the vehicle blazed and ammunition exploded.

But, in any event, Cpl Bryant – the first female British soldier to die in Operation Herrick – had been killed outright, along with three of the men alongside her. Astonishingly, another – later named only as 'Soldier E' – survived.

A lot was later made of the fact that they had been travelling in a thinly-armoured Land Rover. The fact was that the bomb used – which linked two Russian-era anti-tank shells and contained perhaps 45kg of high explosive – would probably have defeated any vehicle in the British Army's inventory.

At the wheel had been Cpl Richard Larkin, a member of the Territorial Army since 1999, a reservist medic and, in the civvie world, a night charge nurse at Evesham Community Hospital. A thirty-nine-year-old father of three from Cookley, near Kidderminster, he was right at the end of his tour. His wife Teresa – his sweetheart since their teenage years as nurses together – was looking forward to his imminent return.

A great family man, Cpl Larkin had been deployed to Afghanistan on Boxing Day 2007. It had been terribly hard for him to leave, but he at least had the memory of having taken his five-year-old twin sons James and Malachy in for their first day at school a few months earlier. It had 'broken his heart, knowing that he would have to leave them', Mrs Larkin would later say. Once in theatre, he had sent home many letters and keepsakes to her and the children, and had managed to get back on R&R in February for the first birthday of his baby daughter Orla. She would take her first steps on the day that her father's body was repatriated.

'The boys have lovely memories of their dad being fun,' Teresa told the *Birmingham Mail* in 2013. 'It's hard for Orla as she has no memories of her dad… She's going for bereavement counselling and I'm putting together a memory box for her. She treasures a picture of her dad returning home for her first birthday. She keeps a feelings book and has written in it that "Mum said dad would be very proud of me."'

Trooper Paul Stout, thirty-one and from Liverpool, was the father of two young children, Mia and Taylor. He was due to marry his partner Sue, their mother, on his return from the tour; Sue would later change her surname to Stout and her title to 'Mrs' in his honour. She would also write an award-winning *GQ* magazine article about the incident, in which she said that the idea of Paul dying 'had never been a real possibility'. They had talked about it, she said, but only in terms of an excuse for him to buy more 'ally' [*flash*] kit.

She wrote: 'I know it's eighty quid, love,' he would say, 'but this could save my life. I could die, 'cos you moaned about me spending eighty quid.'

Once he'd joked about suffering severe injuries, and had asked Sue 'how much of him had to come back for me not to leave him… "What about if I was just a head?"'

She'd replied that she would keep him in a jar, 'like [*in the film*] *The Man With Two Brains*.'

'All the time he told me he was invincible,' wrote Sue. 'All the time, I believed it. I thought *he* believed it; he didn't. So he wrote me a letter, just in case.'

That letter was a last farewell, to be read only if the worst happened. In it, he apologised for dying, and asked Sue to remember that he 'died fighting for you and the kids, because I love you more than anything else in the world.'

Cpl Sean 'Vic' Reeve, twenty-eight and single, was from Patcham, Brighton. In his day job he was a business consultant with a master's degree, but he had given ten years to the TA. An excellent young soldier from a military background, he had enjoyed being in Afghanistan – particularly, he told his family, in dealing with the locals, whom he found friendly and welcoming. He'd arranged for Sussex schools to send over pens and paper, which he had dished out to clamouring and delighted Afghan children.

The day before, he had been stood down to get ready for home. He had spoken to his parents that evening, and had said he expected to be on a flight back on June 22 – the day before his twenty-ninth birthday – unless there was a priority over him.

Indeed, he did return on that day – repatriated to RAF Lyneham, having been killed after volunteering to go back on duty to help deal with the prisoner breakout. The next thing his parents knew, they were answering the door to two men in suits and their world had changed forever.

Like Paul Stout, he too had written a final letter home, which was read out at his funeral.

'I hope that no-one ever has to read this,' it began. 'I want to minimise the pain and distress for my loved ones in the event of my death. I am going to a dangerous place to do a dangerous job, it would be foolish of me to ignore the possibility of being killed.'

He described his mother, Rosaleen, as 'a beautiful and wonderful person. I love her so much that it can't be described. I can't bear the thought of her being sad… no-one has a kinder heart than my mum.'

He wrote that his father, Bob, was his 'idol', and spoke of his love for his sister Heidi and brother Neal.

'Please trust me,' he said, 'that no matter what the circumstances of my death, no matter how fast, no matter how slow, I was strong, without fear and without pain. My only suffering will be the realisation that I will not see my family and friends again. The thing you have to cope with is not the loss of my soul, but the loss of my physical presence. I can live on as long as you want me to.'

But perhaps naturally – because she was the first woman to die on Operation Herrick – the media concentrated most of its attention on the loss of Sarah Bryant.

* * *

SARAH WAS BORN in Liverpool, the only child of Des Feely and his wife Maureen. They moved to the Cumbrian countryside when Sarah was starting infants' school, and she enjoyed the sort of idyllic, old-fashioned, horsey childhood that most youngsters can only dream of.

'She loved being outdoors,' said Maureen. 'It didn't matter what the weather was like – even in hail or snow, she'd just get her wellies on and go outside. And we could be sure that, if there was mud or dirt about, she'd be in it. But although Sarah was a tomboy, she was very petite and very girlie as well.

'She loved the little bit of garden that she looked after herself, and when she got older and a bit more responsible she had animals. She was very good at looking after them from an early age. We started off with a dog and a cat and a goldfish, and then a neighbour asked Sarah if she'd like a couple of guinea pigs that needed a new home. Then rabbits joined the guinea pigs, and then she started helping a neighbour to look after his chickens and geese. Then there were pet lambs that she had to bottle feed. She actually used to walk one on a lead.

'Sarah had a wicked sense of humour from an early age. She would giggle and laugh a lot. On the odd occasion when we had to tell her off, she'd just stand there and giggle at you. She wasn't being disrespectful, in fact she'd say to me, "Sorry, mummy, but I can't help it."'

'Parents always say that their children are little angels,' said Des, 'but, in Sarah's case, she really was. She was just a beautiful child. People would say, "It'll change. Just wait until she's two!" And then, "Wait until she's four!" But none of that transpired. She was a perfect, unassuming little child, who never put a foot wrong and never threw a tantrum.'

Sarah's closest childhood friend, Krista Presch, remembers a girl who 'found fun in everything.'

'She could laugh at herself and at me,' said Krista. 'We giggled a *lot*. We both lived in the same village and attended the same little rural primary school. We became solid friends right from the beginning. We would usually walk to and from school together, spend the day together and then on the weekend we'd be together with our horses. Even before we both had our own horses, we'd pretend that we were show-jumping in her garden or mine.

'We went to separate secondary schools, and leaving each other was a huge thing. But we were still living in the same village, so we went on spending lots of time together. We'd go the country shows and compete at show-jumping events. We weren't really into boys and gigs and that sort of thing during our later teenage years. We were both very innocent and countrified.'

Sarah's interest in the Army was sparked, believes her father, by an experience she had when she was about eighteen.

'In those days,' he said, 'we had the catering concession at Carlisle Airport. The Army and RAF would carry out huge exercises at the airport, and some of the officers took a shine to her. On one occasion, there was an exercise based on [*Israel's famous anti-terrorist operation at*] Entebbe. Sarah and her mum were among those who were selected to play the part of hostages; after being 'rescued', they were thrown into the back of a Hercules and zoomed off into the night for an hour. The excitement really kicked in and I think that made her decide to be a soldier.'

'When she left sixth form college she still didn't know what she was going to do,' said Maureen, 'so she worked in the family business at Carlisle Airport. Then she got a job in the local leisure centre. Then one day when she was nineteen, and to our great surprise, she came home and said she wanted to join the Army. She decided she would try for Sandhurst.

'She still looked more like sixteen – it didn't help that she didn't do make-up, she said the only make-up she wanted was "that green and brown stuff that soldiers use" – but she was invited to an interview, and I drove her down to Sandhurst. They decided that her application should be deferred by a year and then she should try again. But she didn't want to wait. A few days later, she went to the local recruitment office. After exploring a few options, they said to her, "We think you may be best suited to the Intelligence Corps." Perhaps they could see that she was a gatherer of information. At that time, she didn't like to stand up and share it, but she was very good at listening and she could remember things very well.'

She signed up and went to Winchester for basic training in January 2002.

'There wasn't one thing about it that she didn't like,' said Maureen. 'I'd speak to her two or three times a week, and she'd say, "Oh, it's great, mum!" This was despite the fact that, being shy, it must have been hard to go off and live in a room with a lot of other girls. But nothing seemed to bother her. I think that, because she couldn't hide behind anyone else and therefore *had* to speak, the part of her character that had always been there began to emerge. Once she told me she'd had to give a briefing about something. I said, "How did you get on?" and she said, "I *loved* it!" I stood there wondering if I'd heard her correctly. Her school reports had always been very good, except that they often said that she should participate more. She'd say, "I know the answers, mum, I just don't like putting my hand up." I wish I'd been able to go back to her schools and tell them how confident she'd become.'

After basic training – which she completed with a broken foot – Sarah moved on to the six-month course at the Intelligence Corps' base at Chicksands in Bedfordshire. It was there that she met Carl Bryant – a fellow recruit, the love of her life, and the man who would become her husband.

* * *

'I MET SARAH for the first time in April 2002,' said Carl. 'Most of us had completed our basic training together, but Sarah was one of a few new faces. As well as being beautiful, I was struck by how funny she was. She was always up for having a good time, and never let any aspect of the training get to her. I used to get very stressed and downbeat at times, but she just glided along, dealing with whatever came her way with a smile on her face. The first briefing she gave had us all in stitches, and everyone in the squad warmed to her instantly.

'Sadly for me, she started seeing someone else quite early on in training. For the next few weeks, I tried as much as I could to get noticed by her, clowning around or "playing jack-the-lad", as she called it later on, until one night I got a chance. I bought her a drink, and then managed to convince her that I was worth a snog.

'Sarah and I became very close to a few of the other lads on the course, one of whom was Jim Oakland, who eventually transferred to the Royal Military Police. Jim served as an usher at our wedding, he was a member of Sarah's bearer party at her repatriation and funeral, and then the following year he was also killed in Helmand. [*James Oakland, a twenty-six-year-old single man with a long-term girlfriend, whose only brother was going through Sandhurst at the time, was killed by an IED in Gereshk on October 22, 2009.*]

'We would go out a lot and enjoy ourselves, while scraping by in our tests. Sarah was my rock throughout our life together, and that started early on at Chicksands.'

A month or so before the end of training, with first postings about to be allocated, a nervous Carl plucked up his courage.

'We were still single,' he said, 'so we had no reason to expect that we would continue to be posted near each other. We'd become so close that being without her wasn't an option. As it happened, we were deployed to Iraq together in 2003, but that was just luck. I loved serving alongside her on operations, and she was incredible during that tour. She had such a zest for adventure and for all things to do with soldiering. I do remember her becoming very unhappy during Christmas dinner in Basra Palace, though. We all started having a food fight, and it was one of the few occasions she showed her displeasure at something immature I'd done.

'Anyway, I proposed during a trip to London, after yet another Bedford night out. And she said yes. I'm ashamed to say that, as I was a recruit with no money, we went halves on an engagement ring from the H Samuel shop at Victoria Station.'

It was a whirlwind romance – Sarah's parents, by now separated – had never even heard of Carl.

'Both her father and I received phone calls from Sarah to tell us about him,' said Maureen. 'She said to me, "Someone has asked me to marry him!"

'I said, "That's lovely! But who is this *somebody*?"'

'She just said his name was Carl. That was typical of Sarah. She was still very quiet, even with us, in some ways. She'd been home just a few weeks earlier but had never mentioned him. They were married at Holy Trinity Church in Wetheral in October 2005, when they were both stationed in Germany. The wedding was beautiful. Because she was still in Germany, she trusted me enough to organise most of it. She would buy wedding brochures and send them to me with little notes, saying, "I like this, mum. Can you get it please?"

'It was the most amazing day. I know I'm very biased, but everyone who attended said they had never been to a wedding that flowed so easily. Everything was just perfect and, although it was October, it was like a spring day. My little surprise gift was a carriage with black horses to take her to the church. Her face was a picture. She was so happy.'

Soon after the wedding, both Carl and Sarah were posted back to the UK, and moved into married quarters in Shrewsbury. Of course, Army life doesn't run as it might in the outside world.

'Through the first eighteen months of married life we spent less than twelve weeks together,' said Carl. 'In 2006, and thanks to very supportive chains of command, we did both get deployed to Iraq again at the same time. We weren't together this time, but we did manage to have our R&R at the same time.

'In mid-2007, we were both posted to units at Chicksands, and although we knew that Sarah would deploy to Afghanistan at some point it at least meant we had a year living in the same house, and living a normal life. It's so easy to get swept along with military life and lose sight of what actually matters most. I will be forever grateful for that time with her. We had a good-sized house with our dog, Tyson – a rescue dog, that wasn't our choice of name – and we spent our evenings either walking him or eating out and just doing normal, family-type stuff. It brought us as close together as we had been at the very start.

'But Sarah was eager to deploy, and when her build-up training began she was raring to go. It's very strange listening to a girl in pyjamas, enjoying a glass of white wine with her hair down, telling you how to achieve good groupings [*accurate hits*] with a general-purpose machine gun.'

And so Cpl Bryant went off to war. Carl had never served in Helmand and didn't appreciate just how tough conditions were – though he got an inkling during his wife's final pre-deployment exercise.

'A girl Sarah worked with was in tears telling her of her fears about returning to Afghanistan,' he said. 'I was shaken at that. I realised what Sarah might be going into.'

Her mother, Maureen, was similarly unaware.

'When she deployed, the situation there wasn't as bad as it became,' said Maureen. 'It wasn't even in the news that much, even though about ninety soldiers had been killed. So we knew it was dangerous, but it became much worse.

'I remember saying goodbye to her. Sarah had come up to Carlisle to drop off her dog "for his holidays" and to ask if she could have mail order parcels sent to my house. One day after she'd gone a parcel did arrive, and when we opened it we all just started to laugh... it was a holster for a handgun. Sarah had decided that the ones they were issued with weren't that good. I said, "Look at this! Other girls order fashion wear and Sarah orders a holster!"

'I knew she was really looking forward to the posting. Every time she went away, or at the end of each phone conversation when she was deployed, I'd say, "Don't forget your tin hat!" That was just our little joke. She'd say, "Mum, if it was tin it wouldn't do any good." Those were my last words to her in our last telephone conversation, two days before she was killed.'

* * *

ABOVE ALL, SARAH Bryant was a very good soldier, and once in Afghanistan she found herself doing the job she had wanted to do for many years. Because of the nature of that job – psychological warfare and intelligence gathering is necessarily a secretive and serious business – she was able to tell her family and friends back home very little about it. Even Carl Bryant was kept in the dark, as Army protocols dictate. But she sent home many blueys and telephoned as regularly as her work allowed. Usually, she rang her parents on Sundays, though – to ensure she got time on the phone with Carl – they were careful not to use up her allocation of minutes.

'She'd call me three or four times a week,' said Carl, 'and we also kept in touch through blueys and by email. We were so used to being apart that there wasn't that emotional interchange that other couples might have. I'd never tell her I was worried about her, as a civilian partner might, so when we spoke they were just jolly chats about whatever was going on. Obviously, we couldn't talk about her work, though I could tell she believed in the campaign, and in particular she sympathised with Afghan women. She was always very positive, and it was clear she was in her element. But a lot of the talk was about things like a safari holiday to Africa we were going to take when she got back.'

After a few months in theatre, Sarah came home on leave. Unsurprisingly, the experience of being in a war zone had sapped even this most bubbly and effervescent of women.

'She never spoke to me directly about the stresses,' said her father, Des Feely. 'But she was possibly worried. The Army had been going through a period of quite high casualties, and it was getting gradually worse. I think the increasing danger worried her, because she was a target analyst and she frequently went out with the men. She needed to know that the sources and the information on which she was basing decisions were sound.'

That visit was four weeks before she died. On her return, it was back into the action and her working routine.

On the Sunday before her death, as ever she phoned her parents.

'I was in the garden with her dog,' said Maureen. '"I'm outside with your boy," I said. She said, "I wish I was there. I can hear the birds."'

For Des Feely, that was a special day – Father's Day. It's hard to imagine how he felt, his only daughter far from his protection, in a barren country with savage men trying their best to kill her. He made the best of it, as he had to.

'Her calls were always quick,' he said, 'because there would be queues of people waiting to use the phone. She just wanted to wish me a happy Father's Day. It was a light-hearted conversation, as they always were – there was never an instance when Sarah wasn't joking. She talked about how much she missed her dog – she was mad-keen on her animals. We talked about the barbecues they'd been having on the base, and she complained about the heat and the flies. I remember we joked that it was the first Father's Day message I'd ever had from Afghanistan. As it turned out, of course, it was the last.'

Carl Bryant's final telephone call from his young wife was to tell him that she wouldn't be able to speak to him for a few days.

'She sounded excited and up for it, as always,' he said. 'She knew the risks, but never showed any hesitation or fear. That's one of the reasons she was so impressive. She had a wonderful attitude, and she could lift the spirits of those around her. She would never have said that she couldn't do something; she'd always have a go. Plus, she was good at it. Her kit was always squared away, she was an excellent shot, she was fit, and she was determined. She was a natural leader. There is a reason that the men who died alongside her had her in their team that day.

'I was running an exercise when I received the news. A senior NCO called me aside, and then I saw someone walking towards me in a suit and tie. I knew straight away. I said to him, "Tell me my wife isn't dead." It's a very hard job for notification officers, and they have to go through a script. So he didn't answer that question immediately. He just started saying the words he had prepared, so I knew she'd been killed.

'I managed to get hold of relatives and friends of Des and Maureen so that they could tell them Sarah had been killed before they heard about it on the news. Fortunately, Sarah had left me contact details of uncles and aunts, just in case. Talking to them and asking them to break the news to her parents was indescribable.'

Sarah's mother Maureen was engaged in one of those mundane, civilian-world tasks – trying to sort out a visa for a holiday – when the terrible news reached her.

'Carl didn't want people in suits coming knocking on Des' door or mine,' she said, 'so he tried to contact my brother so he could break the news to me. But he was away, so he spoke to my sister-in-law, Jane. As it happened, it was her birthday. He had to tell her the awful news and ask her if she would then tell me. Poor Jane! She had to learn that her favourite niece had been killed on her birthday.

'The only problem was that they lived in Plymouth, so Jane rang a close friend of mine and asked him to tell me. That must have been the hardest thing for both her and him.

'I was living too far away from Des to go around and tell him personally, and I didn't want to tell him over the phone. So I contacted Des' closest friend and got him to go round before anyone else could knock on his door. Once I knew Des' friend was with him, I rang him.'

'My friend and his girlfriend drove about twenty miles to be with me,' said Des. 'He was always one for a few beers, and when he arrived, at about one in the morning, I thought, *Oh no! What on earth can they want at this time?* Then I noticed how ashen-faced he was. She said, "Oh God! He doesn't know." They ended up telling me before the military officer arrived.

'The rest of the night was… well, it was dawn before we knew what time it was again. Then I started to panic, because I didn't know how to tell my mother, and I was worried that the shock might kill her. So I phoned the out-of-hours doctor, and they sent around a whole host of medical people. They took over. It was very good of them.'

Maureen had the same concerns in respect of Sarah's maternal grandparents. 'I was afraid that my parents would find out from the press. My dad would have been eighty-eight then, and my mum was eighty-five. They'd done so much to help bring Sarah up. I remember spending the whole night planning how I was going to tell them. Then at about eight o'clock in the morning I rang them to say I'd pop in on my way to work. I don't know how I could even talk calmly, but I had to.

'I walked in and said, "You must both sit down because I've something to tell you." When I'd been told, I felt as if I'd been lifted into another world; as if it wasn't happening to me. I felt that someone had told me this information but it wasn't meant for me, because it wasn't Sarah they were talking about. Yes, they were saying my name and Sarah's name, but it wasn't anything to do with me. I remember walking all night and thinking this couldn't have happened because, although she was in Afghanistan, she wasn't in any danger. I think their reaction was the same as mine: they heard what I said, but they didn't think I was telling them the truth. Mum said, "No she hasn't." I explained how I'd found out and what I knew, although in fact I didn't know very much at all.

'Later that day, I started to receive phone calls from military people, and suddenly I was, sadly, able to accept it was Sarah they were talking about. My brain had disengaged from reality, but now reality was beginning to dawn. I felt sick and drained of emotion. I remember feeling I had to be strong for Sarah. I thought she wouldn't want me to be in pieces in front of others. *Sarah has been brave*, I thought. *Now I need to be brave for her.* And yet it was the worst thing that could ever happen to me as a mother. Sarah was the love of my life.'

* * *

AS THE HORROR of what had happened sank in over the following days, preparations were made to bring Sarah home.

In the meantime, the media interest was enormous.

'There were ten TV vans outside the house at one point,' said Des Feely. 'I felt under siege. To give them their due, they understood the pressure on me, so they all voted for one TV team to interview me, then shared it. That way I did not have to go through the same experience again and again.

'It seemed like it would never end. Every time the controversy of the Snatch Land Rovers was mentioned in the news [*they were widely considered to be inadequate and gradually removed from use in Afghanistan*], the media would pester the life out of me, asking me what I thought of it all. And I did have an opinion. I was on the Jeremy Vine Show on Radio Two and I said they were tents on wheels. But after the inquest, I realised that no vehicle would have withstood that blast. The wreckage was scattered over a square mile. The press sometimes treated me as if I was some kind of expert. But I wasn't. Even now, when this kind of thing happens, I'm running for an emotional air raid shelter, thinking, *Oh no, not again!* But a week after the funeral, I received a letter from a brigadier at Chicksands saying he was pleased that I was speaking to the press. So I continued to collaborate with journalists. I didn't want my daughter to disappear into oblivion and not be remembered. I also wrote a book in her memory that is sold in support of several military charities.'[10]

Carl Bryant was less concerned about the vehicle in which his wife had died. 'Sarah would have gone on patrol in a vehicle made of paper if that was what was required,' he said. 'She was a brave soldier who knew the Snatch Land Rover wasn't the best, but she got on with it anyway. She would also have detested the coverage she received after her death. She didn't see herself as a female soldier – just a soldier. And she wasn't a victim. She went into this wholeheartedly, and she knew the risks. She would have hated to be seen as a victim of anything. She was a brave soldier.'

Her mother Maureen agrees. 'On all her tours to Iraq and Afghanistan, even passing out with a broken foot, she was determined

76

and brave. And now I just wanted to show her that I could be brave as well. Later, I stood back as much as possible, because Sarah's death received so much publicity. But when I did speak – when I felt I *had* to speak for her – I spoke in the manner that she would want me to. I'd ask myself, *What would Sarah want me to do? How would she want me to react?* Each time I spoke, I would see her smile and it gave me the strength to carry on.'

Sarah returned home two weeks later, in a solemn and dignified ceremony. Seeing the C17 fly past over RAF Lyneham 'was quite unbelievable and stark', said Carl Bryant.

'I appreciated that the repatriation wasn't really for us, the family. It was the Army bringing her home, paying their respects to her, and doing it their way. We had no say in the way this was organised, but it was for them, not really for us. I asked if one of our dear friends [*an officer*] could be a bearer and help to carry her off the aircraft, but they said that wasn't possible because officers could not be part of the bearer party. I could accept that.'

Because of the manner of her death, her family could not see her to say goodbye.

'Sarah was literally blown to pieces and her remains had to be identified by her DNA,' said Des Feely. 'This meant it wasn't possible to repatriate her immediately and the funeral did not take place for another week. So it was about three weeks before we had something tangible to see and touch, albeit just a coffin. The inquest was absolutely horrendous. The Coroner had a special briefing just for Sarah's mother and me, and that's where it got really tough.'

The former Chief of the Defence Staff, General Lord Guthrie, attended Sarah Bryant's funeral, along with other dignitaries and hundreds of soldiers, family and friends. It took place at the church in which she had been married a couple of years earlier.

'It was a beautiful service,' said Carl. 'Military funerals are overwhelming. I felt incredible pride in Sarah, that she had died as a soldier and that she was being laid to rest in a way that can only be done by the military. It was a fitting way for Sarah to go.

'She didn't leave a formal last letter. Her tour was far and away the most dangerous that either of us had done, but we were both very engrossed in our duties and neither of us had lost any friends or colleagues in service at that point. So the possibility of her dying probably wasn't in our minds. I received an email from her just before she went on that patrol, and she said how much she was looking forward to coming home. To me that was as good as a last letter. Sarah had an inner strength and a constantly positive outlook that few people possess. Every phone call we had when we were apart made me smile. She never moaned about anything, unless it was pretty bad. She was chipper and happy. It's some comfort to know that she died as part of a campaign she believed in. She was utterly unique, and I am so proud to have been her husband.'

For Sarah's mother, the pain of her passing was unbearable and has not diminished.

'The sadness never leaves you,' said Maureen. 'She is with me every single day. Even when I'm shopping, I'll see something and think, *Sarah would like that.* And then I'll think, *There's no point in looking at that.* Recently it flashed through my mind that I should ring her about something.

'You can never recover from a loss like this, but you learn to live with it. I go to the cemetery every week. If it's a special occasion, like Mother's Day, and I know she can't come to me, then I'll go to her. She always wanted to give but was never that bothered about receiving.

'I don't regret the life that she chose and I certainly wouldn't have wanted her to do anything other than what she wanted. The fact that it took her from me, yes, I resent that. But she loved the life she had, and what she was doing. I can't say I would have wished for anything different for her. So I'm not bitter. Not at all. The Army can't really do much for us, but they treat us almost as family and I have so many business cards from people in the Intelligence Corps with personal numbers and messages saying to call them if I need anything. Under the circumstances, I don't think we could have been treated any better. There's the Sarah Bryant Award at Chicksands for the best recruit and there's a tree planted in Sarah's name in the Intelligence Corps memorial garden.

'Do these things help? Yes and no. I'm a very private person, and I don't share my feelings a great deal. But I consider it an honour when they contact me as they did last July. Five years on, and they were still including me in events if I wanted to be there with them. They haven't forgotten Sarah, or us. I was proud of her when she was with us and I'm equally proud of her now. If I can help with anything that they want to do in her memory, then I do it. I can imagine her standing there looking on, smiling and giggling.

'I don't think Afghanistan will change for the better in the long run. It'll go back to being ruled by the Taliban. I think we have done a lot of good, especially with opportunities for women, but I don't think anyone achieved as much as they wanted. Perhaps I would feel a little better if we knew there would be peace from now on, but that won't happen. In five years' time it will not be very different to the way it was before we went there.'

Krista Presch never thought her bubbly, optimistic childhood friend would come to any harm. The news of her death, and then the funeral, began a long process of mourning with which she is still struggling.

'During the funeral, I coped by trying to pretend I wasn't there,' she said. 'I was supposed to do a reading, but then it was decided the readings would be by people from the Army. I was relieved – I don't know if I would have been able to do it. I had written a poem to read, but in the end I printed it off and put it with the flowers on her grave.

'I was Sarah's head bridesmaid, and I'd told her that she would be mine when I got married. But she passed away shortly before our wedding. We made sure Sarah was remembered, though. The priest mentioned her during the service, and we mentioned her in the order of service. Maureen was there, which was good, but it must have been very hard for her. I was supposed to have three bridesmaids, but I only had two. We had three bouquets, though, and we gave Sarah's to her mum just before the wedding. Then a day or so later we went to her grave and we put the bouquet on it.

'I think about Sarah every single day. I have the feeling that she's still around, so I have little random chats with her, especially if something bothers me. I don't feel it's futile. She's like a guardian angel. We now live fairly near where she's buried, so I go there often and I put flowers on her grave. I try to make them a bit personal. The last time I went, I picked flowers from my garden and put them in a jar. I think of her smile and her laugh, and it makes me smile. She was always smiling and always laughing.

'I don't know if it gets any easier with the passing of time. I think I might not have accepted that she is gone, because she was away with the Army when she was killed. Perhaps I've convinced myself that she's still out there.'

Sarah's father, Des, is similarly lost without his little girl.

'Given that I was involved in the licensed trade, it was a miracle that I didn't end up a roaring alcoholic,' he said. 'I'd seen so many others in the business go that way, so perhaps there was a voice at the back of my mind saying that this wasn't the way to cure my problems. Yes, there was an element of depression and drinking. And for a while I was under the doctor, who referred me to counsellors. That was a darker side.

'I'm not coming to terms with this. I can only compare my current state with someone who has been hit by a stun gun. You just bounce along from one day to the next, until there is no life left in you. You do come to a point when you try to block it out, though.

'I've haven't worked since Sarah was killed, apart from looking after my mother for the last six years. That was a big distraction, because she had Parkinson's disease and needed my help. That stopped me from wallowing in self-pity. I can remember a time when I would be exercising Sarah's horse, then flying the same afternoon. [*Des had a private pilot's licence, and he and Sarah would often go up for jaunts together.*] What a life that was!

'There are occasions when I can hear Sarah shouting at me and telling me to stop all of this and get on with my life. But my ambitions to do anything more with my life were snuffed out years ago. I've decided to sell up and live in Germany where property can be cheaper. I speak the language, and I've worked there a couple of times. I can survive on what my pension plans pay out and on the State pension when I'm sixty-five. Of course, it means leaving my home of twenty-seven years, with all the memories it contains. And it also means leaving Sarah's grave.

'Do I wish that Sarah had never joined the Army? No. She became a sergeant in just six years and we often joked that she would end up running it. There were so many senior people who said she had a glittering career ahead of her – and these were not platitudes. She really did. You'd only have made an enemy of Sarah if you'd tried to take the Army away from her. She loved every minute of it. I think that soldiers are so dependent on each other that it generates a particular kind of affection between them. This is where her legacy lies: she did her utmost to protect those around her by doing her job well. The soldiers knew it and respected her. They could refuse to take anyone with them, but they would never turn her down if she asked to go on a patrol.

'Sarah had been given a medal and a commendation by some high-flying American officers. They got to see just how good this young woman was. They said she was a credit to the British Army.'

Much time passed before Carl could begin to come to terms with the loss of his wife. 'I don't think I started dealing with her death until at least a couple of years afterwards,' he said. 'I tried to carry on and do anything I possibly could to not think about it. But you can only do that for so long before it eats you up. Life does eventually go on and I have now found great happiness again. But Sarah is with me every day, and always will be.'

CORPORAL ROB DEERING
COMMANDO LOGISTIC REGIMENT ROYAL MARINES
OCTOBER 16, 1975 – DECEMBER 21, 2008

CORPORAL ROB DEERING was a man of contradictions.

He was the toughest of commandos, with 'the heart of a lion and the courage to match', but he was also a 'mummy's boy' and a big softie of an animal lover, who would take the chicken from his plate to feed the stray kittens outside a restaurant.

He was a gym nut who kept himself supremely fit and was inordinately proud of his amazing pecs – he regularly proclaimed himself the best-looking bloke in his troop, and loved to go out on the town wearing a 'spray-on' t-shirt – but he loved his food and had a terrible sweet tooth. He was known for polishing off two or even three puddings after dinner, and wouldn't dream of drinking a 'wet' [*cup of tea*] without a cake or a biscuit, and preferably both.

He was, his mates said fondly, as 'tight as a duck's arse'. He was a car obsessive, and every spare penny he had was put aside to spend on whatever flash motor he was saving up for next. And yet, when push came to shove, he was extraordinarily generous with those he loved.

Above all, he was brave, committed, and professional.

In short, and to use Royal Marine slang, he was – according to those who knew and fought alongside him – a 'hoofing bootneck'.

At twenty-one, Rob Deering actually tried to join the Army – his best friend from childhood, Scott Tombs, had gone into the Parachute Regiment – but they turned him down, saying he had flat feet and was

82

colour-blind. The Army's loss was the Corps' gain, though Rob's pathway to the green beret the following year was not a smooth one. For one thing, he lacked the maths GCSE which is a basic educational requirement for all marines.

Although he was a bright lad, his school career had been chequered, and included a period of serious truancy, to the point where his mother, Karen, was threatened with prosecution.

'He could be very stubborn,' she said, 'and once he decided he didn't like school he just refused to go. Some days he just wouldn't get up, and there were many mornings when we'd fight about it. I have no idea what it was that he disliked so strongly. It crossed my mind that he was being bullied, but I don't think so because I asked him years later what it was and he said even *he* didn't know.

'Perhaps he was bored, because he didn't like maths and English. I knew he had the potential, and I would shout at him in frustration. It came to the point where I was told that we could be fined if he didn't start attending school regularly, and it was a few thousand pounds. So then he took it more seriously, and actually started going.

'But he must have been unhappy, because if he was doing something he enjoyed he gave it a hundred and ten per cent. He proved that when he was told he needed a maths GCSE to join the Marines. He was a few years out of school by then, but he borrowed books from the library and went to classes in the evening, and he did it. He got that qualification. The same determination got him through his Royal Marines training.'

Rob was born in Birmingham in the autumn of 1975, the son of Karen Deering and her husband Dave, who ran a car dealership and garage with his own father. He arrived, said Karen, 'looking about three months old already, and with three dimples: one in each cheek and one in his chin'.

'He was very handsome,' she said, 'and he was always clinging to me. He never bad-mouthed me once, even when he was older, and he was always very affectionate. One of his girlfriends said he was a mummy's boy, and I think he never really changed in that respect. He stayed at home until he joined the Marines.

'From childhood, Rob was always smiling. He had a very cheeky face and an even cheekier grin. He was three years younger than his sister, Elaine, and he was a devil with her. He'd take things from her room just to upset her. Or he'd pretend to cry and say that Elaine had hit him. I'd come in and tell her off, and he'd be grinning at her from behind my back. Of course, I only found that out years later.'

When Rob Deering was ten his parents divorced, and his mother remarried Pete Waspe. Pete had three children, Barry, Andy and Dave, so Rob's teenage years were spent as part of a large, mixed family.

'It wasn't always smooth,' said Karen, 'but the kids left as they got older, until we just had Rob and Barry. Barry has some learning difficulties, but Rob was very good with him. They shared a bedroom for a while, and Barry has a photo of Rob in uniform on his wall. We didn't tell Barry when Rob was killed. We decided he wouldn't understand – I don't think he knows what dying is – but if he ever asked about Rob I would tell him.'

After leaving school, Rob worked with his father and grandfather in their garage for a while, which fitted in nicely with his love of cars. He'd been a keen 'ministock' racer – junior stock-car racing – from the age of about twelve.

'He was good at it and he really enjoyed it,' said Dave. 'He used to race at Birmingham Wheels and Hednesford racetrack. We built the cars at our own garage, and Rob enjoyed working on them as well as racing them. He won a few trophies, and he was one of eight or ten young drivers who featured on a BBC kids' TV programme called *Boxpops*. That was a great thing for him, a real highlight.

'When he was old enough, he bought a motorcycle and I was always scared he'd have an accident. I couldn't wait until he was old enough to have a car. By the time he reached nineteen, he'd decided that garage work was dirty and under-paid, so he went to work at a factory where they manufactured car sunroofs. He earned more there, so he was able to buy the car of his dreams, an RS2000 Ford Escort, which was a road version of a rally car. He always loved fast cars, and he always had something that was a head turner. And when he set his heart on something, he'd work seven days a week, save up the money he needed, then go out and negotiate a price and buy it.'

In 1998, Rob left the civilian world behind when he signed up for commando training.

Dave Deering 'laughed at first'.

'I knew he didn't like getting dirty or being shouted at,' he said, 'but I wished him all the best and I was really proud of him when he passed out and got his green beret.'

Karen led a family group to Lympstone for the big day.

'He was so happy and proud,' she said, 'and the other lads loved him. But the funny thing was that he stayed a big softie. Sometimes you'd never believe he was a Royal Marine. He was a big animal lover. He had a holiday before he went to Afghanistan for the last time. He told us that one day he'd taken some chicken from the restaurant where he was eating to feed a stray kitten he'd found. Unfortunately it was run over the next day, but Rob said, "At least it knew a bit of love for a day." And he would bring home stray dogs. He found one, Goldie, walking in the street... Of course, it stayed with us. Another day he found an Alsatian. He took it back to his dad's garage, and then they found it was pregnant, so then homes had to be found for the pups. I know he fed the strays out in Iraq and Afghanistan as well.'

Rob Deering went to Kosovo on the UN peacekeeping mission soon after earning his globe-and-laurel cap badge. Fresh out of the civilian world, he saw some upsetting sights, including bodies being exhumed from mass graves – but he coped well, according to his father. He even came home with some grimly amusing tales.

'I remember he told us one story,' said Dave. 'As he was the new boy on the block, he was told to go down to the morgue and help fix the generators that powered the refrigerators. He wasn't looking forward to seeing the corpses at all, but when he got there he found they were using the refrigerating plant to keep the beer cool.'

From there he went to Norway, for Arctic warfare training, to Egypt, where he learned to dive, and then to Oman, for desert training ahead of the Iraq war.

That was in 2003. Three years after Iraq, he found himself in Afghanistan for the first time. There was a marked difference between the two tours. He returned from Iraq 'buzzing', after his unit was commended on the job it had done. But, at the same time, the experience of action, and seeing and doing some difficult things, had an impact on the young soldier.

'It was around that time that he began to change,' said Karen, 'and it became more obvious after his first Afghanistan tour. He'd had some scary experiences, and they affected him. One night he was out in Stratford with Gemma, his girlfriend, and some chap in a car said something rude about her. Rob went over to this guy and hit him. That was something he'd never have done before. He was on a shorter fuse.

'But it didn't change the way he treated us at home. He was still very loving. He'd make a point of going out for a meal with Peter and me. He'd take his dad for a drink, and he'd take flowers to his nan and granddad's grave. He did all the right things.'

* * *

OWEN ATWELL HAD been in the Marines for about three years by the time he met Rob Deering, when they were both posted as mechanics in Viking Support Troop on the 2006 tour. Viking is a tracked armoured vehicle built to the Corps' own specifications, and is ideal for the steep scree and soft earth of Afghanistan's hillsides and wadis.

'We were trained to maintain the vehicles,' said Atwell. 'Rob was a course behind me, and I'd heard of him before I met him at Commando Logistics near Barnstaple in early 2004. He was a very confident and good-looking lad, and socially he was larger-than-life. He was always having a good time and, if we were out and about, he'd always be the first onto the dance floor. I'd say he was a loud bloke, but I mean that in a good way. Even if he was taking the mick, or annoying you, he had a beaming grin and you couldn't stay angry with him. Within a minute or two, you'd be laughing.

'Rob lived in Solihull and I lived in Worcester, so on weekends, or if we both had leave, we'd often share a car up and down the motorway. He was mega-keen on his cars and he had a very nice BMW so we usually used his car because mine was so unreliable.

'And at work he was very good at his job. Viking was a great vehicle and a brilliant bit of kit. Rob and I were both involved in trialling it following its introduction to the Marines, and we took it right through to deployment in Afghan itself in 2006. We could take it anywhere we wanted. With a wheeled vehicle, you could expect to get *near* the point where you wanted to be, but you could put Viking right *on* that point. We'd intercept Taliban communications… they thought we were being carried in and out by helicopter because we were moving so fast.

'That 2006 deployment was pretty fluid. We were a small troop of nine men supporting Viking and we weren't always together. When Rob and I were together at Bastion, we lived in a grotty tent, but more often than not we would deploy separately in support of the units using Viking. We had our repair vehicles kitted out with everything we were likely to need in the way of spares and tools, and we went on the operations with the guys, getting stuck in with them. Often we'd be working out of a FOB for weeks at a time.

'The action was very intense at times. In some contacts we got through thousands of rounds, and the firefights went on for three or four hours. In particular, we got into some fairly hairy situations around the Kajaki Dam. But that was very much the sort of thing both of us wanted to do. It was what we were trained for. At times, back at Bastion, we'd been almost fighting among ourselves to go out on a mission. Every one of us wanted to get out and get on with it.

'If you were inside a Viking, it was a pretty happy place to be. I worked with the same Marine company through most of the time they were there, and we only had two casualties, both because a Viking hit an anti-tank mine. The Vikings concerned were immobilised and we had to destroy them, but they saved lives.

'The ops we did were usually in company strength. We'd go off for several days, travelling in a massive arrowhead formation. At night, when it was too dark to be really effective, we'd just pull up, get the ponchos and roll mats out, and get our heads down for a few hours. I look back on that as one of the most amazing times of my life. It was scary fun.

'Sometimes we'd use Vikings to get a company in and out of a FOB, but the job was really to pick fights, especially in the winter when the Taliban weren't so keen. We'd stop on high ground and wait to see what happened. When you saw the women and children leave a village, you knew it was on. It was a good tactic, because we were stopping them from getting any rest. We'd use the Viking's GPMG turrets to support the guys on foot as they went in to clear an area. Sometimes we'd have twelve to fifteen vehicles in a line, each with their turret GPMGs firing. That was pretty awesome.

'The environment was very macho. No-one wanted to say they were scared, but everyone was. So we tended to laugh a lot. Rob would get a laugh out of things one way or another. He'd be like, "I'm only thirty! I'm far too young to die!" That sounds a bit grim now, but it was just marines' humour.

'The IED threat on that first tour was relatively low. There was a place we called IED Alley, and we planned routes around that. But generally the Taliban were using them less then, and they relied more on rifles, RPGs and mortars. Nevertheless, we were aware of the IED threat and we would change routes often to be on the safe side. I think by the end of the tour we all felt we were pushing our luck. But it was a great deployment for doing your job and just soldiering. I would have gone back straight away, and I know that Rob felt the same way.'

In 2008, Rob Deering – promoted to corporal after showing excellent leadership potential on his first tour – was indeed deployed to Afghanistan again. His mother thought it was too soon, but Rob's skills as a Viking specialist were badly needed.

By then, he was in a serious relationship with his girlfriend, Gemma. They had bought a house together, and Rob had traded up – or, as some of his mates saw it, down – from a BMW to a canary yellow Vauxhall VX220, a 'hairdresser's car', as some of the marines jokingly described it. His father was sceptical about the purchase, but Cpl Deering's mind was made up. 'After all,' he said to his mother one day, with grim foresight, 'I could be dead next year, so why not?'

His deployment was delayed by a week when his flight was overbooked, and so he had a precious extra seven days at home. And he was lucky again, when – once in theatre – he placed the names for R&R into a hat and drew out his own first.

'He left in September 2008, and he was away for his birthday in October, but then he was back in early November,' said Karen. 'That was much earlier than expected. I knew he had to go back on November 21, but I tried not to think about that. He crammed so much into that leave. I really feel that it was as if he knew it might be his last. Obviously, he spent most of it with Gemma, but we saw a lot of him too. He went to visit the National Memorial Arboretum in Staffordshire, and he said to me, "I see they've got a wall ready for the next ones."

'I said, "Rob, no it's there just in case." I didn't want him thinking that his might be among the next names engraved on the wall.

'He watched a TV programme [*The BBC's* The Fallen, *from 2008*] which included lots of interviews with the families of men who had died. Bless him, he said to me, "I didn't realise how badly this affects the families who are left behind."

'He'd lost a friend from training and I asked him what it was like when that happened. He said, "It's just strange. You see them around camp, and then you don't see them."

'His sister Elaine was pregnant with her first child at the time, and having Rob home for those two weeks made it an even more happy time, and I know he didn't want to go back after his R&R. He said, "I can't believe that one minute I'm sitting here chilling in the city, and in a little while I'll be back in Afghanistan with all that going on." The contrast must have been awful.

'We all went out for a family meal to an Indian restaurant on the Stratford Road in Shirley. It was a pleasant evening, we were celebrating Barry's birthday, and we didn't discuss Afghanistan. I made a few cock-ups, though. Rob and Gemma were going to visit us in Spain when he came back from Afghan in May 2009. He said, "Don't book the flights," and I said, "No, I won't. You don't know if you'll be back." I quickly added "in time". I didn't mean that I thought he wouldn't be back, but that's how it came across. I suppose I was trying hard not to say the wrong things, but I did. I remember as we were leaving the restaurant, Rob and Gemma walked over to where their car was parked. I was looking across the road at them when Rob turned round, and our eyes met for several seconds. There was a strange look between us. I am not sure what we were both thinking or trying to convey.

'The day before he left, he came to say goodbye to Elaine and me. Unfortunately, Pete didn't get home from work in time to see him and say goodbye, which played on his [Pete's] mind for months afterwards. We tried to keep that visit light-hearted, but it must have been very hard for Rob, knowing what he was going back to. He hugged Elaine. Her bump was bigger by this time, and we joked that the next time Rob saw her he wouldn't be able to get anywhere near her. We hugged and kissed, and I held back the tears because I didn't want to upset him.

'When we got outside he kissed me again before getting into the car. Then we smiled and waved him off. Elaine and I looked at each other and went back inside. I think we both knew we might never see him again. I wanted to cry, but I tried to be brave for Elaine.

'Rob returned to Afghanistan the next day, November 21, 2008. He rang me from the RAF base before his flight, and that was the last time I heard his voice. I don't really remember what we said, but it would have been upbeat. Neither of us would have wanted to worry the other.

'Then, finally, he texted me, saying, "Gemma's gone home now, and I'm just about to get on the plane. I'll see you in March." I was at work when I received his text. I wanted to reply saying how much I loved him, but I didn't, in case he felt that I feared he wasn't coming back. So I never did tell him how much I loved him and how proud of him I was. That's something I have regretted ever since.'

* * *

BY 2008 THE TALIBAN were already switching to more devious means of targeting British soldiers.

In one particularly revolting attack, they killed three marines by forcing or tricking a thirteen-year-old boy into pushing a bomb past them in a wheelbarrow. As the child drew near to the soldiers, the device was triggered, killing the young Afghan and the three Britons.

Rob Deering was also killed by a hidden bomb, but in circumstances so strange as to make one question the fates.

On December 7, 2008, he was deployed as part of Operation Sond Chara – Pashtun for 'Red Dagger', named after the shoulder insignia worn by the men of 3 Cdo Brigade. Supported by the ANA, men from The Rifles, The Princess of Wales's Royal Regiment, The Queen's Dragoon Guards and other units of the British Army, as well as Estonian soldiers and the Leopard tanks of Denmark's Jutland Dragoons Regiment, the marines were tasked with kicking the Taliban out of a number of strongholds near Nad-e Ali, north-west of the Helmand capital, Lashkar Gah. With that goal achieved, the Royal Engineers and their Danish counterparts could then establish two new patrol bases at which ISAF troops could then be stationed.

The eighteen-day operation, which ended on Christmas Day 2008, saw some of the fiercest fighting in Britain's modern involvement in Afghanistan. A combination of Apache and Cobra attack helicopters,

Danish Leopards and British artillery did a lot of damage at longer ranges, but many contacts came at extremely close quarters. At times, the marines were engaging the Taliban at distances of twenty metres, and it was often in terrible winter conditions more reminiscent of the Falklands, or Salisbury Plain, than of the traditional image of dry Afghan heat. The rain poured for days on end, and men could be ankle-deep in water, then knee-deep in mud, then on frozen ground as hard as iron. It was 'Gore-Tex till Endex' said one participant.

By the end of the operation, the enemy had been driven off, at a cost of an estimated one hundred dead and many more injured. But five Britons died, too.

Marines Tony Evans and Georgie Sparks were killed just before the operation began, on November 27. They were on a surveillance patrol, and had put themselves in harm's way by climbing onto a compound rooftop to support colleagues in contact. Tragically, they were both hit by an RPG.

Mne Evans was just twenty, and one of the 'Smiley Boys' of 42 Cdo, with 'a monolithic work ethic' said his grieving colleagues. 'There is nothing about his job that Tony didn't love,' said one, in an official tribute. 'He had a few issues... he couldn't grow a moustache, as hard as he tried, and he was always trying to get himself "massive", hitting the gym twice a day, but he could never find that "chest". But inside was the heart of a lion. On his Cold Weather Warfare Course in Norway he was the winner of the "Good Egg" Award, for being an all-round good guy, which speaks volumes of his character. Always the first man in anywhere, he was eager, especially when asked to knock down a compound wall – in true "Tony" style, he put down most of the compound! He will always be with us forever in our hearts and minds; a true man's man!'

Marine Georgie Sparks was nineteen years old, a 'quiet, understated professional', and a qualified sniper. A fellow marine said of him, 'Georgie [will be] one of us forever... this man's smile could light up your darkest day. His life revolved around his two passions: his family and his shooting. He was the perfect soldier, the perfect friend. His hand was always up for any task, and he gave everything he had, and more. But the first place and last place he remains is in our hearts and in our minds forever.'

Mne Sparks was buried on what would have been his twentieth birthday.

OMLT member and 1 Rifles Rfn Stuart 'Oz' Nash was shot and killed on December 17, while covering comrades from a rooftop. A proud Aussie, Stuart had travelled to the UK to join up and fight, and quickly proved himself one of his regiment's finest young soldiers. Known for his 'gentlemanly manner and thorough professionalism', the twenty-one year-old had been in the Army for only nine months, but had already been identified as a future NCO. A popular man with his fellow riflemen, he was 'a professional and a soldier in the best traditions of Australia and Britain', said one colleague.

LCpl Ben Whatley, from 42 Cdo, died on Christmas Eve, when he was shot as he led from the front under fierce enemy fire. At 6ft 5in the biggest man in his troop, with a 'booming baritone voice' and a calm demeanour, the twenty-year-old was a veteran of Herrick 5 and used to being in contact. 'Immensely strong,' said one tribute, 'he was often to be seen carrying extra batteries or ammunition for the machine-gun and would still not be seen in anything other than a pukka [*correct*] fire position, going up and down the line encouraging the other lads. More than all this he was a great friend… words cannot express what a great loss this has been to all of us.'

One of his mates said, 'Always trying to stitch someone up with a prank, he was without a doubt the craftiest twenty-year-old I have ever met. Always the first one to want to go out for a drink, he was always the last one ready because in his own words, "It's not easy being this essence [*good-looking*]." No matter how much it pains me to say it, he was a maverick when it came to the ladies. With his laid-back attitude it looked like he was never giving a hundred per cent, but Ben loved his job and being a true bootneck was all he knew, and he proved just that on the day he was taken away from us. See you soon Ben, but hopefully not too soon! You're going to be missed by all, especially those closest to you and I'll never forget you.'

His best friend, Mne Tom Curry, had been killed in Afghanistan in January 2007.

In between the deaths of Rfn Nash and LCpl Whatley, on the bitterly cold early morning of December 21, Cpl Rob Deering was travelling in a Viking as part of a convoy returning to Camp Bastion when the lead vehicle was hit by an IED. Three men were injured and extracted by helicopter as the Taliban launched a follow-up attack with small arms.[11]

Cpl Deering – needing to examine the stricken Viking – moved his own vehicle from the rear of the convoy to the front, and dismounted.

He was in the process of assessing the damage when he somehow triggered a second device buried in the frozen ground. He was terribly unlucky. For some reason, it had failed to detonate earlier despite having been driven over by at least twenty-six vehicles, and despite some twenty other soldiers having walked over or very near to it.

The force of the explosion blew the marine into a nearby canal, and two of his fellow marines braved Taliban fire in an effort to help him. Sadly, there was nothing that could be done.

* * *

BACK HOME IN ENGLAND, Karen Waspe had been enduring the ordeal of every mother with a son or daughter deployed to Afghanistan.

'I remember hearing the news of the men killed by the thirteen-year-old suicide bomber,' she said. 'It was just too close for comfort. Those poor guys and their families – and so close to Christmas, as well. Although I knew the families had been informed, I wasn't completely sure that Rob wasn't among them, so I kept checking my phone for any messages or missed calls from Dave, Rob's dad. He was [the MOD's] first point of contact and Gemma was down as second contact, so I relied on them giving me any bad news.

'When Pete came home I was sitting crying about these latest casualties. He reassured me that the families had been informed. I thought, *Yes, this time Rob's safe, but for how long?*

'I found it very hard to sleep. I would lie there thinking, *Can I imagine going to RAF Lyneham for Rob's repatriation, or going to Rob's funeral? No, I can't imagine any of that, so he must be going to be alright.* But despite that, we didn't feel like putting up Christmas cards or decorations.'

On December 20, the family went for a meal to celebrate Elaine's birthday and the news that a scan had shown she was expecting a boy. The following day, Karen and Pete Waspe went to the wedding of a work friend.

'We had a nice day,' said Karen, 'and even a few laughs. Nevertheless, Rob was always at the back of my mind. I just tried not to show it. We were still at the wedding that night, and at about 11.30pm I had this strong uneasy feeling. I wanted to go home. Later, as I got into bed I felt really worried. We hadn't heard anything from Rob for what seemed like a long time. *Surely,* I thought, *he must be going back to one of the forward operating bases for Christmas.* I had an imaginary conversation with him: *I must get some sleep, Rob. I'll have to let the lads out there with you look after you. Me lying here worried sick will not alter things.*

'He was killed while I was lying there worrying about him, when he triggered the IED. Oh my God! My Rob, my beautiful, happy son gone, unrecognisable, blown to pieces, killed instantly.

'The next morning, December 21, still not knowing, we decided we *would* put up the cards and Christmas decorations after all. At about 1.30pm that afternoon, I looked outside and saw that Pete was cleaning the cars. Then I just had this overwhelming feeling that Rob was back home in England. I thought to myself, *How could that be? If he'd come home for any reason I'd have been told.* But it felt like a great relief.'

It being a Sunday, Dave Deering had taken the chance to go out for a few pre-Christmas lunchtime drinks with Rob's girlfriend Gemma, and some of his son's other friends.

'We were toasting Rob's health,' said Dave Deering. 'Unbeknown to us, he had already been killed.

'I lived above the garage then, and when I returned home I was met by two officers from the Royal Marines. I knew then that something was amiss. But I wasn't prepared for the devastating news that Rob had been killed.

'I was totally devastated and dumb-stuck. We all were. We didn't know how to react. We were just numb, heartbroken. To be honest, it really knocked everything out of me. I had the painful task of informing his sister, because I didn't have a contact number for his mum. I was in tears on the phone telling Elaine and then, obviously, she was in tears.'

Elaine gathered herself to call her mother.

'At about 4.30pm, my stepson Dave arrived to bring us our

94

Christmas presents,' said Karen. 'We sat chatting and watching *Deal or No Deal* on TV. I remember the girl who was competing was doing quite well. I was quite cheerful because I thought, *Any day now we'll get a call from Rob.*

'At 4.50, my phone rang. I saw it was Elaine. I said, "Hello Elaine!" in a cheerful voice. But I could immediately tell that something was wrong. She said, "Mum, I have some bad news."

'I thought, *Oh no! She's lost the baby.* Then I thought, *It's Rob! He must be injured.*

'She said, "He's dead." I just fell to my knees screaming, "No, no, not Rob!" And I started banging on the floor. Pete came to me, and Dave just sat there. I don't think he could speak or move.

'I remember feeling really sick. Elaine, I found out later, had been asleep after working Saturday night when she received the call from her dad. She was on her own and five months' pregnant.

'I went outside, because I didn't know what to do. I think a couple of our neighbours had heard me screaming and had come out to see what was happening. One of them, Bob, came up and hugged me. I said to him, "They've blown up my lovely son. He had everything to live for."

'Elaine arrived a short time later. She looked deeply shocked. We all just sat there, not knowing what to do or say. I suddenly thought, *Gemma! I must tell her.* Of course she already knew. But I got through to her answer-phone, and I screamed into it, "They've blown him up!" She must have been so distraught.

'This was too big to handle. I felt I needed to tell family and friends. I wanted everyone to share this overwhelming grief. They needed to know before it was announced on the news. Pete started texting and calling all our family and friends. One of the first calls was to Rob's best mate Scott [*Tombs, by now out of the Parachute Regiment and a civilian again*]. I knew he'd be devastated, because they'd been friends for over twenty years. His mum told me later that when she told Scott he was in tears. It was the first time she'd seen him cry.

'That day we had a few visitors, my brother and sister-in-law John and Paula, and also the matron, Linda, from the nursing home where I worked. I think they were very brave to visit. I can't remember what we said. I just remember sitting in front of the television waiting for them to name Rob as the marine who'd been killed. Until I saw Rob's name on the screen, I felt it could all be a horrible mistake. I knew it wasn't though, because mistakes like that don't happen.

'Gemma's mum rang me, and I could hear Gemma sobbing in the background. It was heart-breaking. She was too upset to speak to me herself, and I was sobbing, too. I'd never heard myself cry like I did that morning and the night before. It was an awful, pitiful sound.

'I don't know how I got through that first night, but I think eventually I did drop off to sleep for a short while. When I woke, though, the pain was still there like a knife in my chest. It really was a physical thing; I had a dull ache in the left side of my chest for weeks.

'The following day I went to our GP for some sleeping tablets. Everyone else was happy and looking forward to Christmas, but I sat in the surgery with Pete, in a daze. I broke down when I told the doctor what had happened and that I needed something to help me sleep. She was shocked and very sympathetic. She also gave Pete some sleeping tablets.

'Those pills worked very well. Within half an hour of taking one, I was oblivious to the pain and nightmare of what had happened. For the first few days I just went through the basics: going to the toilet, cleaning my teeth, and taking a bath. I ate very little. Elaine popped in every day. The first morning she had a big bunch of flowers and a card for me from her boss at work. Everyone was lovely.

'I thought I'd never be happy again. I couldn't imagine ever laughing or smiling. It was like a physical pain. Elaine decided she could not just sit there and said she was going into work to do the night shift. That was amazing. She was trying to keep calm to protect her unborn baby. She couldn't let anything happen to him as well.

'For the first few days we didn't hear anything from the military. We felt left out and unsupported. Eventually, I spoke to the visiting officer looking after Gemma on the phone, and he said to me, "Well, Gemma's the important one here." But I was Rob's *mother*, for God's sake! It seemed they didn't really want to know us.

'Even so, I didn't mind Gemma getting the attention because she was his partner and she was hysterical. She was never very big, but she lost so much weight. It was only after Peter rang the base at Chivenor some days later that we got a visiting officer, and then we also became involved with everything, the repatriation, funeral arrangements, and so on. Parents do get a raw deal sometimes.

'Somehow, we got through Christmas. Elaine came round for Christmas Day. I cooked the dinner, but our hearts weren't in it. None of us ate more than a few mouthfuls. I really can't remember much of the day. I think I just sat watching the television. Well, not really watching it. It was just something to try to focus on.

'In the days that followed, I kept myself busy making a folder of all the letters, press cuttings and so on. I joined Facebook, which has become a life-saver. Being able to talk to other people in the same position and support each other has been so good. We all knew that we weren't alone in our grief.

'After initial slowness to help us cope, the Royal Marines really looked after us. They arranged for us to be picked up and driven to RAF Lyneham for Rob's repatriation on December 30. He was being brought home with a fellow marine [*Ben Whatley*] who had been shot and killed on Christmas Eve.

'On the way to Lyneham, we learned that, because Rob had been so badly injured, his dad and I might have to give DNA samples so the coroner could be completely satisfied that the body was his. It was just horrible, and those thoughts of Rob's injuries will haunt me forever, but in the end it wasn't necessary.

'Everyone at Lyneham treated us so well. Col Andy Maynard, who had been in Afghanistan, was there, along with other senior officers from the Marines. They gave us their condolences individually. It may seem amazing, but only now were we beginning to see another side of Rob, the military aspect of his life. Col Maynard told me Rob had been held in high esteem in the Marines. I was very proud that my son had their respect, from the highest-ranking officers down to the men he served with. Col Maynard said, "He had the heart of a lion and the courage to match." These words are now on his gravestone.

'We watched the aircraft carrying Rob's coffin descend and land. It was a very sad moment. I knew that wasn't my Rob in the coffin, just some remains. I thought the other marine's family was lucky, in a way, because he'd died of a single shot, so his lovely face and body would still be perfect.

'Although I was so terribly sad, I was also very proud to see Rob being carried to the chapel so respectfully by his comrades. We went to the chapel to say our goodbyes. Then the two coffins were taken through Wootton Bassett on route to a hospital in Oxford for a post mortem and to formally identify Rob's remains.

'I remember feeling older, smaller and weaker. I'd been a fit and active person, who went to the gym twice a week and worked four days a week, and I didn't feel like that woman any more.

'Eventually, Rob's body was transferred to a local funeral directors. It had taken quite a while for the pathologist to confirm his identity, so by the time we could visit him at the funeral directors he was beginning to smell. That was very hard to accept. Imagine your son who had been very particular in his appearance, smelling like that.

'We were told we could put some things into the coffin with him, but not personally as we were not allowed to see him. We put in a little Christmas cake that I was going to send out to Afghanistan for him. He loved his cakes and puddings. We also placed some family photos in his coffin, and Elaine put in her baby scan pictures and some car magazines, because Rob loved his cars.

'They let us spend some time in the room with Rob; I ran my hands over the coffin and also hugged it. That was the closest I could get to my son.

'We hung on to the fact that he died instantly. Three guys in that first vehicle were badly injured. I wondered how his fellow marines had been affected.

'We buried Rob on January 14, 2009. I wanted him to be proud of me on that day. I also wanted him to have the best send-off possible. I was going to remain dignified and not cry. It was an amazing drive to the church. We had police escorts and the traffic was stopped for us. I remember feeling very important. The church was packed, so a video link had been installed to the church hall next door, and many people watched from there. There was also a link to the lads at Camp Bastion.

'It was very moving to see all the marines in uniform. Some were still in their desert combats. His company sergeant major and another good Royal Marine friend made speeches. His friend broke down in tears. *Run* [*Leona Lewis's cover of the song by Snow Patrol*] was played. Even today, if I hear that song it makes me cry. I will never voluntarily listen to it again. As we left the church, a party of marines fired a rifle salute.

'Later in the day, Elaine was presented with Rob's medals. Rob's dad received his white dress helmet and belt and I was presented with his green beret. One day that will be passed on to Elaine's son, Rob Junior. Gemma was given the Union Flag that had been draped over Rob's coffin in Afghanistan and had stayed with him until the funeral.'

Rob's boyhood best friend Scott Tombs remembers the funeral as 'a horrible, horrible day'.

'Robert and I met when we were both eleven or twelve and going to the same secondary school in Solihull,' he said. 'We ended up as best muckers – we used to bunk off school together and spend the day playing pool. Neither of us were going to be brain surgeons, but we both made shit-hot soldiers. In our teens, we both developed a thing about fitness, so we used to do weight training and go running together. In fact, one way or another we very nearly spent every second of every day together. He'd often stay at my house and my mum was like a second mum to him. We'd even go on holiday together.

'Obviously we were apart for long periods when he joined the Marines and I joined the Paras, but whenever we were both home on leave, we'd be together. I went to his passing-out parade and he came to mine. We met girls together, too – Robert could always pull the good-looking ones. My partner and I have been together for more than fifteen years, but back then Robert was going out with her sister. We used to have such good fun.

'At one point, he was worried about not getting his corporal's stripe. He said, "I'll give it the best shot I can, but if I fluff it up I'll probably come out of the Marines." But you didn't get many better men than Robert. His attention to detail was second to none and physically, he was in great shape. So of course he passed and got the stripes.

'Robert was the best thing since sliced bread, even though he was as tight as a duck's arse. He was very switched-on with his money. We were out for a run one day when he was home from Afghanistan on R&R shortly before he was killed. I remember him saying to me that by the end of his next tour he'd have saved six or seven grand, and he was planning to buy a new car.'

[*In an official tribute, one Marine NCO, doubtless with a smile on his face, had said, 'The first time I ever saw Cpl Rob Deering was a number of years ago at a petrol station in Barnstaple. I knew that he was a young Vehicle Mechanic who worked in the Light Aid Detachment, and thought,* How the hell can he afford that nice BMW? *As I got to know Rob better, I learnt that he guarded his money extremely tightly. A typical example of this was that during the full six months of his first deployment to Afghanistan he only spent $50!'*]

'He also said it was getting a bit shitty out there,' said Scott Tombs. 'One of the marines had been caught in an IED blast and had lost a finger. It was getting awkward, he said. They were always coming across something. He said, "I couldn't imagine having no legs. If that happened, I could see me pushing myself off a block of flats." But actually he was a really determined bloke, and, if he'd survived, I think he'd have overcome anything.

'I can remember clearly being told that he'd been killed. His family must have got in touch with my mum and she phoned me. I went straight to Rob's house, because he was living with Gemma. It was the most horrible day. I remember wanting to go out and kill every Afghan. They'd killed my best friend, and I was mad as hell about it. I find it hard to describe, but I broke down crying. I went for a walk with Robert's dad, and I felt it hadn't really hit home with him. But it did sink in soon enough and then he took it really hard. I'd lost my best mate and they'd lost their son.

'We had been booked to go on a Caribbean holiday, but we cancelled that so we could be at the funeral. I went with my mother and because the Marines were organising it, I didn't really play a part. I would have liked to have said something, but his parents and his Marines colleagues did it all. It was a horrible, horrible day.'

Owen Atwell was also at the funeral, though he had left the Royal Marines just before the tour.

'When I came back from Afghan in 2007, my mother looked like she'd aged ten years,' he said, 'so I thought I'd give civvie street a go. I joined the police and I'm now a firearms officer. I know I made the right decision because I love my job, I'm married and have a daughter. But when Rob and the other guys deployed again, there was a part of me that wished I was going too. I was still a reservist, so I even hoped I'd be called up.

'It was a Sunday night when I heard that Rob had been killed. I was still in police training at the time, and I was getting ready for the next day's work. I had a phone call from one of our mates who was back on R&R. He told me what had happened. Neither of us knew what to say. We just left it there and said we'd catch up. It was horrible. Gut-wrenching. It's a hard feeling to explain, but I felt bit guilty that I'd left the Marines. If I'd stayed in, I might have been on that patrol instead of Rob. It was a weird roller coaster of emotions.

'I had trouble getting the day off work for Rob's funeral, but in the end I said to my instructor that I was just going. He was a good bloke and said he'd cover for me. "As far as I'm concerned," he said, "you're here." I met another bootneck and we drove up together.

'The funeral was very sombre and the church was so full that I had to watch it on a screen in the hall next to the church. Most of the congregation were bootnecks, and that was quite nice. They played *Run* as they were carrying Rob out, and that broke me up. I play it on the guitar quite a lot now, and it still upsets me. I love the song, but it takes me right back.

'There was a lot of laughter when the beer started flowing, but it was still gut-wrenching. Gemma looked heart-broken. The pain of the family was all over their faces. I looked around during the service and saw all these big, burly bootnecks cracking up, too. That memory will stay with me.'

The memories will obviously stay with Rob Deering's parents, too.

'That Christmas was the most miserable time you can imagine,' said Dave Deering. 'Christmas will never be the same again for us. We don't really celebrate it any more. It's a time for remembering Rob now; a mourning period. There's nothing there to celebrate. Elaine's birthday is on December 20, and she doesn't celebrate her birthday any more.

'In the weeks and months that followed, I went into a kind of depression and lost all interest in life and the garage. The business had to go. I just couldn't come to terms with getting up in the morning and running it. We decided to sell up and move away from the area.

'I don't know where I'd have been without my other half, Maureen. She was there 24/7, doing her best to support me. It's taken me more than five years to come to terms with Rob's loss, and to get back into the human race and start socialising again. But his memory, and all of the things that we did together, will remain with me all my life. I have lots of happy memories.

'Rob's granddad was in the Indian Army in that same part of the world during the Second World War. When the Russians were out there having a go, his granddad said, "No-one will ever win anything out there. The people are tribal and have always fought among themselves. But if anyone moves in, they all band together to see them off. Then they get back to fighting each other again."

'I've always believed that we wouldn't achieve anything there. Wherever we've been militarily over the last decade or so, from the Middle East to Afghanistan, nothing has changed. Iraq is in a terrible mess again. And now we're about to pull out of Afghanistan, and that's going to go the same way. I think if we had left the place alone, Rob would still be with us and things would be a lot better in Afghanistan, too.

'But, to be fair, Rob loved the job he was doing. The Paras had taken a bit of a belting in Afghanistan just before Rob went there for the second time. I said to him, "Don't you think it's time you gave up that job and got back to civvie street?" But he said, "No. That's my job. It's what I do. And what is there for me in civvie street?"

'On November 11 this year, we're going to his camp in Barnstaple. They've built a new remembrance garden for the marines who died. We'll be there for the unveiling of that.

'I've come to terms with it now. He died doing what he loved doing.'

Karen thinks of her lost son 'every minute of every day', she said. 'I think about things he said and I think about what he's missing. There are days when I feel really down, but there are also days when I feel almost normal and can laugh and joke.

'Sometimes, I think he's still away on deployment, and I have to tell myself, *No, he's gone. You'll never see his lovely smiling face again.* I don't really believe in life after death, so I can't think that one day we will meet again. Instead, I take great comfort from Rob Junior. He is so lovely. He looks like his uncle, and he's always happy and smiling.

'At the beginning, I didn't like visiting Rob's grave. I used to think, *What's Rob doing here with all these dead people?* I didn't even like driving past the cemetery, especially when it was dark. I would imagine Rob was there all on his own. I feel better about it now. In fact, I quite like going to the cemetery. I feel close to him there.

'A soldier who saw Rob die said he couldn't get over the amount of blood in the water. He told us he'd been chatting to Rob the day before, which was Elaine's birthday. Rob said to this marine, "It's my sister's birthday today. She's having a baby boy." We think that Gemma had passed that news on to him a day or two earlier. It means a lot to me that Rob knew that.

'Just after Elaine gave birth to Rob Junior, she took him to the grave to show him to her brother. We just stood there in front of the grave. How could a mound of earth respond to her beautiful son? I was heartbroken for her.

'I sometimes think, *How dare life go on as usual without Rob?* People say time is a healer, but it's not true. Yes, the pain is not so raw now, but the reality is worse. I can't believe that life has to carry on without him. I keep asking myself, *What's life for, now?* But then I look at Rob Junior, and I know why we go on.'

ACTING SERGEANT SEAN BINNIE
THE BLACK WATCH 3rd BATTALION
THE ROYAL REGIMENT OF SCOTLAND
NOVEMBER 11, 1986 – MAY 7, 2009

ON THE DAY of his death, Sean Binnie was in high spirits.

Op Herrick 10 had begun in April, and would go on to be a very demanding six months – sixty-nine British soldiers would die, twenty-two in July alone, along with many more of their Afghan colleagues.

But it had been a quiet affair so far. There had been only one fatality to date – LSgt Tobie Fasfous of the Welsh Guards had been killed by an explosion at the end of April, while on foot patrol north-east of Gereshk [12], Nahr-e Saraj – and there had been little contact with the enemy.

It was quiet because it was harvest season in southern Afghanistan. Most of the local people – who were generally friendly, and would often greet the troops with offers of *chai* tea and naan bread – were engaged in bringing in the opium poppy which they grew in haphazard fashion in the green zones along the Musa Qala and Helmand rivers. For now, most of the Taliban were therefore focused on collecting 'taxes' on the crop – in reality, protection money – from the desperately poor farmers, often at the point of an AK47.

They knew that it could not last, but across Helmand British soldiers were enjoying the relative calm. The military's Combined Services Entertainment group – successors to ENSA, of *It Ain't Half Hot, Mum* fame – had arranged a visit to Musa Qala DC to put on a comedy show for the troops there. It was the first – though by no means only – time that the CSE had travelled so deep into Afghanistan. Over at Sangin, the Royal Engineers had adopted a donkey which had somehow got into the compound one night. They'd amused themselves by making him a sun hat, complete with ear holes, and calling him 'Dave'. The Fusiliers were engaged in a moustache-growing competition.

The men were patrolling regularly – there was little in the way of contact, but they were getting to know the lie of the land and looking for the insurgents' arms caches and bomb factories. It was still tough going – the combination of heat and the weight of their kit had to be experienced to be believed, and even then some could not believe it. It would be bad enough just strolling around in combats and boots in fifty degrees, but they were carrying a 5kg rifle, and wearing gloves, Osprey body armour[13] and a Kevlar helmet, adding some 12kg. On top of that, they were carrying another 20kg or more of equipment. This would include five or six loaded magazines, often further ammunition in a bandolier, fragmentation and sometimes 'red phos' smoke grenades, a radio and batteries, medical kit, rations and as much as six or even eight litres of water. Despite drinking so much water, at 'almost tea-temperature', most of it was sweated straight back out; it wasn't unusual for a man to spend six hours on patrol and not need to urinate. A number had suffered heatstroke. One fusilier had even been casevac-ed back to the UK.

When they were not on patrol, they spent their afternoons lifting weights in the shade, listening to iPods or the football on BFBS radio, or just trying to catch some zeds. There were even games of kickabout football, once the sun had begun to dip – and the temperature had dropped with it from the relentless, forty degree heat of midday.

Not everyone was entirely happy at this comparatively peaceful state of affairs. The twenty-two-year-old ASgt Sean Binnie, a career soldier who had served in Iraq and elsewhere, and was on a rapid upward curve, had joined up – partly, at least – precisely in order to experience war fighting, and to test himself under fire. He had been craving action, and his high spirits today were precisely because it seemed he was about to see some.

That Thursday, he and others in his small Black Watch team were due to patrol out to Towghi Keli, north of Musa Qala – and, almost certainly, a spicy meeting with the Taliban.

Sean was part of another British OMLT, living and working alongside Afghan troops and tasked with turning them from a near-rabble into professional soldiers capable of protecting their country when foreign forces finally left. It was a difficult and, at times, dangerous role, as one of his colleagues in the OMLT explained.

'We were stationed in Satellite Station North, a ridiculously small patrol base near Musa Qala,' said LCpl Duncan Milne. 'Conditions were horrible, it was hardly protected, and I remember thinking, *I'm in the middle of nowhere, here, with a little wall around me and the Taliban just over it.* We were mentoring between forty and fifty Afghan guys, and there were only eight of us. You're living in the same compound as people who could very easily pick up their weapons and attack you, and we'd all heard the horror stories about some of the Afghan Army doing just that. That always played on my mind.'

Then there was the added question of the professionalism of their pupils. 'The Afghan army guys used to do most of the guarding of the base, and I'd sometimes lie awake at night, wondering if *they* were awake. We never knew how reliable they'd be in a crisis – though, as it turned out, we had quite a lot of decent soldiers.'

Duncan Milne was 'acting-up' as a full corporal, and Sean Binnie had also been given an extra stripe, the better to gain the respect of their Afghan colleagues. And the team – led by Capt Olly Lever – certainly seemed to have done that.

'Morale was good,' said Milne. 'Each person had responsibilities around the camp, whether it was teaching the Afghans first aid, or weapons handling, or whatever. Sean used to lead quite a few lessons, and he took on the responsibility quite comfortably. He'd only just been promoted to full corporal, so this was very good experience for him.'

ASgt Binnie brimmed with confidence, which didn't endear him to everyone at first sight. 'Sean was a bit like Marmite,' said LCpl Milne. 'He was always very confident, and some saw that as arrogance. And, at the start, I didn't like him much myself. Looking back, I admit I was a little bit jealous. He'd joined up a year before me, and had done well, and he was where I wanted to be. When he became a PT instructor, he had his first taste of authority and a lot of guys were thinking, *Oh, no! Sean's got a little bit of power now!* And, in some PT sessions, he could be a bit of a nightmare. But we could always take the piss out of him. He could take the banter. And when I got to know him – mainly through the nights out that he organised – I saw the real Sean, and I felt very different about him. We became really good friends.'

May 7, 2009 dawned clear, hot and blue, as usual. But there was an unfamiliar buzz about the tiny Satellite Station North.

'Up until then, we'd only had minor contacts,' said Duncan Milne. 'But that day we had orders to head into an area further north than we'd been before, and we knew it would be hostile.'

The OMLT team and their ANA men were part of a bigger operation some way off to the west, on the other side of the river. Their job would be to provide a distraction, and to mop up any Taliban forces fleeing the main attack. The British soldiers and their Afghan charges busied themselves with cleaning weapons, and checking radios, water, and ammunition loads – each man was carrying more ammo than normal – before moving out.

After a while, information came in of a Taliban force not far away, and the Afghan troops pushed on excitedly, becoming separated from the Britons. This was a perennial problem for OMLT soldiers – the keener Afghans could be madly brave, and often a large part of the job involved holding them back as they strained at the leash to get to their foe.

'Our boss, Capt Lever, was annoyed with them, and was keen for us to regroup,' said Milne. 'He was on the radio, telling them to slow down at the front. But then they came into contact. At this point we were buzzing. We were like, *It's kicking off! We're going to get really involved! This is going to be amazing!* I remember looking at Sean and saying, "This is it! It's going to be epic today!" and us high-fiving each other. We were excited about the possibility of seeing some action. Thinking back now, we shouldn't have thought like that, but we were really up for it.'

And so, as the men of The Black Watch have always done, they advanced towards the sound of the guns.

* * *

SEAN BINNIE HAD dreamed of soldiering since boyhood. Born in Dublin, he'd been brought up in a peripatetic way by his mother Jan and stepfather, Allan, a North Sea oil rig worker who had himself served in The Gordon Highlanders, and whom Sean idolised.

'We settled down together while Sean was a baby,' said Jan, 'and he always saw Allan as his dad. He hero-worshipped him. They had a great relationship – he just loved to follow Allan around and listen to his Army stories. Sean was fascinated with it from a very young age – he joined the Black Watch cadets at school, and it was his ambition to join the regiment.'

Jan was understandably nervous about losing her only son – indeed, her only child – to a life in uniform.

'I remember the day Sean came home with his papers for the Army Foundation College,' she said. 'He was sixteen. He said, "You've got a choice, mum. You either support me by signing the forms now, or I'll join anyway later, and you'll never see me again because you stood in the way of me doing what I wanted to do."

'I looked at him and thought, *What do I say to that?* But I'd brought him up to stick by his convictions, so I couldn't stop him. Nevertheless, Allan and I waited three days before we signed the documents. I wanted to know he was a hundred per cent certain. I wanted him to know that he'd be away from home at this military college, with no-one to give him a cuddle, or wipe away his tears. But he knew what he was doing. Eventually we signed, and that was that.'

Sean was on the way to developing into a fine young man.

'Even as a baby he'd never given us any bother,' said Jan. 'He slept through the night quite happily, and was such a happy little baby. The only problem he had was he was allergic to milk for a little while, and he was briefly in hospital, covered in big lumps and blisters. But they put him on soya milk, which made all the difference, and then he just started filling out. He became very mischievous as he learned to get about on his feet, but he was a good boy. He'd never touch anything if he knew he wasn't supposed to. He charmed people. They'd say, "Oh, I'll have him! He's so good!"

'We never seemed to settle anywhere for very long in those days. People said we had gypsy blood, because we were on the move so often. First we were in Aberdeen, then we moved down to Kirkcaldy, where we both worked for the water board for some time. Then we moved to Lowestoft in Sussex to look after my father who was living there, and was suffering from cancer. We ran a pub there for two years, which had always been an ambition of mine. It was a lot of fun at the start, and it was particularly good for Sean – he loved mixing with all the customers, it really brought him out of his shell and, when he joined the Army, years later, he had more confidence than some of the other lads.'

Though not particularly academic, Sean was a bright little boy who overcame significant hurdles in his early educational life.

'Until he was eight, he found school very difficult and he didn't really enjoy it,' said Jan. 'That was frustrating. We knew he understood, alright, but his reading and his writing were poor. Allan had read an article, and he said to me one day, "I've been looking at Sean's writing, and I think he might have dyslexia." I'd never heard of dyslexia, in our day people didn't know much about it, but I went to the school and raised my concerns, and I must say they were very quick off the mark. He was diagnosed with dyslexia, and they got him into a special class and he took off from there. He had the support and understanding he needed, and he just blossomed.'

Not that Sean would have minded too much. By now, the family had left the pub and moved back north to Kirkcaldy, where he was loving the outdoor life.

'He was always out with his mates,' said Allan. 'Getting up to all sorts… swinging out of trees, riding his bike… He'd go swimming a lot, he played a bit of football, and he loved golf. He became very competitive with me about that. He started off just using my clubs, and then one day he came back on leave from the Army, and he had his own clubs and was ten times better than he'd been when he was at home. It turned out he'd been taking it really seriously, and had got some professional coaching. He was determined to come back and beat me, and he did!'

From the day he went to Harrogate in 2003, it was clear that Sean was a high-flier.

'He didn't look back,' said Jan. 'We talked to his instructors on the day he passed out, and they were very complimentary about him, and spoke about his leadership potential. He did everything by the book, took everything in. They did say he was a bit of a cheeky chappy, which didn't surprise us because he was definitely like that.'

Sean went to [*Infantry Training Centre, ITC*] Catterick to complete his basic training, and Jan was naturally anxious about how her son would cope with this new world. She need not have worried.

'Some of the lads were finding the training and being away from home hard,' she said. 'I asked Sean how he was coping, and he said, "Some of these are namby-pambies who can't be away from their mums! Trust me, I'm fine."'

When Sean passed out at Catterick, his parents thought their hearts would burst with pride.

'I was so impressed when I saw him there in uniform,' said Allan. 'He was looking so proud at having achieved so much. I knew what he'd been through, because I'd been in the Army myself. More than anything, he'd really changed into a man very quickly.'

Sean had achieved his life's ambition of joining The Black Watch, one of the most famous and decorated infantry regiments in the British Army, with antecedents going back to the Crimea, Waterloo, and before. Its men fought with great distinction in the First World War, and in every theatre in the Second World War, and have been awarded several Victoria Crosses for extreme gallantry. He valued this heritage and perhaps it spurred him on to make a name for himself.

'We were in the same platoon when I came to the battalion,' said Duncan Milne, 'and from then on we were soldiers side-by-side. He was an effortlessly good soldier, he never struggled with anything. He had an unmatchable determination. Binnie was about being the best, and was an inspiration.'

Others noticed his passion for chess, and his sweet tooth. 'There was hardly a time I saw him without a packet of sweets or chocolate bars on him, or in the vicinity,' said LCpl Jimmy Hutton.

Not long after Sean joined, The Black Watch was amalgamated into The Royal Regiment of Scotland – greatly offending the young soldier's sense of history.

'He actually thought about leaving,' said Jan. 'But he decided to stay when it was decided that The Black Watch would live on as the name of one of the battalions.'

He channelled his passion for 'The Forty Twa' into being the best he could be.

'He never sat still,' said Allan. 'He had his career mapped out. He was going to be the regimental sergeant major as quickly as possible. He had his PTI qualification, then he became a weapons trainer, and he got every category of driving licence. Most importantly, he got his section leader qualification, one of the hardest courses to pass.'

'Sean was very, very ambitious,' said Jan. 'He'd sacrifice leave time, and opportunities for things like skiing and adventure training, just so that he could get another course under his belt, and reduce the time until he could get promotion. I could hardly believe it when he qualified as a physical training instructor eighteen months after basic training. Obviously he was my little boy, and I know they do turn into men, but during the graduation display I saw him climb up this rope so easily... He didn't even break sweat. I was sitting there amazed, thinking, *That's my son!* He'd grown up in the space of three years.

'When he went to Iraq with the battalion in 2006, he filled out again. He came home halfway through the tour on R&R, and I looked at him as he got out of the car, and thought, *That's not my Sean!* He'd expanded in just the few months since we'd last seen him. As he gave me a cuddle, I thought, *Oh my God! My baby is a grown man!* I found it quite hard to cope with.'

It was on that deployment to Iraq that the reality of soldiering intruded.

'I don't know what he saw or experienced, but he had a wee bit of a meltdown when he came back,' said Jan. 'It was his twenty-first birthday, and we'd been out to celebrate. He was sitting on the couch, and he just went into floods of tears. He held onto his dad for dear life. That was the only time I ever saw him like that. He did tell me once that he was involved in an incident with a child, but he wouldn't tell me any more so we have no idea what the details were.'

'I think he had a wee flashback,' said Allan. 'He was a strong character, and didn't like showing weakness, so the tears were probably because he'd had a few beers. After that, I asked him a few times if he wanted to talk about Iraq, but he said, "You had to be there. I can only speak about it to the lads who were there." That's the way it is in the Army. So I said, "Fair enough," and I let it go.'

'He didn't like the basic soldier's salary,' said Jan. 'He said he was going to be on "pop star wages" one day. His CO told us later how he remembered walking through the camp just after Sean qualified as a lance-corporal, and being approached rather abruptly by him. "Oi! Hang about!" says Sean. "I've passed my cadre, and I'm waiting for my promotion and my money! When's someone going to do something about it?" The CO was quite astonished by this, but I think secretly he felt it was funny.

'And, bless him, he did climb the ranks fast. The officers we spoke to after he died were quite astounded at how quickly he had passed his corporal cadre. They said he would have gone on to greater things. It was amazing what he achieved in his short wee life. To be an acting sergeant by the age of twenty-two is amazing. I know that he'd spoken to people about the special forces, and I'm sure he would have gone for the SAS if he'd remained single. But by that time he was also wanting to get married, and I know that he felt it wouldn't be right.'

After spending his teenage years 'playing the field and being a jack-the-lad', in his dad's words, Sean had met and fallen in love with a young Belfast woman – Amanda – who was to become his wife. They dated for a while, and then Sean surprised his parents by announcing that he wanted to get married. Worried that he was too young for such a step, Jan asked him how he knew he was in love.

'Mum,' he said, 'when I'm going to see her, I get butterflies in my stomach. And when I *do* see her, my knees go wobbly.'

'All right,' said Jan. 'You're in love.'

The young couple were married in December 2008.

'He'd wanted to get married in October, after returning from Afghanistan,' said Jan. 'But Amanda wanted it to be before he left. He was worried that if something happened to him she wouldn't be able to cope as a widow, but I said she'd be broken-hearted whether they were engaged, married, or just going out together, and if they *were* married at least she would be looked after by the Army and the Ministry of Defence. I don't regret giving that advice, but I do regret that he got married so quickly. That's only for my own selfish reasons: if he hadn't been married he'd have come home and been cremated and buried here near his nana, where he wanted to be. But it didn't turn out that way.'

Had life worked out differently, Jan and Allan Binnie would probably now be grandparents. Sean was certainly very keen to have children, and joked to his wife that if they had a son they should call him 'Wheelie Binnie'.

'He was a natural with other people's children,' said Allan. 'He could be a bit rough now and again, but I think that was the soldier in him. Kids loved him.'

But in March 2009, Sean was deployed to Afghanistan with his comrades. The news of the deployment left Jan 'absolutely gutted'.

'For some reason, Iraq hadn't really bothered me,' she said. 'But when I heard he was going to Afghanistan, I just had a sickly feeling.'

Unfortunately, as an NCO, Sean was extremely busy in the days leading up to deployment, so he wasn't able to visit his parents before leaving on tour. However, he did find time to phone his mother.

'He called to say cheerio before he had to give up his mobile,' she said. 'He just said a few words, and I don't even remember exactly what they were. His aunt was sitting with me, and when I put the phone down I had tears in my eyes. She said, "What's wrong, you silly bugger?"

'I said, "I'm not going to see him again."

'She said, "Och, Jan, don't be silly!"

'But I had this feeling that I *wasn't* going to see him again. Perhaps it was the disappointment that he hadn't been able to come home to say cheerio. I don't know, but I couldn't shift it.'

Despite her sense of foreboding, Jan was determined not to dwell on Sean's absence. Allan was the same. 'I was worried about him,' he said, 'but you always think it's not going to happen. He'd done Iraq without any problems, so I convinced myself it would be the same. I didn't feel it was right to sit and worry all the time he was away, anyway. It's hard enough for them to do their job without that.'

Sean's opportunities to speak to his family were limited once he was in Musa Qala.

'The satellite phone wasn't very reliable,' said Jan. 'We might have a few seconds of conversation, and then it would cut off. And they were only allowed a certain amount of time on the phone each week. Sometimes, he'd leave a little message for me on MSN to say he was okay. And if he was able to get through to Amanda, she'd phone us. He did try his best to keep in touch, but at one point I sent a note to him asking him to give me a bit more attention. I understood that he was just married, but it's hard when you're used to him depending on you and phoning frequently. Suddenly, he had someone else to phone, and it was difficult. He phoned soon after that. I said, "Sean, if you just phone me and say, 'Mum, I'm safe, I love you,' then put the phone down, I'll be happy. If I'm not there just leave me a message and I'll be happy."

'He did try a bit more after that. I topped up his phone card by £20 and he must have been on to me for about half an hour the day we did that. I asked him whether he had everything he needed out there, because according to the newspapers and TV they didn't. He said, "Mum, get a grip, for God's sake! All you're seeing on the news is a lot of namby-pamby little buggers wanting Gucci stuff. Trust me, we're well kitted-out. I wish you'd stop watching that flaming news and getting yourself all worried." But I couldn't help it.'

* * *

AT THE BACK of his mind, Sean Binnie was worried, too.

'I always thought I would come home,' said LCpl Duncan Milne. 'But some people give the impression that they think they might not, and Sean was one of them. We didn't like to speak about it, but we knew the statistics, and we knew about the threat. I do think he had this attitude that something bad might happen. Despite that, he wanted to go. It was daunting, but, if you're in the infantry, a deployment like that is one of the boxes you need to tick. If you hadn't been to Afghanistan, you couldn't really say you'd soldiered. It was our turn.'

Which was how they found themselves, on that hot day in May, racing to assist the beleaguered ANA with their OMLT colleagues.

A sizeable battle was developing very quickly.

A few months earlier, in January 2009, the gunners of 29 Cdo RHA had achieved a truly monumental task when they had managed to place a 105mm gun on a rock escarpment overlooking Musa Qala. At some 40m in height, the 'Roshan Tower' was a key strategic location, but it would have crumbled under the weight of the 'light gun' – which actually weighed nearly two tonnes – and its many 45kg boxes of shells. So the commandos had the weapon helicoptered to the foot of the cliff, spent four days building a concrete platform on its top, and then carried it to the summit *by hand* under cover of darkness, with Gurkhas watching for any Taliban ambush.

Once *in situ*, it was being employed not in its usual indirect fire mode – firing at out-of-sight targets as much as 20km away – but directly aimed at much closer targets. The gunners had it down to such a fine art that they could acquire, engage and hit targets at a range of two or three kilometres within five seconds. Each shell was sent on its way with a huge belch of flame, which had led the Taliban quickly to nickname it the 'Dragon Gun'. They greatly feared its accuracy and killing power.

Now, as Duncan Milne heard the tempo of the contact ahead ramping up and becoming more aggressive, he heard the Dragon Gun opening up behind him. Simultaneously, his boss, Capt Olly Lever, was on the radio demanding air assets.

The British soldiers were delighted.

'It was getting really hostile,' said Milne, 'but it was everything we'd trained for, and we were loving it. We started pushing forward, came round a corner and saw Afghan soldiers in contact. Two of them had been shot, and were being dragged back to us. Our medics got straight to work on them while Sean made sure that we had all-round defence.

'Rounds started bouncing in and around where the casualties were. We could see some Taliban, and, as I had the GPMG, the boss said to me, "Right, get some rounds down on that treeline!" So I started putting down big bursts. There was a real buzzing atmosphere, and some of the other guys were saying, "I want a shot, I want a shot!" I remember looking at Sean, and saying, "I've got one up on you now! I've got one up on you now!"

'He said, "Don't worry, I'll get my opportunity!"

'I said, "Yeah? We'll see, we'll see!"'

As is often the case, the firefight rapidly became very confusing, with messages arriving to say that a number of ANA men had either been captured or were trapped in a nearby compound.

'If they were captured, we had to go forward to help get them back,' said Milne. 'Fortunately, an Afghan truck had evacuated the casualties, so we could continue on. The Afghan police had also turned up, and they were just shooting everywhere. One had climbed up onto the roof of a building in a compound to try to throw grenades into it, while his colleagues were still blazing away *at the same compound!* We were looking at each other and laughing, like, *This is crazy!*

'By this time, the remaining Taliban were trapped in this small building. There must have been five or six of them. There was quite a lot of fire coming out, and the Afghan army were putting a lot of fire in. There were women and children nearby, but they were shooting all over the place and didn't seem to be concerned about the civilians.

'So we're thinking we need to get in there to rescue these two missing Afghan soldiers, we need to put down some effective fire, but we don't want to get in front of the ANA. So Capt Lever sat back to work out how we were going to become an effective force. Three of us were in a trench about waist deep. Me, Sean, and 'Kenny' Everett. Kenny had a light machine-gun, and I had the GPMG. The Afghans asked us for more grenades, but they weren't trained to use ours and the boss felt we couldn't let them have them. He decided that some of us should right-flank the compound, then put some fire down and attack the front door of the building where the Taliban were. He said, "Right, I'm going to go in with some grenades, and Kenny to put down covering fire. The rest of you stay here and provide more covering fire while I clear the building."

'At this point, Sean famously said, "No, boss, you're the platoon commander. I'm section commander, it's my job. It's my bread-and-butter."

'The boss said, "Right, okay."

Capt Lever would later say that there was no fear in Sean Binnie's eyes, only excitement. 'He was as calm as though we were on a training exercise on Brecon,' said Lever, 'and it was a training grenade.'

'Olly Lever did the right thing. We all knew that. None of us would have expected him to go in with the grenades, because if he was hit then we'd really be screwed. He needed to be getting other troops and air assets involved. It was getting massively dangerous. More assets were getting brought towards us, but it wasn't happening quickly enough. At this point, Sean said to me, "This is it! I'm getting involved!" I remember him looking at me as if to say, *I bet you're jealous.* And I *was* jealous. I wished I was going into this with him. I remember saying to the boss, "Can I go? Can I go?"

'He said, "No, I need you here."'

With rounds zipping everywhere, Sean Binnie and Kenny Everett left the relative safety of their foxhole and headed towards the enemy, while their comrades tried to get the Afghan police and ANA to stop shooting at the compound. They clambered over a wall, and quickly established that no ANA men were in fact being held. But, by that time, the die was cast: ASgt Binnie was committed to clearing the building from which the Taliban were firing.

'We couldn't see Sean and Kenny at this point because of the wall,' said Duncan Milne. 'I just remember hearing a large burst of fire from Kenny, and then a grenade went off. Then there was silence. The Afghan Army were still shooting at the compound, but there was no fire coming out any more. Something had obviously happened. If there was no fire coming out, Sean must have killed whoever was inside. But why wasn't Sean on the net, saying "Building clear!" as we'd expect him to?

'I was on my personal radio, going, "Sean, send me a sitrep! Sean, send me a sitrep!" Nothing. Everyone was panicking, guys were shouting, "Sean! Sean!" The next thing we heard was Kenny shouting, "Medic!" The boss wanted to shoot right off and get down there as quickly as possible, but I remember standing up and saying, "I'm going, I'm going now!"

'We had a Gurkha colour sergeant with us, and me and him shot off. I had the GPMG with me, but the adrenaline took me over those six-foot walls easily. I just had to get to Sean as quickly as possible. I saw his ECM kit on the ground, and then I saw his weapon. I went around a corner, and there was Kenny with Sean. Kenny had ripped open Sean's body armour and he had his top pulled up. I could see where the round or rounds had gone into the side of Sean's chest [*just missing his Kevlar protector*]. Kenny was trying to put a bandage on and checking his airway.

'Sean was unconscious, and so pale. That terrified me. I grabbed his top, and I just shook him. And then he made this horrible sound, as if he was taking his last breath, and that was it. There was no movement from him after that. I remember shouting into the radio, "Medic! Get the fucking medic here now!" But nothing was happening, so I stood up and screamed, *"Get the fucking medic here NOW!"*

'The Afghan Army guys were just looking at me blankly. It's easy to communicate with the Afghans when it's calm, and you have the interpreter, but when things get active it's another matter entirely. I remember thinking, *This is the most horrible thing in the world*. But if they'd been British soldiers, the message might have got through straight away, and there'd still have been nothing anyone could do.

'I dropped the GPMG, picked up Sean's weapon and went back over the walls to the boss and the medic. I said, "Getting fucking round there now!" So then everyone did get around to where Sean was. We looked at the medic and expected him to work wonders. I was ridiculously angry, then I was crying, then I was angry again. I started shouting at the medic, "Just fucking *do* something! There's got to be *something* you can do!" He knew straight away, but he also knew he had to try. He tried to put fluids into Sean, but of course he was dead.

'The others tried to calm me down, and then I said, "Okay, I'll keep a watch, I'll make sure there's no more threat. I don't want to look."

'I remember feeling this horrible sense that there was nothing we could do. Part of me wanted to run off and get some kind of revenge. There was still some weird part of us all that thought, *Maybe if we can get him to the medical helicopter…* Anyway, we wanted to extract Sean as quickly as possible. The boss managed to get two American Blackhawks with med teams on board.'

They wrapped Sean's body in a woollen blanket and placed him in the back of an ANA pick-up. With sporadic fire still ringing out, they walked alongside their fallen comrade to a nearby cornfield. Olly Lever watched the Black Hawk come in, its downdraft blowing the half-grown maize around 'like something out of a Vietnam war film'. As it touched down, they hurried forward with Sean Binnie's body, said their final farewells, and watched it lift away with him.

Later, Capt Lever would ponder how different life would have been if he had ignored Sean's request to hand over the grenade, and gone forward himself. But for now they still had to make it back to the FOB in one piece.

'I pretty much cried the whole way back,' said Duncan Milne. 'and there were other guys crying. It was such a weird, emotional thing. When we got back, all the guys who'd come to help just left us, and it was just the five or six of us left there. We just stood there in silence, just crying and hugging each other.

'I had Sean's blood all over my hands, all on my clothes. Kenny had blood all over his boots and clothes. It was horrible. I'd been feeling enthusiastic for the fight just a little while before. Now I just felt almost guilty.'

Kenny Everett was later able to talk his comrades through Sean Binnie's death. Sean had approached the doorway of the building and thrown a grenade inside. As he did so, the end of a weapon appeared and a round was fired. Sean Binnie turned around and said, 'Oh, shit!' Everett assumed that he had bumped himself, but he watched Sean walk around a corner and collapse. This all took two or three seconds – at the end of which the grenade thrown by ASgt Binnie detonated. It killed the remaining Taliban fighters, including the man who had shot him.

His actions had spoken volumes as to the character of the man – he was posthumously Mentioned in Dispatches, and was truly, as his OC Capt Ollie Lever described him, an individual of the 'highest calibre' who demonstrated 'incredible and sustained bravery'.

* * *

BACK HOME IN SCOTLAND, Jan Binnie was preparing dinner and wondering why she hadn't heard from her son or his wife for a while.

'Sometimes Amanda would phone me several times a day,' said Jan. 'Not because she was particularly worried – we just got on really well. But that day she'd phoned me a few times, and each time she said, "He still hasn't been in touch."

'I said, "He's obviously been on patrol. He'll probably phone soon as he gets back to the base."

'I was in the kitchen making tea when she rang again. I said, "Hiya, hon! Hang on, I'm peeling tatties, give me a minute."

'And I put her on loudspeaker. She said, "No, Jan! It's the Army. It's Sean!"

'I said, "What about him?"

'She said, "He was shot and killed at six o'clock this morning!"

'I remember expecting Sean to come on the phone and say, "Ha ha, gotcha!" because he did play practical jokes on me. But instead, this man's voice came on, someone from the Army. He said, "I'm really sorry, Mrs Binnie." From that point I don't remember much, except I was screaming.'

Somehow, she managed to dial Allan's work number.

'One of my workmates took the call,' he said. 'Jan was hysterical. All I could understand was that Sean had been shot. That was it. So I drove home, hoping he'd just been injured. But as soon as I saw Jan, I knew. After that, it was just a nightmare. The two of us were just numb for hours.'

The Army's initial support was focused on Sean's widow, Amanda. 'I wasn't being told anything, and I was desperate to know more,' said Jan. 'I phoned the Army and asked them to sort something out. "It's my son were talking about here," I said, "and I'm not being told anything." Soon after that, Capt Brian Hermitage, who ran the TA in this area, was at my door. He was a lovely man, and he took care of everything on our behalf.'

He was also able to tell the Binnies a little about how Sean had died.

'It made me very proud,' said Allan. 'He had no fear in his eyes at the end, and he died the way a soldier would want to die, in the thick of the battle. He was careful not to kill or injure the women and children in the compound. He did what he had to do.'

'As someone from the regiment said, "He died in the true manner of a Black Watch soldier, taking the fight to the enemy,"' said Jan. 'His friends were there with him, the likes of Duncan Milne and Kenny Everett, and I'm glad he went quickly, and that he had close friends there.'

Nonetheless, the first few days after Sean's death were extremely traumatic for his parents. 'Allan and I had each other,' said Jan. 'But it's difficult to help each other when you're both under the same awful stress. We tried, but it was hard. I wasn't coping at all. I remember wrapping myself in Sean's coat, and throughout those first days we never slept and hardly ever ate. I smoked about a hundred cigarettes a day. I didn't want to get up, or get dressed. I was that bad that my auntie and cousin came up to see me and stopped at Asda to buy a top and trousers on the way. Then they helped me to get dressed. For the first time in days.

'I'm not even clear about how long it was before Sean's body was brought back. I guess it was a matter of days. I just remember the house being full of people for most of that time, even though I just wanted to be on my own.'

In fact, Sean's body was brought home on May 13, along with those of Cpl Kumar Pun of The Royal Gurkha Rifles, Sgt Ben Ross of The Royal Military Police, and Rfn Adrian Sheldon of The Rifles, who had also been killed in Helmand on the same day.[14]

For Jan, her only son's repatriation through RAF Lyneham was 'the most horrendous thing I have ever experienced'.

'We were quite unprepared for it,' she said. 'I was okay while the aircraft was landing, and while they were taking the coffin off, but the moment the pallbearers turned towards us with the coffin on their shoulders, that was it. I just crumbled.'

For Allan, it was only at that moment that he really accepted his son was dead.

The four bodies were driven through Wootton Bassett, the families following behind, numb with grief. Later, Jan and Allan were able to see Sean in his coffin. 'There was some opposition to that from some people,' said Jan, 'but I brought him into this world, and I was damned if he was going out without me seeing him. They did him proud. He looked like he was ready to open his eyes. His shoes were shining... He really looked good. I tucked a letter and some photos into one of his pockets, and I put one of his favourite sweets, a Crunchy bar, under his kilt.

'At the funeral, Allan and his brother were the lead pallbearers, and when they got to the grave, Sean's boys, the men he'd fought alongside, lowered him down. That felt like the right way to do things.'

Such unthinkable tragedy can sometimes poison family relationships and friendships, and Sean's death caused a grievous rift between Amanda and his parents. The funeral took place in Northern Ireland, where Amanda is from; Jan and Allan believe he wanted to be buried in Scotland, next to his grandmother.

'We feel strongly that he never came home,' said Jan. 'That hurts me still. He married Amanda just a short time before he went to Afghan, and she chose to have him buried in Northern Ireland, where she lives. But Sean had never lived there, and we knew that if he was killed he wanted to be cremated and buried near his nana in Aberdeen.

'Our relationship with Amanda hasn't gone well since Sean's death, mainly because we couldn't agree with him being buried in Northern Ireland, and because we felt very left out of everything. But when I met Amanda I thought she was amazing. She's such a beautiful girl. I remember Sean saying, "You have to tell her you like her. You have to tell you love her." That was so important to him. I did love her, and I suppose I still do.

'After the funeral, Allan and I lingered at Sean's grave. We'd taken soil there from all the places where he'd lived in Scotland, and we'd also put some thistle seed in his grave. We were hoping that the thistles would grow through, but five years on they still haven't. It was very hard to walk away, but eventually we had to. As we did, I heard Sean screaming, "Please, please, mum! Don't leave me here!"'

'I know it sounds incredible,' said Allan, 'but we both heard it. I said to Jan, "Did you hear that?" I was amazed, because Jan said, "Aye!" It was a horrible, horrible feeling. I don't know if it was in our subconscious, but for the two of us to hear it at the same time was very strange. We felt awful leaving, but we had to.'

Illness meant Jan could not visit her son's grave for the first year, but after that she would fly across the Irish Sea to visit it every two weeks – usually alone, with Allan away on the rigs. Financial pressures meant she eventually had to reduce the frequency of those visits, but she still goes as often as she can afford. 'I get a lot of comfort when I visit his grave,' she said. 'I feel close to him, and I get a horrible feeling when I leave. But I no longer hear his voice asking me to take him home.'

It's the tritest of trite phrases, but life must go on; Jan and Allan Binnie are certain that that would have been Sean's wish for them. 'We're trying to have a happy life together,' said Jan, 'because we honestly believe that's what Sean would want. Sean's Army friend Michael Spencer insisted that we "adopt" his two boys, Dylan and Riley, as our grandchildren. Having them to love and enjoy has been wonderful. They come on holidays with us and sometimes they come with us to Northern Ireland to visit Sean's grave. They help us to replace the old flowers with new ones, and then we look for the swan that we saw on the lake near the cemetery on the day Sean was buried. If they see a swan, the children think Sean has joined us, and they shout, "Hello, Uncle Sean!" If we're lucky, it will paddle over towards us.

'It's been five years since we lost him, but I still find it extremely difficult. I always carry a lock of his hair in a locket around my neck, and he's never far from my mind. I try not to show it to Allan all the time, and sometimes I just disappear into my little world, but there are times when Allan's on the rig when he'll phone me, and I have a bit of a meltdown. But I pull myself together. I still have difficulty sleeping, and I still have nightmares, though a little less often now. I know it sounds strange, but I see myself in the middle of this firefight, and I see Sean running. Then I see everybody running to him and I'm standing over them. He's looking at me, and then his eyes just roll. And all the time this shooting is going on in the background. I can hardly make out what else is being said, but what I can hear is Sean screaming, "Mum, please! Mum! Please!"'

'We've spoken about it a lot over the years,' said Allan. 'We have to live a decent life, because Sean wouldn't have wanted us to live a life of misery. So we try to do as much as we possibly can with our lives. It took quite a while for Jan to accept that, because she was very down, for a long time. But now she has the adopted grandkids, and she spends as much time as possible with them. The regiment has told us to call on them any time, but I sometimes think we have to let them move on. We're a constant reminder of what happened. But we're very close friends with Sean's regimental sergeant major, who's now a captain, and we see a lot of the lads who were with Sean in Afghanistan. They come to see us from the camp, dump their washing, and say to Jan, "What are you making for tea, mam?" We like that.'

Jan and Allan are still wondering whether Afghanistan was worth the price they and hundreds of other families have paid. 'Sean swore allegiance to his Queen and country, he fought for his Queen and country, and he died for his Queen and country,' said Jan. 'I am proud of him and I always will be. But I used to wonder if we were right to be there. I asked him once why we were fighting there. He said, "Mum, do you think we're out here just fighting? Our boys are out here building schools, we're sorting out water supplies, we're getting rid of drugs, and we're giving the Afghan people a better quality of life."

'I said, "Right, but how do you feel about it?"

'He said, "I feel good about it. And I want *you* to feel good, because I'm out here doing some of that work." I did then see it in a different light. But, at the same time as a mum, sitting here now after losing him, I still wonder.'

123

Every Remembrance Day brings a special poignancy for the Binnies: Sean's birthday was November 11.

'We go to Kirkcaldy and attend the service at the war memorial which bears his name,' said Jan. 'It's a more traditional form of remembrance there – the way it should be. The pipes and drummers play, and it seems like all the town turns out. Amanda gave us Sean's medals and his Elizabeth Cross. We also have his watch and his aftershave and his mess uniform. They were things we thought we'd never see again, so we're grateful for them. One day the medals will go to the Black Watch Museum, but meanwhile, when we go to Kirkcaldy, the place where Sean joined the Army, I wear the Elizabeth Cross and Allan wears his medals.

'We're with family there. People try to console me by saying things like, "Your laddie, he was a braw young man." They show us a lot of kindness, and it helps. But I don't think there'll ever be a November 11 when I don't cry.'

[*Amanda Binnie did not take up the opportunity to be interviewed for this book, and no criticism of her whatsoever is intended.*]

RIFLEMAN CYRUS THATCHER
C COMPANY 2nd BATTALION THE RIFLES
JANUARY 13, 1990 – JUNE 2, 2009

BEFORE HEADING OFF to Afghanistan on the tour that would end his life at the age of nineteen, Cyrus Thatcher wrote a secret farewell letter to the family he loved more than anything in the world.

He told his closest Army friend, Rifleman Stewart Elliott, that he'd hidden the letter in the kitchen at home, and made him promise that – if the worst happened – he would tell Cyrus's mother and father about it.

On June 2, 2009, not far from his forward operating base near Gereshk, in Nahr-e Saraj, the worst *did* happen, when the irrepressible teenager triggered a hidden IED and was killed instantly.

It was a terrible moment for the men of 10 Platoon. Cyrus was one of its most popular members; even in the heat of a firefight, his friends would hear him cackling across the battlefield at some joke he had just cracked. Leon Smith, Cyrus' platoon serjeant – The Rifles' spelling of the NCO rank – was himself badly injured in the same explosion. In an official tribute released by the Army, Sjt Smith described his fallen comrade as 'a ray of sunshine… always giggling and joking, making the blokes smile. I am going to miss that laugh, and that Rifleman. Rest in Peace, my brother.'

In the same tribute, Stewart Elliot said it had been an honour to have known and served alongside Cyrus. 'When he first joined the platoon, he was quiet and shy,' said Elliott. 'But it didn't take him long to show his true colours for the rascal he really was. He made me promise that people would remember him the way he was, not to feel

125

sorry for him but to remember the good times. Goodbye, my brother, rest well.'

Cyrus's platoon commander was Lt Paul Mervis – a former journalist at *The Spectator* magazine who had joined up out of a thirst for adventure.

'There are many good men out here,' said Lt Mervis, 'but Thatch was one of the best. We have lost a good man, one whom I will never forget.'

In a private letter to Cyrus Thatcher's heartbroken family back in Caversham, Berkshire, he told them how he would cherish the memory of the young soldier 'until the day I die.'

Cyrus's grieving parents immediately wrote back to Lt Mervis to thank him for his kind words.

He never received the letter. The day after it was posted, and ten days after Cyrus Thatcher's death, Paul Mervis was himself killed in an explosion. He was twenty-seven.

* * *

'HELLO ITS ME,' wrote Cyrus Thatcher, in that final letter.

'[T]his is gonna be hard for you to read but I write this knowing every time you thinks shits got to much for you to handle (so don't cry on it MUM!!) you can read this and hopefully it will help you all get through.

For a start SHIT I got hit!! Now Iv got that out the way I can say the things Iv hopefully made clear, or if I havent this should clear it all up for me. My hole life you'v all been there for me through thick and thin bit like a wedding through good and bad. Without you I believe I wouldn't have made it as far as I have. I died doing what I was born to do I was happy and felt great about myself although the army was sadly the ending of me it was also the making of me so please don't feel any hate toward it. One thing I no I never made clear to you all was I make jokes about my life starting in the Army. That's wrong VERY wrong my life began a LONG time before that (Obviously) but you get what I mean. All the times Iv tried to neglect the family get angry when you try teach me right from wrong wot I mean to say is I only realised that you were trying to help when I joined the army and without YOUR help I would have never had the

BALLS, the GRIT and the damn right determination to crack on and do it. If I could have a wish in life it would to be able to say Iv gone and done things many would never try to do. And going to Afghan has fulfilled my dream ie my goal. Yes I am young wich as a parent must brake you heart but you must all somehow find the strength that I found to do something no matter how big the challenge. As Im writing this letter I can see you all crying and mornin my death but if I could have one wish in an 'after life' it would be to stop your crying and continueing your dreams (as I did) because if I were watching only that would brake my heart. So dry your tears and put on a brave face for the rest of your friends and family who need you.

I want each and everyone of you to forfill a dream and at the end of it look at what you have done (completed) and feel the accomplishment and achievement I did only then will you understand how I felt when I passed away.

[To his brothers:] You are both amazing men and will continue to be throughout your lives you both deserve to be happy and fofill all of your dreams.

Dad – my idol, my friend, my best friend, my teacher, my coach, everything I ever succeeded in my life I owe to you and maybe a little bit of me! You are a great man and the perfect role model and the past two years of being in the army I noticed that and me and you have been on the best level we have ever been. I thank you for nothing because I no all you have given to me is not there to be thanked for its there because you did it cause you love me and that is my most proudest thing I could ever say.

Mum, where do I start with you!! For a start your perfect, your smell, your hugs, the way your life was dedicated to us boys and especially the way you cared each and every step us boys took. I love you, you were the reason I made it as far as I did you were the reason I was loved more than any child I no and that made me feel special.

Your all such great individuals and I hope somehow this letter will help you get through this shit time!! Just remember do NOT mourn my death as hard as this will seem, celebrate a great life that has had its ups and downs. I love you all more than you would ever no and in your own individual ways helped me get through it all. I wish you all the best with your dreams.

Remember chin up head down.
With love Cyrus xxxx

* * *

'CYRUS WAS BORN kicking and screaming, and that's how he continued,' said his mother, Helena Tym. 'We had three boys. Zac is the oldest, then there was Cyrus, then Steely. There were only four years between the three of them. When he was a teenager, he went through the angst that a lot of teenagers go through. He wasn't particularly academic, and he struggled with school. With the help of the school and the local education authority, we ended up with a plan that enabled Cyrus to go to school for two or three days a week and spend the rest of the time working in his dad's building business. But it was still a challenge getting him to go to school for just those three days.'

'He was bloody hard work when he was young,' said his father, Robin Thatcher. 'But I was the same – I hated school. I think he just didn't grasp it. If they were studying French, he'd think, *What's the point of doing this when I'm not even very good at English?'*

'He struggled to read and write well,' said Helena, 'and I think he was angry at his inability to sit and learn. Socially, he was absolutely fantastic. If you spoke to his teachers, not one of them had a bad word to say about him. He just couldn't cope in a classroom. Eventually, he began receiving one-to-one lessons, which helped, and he left school with three GCSEs, which was fantastic and enabled him to join the Army.'

His parents have tremendous memories of Cyrus and his brothers growing up in Berkshire.

'Cyrus was great fun,' said Robin, 'and that's probably what we miss the most. His laugh was so infectious. He could be childish at times, but very adult at the right moment. He was a lovely person. I loved outdoor pursuits – trials bike riding, fishing, certain kinds of shooting. I used to involve the boys in all of it, and, although they each had their own characters, they loved it, too. The boys were everything to us, and we planned everything around them. We wouldn't even go out for a meal without them. And whatever we were doing, Cyrus was the most determined and the most demanding. He *always* had to win. He was so competitive, he wouldn't even give his younger brother Steely a chance, and Steely was not as fit and agile as Cyrus. Cyrus would elbow him out of the way to make sure that he got to the top of a hill first. He'd do it even though he knew I was going to give him such a bollocking. "What is your *problem*?" I'd say. "You *know* you can beat him. Why do you have to prove it?"

'But he was also very sensitive. He always wanted to know that he was loved. "Tell me that you love me, mum," he'd say, and Helena would say, "Of course I love you!"

'"But tell me that you love me more than the other two!"'

The caring side to Cyrus's nature – which would later show itself in his readiness, even eagerness, to distribute goodies from his regular parcels to less fortunate soldiers in Afghanistan – was often to the fore.

'Cyrus was very observant,' said Helena. 'If I bought a new perfume, he'd notice. If I'd washed the windows, he'd come along and put kiss marks all over them. And he always had to have the last word. That was absolutely his thing.'

'After an argument that had gone on for a bit too long, I might say, "That's the end of it, and I don't want to hear another word. Understood?"' said Robin. 'He'd say, "Yeah, understood." Then there'd be a little silence. "I was right, though, wasn't I!"'

Robin and Helena will never know what made their middle son decide to join the Army, though an outdoor childhood spent playing with his Action Man and his BB guns must have contributed. 'Things like caving, getting soaking wet and wondering if we were going to get out, would have given him a great sense of achievement,' said Robin. 'Perhaps that was similar to the Army experience. Anyway, he suddenly announced that he wanted to join up. I don't think we took his plans too seriously, to start with.'

'Working with Rob would have been the easy route, but he didn't enjoy building and I think he wanted to prove something to himself,' said Helena. 'He joined in March of 2007, when he was seventeen. We tried to persuade him to pick a type of soldiering that would give him a profession when he came out again, but he wanted to be on the frontline. He had it in his head that he was prepared to face anyone and take on the world. So once he had decided to be in the infantry, that was it. Even if we'd said he couldn't join, he'd probably have done it anyway. It was far better that he went to the Army knowing that he had a hundred per cent support from us.'

Cyrus's father said his son relished the prospect of one day confronting the enemy face-to-face.

'Perhaps it was that I'd succeeded on my own, and he wanted to prove that he could do the same,' said Robin. 'He didn't need a handout from his dad. When we were driving him up to Bassingbourn to begin his training, I heard him say quietly, "What the fuck have I done?" I said, "Sorry, mate?" He hadn't realised that he was talking out loud. He said, "Nothing!" But Helena and I were sitting there thinking, *Oh, God! He's having second thoughts.*

'We pulled into the base and were asked in for tea and coffee, and Cyrus was told to wait by the bus stop. We looked around as we were served our tea but he'd gone. We'd had a quick goodbye, but no more. After twelve weeks, the recruits were entitled to go home on leave, but he refused to come home. We think he knew that he would have had a hard job leaving his friends and family again. One of his officers said, "What's the matter, Thatch? No loving at home?" He said, "No, sir, exactly the opposite."

'The Army Recruitment Officer actually told us that they would break him and then rebuild him, and he would learn that, even when he thought he had given everything he had to give, he would be able to find that little bit extra. In one exercise, he raced to the top of a hill, and he was then dragged back down again by his feet and told to do it again, this time making sure that those who were lagging behind were with him and safe. He was scratched and bruised, but he'd understood the lesson.'

Helena said, 'One of his corporals told us that, by the end of training, Cyrus was pushing his slower mates up the hill, and he would be carrying two backpacks. He pointed to the hill where he had to be dragged back down, and jokingly said, "We call that Thatch's Hill."'

Although slight in build, Cyrus was chosen as a GPMG gunner.

'He could carry that weapon without a problem,' said Robin. 'He could keep up with anyone. He'd have loved to have been that fit in the civilian world, but he needed that drive and push that the Army gave him.'

He was proud of what he had achieved, too. During one spell of leave, he flexed his arm and said to his mother, 'Do you know what that is?'

'I said, "Yeah, it's a muscle,"' said Helena. 'He said, "No, it's fucking hard work!" That's how he was. After he'd finished his basic training, he visited his old school, in full Army uniform, and gave a talk to the class of children that would have been leaving school that year. He said, "Look, there's another world out there. You still need to get your basic education, but it's not all about being academic." Most of all, though, he was able to stand there proud, and the teachers could see that he had made something of himself.'

Cyrus Thatcher was posted to Northern Ireland when he turned eighteen in the January of 2008. His first operational tour was to Kosovo later that year, where 600 men of 2 Rifles were involved in the UN peacekeeping mission.

'He absolutely loved it,' said Helena. 'He really felt he was a soldier. He enjoyed meeting the people in Kosovo, especially the children. He loved children, and he was very good with them. Cyrus had a very sensitive and nurturing side to him, and we've always been a very tactile family. There's never been any embarrassment about showing that we cared for each other. And he was like that with his friends, too. He didn't have any particular girlfriend, although he had lots of friends who were girls. This hurts a bit now, because we know that a lot of his old Army friends are now married and having children. It's quite likely that Cyrus would be settling down by now. People talk about their grandchildren, and we know that Cyrus won't be able to give us any. When the time comes with Zac and Steely, it's going to be hard. Cyrus would have been so good with his own children, and theirs.'

The Rifles' deployment to Afghanistan rolled around all too soon. It had long been on his family's horizon – and Cyrus's.

'He'd said, "Great, bring it on!"' said Robin. 'He was an adult when he took that final oath, and he went with his eyes wide open. There was a pre-Afghan deployment talk for families, and we had the opportunity to query the quality of their equipment, or the helicopter and medical support, if we wanted to. We didn't have any queries. We felt that he'd been trained by the best, and the equipment he had was as good as any available and that budgets would allow for. Cyrus wanted better boots than the standard issue ones, and so we found some in a shop in Manchester. But we didn't have a gripe about that. Whatever the standard issue, people will always think they can have something that's a bit better.'

Cyrus was a young man who was neither afraid to admit his fears, nor to confront them. After one training exercise, three months after joining 2 Rifles, he won a battalion award for valour, the prize for which was a tandem freefall jump from twelve thousand feet. Lt Col Rob Thomson, his CO, said later, 'As he received the prize, it was all he could do to utter that he hated aeroplanes – passionately so. To his huge credit, he jumped and, not only that, he ensured that his family was there to record the event for posterity.'

He landed with just about the biggest grin anyone had ever seen.

Cyrus took the same attitude with him to Afghanistan, said Helena. 'I remember he said to me once, "Of course I'm scared. Anyone who says they're not scared is a liar. But I'm not afraid to die." Cyrus was fully aware, and we were aware, that people would be trying to kill him, and he would be trying to kill people. That's the mind-set you have to have.'

* * *

ONCE HE REACHED Afghanistan, and in the two months before his death, Cyrus did his best to keep in touch with his family back home.

'I think he managed to phone us four times and he wrote seven blueys,' said Helena. Those letters were full of fun and life. In one, dated 27 April, he wrote:

> *Hello Mum*
> *I've just got your bluey (the 1st one) yea you are right it does get fucking hot, I can't work out wether I'm tanned or just burnt to fuck!! I've spoke to you on the phone so you no what I've been doing... We'v had the same shit maybe a month now. Everyday a Monday out here. You kind of loose track of days. I cant quite work out if its going fast or slow. This pen is shit its doing my head in!!*
> *Iv been thinking of loads of things and places to do, go and see. Me*

132

and [Rfn Stewart] *Elliott are gonna go to Amsterdam after this.*
THINK WE MAY HAVE DESERVED IT!! It should be a good day
(November 5th) [the date of the 2 Rifles homecoming parade].
On the 6th we can go Belfast Iv'e got loads of sad things I wanna buy
ie Sky+ Big TV. Get the old man to help me rearange my room and
help me fix my shelves. Im not the DIY type normally resort to celler
tape or blue tack. HA HA HA.

Hope everyones safe at home. Complete detox out here – water no
drink. So my dance moves might involve a bit of stumbling when I
return! Im coming home 2 weeks earlier now so that's kinda good, it
might be worth Zac picking me up give me a bit of chill out time so I
don't try stab a gobby civvi plus he's a good listener, sumtimes I wonder
if he's listening or thinking of sumthing completely irrelivant.

Well pass this round the family so they can all admire my extream
spelling (infantry eh!). Lots of love to all the nearest and dearest. Love
Ya!! Xxxx

Four days later, he wrote:

Hey Mum + family
Everything is good up this way getting hotter, still moving at a million
miles per hour (HA HA HA) I think Iv'e stopped burning Im slowly
going brown and my hair is getting ridiculous just wait till I come
home ill look like a fucking wooky?! I was gonna write to granny +
grandad but to be honest with the few spare hours I get Id'e rather
write home ey? BTW send my regards to Daphne, Joan, Brian etc. Let
em no how Im doing?

Every so often we get old people and churches send us little gifts
like baby wipes, razors, sweets and stuff so its quite a good bit of moral.
Got some really good photos ill have to bring my camera back so we
can get that Kosovo collage on the go, to bring back on the 5th of
November. If you saw what and where Ive been sleeping you would
be shocked!! So pictures will back me up!

Unfortunately 3 blokes died 2 days ago in an IED explosion in one
of the FOBs bout 2 kilometers away [this was probably a reference
to the IED deaths of Welsh Guardsman Tobie Fasfous and an
Afghan interpreter called Popal Shah]*– we visited that FOB 2 days*

133

before the attack – fucking mental quite scary actually! We'v had a rest day so Im doing a bit of hand washing and fitness! God you'd be so proud Ha! Ha! Ha! We've still had spam, rice, beans and unflavoured noodles every day – promise me actually I promise you if I see spam in the house ill fucking destroy it!! Im getting pretty good at making flat bread and we bout a goat of a local for 200 dollars and we slaughtered it. I got a good video. Its either catch it, kill it, or make it out here or else you go hungry LOL!! The showers are also freezing whilst Im on the subject of moaning?? Id'e best go again BUT ill keep writing when I get the time + ill be home in a couple of months. Love you'zzz all don't worry bout me to much. Theres only 3 things that kill people over hear BULLETS, BOMBS + EGOS so I might go down with a bad case of swollen head!! Ha Ha Ha Ha Ha. Love ya xxxxx

On 12 May, he wrote:

Hello Mother
Yesterday was a massive day for moral an american chopper came in yesterday. I got 5 blueys one from Zac, Daphne, I think Sharpie sent one and Dad?? With some pictures that was great. I stared at them for about an hour I cant explain how good it is to get pictures and stuff you get grown men close to tears at the sight of there kid or a good night out its really strange how this place fucks with your head and emotions.

A BIG ONE that I NEED you to try do (get started ill help when I get back) is appeal to local charitys, churches, major companys ie Zoo, Cadburys, boots you name it. Write to them and explain my whereabouts and they do send gifts, chocolate, sweets, magazines you name it trust me a lot of the lads parents did it and they've got clothes, the lot. Trust me Red bull, lucazade, fags AND SWEETS are wicked just keep sending them and URGE people to send photos they keep the moral SKY HIGH.

I thought [the photographs of] *Steely and Zac in the garden were quality. I can only prove how much a letter or small parcel means by finding time to right back – that's probley the most precious thing I have and Id'e trade hours for a letter.*

On some much sadder news one of our rifleman died a few days back [a reference to the death of Rfn Adrian Sheldon on evening

134

of May 7, 2009 when his Jackal vehicle was blown up], *we had a parade and a few minutes silence its so strange how many emotions you go through living in these conditions its like everything wants to beat you and rewin your day. Its about not letting it get to you and don't worry nothing fucking gets to me. Well Im off I love you all loads thanks for my parcels and letters. Lots of love xxx*

Just a couple of days later, Cyrus was writing again:

Hey Mum!
Its just gone 10 in the morning here Im on a stag rotation for the next 7 days guarding the FOB. Its 6 hours on 3 hours off so not much sleep. (Im already an hour in). If you could see what Im looking at now you'd be pretty shocked. Its pretty stunning to be honest. I could probley sling shot a stone from where we were last contacted from Ha! Ha! Ha! Pretty fucking crazy huh? I shouldn't really tell you this but its safer than on the phone – were leaving this place. Its gonna be a fucking massive operation moving this lot + a lot of helicopter rides. So when I come back after R&R ill fly to bastion then out to our new FOB. You don't really do much on stag. Swetting my tits of its gonna hit 50 degrees today. AAAAH Shit my grenade just fell out of my [body armour] *– we wont mention that to any higherarcy will we now.*

37 days ill be home – not that Im counting or anything??? THINK there's a bird [helicopter] *coming in today at 13.30 so this bluey will probley arrive with the others – well as always gotta go ill try ring when I get a top-up of minuets on Monday. FUCK knows what day it is I thought it was Sunday today. Ha! Ha! Well lots of love to you all!*

As was often the case, the tour had started fairly quietly. To the north, in Sangin, soldiers of 2 Rifles felt safe enough to organise a charity event on the two rowing machines at the FOB, where eight of them had set about rowing the distance from Sangin DC to Pegasus Bridge in Normandy, a total of almost 6,000 km. Not easy, even in the relative cool of the morning or afternoon, but they were hoping to help raise the money needed for a memorial on the bridge to commemorate the D-Day landings.[15]

135

On June 2, the young rifleman was part of a 2 Rifles QRF which was supporting an American IED clearance unit. A fellow soldier, Cpl Llewellyn Bryan, triggered an explosion, but somehow escaped unscathed. Cpl Bryan told a later inquest, '[Cyrus] told me how lucky I was. He stood up, he turned away from me to face the direction of the FOB, and I then heard a massive explosion, and immediately knew it was another IED.'

Cyrus had triggered a device containing between 8kg and 13kg of explosives. Sjt Leon Smith told the inquest, 'I was four or five metres away. It blew me off my feet and my weapon out of my hand. I was on the floor, and the next thing I remember was a pool of blood on the floor coming from my face. There was smoke and dust everywhere. It became obvious that somebody had been killed by the blast.'

Back at home, it was ten o'clock and Robin and Helena were turning in for the night.

'We saw the security light come on outside,' said Robin. 'Helena looked out the window and saw two men in suits walking up the drive. At first, I thought it was the police. But when I opened the door they introduced themselves, and showed their MOD identification cards. They asked if they could come in and sit down. Then we started asking questions: "What's wrong? Is he okay?" Helena said she wouldn't sit down to be told that Cyrus had been killed. I said, "The sooner you sit down, the sooner they're going to speak to us."

'They said, "At 9.15 this morning your son, Cyrus Thatcher, was killed by an IED in Afghanistan."

'The only details they could give us were quite sketchy, but they did ask us when we would like them to bring him home, and we said as soon as possible.'

'We weren't given any gory details,' said Helena, 'but before we went to the inquest sixteen months later we were given the opportunity to look at the folder of information about the incident. We felt we didn't need to compound the horror by reading those details. All we knew was that Cyrus died because of catastrophic lower body damage, and that he died instantly. They said he would have been rendered instantly unconscious. If we ever really want to know more details, we can have them.'

Lt Paul Mervis, Cyrus' OC, wrote immediately. In his letter, he said:

My last memory of Thatch, and the one I will cherish for the rest of my life, is of one evening in the FOB. I was the night watch-keeper, which meant I had to stay up all night in case something untoward happened. Joe, who, like me, had known Thatch from the beginning, and had always been Thatch's section commander, was the guard commander. We were sitting in the operations room when we heard Thatch and Pricey's voices on the radio from Sangar One. We told them to make us brews, and they told us to get lost – the usual banter. Joe and I decided we would go down there and give Thatch a dig. He used to bring out all our inner children. We caught him on the way back to bed. He stopped, gave us that same cheeky smile and sprinted away, laughing. I chased him. There wasn't a hope in hell of me catching him, though.

We were there in the Green Zone, in an IED belt, casualties were being taken across the battlefield, and the Taliban were closing in. But that night, in that part of Afghanistan, the FOB echoed with the sound of his laughter. I will cherish that memory until the day I die.

Tragically, that day was not long in coming.

'Paul Mervis never got our reply,' said Robin, 'because he was killed on Friday, June 12, the day after *we* received *his* letter. 2 Rifles were hit very hard on that tour, they lost thirteen men, and of course there were many more injured. Cyrus's serjeant was injured in the same blast, and his injuries were serious enough that he had to be medevac-ed out. But he actually managed to come and speak at Cyrus's funeral. He was quietly-spoken and still obviously very shaken by what had happened. He was kind, and very sad for us and for the platoon. We've kept in touch ever since.'

Cyrus' parents asked to see their son's body after it was flown home.

'We weren't sure if we would be able to,' said Helena, 'because he'd been killed in an IED explosion and they didn't know what condition he would be in. But that didn't mean anything to me. I wanted to see him one more time, and it hadn't occurred to me I might not be able to. We saw him the day before he was buried. It was really hard, but you could say we were fortunate to be able to see him, as there are families who are unable to see their loved ones.'

'It's the most awful thing,' said Robin. 'We felt we had to do it, but to actually open that door and see him lying there was the most disgusting thing ever, because that was the last vision we have of our son. I have no regrets that we did it. But it was awful. He was just lying there, it could have been a wax model of the son we had. It wasn't him. But that was our one last chance to be together as a family, it had to be done and we wouldn't have had it any other way.'

A distraught Rfn Stewart Elliott had sent Cyrus' family a bluey home with the coffin. In it, he told them about the letter Cyrus had written to his family, which was only to be read if he was killed.

'I took our kitchen apart to find it, but it wasn't there,' said Robin. 'But then, just after we had come back from seeing Cyrus for the last time, Steely found it. Cyrus had actually put it in a small chest by the side of his bed. I remember Steely running down the stairs shouting, "I've found it! I've found it!"

'Through this letter, he was talking to us in a way which was strangely comforting so soon after having seen him for the last time. Steely read it to us all. He was so choked up, but still he read it. I don't know how he did it. He was only seventeen. Tears were streaming down our faces. I can't remember what happened after that. I think we just sat there in a complete daze. I think somehow Cyrus knew that, if something happened to him, that would be it. He'd be gone for ever, so he had to say things. It seems amazing that he could imagine being gone and being able to say the things that he did.'

'He was acutely aware of the relationship he had with each of us,' said Helena. 'He'd never have wanted to hurt us like that. He needed to tell us that it was okay. He was very articulate. I think that because, in the past, he'd struggled with reading and writing, his verbal skills were very good, and that comes through in this amazing letter that we now treasure.'

* * *

CYRUS' FAMILY HAVE suffered terribly as a result of his death.

'It's ruined us,' said Robin. 'I can't see that we will ever have the ultimate happiness that we had. We have a house in France, and I remember us all being there once while Cyrus was on leave. We had a bonfire going, and we had the motorbike out and we were jumping over the fire, sneaking around with BB guns, we had fireworks, and we were drinking Sambuca, and eating and laughing. We'd hit the ultimate in happiness as a family around that time, and we'll never have that happiness again. There's a huge hole in our family. We're not who we were, or what we were.

'It's certainly affected my relationship with Zac and Steely, because I only have so much energy, and everything I've got goes into thinking about and trying to deal with the one who's not here. The boys have handled losing Cyrus in different ways. Zac was affected very, very badly. He's very emotional. He said, "It's my fault. I should have been there to protect him." That's still Zac's take on it, four years later. Steely's a different character. He went off to America to a music college in Los Angeles. He is determined to be a drummer, and he was with people who didn't know his story, so I think that helped him.

'We've hardly taken any photos since Cyrus was killed. We can't look at them. If we see a photo that has Cyrus in it, we tend to see only Cyrus. If there's a photo that *doesn't* have Cyrus in it, we notice that he's not there. Every day is a day longer since I last saw him, so I miss him even more. I can't stop thinking about him. I cannot. Friends have said, "Well that's not a bad thing, is it?" Trust me, it's almost torture. I open my eyes at night, and the first thing I think about is Cyrus. If we've been to the house in France, the first thing we do when we come back is go to the cemetery to put fresh flowers on his grave and pat the headstone. If we go away, we pop up to see him before we leave.

'The what-ifs bother me. Forget it, though. It's over. He's gone. It's not going to happen. But we can't switch off as a family. Every birthday, every Christmas, every celebration, every single day is a day that he's not here. We miss him so much.'

Christmas is particularly tough.

'Cyrus loved Christmas,' said Helena. 'It was his favourite time of year, and his birthday was very soon afterwards. He had to have the biggest stocking, more presents than anyone else.'

'We haven't had a Christmas tree since he was killed, and we haven't sent any Christmas cards,' said Robin. 'That might sound awful, but who do we say they're from? We've always sent Christmas cards from Robin, Helena, Zac, Cyrus and Steely. Do we leave him out? Last Christmas, Steely was in New York, so we went down to our place in

France with Zac, who wanted to get away as well. On Christmas Day we took a flask of mulled wine to the woods and had a bonfire. We had spaghetti and meatballs, and that was our Christmas dinner. We just wanted to get away from Christmas.

'I have no motivation. I still need to be bringing in an income, but I don't employ people any more. Zac works for me, and that's good because I'm helping his future, and Steely needs help with finance. I've reduced the size of the business. We're not VAT-registered any more. I won't let anyone down, and I do what I have to when I have to do it, but I don't go out to talk to customers in the evenings or on the weekends any more. I just can't be bothered. I feel like crap all the time. There isn't even much escape in sleep. I keep having this dream in which I see Cyrus. As he smiles, there is a flash of light and he's swept away. That's when I wake up, and then I have to put the TV on or do anything to stop myself thinking about the last time I saw him, the last thing we did or the last things we said.'

Helena suffered with bad dreams, too, but they have faded with time. 'I haven't had a really bad nightmare for a while,' she said, 'but they were horrific. He'd always be dead, and he'd be saying, "There's no point in talking to me, mum, because I can't hear you. My ears have been damaged." It's that awful thing of him being just out of reach. I've had a couple of dreams when I've felt him physically on top of me, and I believed he was here with me. I woke up thinking, *This is ridiculous*. I don't have such bad dreams now, but they're still nightmares because I dream he's alive and wake up knowing it's not true. He's more likely to be young in my dreams now, about ten. Before I wake up, though, I see the face I saw in the coffin, so I know he's dead. But I don't wake crying and sobbing every night now like I used to.

'I wake up in the morning, and I have all these things on my mind that I'm going to do. But I'm lucky if I do any of them. In the beginning, it was hard even thinking about getting up. But, equally, I couldn't stay in bed. If my socks didn't match or I hadn't washed my hair, I'd think, *Who cares?* That has slowly changed, but I still have days when I wake up and think, *I really can't bothered to do anything*.

'We do have happy times with the two boys. I think they're slowly coming back. But it's different. When you laugh, you laugh through pain, and all we think is, *How Cyrus would have loved this*. We don't say it, we just think it.'

'We know that this is with us for life,' said Robin. 'We're coping. We have a lovely garden, and we look after things, but we're doing it through an absolute agony of pain. There's a knot in our chests all the time. We are as happy as we can be being sad, if that makes sense. We just drift along. We still get up early every day. We have a dog we love dearly, and he's always pleased to see us. He doesn't judge. He's just there, and all he wants to do is go for a walk, which is good for us. We go out into the woods and we talk, and we have a cry, or we smile about things.'

The support they have received from the regimental family has helped.

'If we want anything, we only have to ask,' said Robin. 'We were invited to a curry evening at The Rifles Club in London, which we went to, but very few other bereaved families went.'

'I think we've been fortunate, in that The Rifles are extremely good in the way they treat the bereaved and seriously injured,' said Helena. 'Colonel Rob Thomson – he's now a brigadier – keeps in touch with us. General Nick Parker told us at the repatriation, "You're part of the Rifles family now until you tell us to go away."'

Helena and Robin are content that Britain was right to go to war in Afghanistan.

'Had we not gone there to try to stop the Taliban getting a foothold again it would only be a matter of time before they were a force to be reckoned with, and we'd be facing more attacks like 9/11,' said Robin. 'We weren't happy that we were there, but somehow we felt it was right. And you can't tell me that the Army were not doing their utmost, and all within their power, to ensure that soldiers were not killed. Sometimes people do feel they have been let down by the system, but the truth is that there are always going to be casualties.

'Cyrus made the right life decisions for him. He never chose devastation for us; he chose a life for himself. Our only regret is the final outcome. We don't have any hatred. We just have terrible sadness. The sadness is enough to bear without being angry.'

LANCE CORPORAL DANE ELSON
FIRE SUPPORT GROUP 3 1st BATTALION THE WELSH GUARDS
SEPTEMBER 28, 1986 – JULY 5, 2009

IT WAS JUNE 20, and D-Day +1 of Panther's Claw, an operation designed to take control of key crossings over the Helmand River and allied irrigation canals to the north-west of Lashkar Gah,

The idea was to squeeze the Taliban in the area into a large killing zone – and then kill them. That, it was hoped, would clear the way for local people to vote in the forthcoming Afghan parliamentary elections.

The operation would involve hundreds of British, Estonian and Afghan troops, and 'Jægerkorpset' special forces and Leopard tanks from Denmark. A dozen Chinooks were used to airlift the soldiers into position, and British and American Apache attack helicopters, Harriers, drones and an AC-130H Spectre gunship provided air support.

By the end of the operation, several hundred Taliban would indeed be dead, and the area placed under ISAF control – much to the delight of most locals, who were angry at having their supplies taken, their homes violated, and their fields laced with IEDs by the insurgents, many of whom were believed to be foreigners from across the border in Pakistan.

But that success would have come at considerable cost.

The previous day, June 19, had been a traumatic one for the Welsh Guards family: a charismatic company commander, Maj Sean Birchall, married and the father of an eighteen-month-old son, Charlie, had

142

been killed when an IED hit his open-topped Jackal armoured vehicle as he moved between patrol bases a few kilometres north of Lashkar Gah.

More men would perish during the op, including Lt Col Rupert Thorneloe MBE, the CO of 1 Welsh Guards and the most senior British officer to die in Afghanistan.

On July 1, 2009, Lt Col Thorneloe would leave Battle Group HQ on a resupply patrol – vital if the men on the ground were to be kept 'bombed up', fed and watered. As they travelled along a track next to a canal, the patrol sensed that there might be IEDs ahead – a vehicle had been lost on the same route two days earlier. Thorneloe, a married father of two young girls, dismounted from his Viking to take part in 'Operation Barma', the codename for the dangerous but everyday job of sweeping the ground ahead for hidden devices with 'Vallon' mine-detectors. It was not the sort of task normally carried out by a battalion CO, but Thorneloe was insistent that he would not ask his men to do things which he himself would not carry out. It took some time to clear the route, but eventually, satisfied that this particular stretch was clear, he returned to his Viking, along with other members of the Vallon/Barma team. Unfortunately, some way further down the track, a device – perhaps primed by watching Taliban, as the British soldiers Barma-ed a few hundred metres away – was detonated under Thorneloe's vehicle. He was killed almost outright, and one of the Barma team – Tpr Josh Hammond, of the Royal Tank Regiment – also died. Tpr Hammond was eighteen years old, and excited about his impending marriage to his childhood sweetheart.

But on June 20, all that tragedy, and more, lay in the future. As the sun set, Dane Elson and his good friend Paul Liddy were chilling out in a compound which they had helped to secure earlier in the day.

'It was just the two of us in our little corner,' said Liddy, a guardsman for fourteen years. 'I remember we were listening to Bryan Adams's theme song to *Robin Hood* on Dane's iPod. The locals were growing cannabis in this compound, and we were surrounded by the stuff. I remember one of them telling us that we couldn't get high on them because they were female plants. Listening to that music among the cannabis plants: that's stuck in my mind ever since.'

Dane Elson had joined the tour a few days late, after breaking his wrist during quad-bike training. He'd been so keen to deploy with his mates that he had suggested to his section commander that he should cut off his plaster and pretend that the wrist was fine. To his disappointment, he was told that this was not a good idea.

Eventually, LCpl Elson arrived and joined up with his mates in Fire Support Group 3, which was attached to B Coy 2 Mercian as part of the Light Dragoons Battle Group. His role was to operate the Javelin anti-tank weapon, which was used against Taliban firing positions in the otherwise seemingly-indestructible mud walls of the area's many compounds, and – because of its excellent sights – for surveillance. Paul Liddy was a fellow member of FSG3.

'Throughout Panther's Claw, we were always on the move,' he said. 'We pushed forward for three weeks, non-stop. We'd pitch up somewhere, take over a compound, stay the night and move on. We wouldn't really sleep much. There were IEDs everywhere, but we still had to move. Oz Schmid was with us for a lot of the time. I lost count of the number of IEDs he defused. He used to say, "You just have to think about where they'd plant them." He was a really good bloke, you felt safe with him. He slept near us, too, just to keep our morale up, and he'd let us use his satellite phone to pass on messages to our families. We were devastated when he died.'

[*SSgt Olaf Schmid, an AT in the RLC's 11 EOD, disarmed hundreds of IEDs and saved dozens of lives before he was himself killed by an IED on October 31, 2009. He was posthumously awarded the George Cross for his extreme bravery.*]

'Finally, early in July, we set up a permanent PB and stayed there until the end of the tour,' said Liddy. 'Eventually, it was named PB Falcon-Laws, after Dane – because his second name was Falcon – and Pte Robert Laws of the Mercians, who had been killed the day before Dane.[16]

'We were fighting every day. The only day I didn't fight was the day I left to go home on R&R. A couple of journalists came to see us at the PB. They were supposed to be staying with us for a long time, but they only lasted a day before they went back to Camp Bastion.

'I have to say, we loved the firefights. You'd get a good buzz out of them. Except [LSgt] Dan Collins, a good friend of mine and Dane's – he got shot twice. Once his body armour stopped a round, and once a round grazed his ankle. We laughed about him being a bullet magnet.

'Dane and I always did night stag together. Our main worry was the wild dogs. We weren't scared of the Taliban, but we were worried that we'd have to shoot the dogs if they came at us. We'd keep each other going throughout the night with banter and jokes. There was nothing else you could do except have a laugh.'

On July 5, with Panther's Claw well under way, LCpl Elson and his FSG team, along with men from 2 Mercian, were engaging the Taliban near Babaji, a village approximately 15 kilometres southwest of Gereshk.

The day had an ominous feel to it, said Paul Liddy. 'We knew it was going to be bad. It was super-hot, and everyone who could was trying to get out of the place. The press wanted out, and there were a few people who said they had diarrhoea and vomiting. And I believe Dane knew he was going to die that day. We'd already been hit by an IED that morning, which was when the journalists said they had to get out. We were on stag while the vehicles were coming in to pick them up. Dane said, "I've got a bad feeling about today."

'I was like, "Yeah, and me, man."

'Then Dane said, "If I die, make sure my Welsh flag is buried with me."

'I said, "Shit! You're not going to die. Nothing's going to happen. I'll look after you. But if I die, look after my missus. Just don't get off with her, okay?"

'We were still managing to joke a bit, but we had this sixth sense. Things didn't seem right, and we were just waiting for something to happen.'

* * *

DANE ELSON HAD been born in Zimbabwe. His auntie Joanne suffered badly from asthma and eczema, and her father thought the hot, dry African climate might suit her better than their native Derbyshire. It worked out well for Joanna, but less so for Dane's mother Debby, who was involved first in a bad car accident which broke most of the bones in her face, and left her blind for a while, then suffered a benign brain tumour, and then a condition known as Ménière's disease which causes loss of balance and nausea. It was during this series of health crises that she met Dane's father, Stuart.

'I looked awful at the time,' she said, 'but he must have seen something in me. I was twenty-one, and a short time later we got married. My first child was Rowenna. Dane came along eighteen months later. I used to love *The Thorn Birds*, and one of the characters was called Dane. I gave him the middle name Falcon after Scott of the Antarctic, who was Robert Falcon Scott.

'People were just amazed at how good he was. "You're so spoiled," they'd say. "Have another, then you'll see how tough it is!" He hardly ever cried. He'd have his feed at about five o'clock, then he'd go to bed and we'd have to wake him up at eight the next morning. He was fabulous.

'He was always an affectionate boy, and he didn't change as he grew up. He was never ashamed to show he loved me. I used to say, "Here comes mammy's little soldier," as he walked into the pub to join us on a Friday night. But that wouldn't have embarrassed him. He was happy for people to know how he felt. He'd come through the door, and give me a big hug. He would often tell me that he loved me, and he didn't care who heard him say it. Behind that soldier's toughness, he had such a soft nature.'

The Elsons had come back to the UK not long after Dane's birth, with Stuart finding work first in Beaconsfield and then in South Wales. Stuart and Debby split up a short while later, and both remarried.

'It was a happy outcome,' said Debby, now Morris. 'My new husband Terry was a fantastic dad to Rowenna and Dane, and we've lived in Bridgend ever since. Dane was never going to be a lawyer or a doctor, but he excelled in whatever sport he tried, and he had a great personality. He was so full of life, and his schoolteachers loved him for that. They knew he wasn't the brightest, but his personality would always carry him through. He was always such a happy boy. He's beaming in almost every picture that we have of him.

'As a child, I can't say he was always well-behaved, especially at school. I remember being called to nursery because he'd said something cheeky to one of the dinner ladies. And yet, when we went

Capt Jim Philippson was perhaps always destined for a life in uniform. He started out in the Cub Scouts and ended up as a Commando and airborne-trained gunner.

Cpl Mark Wright GC manning the .50cal at Sangin, spent cartridges at his feet, before his move to Kajaki.

Mark was 'always a loving wee boy', said his mother Jem.

LCpl Stu Hale (left) and Cpl Stu Pearson with three comrades on the hillside at Kajaki. The runway-built village of Tangi is visible behind and below the men.

You can go, but be back soon: Jake Alderton with his mother Lesley at the farewell party his parents threw before he left for Afghanistan.

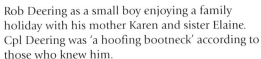

Rob Deering as a small boy enjoying a family holiday with his mother Karen and sister Elaine. Cpl Deering was 'a hoofing bootneck' according to those who knew him.

Cpl Sarah Bryant in playful mood with her father, Des.

Sarah and her mother Maureen on Sarah's wedding day. Her funeral would take place at the same church.

ASgt Sean Binnie takes a breather alongside colleagues from the ANA.

Sean hugs his mother Jan during a family holiday: he was a mischievous youngster, always grinning.

Pte Cyrus Thatcher in two entirely typical poses. 'Thatch', seen here manning a GPMG in a sangar, was relentlessly upbeat on the battlefield and absolutely loved soldiering. But he was also a great family man; here he hugs his mother, Helena.

Cyrus and his mates pose for a team photo ahead of another difficult patrol in the heat and dust of Gereshk, in Nahr-e Saraj.

LCpl Dane Elson and his mother Debby when he passed out. She was 'so proud' to see her baby in his Welsh Guards uniform. Soon her baby was on operations in Afghanistan.

LSgt Dan Collins, one of Dane's closest friends, was unable to cope with the pain of having had to collect up Dane's body parts after his death in an IED blast.

Pte William Aldridge: at just six weeks past his eighteenth birthday, William was one of the youngest British soldiers in Afghanistan, and the youngest to die.

William with his mother Lucy, and brothers George and Archie.

out, we were always complimented on the kids. It was when he was out of my sight that the naughty streak appeared. He joined Rowenna at Llangan school when he was nearly five, but he fell in with the older boys and if they dared him to do something he would do it. I lost track of the number of times the phone rang, and it would be Mr George the headmaster: *Get up to this school NOW!* One time, the deputy head brought her new car to school, and one of the older lads had said to Dane, "Why don't we jump on Mrs Hunt's new car?" He was happily dancing on the roof when Mr George arrived, and of course all of the other boys had run off.'

At the age of six, Dane went to live with his father in Gloucestershire, at the suggestion of his frustrated headmaster.

'He said, "Don't you think it would be a good idea to let him go and live with his dad and attend another school?"' said Debby. 'I wasn't keen – he'd been only eighteen months old when his father and I split up, and they hadn't developed much of a relationship at that point. But I was having terrible trouble with my balance, because of the problem with my ear, and I'd been in hospital for six weeks. Terry was working long hours, Dane was a handful, and I was really stressed. I just couldn't manage. Eventually, I gave in. I thought, *What harm can it do? I'm not letting him go to live with a stranger.* My father didn't speak to me for two years because I let Dane go to Stuart. Terry was dead against it, too. But I did what I thought was best.

'One thing he did get out of going to live with his father was his interest in rugby. Terry didn't have time for sport, but his father was always rugby-mad, so he instilled into Dane the idea that, whatever sport he did, he should do it well. That's one reason why Dane was such a great rugby player.'

After leaving school at sixteen, Dane went to work in the kitchen at a local brasserie, and the chef urged him to think about a career in catering. But his heart was set on the armed forces.

'His grandfather on his father's side had been in the Navy and was quite a disciplinarian, which had helped Dane to some extent,' said Debby. 'I think he wanted to prove something to his grandfather. He tried for the Navy, but wasn't offered a place, so he moved on to the Army, and went to Harrogate in September 2003. And I was so proud when he passed out, wearing the Welsh Guards cap badge. He still seemed such a baby – he was only seventeen – but at that point I wasn't very worried about it.'

In December 2004, shortly after his eighteenth birthday, Dane Elson went to Iraq. He was 'champing at the bit' to see some action, said his mother, but the country was then relatively calm before the later storm, and his team were contacted only once. Still, he phoned home full of excitement at having got some rounds down.

After Iraq, Dane went to Kosovo, where near-disaster struck when he tested positive for drugs.

'He was devastated,' said Debby. 'I received this phone call: "You've got to help me, mam!" He put me on to an officer who said that Dane had tested positive for ecstasy. I said, "I can guarantee you that Dane does *not* do drugs. I know every mother will say that of her son, but it's true. He's such a sportsman, he just wouldn't do it." The week before he left, he'd gone out drinking with the boys and I think someone slipped something into his drink. Anyway, the officer was sympathetic. He said he'd send him to Bosnia, where there was another Welsh Guards detachment, while they waited for his hair to grow. They needed a sample to analyse to find out whether he was a habitual user, or it was a one-off.

'Eventually, he was brought back to Abergavenny for more tests which proved he'd consumed a single ecstasy tablet, and there was no sign of habitual use. So he was allowed to stay in the Army. It emerged that there were quite a number of officers who thought a lot of Dane and didn't want to lose him. He didn't have any more similar incidents, and he was very fit, even though he smoked. He became quite well-known for always giving a hundred per cent, and I think this must have contributed to him being made a lance-corporal at twenty-two.'

After Iraq and Kosovo, the battalion moved to Wellington Barracks in London, where they carried out ceremonial duties.

'We all went to see the Welsh Guards Trooping the Colour,' said Debby. 'I was so proud. He told us roughly where he'd be in the parade, but they all look exactly the same. Later, he said, "Mam, you were looking in totally the wrong direction!"

'Dane loved London. He'd ring up and say, "Me and the lads are going to church today, mam." I'd say, "That's nice dear," but I was surprised because he'd never been to church before.'

Little did she know that The Church was one of London's most infamous alehouses.

'But he came home to Wales almost every weekend. He'd phone me from the motorway on Friday afternoon, stuck in traffic, and I'd tell him how to avoid the jams. I know the roads well, because our family business is delivering vehicles all over the country. After a while, he'd call me again. "I'm not too far away now. If you've gone out before I get home, bell me, and I'll meet you at the pub."

'So he'd meet us at the pub, then get a curry and a taxi home, then start rolling around on the floor with our dog, Cookie. He absolutely loved her. Then he'd go on the Jack Daniels and Coke.'

Eventually, the news came that Dane and his mates were going to Afghanistan.

'I worried about it a lot,' said Debby. 'It seemed like British soldiers were being killed there almost every day, but there was nothing I could do about it. I'd been visiting a spiritualist after my brother died, and I found it comforting, so I thought I'd ask her if Dane would be all right. She paused, and said, "Oh, he'll be fine." But the fact that she had paused made me think.

'As I was walking out the door, she said, "Oh, by the way, your son's going to Mexico." I thought that was strange, but I was just getting into the car a few minutes later when my phone rang, and it was Dane. "Mam, guess what! I'm going to Mexico!" Turned out they were going to Belize for training, and after that they'd have a week in Mexico.'

As it happened, Dane missed Belize – and Mexico. He had developed a benign growth on his neck – he jokingly called it 'Bob' – and the scar left by an operation to remove it had not healed sufficiently. Then, just before deployment, he broke his wrist in that quad-bike accident.

'He was absolutely devastated,' said Debby. 'He was back home for six weeks when he wanted to be with the men. He threatened to take his cast off and I said I'd phone the regiment and report him if he tried it.

'Around that time, we sat down, and I said to him, "I don't want to have this conversation, Dane, but if anything happens to you, what do you want us to do?"

149

'He thought for a bit, and he said, "I want to be buried."

'I was so shocked. I'd assumed he'd want to be cremated. I said, "Are you sure?"

'He said, "Yes, mam, I'm serious. I want to be buried at Pencoed."

'I suppose Pencoed made sense, because all his friends were in Pencoed and there isn't a cemetery around here. So we agreed on that. Sometimes I think he did have an inkling about what would happen. He was certainly closer than normal during that last period at home.

'He finally had his cast removed, and he was so pleased that he could join the lads, particularly those who were in his charge. He really cared about those boys. I heard later from a soldier who was in FSG3 but who wasn't a Welsh Guardsman. He said, "Your son took me under his wing and made me feel like one of his boys. You should feel so proud of him."'

Dane left home early one Monday morning.

'Saying goodbye was very hard,' said Debby. 'We were all hugging, but Dane was making light of it because he was so excited. He was just full of it. I told him I loved him, and to keep his head down. "Don't be silly, mam," he said. "I'll be fine."'

He had registered his mother for a service which informed her of any serious injuries or deaths.

'I would receive a text a little bit before it appeared on the news,' she said, 'and, most importantly, I would know it wasn't Dane. We all knew that if anything happened to him we would be told about it personally, before it was reported. At one stage, I was receiving two or three texts a day. It didn't do much for our nerves but – and I know this sounds selfish – I would think, *Thank God it's not my day*. As well as the texts, every time a Welsh Guardsman was injured or killed I'd get a phone call from Dane. Tobie Fasfous was the first to die.'

Twenty-eight year-old mortarman LSgt Fasfous was killed on April 28, 2009 in an explosion while on a 'reassurance patrol' with ANA troops near FOB Keenan [*later renamed Khar Nikah*], north of Gereshk. Lt Col Rupert Thorneloe was one of those who paid tribute to 'this outstanding Welsh Guardsman'. Fasfous, a sniper, was also described as 'an officer's worst nightmare… A soldier with brains who was possibly more intelligent than you.' He had gone on tour fearing that he might not return, and had left instructions with his partner, Kelly, as to how to arrange his funeral. In the event, some 500 people attended Salem Chapel, Pencoed, for the service, many in sports tops, rather than funereal black, as he had requested. Kelly herself wore a vivid pink Cardiff Blues rugby shirt.

'Dane called me,' said Debby, 'and said, "Mam, something's happened. I can't go into it, but it's Tobie." He sounded really shocked. He thought the Welsh Guards were invincible. For something like this to happen so soon after they got there was really a wake-up call.'

Despite this, Dane managed to remain upbeat for his family. One e-bluey, sent to his 'mammy' and signed *'miss ya millions ur little boy xxxxxxxxxxxxxxxxxxxxxxxxxx'*, said he was fine, *'on watchkeeper at the mo tan looking good'*.

Another, sent at 2030hrs on May 10, provides a vivid insight into the contrast between life in Afghanistan and the normal world back home. On the one hand, Dane was concerned about the heat, the rations and the increasing Taliban activity; on the other, he was planning to upgrade his wheels when he arrived back in Wales:

> *mam, dad, row and cookie*
> *hey all just to let you know im ok and don't worry, weather so hot out here now its rediculous its nearly in the fifties. i don't think i have ever drunk so much water in my life... the detox is goin good lol but cant wait for a nice pint of strongbow and a jack daniels to top it, its started to get a bit hairy now because they started to cut the poppy down for the opium, I still havent had any letters from anyone but it shouldn't be to long before I do, they still havent sorted my 30 minutes a week for my phone calls but the boss is still on it. rations are getting boreing so could you send me some super noodles and stuff like that... can you speak to danny and ask him if devons still selling his transporter and how much does he want for it? because its quite smart, hope cookie behaving herself!!! and row lol hope your all ok and i will speak to you when i can, say hey ya to everyone for me and i will see them in july so make sure they have enough money on them to get the drinks in lol the army wont give us hire cars when we come home for r and r because we will be to tired from the flight don't know how tho because all you can do is*

*sleep for six hours so i will have to catch the train from swindon.
miss you all loads love you millions your loving son, brother
Dane xxxxxxxxxxxx*

'He didn't really tell us much about the conditions or what he was
doing,' said Debby. 'I suppose he didn't want to worry us. The few blueys
he sent were so like Dane – upbeat, and all about his plans for R&R.

'The second from last time that he called, neither Terry nor I were
at home. Fortunately, Rowenna was, so she called me on my mobile,
saying, "Mum, get home quick. Dane wants to talk to you and he can't
get through to you on your mobile."

'We came home immediately, and within five minutes Dane was
on the phone again, and I was talking to him. That was July 1, the
day that Rupert Thorneloe died. He said, "Mam, things are getting
scary. The CO's been killed, and there are going to be so many more
dead bodies now." Mr Thorneloe was so respected by the boys. His
message was always, "I'm not expecting you to do things that I'm not
prepared to do. I don't expect you to walk over a patch of ground
which might have an IED if I'm not prepared to do it, too." He died
because he put that principle into practice.

'It was a terrible blow, and Dane felt it deeply. I said, "Promise me,
baby, that you're not going to be one of them." He said, "I promise
you, mam, but everyone's scared now."

'The following day he called again to say that we wouldn't hear
from him for some time. He couldn't say why, though we found out
later it was because of Panther's Claw. I was so frightened. We knew
something big was going to happen, and we knew how dangerous it
would be. After that we were waiting on tenterhooks.

'Three days later, they lost David Dennis, "The Duke" as they
called him, who was a member of The Light Dragoons but working
closely with Dane and his mates. Then, a day later, Dane was killed.'

* * *

AS OP PANTHER'S CLAW progressed, the men of the Welsh Guards,
and their comrades from the Mercians, the Light Dragoons, and other
regiments, were fighting hard.

Teenaged soldiers were risking their lives every day, for the princely sum of £1,150 a month – 'about £250 more than I was getting stacking shelves at Costcutters' said one. Everyone accepted some level of risk – this was a war, after all – but if a lieutenant colonel could be killed, how could a young private feel safe? Sometimes, the NCOs had to almost force them to go out on patrol. Then, when they were out on the ground, the more experienced men had to watch for their young charges freezing under fire. But they never let themselves down.

'Weeks later, when it was all over,' said Gdsm Paul Liddy, 'the boss called us "warriors", because we'd kept pushing and pushing. To be honest, though, the adrenaline just takes over. It's weird. Keeping morale up was really important. The younger lads were getting scared, and the older blokes like me, Dane, Dan Collins, Michael Bunce, guys who'd been around longer and had previous deployments, needed to take that fear away. Sometimes some of them would refuse to move, and one of us would say, "You've *got* to move, or you're gonna get shot!" Then later, when we were having some downtime, we'd all have a laugh about it. Mostly, it was the IEDs. The Taliban knew that was the only way they could beat us, and when the CO died they were starting to shake us up a bit.

'On the day Dane died, we'd been fighting forward through a village called Babaji. It seemed like it was taking forever. Then the Mercians had an IED strike and came under contact. We were called forward to clear casualties, and we had to fight through, because we'd all become pinned down. We used some snipers, and then did a section attack to take a compound. We cleared it with grenades and went firm there, because we were knackered and dehydrated.

'Then we were told over the net that they wanted our IED men to go about a hundred metres back the way we'd come to re-join the Mercians and clear a route. Why they didn't use the people who were already there, I don't know. Anyway, Dane and [*Gdsm*] Gareth Bisp went back with the kit, while we pushed out to give them cover. There were just eight of us in FSG3 that day. There'd been twenty-three originally, but the numbers had dwindled for one reason or another.'

What happened next perfectly illustrated the fragility and capriciousness of life for a British soldier in Helmand. Dane Elson and Gareth Bisp 'went firm' along the side of a compound and awaited further orders. As the order came in for them to go forward and Vallon a track, they began to get to their feet. The next thing Bisp knew was that he was lying on the floor with his ears ringing. He looked over to where Dane had been sitting; all that was there was a smoking crater and smashed-up pieces of a weapon and body armour. Dane's body had been blown twenty metres by a bomb which must have been inches from him from the moment he sat down. He had been killed instantly.

'He was a hundred metres away from me,' said Paul Liddy. 'Dan Collins was there with me, and we heard it go off. We started desperately trying to get hold of Dane on the radio, but he didn't answer.'

The loss of such a respected and talented NCO hit the FSG and their colleagues hard.

'We just couldn't believe it,' said Liddy. 'We were devastated, gutted. One of the boys just started crying. We had to look after each other and lean on each other's shoulders, and just keep on going. There was no choice. Dan said, "Get a grip, Paul. You've got to step up and be 2IC to David Haines." Dane had been David's 2IC. I didn't mind the extra responsibility, because I knew what I had to do, which was copy Dane. He'd had this really responsible attitude about his men. We could have a laugh, but when he was working, he was working. If there was an IED or a mortar attack, he'd be the first one on his feet, running to help. He was the team medic and he'd be there immediately helping with the medevac. I remember the CO seeing him in some bad situation, and saying, "Bloody hell, it's you again!"

'Anyway, a casevac Chinook was called in with a medical team [*other men had been injured in the explosion*], but we weren't allowed to put Dane on it, even though he was one of ours. I guess that was because they didn't want us to see him. I think it was our platoon sergeant, Sgt Lewis, who took him onto the helicopter.

'After Dane was killed, Dan got shot again, although he wasn't badly injured, and our little medic Kerry Smith was shot, too. Kerry was like our little sister. I'd help her to get over ditches and walls on patrol, and we used to escort her to the toilet and showers so she could have some privacy. Kerry was shot [*twice*] in the leg, and she also lost two fingers. Big Mike Bunce saved her life by putting a tourniquet on her, and giving her morphine. Kerry was instructing him, saying, "Do it tighter! Do it tighter!"'

[*Female soldiers are not supposed to be employed as front-line combatants in the British Army, but Pte Smith later told* The Sunday Times *that it had been unavoidable at times during the tour. 'It was always a last resort,' she said. 'As a medic, I'm a non-combatant. That said, I carry a rifle for a reason. The fighting was so intense around our objective that sometimes I had no choice but to use the weapon. It could have been dangerous for all of us if I'd refused.'*]

LCpl Elson's FSG3 colleagues were not able to accompany his body back to the UK; in fact, their specialist role meant they didn't even leave with the rest of their battalion at the end of the tour, but instead stayed on to support the Light Dragoons and Mercians.

'We were fuming,' said Paul Liddy. 'The CO said he'd do his best to get us home, but we missed the battalion's homecoming. They marched through Cardiff and paraded at the football ground while we were still in Afghan. I was at least able to go back to Bastion for Dane's repatriation.

'On our very last patrol, we saw a falcon flying over us and we all thought the same thing. Dan Collins turned to me and said, "Look at that! That's Dane! He's been with us all along." It was hard to believe, but we do believe it because we'd never seen a falcon – we'd hardly seen any birds – until that day. It was strange, and spooky.'

* * *

THE MOMENT ALL parents dread came late on Sunday evening.

'Terry had just gone up to bed, I was watching telly and someone knocked on the door,' said Debby. 'It was nine o'clock. Rowenna went into Dane's bedroom, looked through the window and said, "Mam, there's someone at the door, but I'm not letting him in. He's wearing a suit, and carrying a briefcase." I believe she knew straight away.

'I hung back for a little while, but then I had to open the door. The man was an Army captain, Glen Neale. He said there'd been a fatality out in Afghan.

'I said, "Well, you've come to the wrong house."

'He said, "Unfortunately, I'm sure I haven't. I have to say that it is Dane who was killed. It was an IED at about 4.30 this afternoon."

'After that I don't remember very much. All I know is that my sister and mother arrived in the early hours of the next day. I know that Rowenna phoned Pencoed to let Dane's father know, and he and his wife came over, but I don't remember them arriving. Later that morning, Captain Neale introduced us to the visiting officer and the regimental welfare officer from Aldershot, who knew Dane well. He was Captain Pridmore. Those guys were absolutely marvellous. Captain Neale told us about the circumstances of Dane's death. They'd just provided fire support for an assault on a compound, and Dane and Gareth Bisp were sitting against a mud wall. Gareth, who was junior to Dane, had just been called to the front of the team to handle the Vallon, but Dane said to him, "I'll go, because you're married and you've got two kids."

'Gareth said, "No, it's me who's been called."

'But Dane said, "No, I'm pulling rank."

'He got to his feet, bent down again to pick up his rucksack, then stepped back, and the IED was detonated. He was the only one killed in the blast, and he died instantly. I know he lost his right arm and was very badly damaged from the waist down. I just went to pieces when I heard that. When we received the official coroner's report, Terry [*Dane's step-father*] asked if he could read it first. Afterwards, he said, "Do me a favour, Debby. Promise me you'll never read that. If you do, you'll never sleep again." It's some consolation to know he wouldn't have suffered.'

Dane Elson was repatriated with four other soldiers, reflecting a terrible week for the Army. LCpl David Dennis of The Light Dragoons and Pte Robert Laws of the Mercian Regiment had died the day before Dane, on July 4. Capt Ben Babington-Browne of the Royal Engineers died the day after him, on July 6. Tpr Christopher Whiteside of The Light Dragoons died on July 7.[17]

Debby Elson found the repatriation extremely hard.

'We were allowed ten minutes with Dane in a private chapel,' she said, 'and then we went aboard the plane to meet the crew who had brought the boys back. There were two warrant officers on the plane, and they told us that Dane was not left alone for one second during that flight. One of them would always be sitting with the lads in those coffins. I thought that was really lovely, and somehow comforting.

'After a short service, all the hearses drove through Wootton Bassett where people paid their respects in the usual way. The Welsh Guards were absolutely amazing. They organised the funeral and we didn't have to do anything, except decide on the order of service. It was all orchestrated to military precision, and it was a funeral fit for a king. But then Dane deserved that.

'We buried him about five miles from home. We go there at least once a week, and put fresh flowers down. His friends go down there often and have a beer with him, so Terry takes an empty carrier bag with him whenever he visits, and he picks up the cans and the fag ends. Some people would find that disrespectful, his friends leaving their litter there, but I think it's nice. They go down there after they've been to the pub, and they include him in their chats.

'His mates from the Fire Support Team have left flowers, and a plaque, and the Welsh flag. But, to be honest, I get more comfort going to the National Memorial Arboretum near Lichfield. It's just so tranquil and beautiful. There's a bench engraved with his name, trees planted in his name and a slab with his name to be laid on the heroes walk. It's where all the heroes are; they're all in one place. I think it's because Dane is with all the others that I find it so comforting. I could stay there all day.

'Dane wrote letters to Rowenna and me, but we never got them. He was going to send them home, but then he changed his mind and decided to keep them with him. I think they must have been in his pack when he was killed, which means they were probably destroyed. It would have been lovely to see what he'd written, but it didn't change anything because we knew how much he loved us. We did get a lovely letter from Capt Phil Durham, one of his officers. He said Dane was the best soldier in the platoon, and that the boys found comfort and inspiration when he was around. Phil Durham was only a few metres away when the IED went off, so that letter means a lot.

'I saw the spiritualist again after Dane died. She was able to tell me he's happy, that he loves me, that he kisses me goodnight every night, and that he's a "walking spirit", which means he's always concerned about other people and he tries to help people down here. I found that comforting.

157

'The lads from FSG3 had to stay over in Afghan for another six weeks after the bulk of the Welsh Guards returned home, but as soon as they got back they came down to visit Dane's grave. Dewi sang a song from the valleys, and Mac [*a Fijian Guardsman*] sang two lovely songs from his island. Dan Collins said a few words, Chris said a few, and Rob read a poem he'd written. His comrades, his brothers, are absolutely amazing. They've been the support in our lives. We have one or more of them here with us most weekends, and every year on the anniversary of Dane's death we have lots visiting and sleeping wherever they can find space. Smudge, Sam, Nathan, Simeon, Mole, Ray, Paul… Just to name a few. I think they get as much comfort out of us as we do out of them. It's like we have a whole new family.

'If I've been sobbing my heart out at two in the morning, when Terry and Rowenna are asleep, I'll phone Smudge or Paul or whoever. A few days later, the phone might ring in the middle of the night, and it'll be Paul Liddy, terribly upset about Dane. We have an incredible bond.

'It's nearly five years now, and I still can't quite believe it. My brain can't really process the fact that he's gone. I still feel so close to him. I was on medication – I took myself off it, but Terry and I have discussed it, and I think I'm going to have to go back on it. I don't know how Terry ran the business for the first two years. We were working together, and I would do the long-distance car deliveries. I was barely eating and I was drinking too much, although the alcohol was having no effect. I lost so much weight, and I wasn't interested in anything. I would have just stayed in bed all day, every day. To be honest, if I didn't *have* to get up to do things, I'd *still* stay in bed all day. Even now, nothing comes naturally. Everything is forced. I say to myself every morning when I wake up, "Come on, you've got a job to do." Or if I don't have a job to do, I'll say, "Come on, then! Go to town, or go for a swim."

'I don't think it's got any better over the five years. I don't think it will ever be the same again. I just think I'll learn to cope with it a bit better. We've always been a close family, and if anything we're even closer now. Perhaps Rowenna stays with us partly because of this. She's kept a lot in, because she doesn't want to upset me by talking about it. She's found it very hard to cope, but she's doing well at work and has tried to convince me to have counselling. I've thought about it, but I can't see that talking to someone is going to change things.

'I don't believe we should ever have gone to Afghanistan. It wasn't our war. There's too much in our own country that needs to be addressed before we go and sort out other people's problems. But Dane wanted to go. The ferocity and danger just made it more exciting for him. When he wrote or called, he never said, "We shouldn't be here." He felt he had a job to do, and orders to obey, and that was that. And, strangely, now we're pulling out, I do find myself wondering if we're doing the right thing. I know that things have been better for a lot of Afghans because of improved security, and some people have benefited from improved education and medical care, and things like that. But I fear it will soon go back to the way it was. In which case, what was that for? Why did my son die there?'

RIFLEMAN WILL ALDRIDGE
C COMPANY 2nd BATTALION THE RIFLES
MAY 23, 1991 – JULY 10, 2009

IF THE WEEK which claimed the life of Dane Elson and the other men on his repatriation flight was bad, then July 10, 2009 was a particularly black and infamous day – a date which is seared into many memories.

It was 4am, and the men of 9 Platoon, C Coy, 2 Rifles were preparing to patrol out from their base, FOB Wishtan, in the blood-soaked streets of Sangin. The early start meant they could be out and about before the mercury started climbing too high, and while Taliban 'dickers' might still be slumbering, or on their way to morning prayers.

Wishtan, a few hundred yards along a dusty track known as Pharmacy Road from Sangin's main base, FOB Jackson, was called 'The Devil's Playground' by some. It had been bought and paid for in British lives, and, with typical squaddie humour, many of its veterans liked to wear *Wishtan you were here?* t-shirts.

The area was a maze of alleys and wadis and little rat-runs, with enemy IED teams spoiled for choice as to where to plant their bombs. Over recent weeks, there had been several late night explosions, when Taliban bombers had blown themselves up in error as they tried to lay their devices, but more careful and cunning insurgents were bound to have set a trap somewhere. The only question was where.

There was every possibility of ambush, too. The poppy and wheat harvests of May – done the old-fashioned, back-breaking way, with scythes and donkey carts – were long since completed, and the fields in the green zone had been sown with curry beans and maize. With the sun beating down on the fertile earth, and the irrigation channels flooded, the sweetcorn shot up. You could almost see it grow, day-by-day, and it was already high enough to offer decent cover-from-view for anyone who wanted to have a pop. In denser parts of the green zone, it was not at all unknown for British troops literally to walk into their enemy, and to engage them at distances of a few metres. Equally, the Taliban were quite likely to take a few shots from a hundred metres away and disappear into the foliage. With an AK47's 7.62mm round travelling at around 700 metres per second – twice the speed of sound – a well-aimed shot meant you were dead or injured before you even heard the crack of the rifle. Even if it missed, and the round zipped harmlessly overhead, you had no chance to react before the shooter dropped out of sight, either into the maize or to blend in with local non-combatants.

Commanded by a young Old Etonian, Lt Alex Horsfall, the patrol – partly designed to reassure locals, partly to put the insurgents on the back foot, and partly to familiarise some reinforcing troops with the lie of the land – was a mixture of seasoned soldiers and the relatively new.

Cpl Jonathan 'Jay' Horne, from Walsall, was one of the former. Due to turn twenty-eight the following day, he had overcome a heart murmur to join the Army in 2004. He was a veteran of Northern Ireland, Kosovo, Iraq – where he had been injured by a roadside bomb in 2006 – and Afghanistan. One of the company's big leaders, he was a very competent and tough but caring NCO. That and his wicked Black Country sense of humour made him highly popular among the men, who fought to get into his platoon. Cpl Horne was the father of two girls, nine-year-old Frankie-Jane, and Jessica, born not three months earlier. 'He was a big family man,' his mother would later say. 'He loved his kids, and adored his wife. We used to call them the Posh and Becks of Walsall, because he was always buying her presents.'

Somehow, Jay Horne always managed to wangle his way into the Corporals' Mess football team; no-one else thought he was as quite good a player as he himself did. Perhaps his fitness was the key. 'He would pass his spare time in the gym lifting "big boys' weights" and admiring his body in the mirror,' said 9 Platoon Serjeant Jamie Moncho. '"The body of a God" he would call it – it was a matter of some debate!'

Rfn Daniel 'Simmo' Simpson was the platoon signaller. The twenty-year-old from Croydon, later described as 'a big, hard, bouncer-lookalike' and a 'South London geezer', was a keen Arsenal fan – though he'd had trials for West Ham – a handy boxer, and an even better shot. He could carry the weight of ten men, and often did, according to his ops officer, Capt Ed Poynter. His fellow riflemen loved him for his bad dancing, good jokes and endless *joie de vivre*. He was the father of an eight-month-old son, Alfie.

Rfn James Backhouse, a gritty eighteen-year-old Yorkshireman from Castleford, and one of four brothers, was lead scout. It was a dangerous and demanding role, with multiple threats to consider, but the young soldier's sharp eyes and brain made him a natural. A keen rugby player and footballer, he harboured ambitions of becoming a PTI. 'It would have been right up his street,' said Lt Col Rob Thomson, CO of the 2 Rifles battlegroup. 'He had lungs big enough for the rest of his platoon.'

Rfn Joe 'Murph the Smurph' Murphy was an eighteen-year-old light machine gunner from Castle Bromwich in the West Midlands. An excellent young soldier, he was best known for his love of Aston Villa and his brilliant drawing. After a night on stag, his artwork – proclaiming his footballing allegiance – was often clear for all to see.

Rfn William Aldridge was also there that day, and was thus achieving his life's ambition. Nicknamed 'Baby' by his protective mates, William was the youngest soldier in the platoon, if not in all Helmand. In fact, he'd been too young to deploy on active service with everyone else, and had kicked his heels with the rear party back at Ballykinler until he'd turned eighteen on May 23. He'd boarded the flight to Afghanistan just six weeks earlier with the biggest smile imaginable.

'He was jovial and happy, but naturally quite quiet at first,' said his boss, Alex Horsfall. 'But he was inquisitive, and he was very competent. Soldiers like that, especially if you're fresh out of training. You do get some gobby soldiers who rattle the cages of the corporals, but William was quite the opposite.'

Two days earlier, William had telephoned his teenaged sweetheart Zeta Price. 'I promise you I'll be okay, babe,' he'd told her. 'I promise you I'll be back. Love you.'

He dreamed of a distant future in which he would undertake selection to the SAS. Apart from anything else, if he succeeded he'd be based closer to his beloved mother, who lived in Bromyard, Herefordshire.

But in the here-and-now, it was another difficult patrol in the relative early morning cool of Helmand.

* * *

WILLIAM WAS BORN in 1991, when his mother, Lucy, was twenty-three.

'I was a single parent,' she said, 'but I had a very close family network, and William was just a joy. He was a very happy little boy. He had an idyllic upbringing, we lived rurally, and he went to a tiny village school, so he grew up with that sense of family, of belonging, and of being there to help others. I think that formed the type of person he became. He was very caring, and that quality stayed with him right up to his actions on the day his life was taken.

'At his funeral, his old primary school vicar mentioned what he called "William's noble ability to help others." William would often come home from school with the children no-one else wanted to play with. I'd often find the house full of the less-popular children. That was William. He made friends easily, and he always maintained his friendships.

'He wanted to please. He was always polite, and he respected his elders although he was confident with them. I think this was because he was the first-born grandchild. He didn't have any cousins or siblings until much later. He was as happy talking to somebody in their seventies as he was talking to someone of his own age or younger. He was also a very affectionate little boy. If I got the occasional opportunity to go out for an evening, and was getting glammed-up, he'd say, "Mummy, you look *beautiful!*" It made my heart swell, and it demonstrated that he was appreciative of people and things around him. He took notice of details.'

William was an outdoors boy – his mum was a cub scout leader, and he loved going off camping, and cooking over an open fire, and it was no surprise when he joined the Army Cadets, aged eleven. Lucy

Aldridge had 'very mixed feelings' about that. 'I was one of those mothers who didn't like their children playing with toy guns,' she said. 'But boys have an imagination, and they watch the TV. William would spend many a happy hour in his grandmother's orchard, playing with sticks and pretending he was a member of the SAS. At school, his history teacher used to say, "If only he'd apply as much enthusiasm to the Industrial Revolution as he does to the First and Second World Wars!" He was just so focused on military history, and the Army was always in his mind.'

As soon as he reached sixteen, William said he wanted to attend the Army Foundation College in Harrogate, a course that would lead to life as a soldier.

'I argued a little bit with him,' said Lucy, 'but I knew that it was what he loved, and what he wanted. I felt it was my responsibility to support him in achieving his dreams. It wasn't about me, it was about him, and, if I did anything right as a parent, I brought him up to be independent, to know what he wanted, and to strive to achieve it. He could have gone on to university if he'd wanted to, and the Army recruitment office looked at his projected exam results and mentioned officer training. But he wanted to be one of the boys, in the thick of it, and he wanted to earn his rank.'

The Army careers officers tried to steer William towards the REME, to give him a post-service trade, but, to him, soldiering meant infanteering.

'He knew he'd be on the front line,' said Lucy, 'but he had fantastic field and survival skills. You could have given William a knife and piece of string, and he would have gone into the wilderness and survived. That was what fascinated him.'

So it was that, in September 2007, after sitting his GCSEs and spending a final summer holiday as a boy at home, William went to the Army Foundation College.

At first, he was a little homesick.

'He'd never spent so much time away from home before, and it played on his mind a bit,' said Lucy. 'He missed his two little brothers, George and Archie. As a little boy, he'd often said, "Mum, can I have a little brother or a sister?" I used to say, "Well, it's not quite as simple as popping along to Tesco, sweetheart, and picking one off the shelf."

So when George came along, he was absolutely overjoyed. He'd been an only child for twelve years, and he just threw himself into being involved in his brother's life. He would change his nappies, he'd bottle feed him. Occasionally, I'd feel I really could do with putting my feet up for half an hour. William would say to me, "Mum, you go along and have a rest, and I'll look after George." He'd be happy to take on the responsibility, despite his age. Archie, the youngest, was only two when William joined the Army, and they were very important to him.'

After a while, William settled in at Harrogate.

'All the lads are in it together,' said Lucy. 'They find their own little pecking order. They find out what their strengths are, and they play to them. William made some incredible friendships there. I think that's one thing that's special about the military: the friendships they make are stronger than any in civilian life, and they're life-long. He passed out the following August, aged seventeen. I was so incredibly proud of him. He'd done what he set out to do. That would make any mother proud.'

He 'absolutely loved' his brief time in the Army, she said.

'It was everything that he wanted it to be. He was outdoors; he was testing himself. He passed his field medic's course. He enjoyed the training and the demands on his fitness when they were on tabs and exercises, even though it was exhausting. He rang me one day, and said, "Mum, I have discovered that it is possible to breathe through your arsehole." By that he meant that, when you feel that you have given all you can give, and your lungs are burning, you can still push yourself that bit further.'

In December 2008, William joined his unit in Northern Ireland. His first choice had been 5 Rifles – a mechanised infantry battalion, which operates the Warrior armoured fighting vehicle – but he was offered and accepted his second choice, 2 Rifles. The battalion went to Afghanistan shortly afterwards, William joining them once he reached eighteen – the British Army does not allow soldiers to serve on the front line below that age.

For Lucy Aldridge, it was a moment of truth.

'William had made me confront all of my fears,' she said. 'I am a complete pacifist, and the possibility of my own child taking a life preyed heavily on my mind. But he said to me, "Mum, I'm not joining the Army to *kill* people, I'm joining to *protect* people." That was the role he felt he would be fulfilling: protecting those who couldn't protect themselves. He said, "I'm doing this for you, I'm doing it for George, and I'm doing it for Archie, because someone has to make the world a better place."

'He tried to stop me worrying. He said, "If you hear on the news that a soldier has been killed, it's not me, because you would have had the knock on the door. So please don't sit there watching the news every day."

'And he was fulfilling his dream. On his Facebook profile, it says, "Hi, I'm Will. I'm in the British Army. 2 Battalion the Rifles is where I belong." His Facebook profile still exists, by the way, and his friends still leave messages. I occasionally write something on it, usually around the anniversaries.'

* * *

BY THE TIME William Aldridge arrived in theatre, his mates were already heavily engaged in fighting the Taliban.

It hadn't always been like that. Sangin had long been a highly-contested area, but it had been reasonably quiet at the beginning of the tour.

'Quite early on, a peace deal was brokered between the Taliban and ISAF,' said Lt Alex Horsfall, 9 Pl commander. 'It enabled the Taliban to deal with the poppy harvest, and it was good for us, too, because we then had the chance to patrol and get to know the area, without facing too much risk of attack. They were still keen to test us, so they would plant fake IEDs to see how we would react, and at night we'd get a few opportunistic shots fired over our heads. But there was nothing threatening. We were in our base, we were in charge.

'This went on for a month and a half. It was weird, because everyone started to get a bit restless. Some of us were thinking, *Come on! This is supposed to be a highly kinetic area.* No-one seemed to want to come and fight. I remember one of the guys said something along those lines to me, and I said, "Just wait. In a few months you'll wish you'd never said that."'

It was a horribly prophetic warning.

Alex Horsfall was confident in his men, though – as many young officers do – he occasionally doubted his own ability.

'Some platoon commanders rocked up in Afghanistan never having met any of their men,' he said. 'But I'd deployed to Kosovo with 9 Platoon not that long before, so I knew most of them very well. They were a good, generally happy bunch, with some strong NCOs – we were, after all, considered the top platoon in the company. For my part, I didn't know if I was going off to do something that was within my capabilities, but that wasn't a bad thing because I spent more time thinking about how I was going to command than I did worrying about people who might try to kill me.'

When they heard they were going to Sangin, the Riflemen were jubilant.

'We all knew what we were in for,' said Horsfall. 'But I don't recall people saying, "Oh shit! We're going to Sangin." Rather, it was a mixture of glee that we were going somewhere exciting, and a little bit of apprehension. We felt we'd been given a wonderful challenge, in that we were by ourselves with our own area of responsibility. We moved patrol bases a few times, but for the most part we were in FOB Wishtan. This was an urban area that ranged from some quite nice-looking compounds to sheer poverty. The compound walls could be as high as twenty feet, and that often stopped us from going to the left or right of the roads we were moving along. This had the effect of channelling us, and the Taliban seized on this opportunity quite effectively: if they were able to channel us, why not use IEDs? And they did so, very well.'

After the brief phoney war of the poppy harvest, the soldiers slowly started finding more IEDs, the rounds began to fall closer to the FOB, and the ANA were being targeted more. The Taliban mined the streets, and the walls and the doorways of compounds. When they saw that British soldiers were using ladders to allow them to get over walls – and to avoid the doorways – they placed devices on top of walls. Sometimes, the insurgents – who were fighting a hearts-and-minds campaign of their own, of sorts – would tie purple ribbons to alert locals to the presence of an IED planted in a given location. Other times they would tie ribbons where there was no bomb in order to channel patrolling troops towards an ambush zone. Or they would build convincing dummy devices, or simply block off alleyways, to achieve the same result.

In such circumstances, and in such terrain – narrow, claustrophobic streets, full of dead ends, corners, and cut-throughs, facing an enemy who is utterly indistinguishable from the civilian population – even the best-trained, best-equipped and most watchful soldiers will come to grief eventually.

On June 29 a twenty-year-old Sapper from 33 Engineer Regiment became the first Wishtan victim of this deployment when he lost three limbs to an IED which had been planted under the threshold of a compound doorway. Early in July, the enemy mounted a complex attack on the FOB itself, firing from several points and leaving one soldier badly injured. Despite that, the men of 2 Rifles remained confident.

'It was generally starting to spice up,' said Horsfall, 'but we were still very much on top of things. We were finding the IEDs before they were finding us, and we genuinely had control of the situation. Our patrolling was slow, but methodical. We were usually greeted by friendly faces, although they were averse to talking about the Taliban – and the Taliban were everywhere. We'd talk to the locals and see if there were any serious issues we could help with, but in hindsight we probably ended up talking to quite a few Taliban without knowing it.'

Many local people seemed happy that the British were there, because the security they brought was preferable to the cruelty and barbarism of the Taliban. But it was a fleeting security. The British could patrol, but they didn't have the numbers to hold the ground. All the insurgents had to do was blend into the background; then, once the soldiers had returned to base, they ruled the roost once more. It was a small-scale example of the oft-quoted Taliban maxim, that the west had the watches but they had the time.

'It was only by continual patrolling that we could achieve anything,' said Horsfall. 'We'd patrol perhaps twice a day, and each patrol would be eight to ten hours long. We were doing this all the time.

'By the time William joined us, there'd been a fairly rapid escalation. We'd be very fortunate if we went out and did not encounter one or multiple IEDs. We had one EOD [*Explosive Ordnance Disposal*] team for the entire company, and they were working their socks off. At the beginning, we'd find an IED, mark it, and get the EOD people out to clear it. As things got worse, we just had to mark and avoid them. The quantity of IEDs just could not be dealt with. As a result, our patrolling was very slow. The Taliban would watch to see how we reacted to events, and then improvise to take advantage of that. They knew we used [*Vallon*] metal detectors, so they started using devices with very low metal content. At least one pressure plate was made of graphite, which conducted electricity but couldn't be detected.'

By July 10, the Taliban had refined both their devices and their tactics to such an extent that they were able to lay a near-perfect trap for Lt Horsfall, Rfn Aldridge and the rest of 9 Pl.

'The company from the upper Gereshk valley had just moved into Wishtan, to increase its size,' said Horsfall. 'We were to take some of them on a familiarisation patrol. The ANA would be joining us during the patrol, but we'd given them more time to get organised. With hindsight, I believe that an ANA soldier must have leaked our plans, because it seemed like the Taliban knew our exact movements. We were heading into an area that we didn't visit often, and yet they had planted a pretty well-thought-out IED minefield.

'Just the day before, we'd had the biggest attack so far on the base. We were attacked from four or five positions with small arms and RPGs, and Cpl Walker was shot in the shoulder and had to be evacuated. We were just over four months into the tour, and until that point we [*2 Rifles*] had had no serious casualties.

'As we left the base, I just thought, *okay, this is going to be a fairly standard patrol*. There was a chap living in a nearby wadi who we suspected of manufacturing IEDs, and we wanted to pay him a visit with the ANA to let him know that we were keeping a beady eye on him. We didn't have any proof of his involvement, so we couldn't do more than that. But the main purpose of the patrol was to familiarise some of the commanders from the new company.'

They moved out of Wishtan in three sections and headed in the general direction of the Wishtan Bazaar road, tracking it through back streets which should have been safer. Before long, the Vallon man held up his hand. He'd found a buried device.

'We marked it, recorded it, and moved on by another route,' said Horsfall. 'Then we found another one. We tried about three different

169

routes, and each of them had potential IEDS. I was with the lead section, and we ended up climbing over a wall into a compound. I'd just sent another section down into a little valley, with the intention of sending them up the other side to some slightly higher ground from where they could give us overwatch. I remember seeing them going into some dead ground, and thinking that we should move around a little bit so we could keep them in sight. At that point, there was an enormous bang as the first of the IEDs went off.'

It is perhaps impossible for anyone who has not experienced an IED blast to understand the fearsome power and havoc they unleash. In an instant, an IED produces a devastating and superheated shock wave which moves outwards at – depending on the size of the charge – a pressure of several hundred tonnes per square inch, and a temperature of perhaps 2,000°C. It takes with it loose stones, dust, bits of rifle and body armour in a haze of semi-molten shrapnel which travels at many times the speed of sound. The whole thing is accompanied by a giant bang, and followed by a momentary silence – the product of damage, temporary or permanent, to the hearing of nearby survivors. The air is filled with rubble falling back to earth and then a choking cloud of dust. It is massively, bewilderingly disorientating.

This first explosion devastated the command chain.

'It hit myself as platoon commander, and the incoming company commander who was with me,' said Alex Horsfall. 'It also hit a section commander and a rifleman who was a section second-in-command. And it hit the interpreter.'

Horsfall had lost his left leg and three fingers from his left hand. He had a broken jaw, arm and eye-socket, and had gaping flesh wounds all over his body, and was momentarily stupefied by the noise and the shockwave. Worse, though, the blast had killed eighteen-year-old Rfn James Backhouse.

'A daisy chain of three or four IEDs had hit us, and they were in a circle,' said Horsfall. 'A few of us were within the circle itself. I don't know if James had been standing right on top of a bomb, or if the one that was nearest him was more powerful, but it killed him outright. At that point, we also came under fire from three or four different angles, and the section that had moved down the valley started returning to where we were.

'My serjeant, Jaime Moncho, was to the rear of our section, but he immediately came forward, and he took over command at that point. He was not only in a firefight but handling an enormous number of casualties. He was, quite rightly, decorated for his action that day.'

[*Sjt Moncho was later awarded the Conspicuous Gallantry Cross, second only to the Victoria Cross, for his 'supreme courage'.*]

'A quick reaction force left the base to help us, and that included the sergeant major with a quad-bike trailer for some of us who were more seriously injured. At that point, we had serious casualties – me among them – and we'd lost one rifleman. I suppose there were a few people in shock and thinking, *Jesus, what the hell has happened?* This was the first time we'd lost someone to an IED. But we were still on top of the threat. The Taliban are not renowned for their accurate shooting, and we carry far greater firepower anyway.'

Except in the direst of circumstances, movement was always slow in Helmand. Patrols never went from A to B: they went from A to Y, to G, to P, to B, taking the hardest and most unfeasible route, never the obvious one, the Vallon men doing their level best to find the hidden bombs. This necessary caution meant that, an hour or more after leaving the front gate, the patrol was still only about three hundred metres from FOB Wishtan. Now they needed to get back as quickly – and safely – as they could.

'The decision was made to call a helicopter in to the compound to pick up the casualties,' said Horsfall, 'but when we started sweeping it for IEDs we kept finding more and more of them. It became clear that a helicopter couldn't get in, so we decided to get back to the PB and call the helicopter in there.

'This was where I became very lucky. I was in a very bad way – I know the doc, Cpl Thomas, had shoved a tracheotomy into my throat – and because of that I probably got priority treatment over those with lesser injuries. Cpl Thomas grabbed William Aldridge – who had nasty shrapnel wounds himself – and told him exactly what to do with me.[18] He and another rifleman were trying to patch me up as best they could, applying tourniquets and so on. I know they had to force me down, because I was being a terrible casualty and wriggling a lot. Then they put me into the sergeant major's quad-bike trailer for the journey back to Wishtan.

171

'We left the compound through a hole in the wall, and from there a road went back up to the base. Behind us was a group of guys, including William, carrying some of the other casualties on stretchers. He was helping even though he was himself injured: huge credit to him for carrying on.'

All this was taking place with enemy rounds pinging overhead from various murder-hole firing positions in the nearby compound walls, and with the air thick with dust, the sounds of injured men, and the smell of blood and explosives.

Unfortunately, the Taliban had planned their attack with some skill, predicting which route the British troops would take back to the FOB.

'The quad-bike had to take a fairly wide berth around the corner of the compound,' said Horsfall, 'but the guys behind us probably cut the corner, and in doing so they set off another series of daisy chain IEDs buried in the wall at pretty-much head height. That took out four more guys, including William. [*These were Rfn Dan Simpson and Joe Murphy, and Cpl Jay Horne. William died later, at Camp Bastion.*]

'It was carnage. People were picking up body parts and bits of kit, and we were still being engaged with small arms fire.'

More troops had to come out from Wishtan to help – some running out in their shorts, not taking the time to don body armour or helmets, so desperate were they to get to their mates. Eventually, of the 110 men who had been at the FOB that morning, only five remained at the base – four on the wall defending it, and one in the ops room, trying to co-ordinate the rescue effort and liaise with FOB Jackson and HQ.

'Jay's body had been blown over a wall,' said Alex Horsfall, 'and I'm told that it was only when everyone else had got back to the base that they realised he was missing. So the guys went out again to try to find his body and bring him back. That meant sweeping for more IEDs, but they managed to lift him out of the compound. It took three helicopters to evacuate the casualties, and they were also carrying the dead in body bags.'

The next thing Horsfall remembers is waking up in Selly Oak Hospital in Birmingham, and the nurse telling him that he had been in an IED incident.

'The opening three days in Selly Oak, I was so high on ketamine and morphine that I didn't realise I'd lost a leg, and I didn't realise I'd lost any of the riflemen,' he said. 'I was dreaming of Afghanistan, and that I was still in charge. I remember my father telling me that Rfn Simpson had been killed, but I assumed he was wrong because I'd seen him five minutes before in an hallucination. So it took a while to understand the gravity of the situation.

'There was a wonderful chap there called Rfn Percival who'd been injured and flown back earlier, so I started talking to him. It was difficult for him, because those five guys who died were very much his best mates. They meant a lot to me, too, I'd got to know them hugely well, but I was their platoon commander, whereas he'd been through training with them, and had seen them almost every day of his adult life.'

* * *

WILLIAM ALDRIDGE WAS the youngest British soldier to die in Afghanistan.

In the two weeks before his death, Lucy Aldridge repeatedly dreamed that she was witnessing her son being blown up by an IED.

'I had a sensation of my own body burning,' she said, 'and I would wake up in a hot sweat. The smell of burning and feeling of dust in my mouth was so vivid. I was never truly asleep when I was having this dream, but, just at the point of being able to see William's face, I'd wake up. I would see more than one explosion, and it scared the life out of me. I made an appointment to see my doctor. He told me I was projecting my fears. It was quite natural, he said, and he prescribed me some sleeping pills. But to me, that didn't explain why I was able to taste, smell, and hear names being called. I still remember those names, and the shouts and screaming. There was an acrid smell that I couldn't get rid of.

'Just before he died, William telephoned me. I was in a hell of state, dreading going to bed because of the dream. But, strangely, I didn't have the dream that night. Then he phoned again in the morning. There was his voice on the end of the phone, but I didn't feel that it belonged to him. I said, "Is that you, Will? Because it doesn't sound like you. Are you okay?"

'As he was talking, I just felt that something was not right. I couldn't put my finger on it then, and I still can't. I could hear the words he was saying, but I wasn't really listening to them. He said he was sorry he'd not been in touch a bit more. "You must have been out of your mind with worry," he said, which I was. I tried to lighten the mood a little, and actually made him laugh. I'd stubbed my toe the day before and broken one of the smallest bones in my body in three places. I said, "I'm glad that you're okay, but your mum's been in the wars."

'He said, "What are you *like,* mum? You seriously need someone to look after you."

· 'He said they were having a tough time at the patrol base. Resupply was difficult. They were low on ammunition. They were even sending a local out to the market to bring back water. He sounded extremely tired. He didn't sound like himself. I actually found it hard to believe that it was William I was talking to. He sounded totally different compared to conversations we'd had before he deployed to the patrol base. I remember saying, "Is everyone okay? Has something happened, Will?"

'He said, "No, no. I'm just absolutely dog-tired. We've been out on patrol every day."

'I was alarmed. Although I had obviously been concerned throughout for his safety, at that time none of the families knew exactly how dangerous Sangin was. And it's probably just as well that we didn't. The Army told me later that the patrols were about gaining hearts and minds among the local people, and I believe they did help to bring some of the locals back to the area. But in that last phone call William said, "Mum, I don't know why we are here. Every now and again, you see someone herding goats or something like that but otherwise there *are* no locals. It's like a ghost town."

'Whenever we spoke, I told him that I loved him. And he was never afraid to say that he loved me. Even if his mates took the mick, he would say, "Mum, I love you." And we both said we loved each other in that last phone call.

'I said, "Keep your head down and stay safe. I love you, sweetheart." For some reason, I then said, "No heroics." We have a little in-joke from when he first became a teenager. I'd bought him a t-shirt with the words, *I hear you, but I'm not listening.* That was our joke. His stock response when we joked like this was, "Yeah, yeah!" That indicated,

"I hear you, but I'm not listening." His very last words to me were, "Yeah, yeah!" in reply to my, "No heroics."

'I knew that, if the opportunity arose, William would be William, and as it turned out, he was. If that day happened a million times over, the result would be the same, because William would have given his life for his friends every day of the week, and that's precisely what he did. He didn't care about his own injuries.

'Two days after that last phone call, someone knocked at the door. I peered out of the window and saw a man and a woman on the doorstep, and I knew before I even opened the door what they were here to tell me.

'I was told William's funeral would be on a particular day, and I said that it wasn't a good day, because it was my stepfather's birthday, but it had to be then because there were four other men. It had to be orchestrated by the military. I could have said that I didn't want a military funeral, but in a sense I was glad that somebody was advising me, and holding my hand through that process.

'William was cremated, and I delayed the burial for quite a while until the rest of the regiment returned from Afghanistan. Then fifty guys came over from their base in Northern Ireland, and they participated in the whole process. It was very moving. One soldier had been nominated to place Will's ashes in the ground. Another held the tree we were planting, while a third man backfilled the hole in the ground. What happened next, though, was just a natural phenomenon. The guy who was filling the hole was tapped on the shoulder, and he handed the shovel over, and in turn each of the men who were there played a part.

'Then I did what you do with squaddies: I put a few hundred pounds behind the bar of the local pub, asked them to put on some hot pork rolls, and let them drink and eat. It gave me an opportunity also to meet and talk more freely with some of the young men who had served with Will. The burial ceremony had the effect that I wanted, which was to allow the lads to say goodbye.'

In all, The Rifles lost thirteen men on the tour, out of the sixty-nine British fatalities on Herrick 10.

'They weren't just saying goodbye to Will,' said Lucy. 'They were saying goodbye to all the men they'd lost. The guys never really get to say goodbye when someone dies on operations. They just have to get

175

on and do their jobs. Then they come home, and all they can do is visit their friends' graves.

'Some of the lads told me more about the incident after they returned. They said that, in all the chaos after that first blast, William was the calmest man there, and although he was the youngest man in the patrol he was telling everyone else that it would be okay. He had belief in himself, and he had faith. I never brought William up religiously, but he was a Christian, and it meant something to him. He was one of the few people I know who actually enjoyed religious education at school, bless him!

'Since the burial, the lads who William served with have kept in touch, and some of them call me mum, which is lovely. A couple of them will send me a Mother's Day card, for William.'

Unsurprisingly, her eldest son's death hit Lucy extremely hard.

'The only thing one can liken it to is the murder of a child,' she said. 'It's sudden death, and violent, and, for a mother, it has to be the hardest thing in the world to come to terms with. You knew your child for nine months before they were even brought into the world. You had a bond that, even in death, is unbreakable. But you feel so helpless. Because your child is a physical part of you that has been taken. When a child dies, a part of you dies with it.

'You do understand that there are risks involved in your child joining the military. Of the tens of thousands of British troops who have deployed to Afghanistan, there have been a relatively small number of deaths. But for the families, their lives have been shattered beyond recognition.

'Somehow, I had to explain to Archie and George, who were four and six at the time, that they would never see their big brother again. It took me two weeks to find the words, but I had to do it. They knew that William was a soldier and spent a long time away from home, so they were quite used to waving goodbye to him. But when they saw him walk back through the door again, they'd go absolutely mental and jump all over him. William referred to this as "the 24-hour love factor". They also knew that he had gone to a country called Afghanistan, because I'd shown them on the globe. I'd told them that he was going there to help the people of that country. I knew they could understand about helping people.

'When I explained his death to them, I said, "You understood about William going to help other people in another country? Well, he's been chosen to do an even more special job, because he needs to help even more people, and that job is to be an angel."

'They were only babies, but I wanted them to attend the funeral, because I felt that seeing the coffin would at least give them some understanding of the "forever" aspect of what had happened, because children don't have the same understanding of time as adults do. George, the older of the boys, seemed to be more affected than Archie. At the funeral, he asked me if William was in the coffin. I said, "Yes. William's shell is in the coffin, sweetheart. But it's just his body."

'I tried to keep the details of Will's death from Archie and George, but they were going to hear something. George said to me one day, "Mummy, William was killed by a bomb, wasn't he?"

'So I said, "Yes, sweetheart."

'He said, "When a bomb goes off, there's fire, and water puts out fires, so if I'd been there with a bucket of water, he wouldn't have died."

'I just couldn't believe that my six-year-old believed he could have done something to prevent his big brother's death. He was attempting to shoulder that burden, and I think that was what made me realise that I had to pull myself out of the depths of grief that I was suffering and be a better mother. Because otherwise I was going to lose another child. My life had been totally shattered. After a loss like this, you can't ever be the same person again. But I had two much younger children, and I've tried really hard to give them their childhood back. It was taken from them, and they didn't deserve that. I've worked really hard at being the best mum I can be.

'I enrolled the boys in out-of-school activities, and one of the activities they've taken up is tae kwan do. Their big brother used to do ju jitsu, so I thought I would encourage a martial art. That way they would do something that was following in his footsteps. And they love it.

'With some of William's death-in-service money, I bought a little caravan in North Wales so that I have a safe haven for the boys. We'd go there to try to find our feet again without William. We still go when we can, and the boys can play on the beach in total freedom. No-one knows us there, and nobody knocks on the door. We have a place where we can escape to.

'I remember every anniversary in William's life and his death, including his repatriation, his funeral, and his burial. But the only one that I really encourage the children to celebrate is his birthday. To them, birthdays are happy occasions. I've worked really hard to keep all the negative things away from them, so that they can have their childhood back.

'When you're grieving, it's quite a selfish emotion. You don't do it intentionally, but everything turns inward and, although other people are grieving around you, you can't understand their grief because it's such a personal thing. We all carry our own scars of our loss, and it can make relationships very difficult. I understand why couples sometimes split up, or wives and mothers-in-law sometimes have issues. No-one has written a handbook for this journey, and nobody can tell you how to deal with it.

'I felt a great draw to be wherever William is, if he is somewhere else. If I didn't have my two other children, then I wouldn't be here. I had a wobble just over a year ago. I took an overdose and I ended up in hospital. I can't explain why I did that. I'd struggled very early on with the conflict between wanting to be here for my other two children, and just wanting to be with William. I tried not to give in to an overwhelming feeling that, *I can't do this!* For a long time, I felt I was on automatic pilot as a mother to George and Archie.

'I had an enormous sense of guilt. It wasn't just the guilt that comes from wondering if things would have been different if I hadn't signed the piece of paper giving my consent for Will to join the Army. I questioned every decision I'd ever made as a parent. Did I do the right thing? Did I *say* the right thing? Am I going to let my other children down?

'After my suicide attempt, I was referred to a psychiatric nurse for counselling, and she basically ended up saying to me, "I can't even relate to what you've been through. I would be patronising you if we continued."

'I ended up pulling myself out of my grief. I just had to switch it off. I know that means I haven't fully grieved for William, but I still have to carry on living for my other children.

'Parents are supposed to inspire their children, but my son always inspired me, and he continues to do so. I often find myself thinking, *What would William say? What would William have thought of that?* Because he had something profound to say about most things. He'd kick my arse if I wasn't here to look after his little brothers. He knew that I could get very passionate and very stressed about things. One of his favourite sayings was, "Mum, you need to take a chill pill." I find these little things now just pop into my head when I'm getting a bit uptight.

'I don't believe that the invisible umbilical cord between a mother and her child is ever severed, even through death. William's still advising me. He had such a mature head on his shoulders. He said to me just before he went to Afghanistan, "Mum, I love you to bits! You're so passionate about injustice and other things that matter to you, but you'll never change anything if you don't have an audience."

'I've followed his advice, and I'm very pro-actively campaigning for the rights of service personnel. For example, I helped to persuade the MOD that the standard will form needs to be modernised. I worked with other bereaved families to persuade the MOD to recognise the role that RAF Lyneham played in repatriating those who died in Afghanistan. There will soon be a memorial garden and a permanent display in a museum outside the base.

'I also do what I can to raise money for Forces charities. I've done five parachute jumps with military amputees, even though I'm scared of heights. I think William would laugh his socks off at that! I've allowed the boys to be a part of it all because these are very positive activities. I spent £20,000 of William's death-in-service payment to set up a foundation in his memory to support bereaved military families. All of this has given my life some purpose.

'I have mixed feelings about Afghanistan. When a country asks for assistance, we have to think long and hard about how we would feel if we were in the same position. I believe we would want help. But I think the whole campaign was mismanaged. There wasn't a big enough budget, and there were just so many things that went so horribly wrong.

'But whether the campaign is won or lost, I know that William didn't die in vain. He was running a relay, and he handed the baton to me. He said, "Run with it! Do something! I told you to find an audience and a platform!" That's what he has given me.'

* * *

FOR ALEX HORSFALL, lying in his Selly Oak bed, the hardest thing was the sense that not only had he failed to bring his men home safely, he had left others behind to do his fighting.

'I knew the tour was getting harder and harder,' he said. 'People continued to die and be badly injured.'

Indeed, his own replacement, 2nd Lt James Amoore, was himself blown up a fortnight later. In Amoore's case, the explosion bent the barrel of his rifle back on itself, hurled him thirty feet into the air, and wrecked his legs, jaw, and left hand. Shrapnel left him partially sighted. Incredibly, after spending what must have seemed like an eternity in intensive care and learning to walk again, he went back to Afghanistan for more. Such astonishing bravery was, if not commonplace, then certainly not unheard of.

Later promoted to captain, Horsfall has since left the Army. But he will never forget William Aldridge and the others who died that day.

'The tenth of July is a date I remember even more clearly than my own birthday,' he said. 'I still think about it and dream about it – not in an emotionally-damaging way, but it's always a fresh memory.'

That terrible day claimed another life in May 2011, when Rfn Allan Arnold – a very good friend of William Aldridge – hanged himself in a copse near his sister's house while on leave. He was twenty. Rfn Arnold's mother, Nickie Smith, later told the BBC that her son rang home from Afghanistan after the incident.

'He informed me his closest friend had died,' she said. 'He was crying. There was nothing that I could do to make it easier for him, I couldn't cuddle him, I could just listen.'

Alex Horsfall and his men still keep in touch and meet up now and then; one of those occasions was at Allan Arnold's funeral. Another was while working on a BBC documentary about the platoon.

'I managed to get a few of the guys back together,' he said, 'and we ended up having a wonderful, black-tie piss-up. It's always good to see and hear from them. I email them from time to time, and we keep in touch on Facebook. I have a slight feeling of guilt, not because I consider myself responsible for what happened, but because it was my responsibility to get my people back in one piece. That has always been at the back of my mind. I thought I'd have a fair amount of explaining to do to the families, but they have all been thoroughly supportive, and that's really helped me.

'I got to know William better than a lot of the platoon because, for a brief period at one PB, we were just half a platoon, and he was one of the guys I had. We weren't hugely busy at the time, but we did run out of water at one point, so I remember William and me trying our best, with our Bear Grylls survival skills, to create a water filter. We got some water from a nearby well and filtered it through this thing we'd made. We both had a good swig, and then immediately regurgitated it, because it tasted of cow urine.

'He was the youngest British soldier to die in Afghanistan. I don't think he realised how young he was, probably because he picked up the nuances very quickly, even though he joined us after we'd been there for a while. He was a very competent and confident young man. You never had to ask him to do the same thing twice. He was joyful and always had a smile on his face. I have great memories of him.'

CORPORAL CHRISTOPHER HARRISON
BRAVO COMPANY 40 COMMANDO ROYAL MARINES
MARCH 26, 1984 – MAY 9, 2010

TEN DAYS BEFORE his tragic and untimely death in an IED blast, Chris Harrison – a larger-than-life extrovert, with unique dance moves and a keen sense of humour – wrote a last letter to Russell, the older brother he had looked up to since childhood.

The two were very close, and shared almost everything with each other. Russell said later that just about the only thing he had not known about Chris was how desperate he and his wife Becky had been to have a baby. So the letter, fondly addressed 'To Bruv', was full of little in-jokes and nuggets of information about Cpl Harrison's life in Afghanistan, where he had arrived a month or so earlier on his second tour of the country.

He talked about his acclimatisation week at Camp Bastion – it was 'fucking mahoosive now', he said, 'about ten times the size it was a few years ago, about 8k from the two furthest points.'

Its toppers [Royal Marine slang for full] *with yanks, dutch, norgies* [Norwegians], *estonian nutters and a few of us. I spent about 7 days in Bastion acclimitising to the heat and altitude and conducting some up to date training cascaded from the rifles battle group. Most info was relevent, a few doozies though! I then flew forward in a CH-47* [Chinook helicopter] *to fob Inkerman, spent a few hours there, then moved in a Mastiff convoy (best wagon in theatre) about 4k south to patrol base Shuga.* [The PB is] *surrounded on 4 sides but is well*

182

defended by us with good arcs [of fire] *into the neighbours compounds which they love and repay us by chucking the occasional grenade over the wall!*

Its very basic but is improving every day. We all live in little caves dug out of the thick compound walls which are made of mud and horse shit!

We've been patrolling every day, sometimes in the green zone other times on the heavily compounded desert side.

We got contacted 5 metres out of the front gate on my first patrol! Fuckers! Going well so far, mega hard work with ridiculously heavy kit but having fun though. Just got to win some hearts n' minds...

Russell was at home with the military jargon, having himself been a soldier. In a way, it was down to him that Chris was in Afghanistan with the Royal Marines in the first place. The Harrison brothers had both been 'Army barmy' as youngsters at home in Watford, comrades-in-arms in endless, youthful games of soldiers.

'We used to get through the neighbours' fence and sneak around,' said Russell, the elder by two years. 'We spent all our pocket money on military kit from the surplus stores, and we'd spend nights camping out in the garden. We'd do sentry duty in the garden, although I don't know what we were guarding against. Because I was bigger, I'd sometimes pull rank and get him to stag-on and do my duty!'

There was never much doubt that they would end up in uniform and, in the event, Russell Harrison joined the Army at seventeen. His younger brother went to his passing-out parade, filming it for posterity on the family video camera. At one point, he turned to his mother and said, 'I'd like a bit of that!'

At fourteen, Chris had had plans – recorded in his school yearbook – to become an Army officer. But then he asked Russell for advice on where he should sign up, stressing that he wanted to be wherever the action was.

'I'd gone into the Royal Green Jackets,' said Russell, 'but there was nothing particularly elite about that. If troops need to be deployed urgently, it's usually the Royal Marines or the Parachute Regiment who are sent first. So I recommended that he should join the Paras or the Marines.'

Chris Harrison took his older brother's advice, and went to Lympstone for commando training.

There has always been rivalry between the Army and their comrades in the Royal Navy, and once Chris earned the coveted green beret there was plenty of opportunity for good-natured banter between the two brothers. Perhaps that explains the humorously over-the-top way in which he signed off his last letter to Russell: 'Love Chris (Corporal, Royal Marines, Indirect Fire Specialist, Forward Observer, Team Medic, MFC [*mortar fire controller*] and Jungle Warfare Trained).'

But there was no real sense of competition between the two of them. Russell, by now out of the Army, would tell Chris stories about his posting to the Balkans; Chris would fire back with tales from Iraq, or his first trip to Afghanistan.

'There was never an edge to it,' said Russell. 'We'd just be trying to make each other laugh.'

Just as in that final bluey, which Chris wrote on April 29, 2010.

The British Forces Post Office leviathan grinds slowly, and the letter still hadn't arrived on May 9, by which time Russell had heard the dreadful news about his beloved brother's death and was on his way to Chris and Becky's Taunton home, to support his parents and sister-in-law.

It finally arrived a few days later, when he was back at home.

'I was really nervous when I saw who it was from,' said Russell. 'I sat looking at it for quite a while before I opened it. I made sure I was ready. And it was tough to read. But the content was really positive, it was light, and chatty, and he even talked about having fun. I found that quite comforting, in a way. I never expected to be able to speak to Chris again, so this last letter was good. It was like the opening of a conversation, even though we'd never get to finish it.'

* * *

GILL HARRISON REMEMBERS the day her younger son told her he was applying to join the Royal Marines.

'I said, "Please, no!"' she said. 'I begged him not to. I *really* begged him. It was the danger that worried me.'

But once Chris Harrison's mind was made up it was hard to change it, and he was determined to press on. He knew he had to develop his upper-body strength in order to be selected for the tough commando course, but that simply brought out the steel in his character. His supreme determination to succeed was demonstrated one day when his mum came home from work and found her son's legs dangling through the loft hatch.

'He'd put a bar across the opening, and was doing pull-ups on it,' said Gill. 'He was very determined to be accepted on to the course, and he was. If he said he was going to do something, he would bloody well do it!'

Another demonstration of that determination came during the four notoriously challenging commando tests, which arrive at the culmination of thirty weeks of training. Recruits have to pass the tests in one week, all while carrying a 10kg Bergen and a rifle weighing a further 5kg. The first is a six-mile endurance course – a series of tunnels, one filled with water, followed by a four-mile run back to Commando Training Centre (CTC). The second is a nine-mile speed march, which must be completed in ninety minutes. The third is the 'Tarzan' assault course, a series of high obstacles, ropes and jumps which must be finished in five minutes. The final test is the toughest of them all – a thirty-mile march across Dartmoor, starting before first light. Recruits have eight hours – officer recruits an hour less – and those who succeed receive their green berets at the finish line.

It is said to be the world's hardest non-Special Forces training regime, and the thirty-miler in particular proves an insurmountable hurdle for many men. In Chris Harrison's case, his feet were covered in painful septic blisters, so bad that the training staff recommended on medical grounds that he 'backtroop' to the next cadre of recruits in the pipeline. But Recruit Harrison gritted his teeth, slogged on through the pain, and collected his beret. One of his officers later remarked that when he had finished the thirty-miler he had resembled 'a skeleton with hair'.

This spirit had been obvious to his parents from childhood.

'He was very keen to start school,' said Gill. 'I'd take him with me when I dropped Russell off, and he'd often be in tears. Once, someone saw him crying, and said, "Poor little mite! He doesn't want to go to school!" I said, "That's the trouble – he *does* want to go, he's upset that he *can't*."

185

'Eventually, his first day came round and I took him into the cloakroom, put his plimsolls on, and took him to his little table. I was fidgeting around, making him comfortable, and he just looked at me and said, "Shove off, mum!"

'He was quite easy as a little boy – in fact, after Russell, who was difficult, he was a piece of cake. He was more daring, though. If I said to them both that they shouldn't leave a certain room, Chris would just sneak one foot out to see what he could get away with.'

The Harrisons fought hard to get both brothers into the always over-subscribed Parmiter's School, where Chris's academic career was solid but unspectacular. Nevertheless, he was an intelligent young man who could easily have gone on to university. But that military bug was in his brain.

'Most teachers liked him because he made them laugh,' said Martin, his father. 'They just used to say he should apply himself more. But he pulled himself together and got some good GCSE results, which showed he could do it when he tried. He was very popular – his school friends still meet up on his birthday – but quite late developing an interest in girlfriends. Of course, that changed with Becky.

'He was a bit indifferent to most sports at school, but he was good at rugby. He was a big lad – 6ft 3in tall by the time he stopped growing – which helped. He became a bit of a school rugby star, and the county youth squad were interested in him for his lineout skills. But he lost interest in rugby after leaving school, and felt his military training was more important.

'Gill worried about him when he joined up, but I was resigned to it. It was always in the back of his mind. He and Russell both had officer training potential, and I did try to persuade them to go that way. But they wanted to join the ranks and work their way upwards. I just thought, if he was going to do that, the Royal Marines was a good choice.'

Chris Harrison passed out in 2003 with a reputation as a very fit and promising young bootneck, and one who was not averse to taking the mickey out of his bosses. He was famous for his uncanny impressions of senior NCOs and officers, so much so that the officer who presented him with the famous beret remarked, with a smile and to warm laughter, 'Chris Harrison is well-known for his impersonations… Just about the only figure he hasn't been able to impersonate yet is a good Royal Marine!'

Mne Harrison was still getting to grips with membership of one of the country's elite fighting forces when, in 2004, he met the woman who would become his wife. Becky Yates was a nurse on a night out with friends in Watford when the young marine approached her in a bar.

'He was very tall and good-looking,' she said, 'and he was quite shy when we first met, which wasn't typical of him. He certainly wasn't shy normally!'

Becky didn't give much thought to the dangerous nature of her new boyfriend's life.

'I get asked this a lot: whether I knew what I was getting myself into with Chris,' she said. 'The truth is, I didn't even think about it at first. I was very young. And then you fall in love, and then it's too late to change anything.'

Soon after they met, Mne Harrison was posted to the Fleet Protection Group – a specialist unit responsible at home for guarding the country's nuclear weapons, and used at sea to board suspect ships via offshore raiding craft. He was involved in numerous such interceptions in the Arabian Gulf, and later told his father how exciting it had been. But it was action on land that he really craved. Soon afterwards he transferred to 40 Cdo in Taunton.

By then, Afghanistan was starting to warm up. It was in the period before Chris Harrison's first Afghan deployment – on Op Herrick 7, between September 2007 and April 2008 – that he and Becky became engaged.

'By the time he went to Afghan the first time, we'd moved in together,' she said. 'I still don't think I really knew what to expect. I was only twenty-three, and it wasn't until I started hearing things on the news, that I started paying attention. Suddenly, someone I loved was out there. It was hard, especially when three guys from 40 Cdo were killed late in that first tour. That was when it really hit home how dangerous it was. But then he came home just a few weeks later. I was so grateful for that.'[19]

Chris Harrison's close friend Terry Holland, himself a veteran of Herrick 5, was on that tour with him.

'Chris and I met in the summer of 2007, shortly after I transferred to 40 Cdo mortar troop,' said Holland. 'We hit it off straight away. We did a few exercises, we went out and did some heavy drinking together, and were soon firm friends. Then, in the September, we deployed on Herrick 7.

'Chris was a bit OCD, in the sense that, before going away, even on short exercises, he'd pack and repack his stuff, adjusting it slightly every time. But his job tended to breed OCD, so it wasn't a bad thing. It made him very slick, and he was a very competent mortar man. And he was always trying to improve. At weekends, he'd go off to the Quantocks with a tent, and navigate and yomp around on his own, or maybe with Becky. When he was doing his twos – the course to become a forward controller – he had flash cards to help him learn. He even had a pack of them in the toilet to put that time to good use. And he was always happy to pass on any little tips and tricks he'd discovered. He helped me a lot.

'Although he was younger than me, I looked up to him. Not that age mattered much; it sort of blurred between us, because the older guys would act younger and the younger guys would act older. We'd meet in the middle. But I looked up to him because he was, physically and mentally, very capable. He was just a very professional soldier.

'Chris and I were stationed at Kajaki from September 2007 to April 2008. The company commander was excellent, and we also had an OMLT team – a couple of Army guys and about twenty ANA. We had an Army medic, as well, but apart from that we were a company of marines.

'The task was to secure the dam there [*as the late Cpl Mark Wright GC and his fellow paratroopers had done earlier*]. Kajaki was the furthest outpost from Bastion, and we were the only company in that area. But by the end of it we'd had a lot of success. Tangi village was a hundred metres or so from us, and the Paras had driven everyone out of the village after the enemy infiltrated it. We pushed the forward line of enemy troops out to about five kilometres, which was a huge area by Helmand standards. Once we'd established dominance, the locals moved back because they felt safe under our care.

'Life on the FOB was pretty good. Mortars are always extremely close teams. The guys have done their time in a fighting troop, and they're a bit older. In Kajaki we were very much our own entity. If the guys weren't out on patrol, our days were largely spent eating, exercising, and sleeping. But when a patrol was out, we'd have two forward controllers deployed, one on the high ground and the other with the lead section of the friendly forces. Both Chris and I were number ones on a mortar, basically controlling it.

'Throughout that six-month period, we made no movements in numbers less than a hundred, with air support. It was very kinetic – I'd say that guys were patrolling three days out of every four, and they encountered the enemy to some degree every time they went out. We fired something like 28,000 mortar rounds, which was said to be the most in that sort of period since the Second World War. We did suffer three serious casualties, but it was a lot more successful than later tours. We were getting to do our jobs, and morale was good.'

* * *

CHRIS HARRISON HAD called home and written often while away, always keeping the conversation light and upbeat – particularly with his mother, whom he called 'Muv'.

'I wouldn't say he poured his heart out to me,' said Gill, 'but I loved getting his letters and e-blueys. It was just the best thing. I learned to use a computer to read his e-blueys. Thank you for that, Chris! He was always affectionate, though perhaps not as much as Russell when they were children. Russell always worried about me, even if I was just out late. Chris would say, "Stop worrying! She'll be back soon!" But when they grew up they changed, and Chris became the more affectionate one.'

Martin Harrison got a little more of the nitty-gritty.

'He tended to speak to me more about work,' said Martin. 'He didn't want Gill to worry, and I can understand why. One day, he played me a video [*of action from Herrick 7*] on his laptop – you could hear the bullets zinging past. He laughed about that and said it was just normal. I could laugh a bit, too, because, obviously, he'd survived. But he wouldn't share that with his mother. There's a different language between sons and mothers and sons and fathers, and a desire to reassure the mother which was reflected in his language with Gill. He was very good with her. He'd spend time with her when he was on leave, reminiscing about his childhood, and watching the TV quizzes with her, each trying to beat the other.

'From what he told me, he liked a lot of the Afghans. He just liked the simplicity of their lives, and I think that helped him to rationalise the war in his own mind. During Herrick 12, he befriended a painfully thin young lad who worked as an interpreter for them. This lad was impressed by the marines' physiques, so Chris started teaching him how to use the gym equipment so he could build up his body to look like a marine.

'But there were some terrible things, too. Up near the Kajaki Dam, he his colleagues were returning to their base after a patrol, and they took the time to help a local farmer unblock an irrigation ditch. They didn't ask him if he wanted the help, they just did it. The next morning they checked on the family and found that the Taliban had murdered all of them, including five children. The incident horrified Chris. He and his friends had only been doing something simple to help some local people. It showed the complexity of trying to help the Afghans. Even if you thought you were carrying out a simple humanitarian act, the consequences couldn't be foreseen.'

In 2008, Chris and Becky were married. They settled in married quarters at Norton Manor, the Corps' base near Taunton, in Somerset. There followed a period of normality – or as close to it as the Royal Marines can offer a young couple. Martin and Gill spent Christmas 2009 with them at their house, along with Becky's mother, Elaine, her two brothers, Iain and Richard, and Chris's brother, Russell.

'It was the first time they'd entertained anyone for Christmas,' said Martin, 'so it meant a lot to them, and us. They obviously enjoyed it, and married life, and settling down. It made us smile to see them together. They'd stand at the sink working together and high-fiving each other. They were extremely happy. We're so pleased we had that time with them.'

With his new responsibilities – and trying for a baby – Chris considered leaving the service. But he and Becky decided it was who he was, it was what he loved, and that he should stay in. So he threw himself into work, passing various courses with flying colours. He completed a ten-week, all-ranks, forward controller's course, in which he was the top student and missed a distinction by one per cent. He also undertook his three-month junior command course, in which he secured an A grade and an instant promotion to full corporal.

In between, he and Terry Holland went on a jungle training exercise in Brunei, during which Chris came close to death when he was bitten by a krait [*a jungle snake*]. Unless treated promptly with anti-venom, eighty per cent of krait bites are fatal, usually within six hours. Victims often suffocate following respiratory failure brought on by paralysis of the nervous system.

'I wasn't a fan of the jungle,' said Holland, 'but Chris was into any kind of soldiering, really. That said, he didn't anticipate being bitten by a snake. Once the poison took hold, he said it was like being hit by a sledgehammer. He was still quite confident, but it was a bit touch-and-go.'

Communications were down, and the marines were not carrying anti-venom, so getting him out of the jungle and to medical attention became a matter of life or death. He was too heavy to be carried through the dense vegetation, so – almost incredibly – he 'yomped' out. [*Yomping is Royal Marine slang for a long-distance march, across country, usually in full kit; it is analogous to the Parachute Regiment's 'tabbing'.*] They eventually reached civilisation, and medical care – many hours by now having passed since the bite.

'A doctor asked when he'd been bitten,' said Holland. 'When he was told he started panicking. Chris was out of hospital in forty-eight hours, but he could easily have died.'

The theory was that he had survived because of his size – the poison had had further to travel. Whatever, it left him with a great story to laugh about.

Herrick 12 soon rolled around. It was clearly going to be a very different tour from the Commandos' earlier visit, not least because they were headed for Sangin. Towards the end of March 2010, a couple of weeks before deployment, Gill, Martin and Russell went to Taunton to stay with Chris and Becky, partly to celebrate his birthday and partly to say their farewells. At one point, when he was alone with his father, Chris Harrison confided in him.

'He said, "It's going to be really tough, dad,"' said Martin. '"It's going to be worse than before. Everything I've heard suggests it's going to be

191

hairy." He was straight with me, so I know he felt a bit of trepidation. He knew Sangin was a Godforsaken area. But then, this was what he'd joined up for. I remember him saying, "I'm good at what I do, and I don't take unnecessary risks." He knew the statistics. His logic was that there was more chance of surviving than dying. So he talked in a positive way, reassuring himself and me.'

Gill hadn't worried too much about the Gulf, or his first tour of Afghanistan.

'I just thought, *okay, you're doing your job*,' she said. 'But I didn't know much about it. I felt very different about his second tour. I thought, *You've survived once...* I told him how scared I was, but he said, "Don't worry, mum, I'll be alright."'

He used the same tactic with Becky.

'I remember on his first tour I had little blips a couple of times,' she said. 'I was scared and upset. Chris had this way about him. He'd say, not in a harsh way, "Come on, pull yourself together! It's not going to happen." He'd make it into a joke. He had this line: "I'm hoofing! Nothing's going to happen to me!"

'The second time, our conversations were different. He was more serious, he gave glimpses of how he felt. I remember him saying, "You know, this is going to be different to the last tour." I think he was subtly trying to make me aware of the dangers, but every time I started to talk more realistically, and more seriously, he'd still play it down. "Oh, I'll be alright," he'd say. We always stayed positive. In his position, you never really believe it's going to be you.'

Russell Harrison remembers feeling uneasy about the dangers his brother faced as they said their farewells in Taunton.

'He used to joke about coming back with chicken dippers for arms,' said Russell. 'Just typical marines' black humour. But when we said goodbye that day, there was something different. I said, "Take care of yourself, and be careful." He said he wouldn't take any risks. It was the handshake, though. I can't put it into words, but it did worry me. Everything was said in that handshake. I could feel it.'

Any soldier returning to Afghanistan must feel the odds stacking up against him – the more tours you go on, logic dictates, the greater the risk. But Chris Harrison's concerns were rooted in more than mere numbers. Terry Holland – now promoted to acting corporal – said,

192

'Before we deployed, we were told we'd be patrolling in section-strength, only about eight men, as opposed to the company-strength patrols of the last tour. On top of that, [*US General Stanley*] McChrystal, who was in command of ISAF at the time, was saying we'd operate under a policy of what he called "courageous restraint", which seemed to mean that, even when we were being shot at, we wouldn't shoot back, or at least we wouldn't call in heavy firepower. That way, hopefully, the Afghan people would realise we were friends, not enemies.

'I remember being at Chris and Becky's house for dinner and laughing about it, saying it couldn't possibly happen. I thought they were telling us a fib just to make us take the deployment more seriously. To me, it just seemed crazy – casualty rates were going up and they were talking about scaling down air support and the number of guys on the ground. It was mad. But I think Chris realised they meant what they said, and that "courageous restraint" was going to cause us a lot of problems.'

But Royal Marines, like all service personnel, go where they're told to go, and make the best of a bad hand of cards. And so it was that Gill and Martin Harrison's final sight of their son was as they left his home near Taunton after that weekend together.

Chris and Becky stood in their doorway, smiling: Chris gripped Wilson, his black retriever-collie cross, in his arms, the dog's legs dangling, tongue lolling. Becky held her spaniel pup, Ellie.

They were using the dogs' paws to wave goodbye.

* * *

ONCE IN AFGHANISTAN, as mortar men Chris Harrison and Terry Holland were attached to different companies – Chris to Bravo Coy at PB Shuga, Terry to Alpha Coy at PB Almas – and based a couple of kilometres apart in the Sangin area.

They had a week together at Camp Bastion, acclimatising. There were briefings to attend – some soldiers referred to it as 'death by PowerPoint' – equipment to check, and trips to the coffee shop in the evening for general gossip, discussion of the sloppy drills of officers on the ranges, and to swap rumour and conjecture about what lay ahead. After that week, they went their separate ways. Terry Holland never saw his mate again, though he soon discovered that 40 Cdo had, indeed, landed in a very sticky situation.

'I remember being told at Bastion that, at my PB, they'd almost stopped patrolling because the situation was so bad,' he said. 'Royal Marines have a terrible habit of believing that they're better than they are, so we thought we'd do it better. As we found out, that wasn't the case.

'We didn't have much contact between us while we were at the bases. I'd sometimes hear Chris on the radio, maybe as his patrol was heading back, but the most you can get away with is a quick, "Alright mate, hope all's well, take care of yourself!" over the net. I wrote him a couple of blueys, but he never received them, because they had to go all the way back to the UK before being sent back out to theatre. By the time they covered all that distance, he'd been killed.

'Almas was right in the green belt through the centre of Sangin, near the river, and Chris was further into the built-up area, near the outside of the green zone. There were quite a lot of supplies at Almas when we arrived, which was fortunate because we went weeks at a time without any ground resupply and the helos refused to fly to us. One Chinook did try to fly in to drop an under-slung load, but the Taliban nearly took it out with an RPG as it touched down. That was just a single opportunity shot – I suppose they knew a helicopter would eventually come in, and they probably had an RPG stashed nearby to grab and take a shot. It only missed by a matter of metres and, after that, the RAF said "No, we're not doing it." Actually, after about ten weeks, one helo did come in with food and a generator to run the water filtration plant.

'They'd come in if someone was injured, but not for resupply, or even if someone had been killed, because they felt it was too dangerous. We took three KIA at Almas. One of them was alive when he left us, and another had a T1 casualty with him. So they *were* flown out. But in the case of the third guy, who was killed instantly, they wouldn't come in for him as there was no longer a threat to life. That left us only one option – to carry him on foot to our FOB, Nolay, which was about 1100 metres from Almas as the crow flies. There was only one route in and out, which we called Route Onion. Very apt, because I hate onions. It was heavily strewn with IEDs – it was on or very near Onion that all three guys we lost were killed, as well as others who were more fortunate and survived, minus a limb or two – and to carry a body that distance along that route would have been extremely difficult and dangerous.

'But you can't have a dead man at the PB – it's terrible for morale. Particularly the younger blokes, they like to think they will be treated with respect and dignity if the worst happens. We had placed him in a body bag on our little air head [*landing zone*], which was in the perimeter of the PB but not in the compound, and placed an armed guard on him while we waited for the air to come and take him home. Eventually, we were told they wouldn't come, which led to a heated and emotional argument over the radio.

'By that time, it was too late for us to move him on foot. Movement was extremely slow, and we would have been out in the dark, making all visible ground sign [*of IEDs*] invisible. Plus, we had no air support. It would have been an extremely arduous mission after a hard patrol that day, which had resulted in one of our senior marines being killed.

'Fortunately, the Americans got wind of the situation and they came and got him, maybe eight or ten hours later. All the crew except the pilot came off the helicopter and stood in two ranks as we carried him on.'

Their situation was made worse by the policy of 'courageous restraint'.

'When we were shot at we couldn't engage unless there was an extreme threat,' said Holland. 'Essentially, our right to self-defence was taken away. Our entire training was about reacting to enemy fire, so it didn't make any sense. We ended up questioning everything. I was on the radio in our little Ops room one day, and a guy in one of the sangars radioed down to say he'd just had a shot fired at him. We had Boomerang [*an incoming-fire direction locater*] on top of the sangar, so we knew it had come from a nearby copse. The guy in the sangar asked permission to engage the treeline with a burst of GPMG fire, which had been standard procedure. I was about to say yes when the boss came through and said he would radio HQ at FOB Nolay and check with them. While he did this, a second round was fired, and that one went just above our firing point. It was ranging fire, so we could expect the next round to be on target. The OC came back and asked if we could identify a weapon. We explained that the guy was hiding in some trees. Because we couldn't see him we were told that, under the rules of engagement, we couldn't engage! There were so many situations like this.

'The enemy was so much more aggressive than I'd experienced before, but given that we couldn't engage them properly that was no surprise. Guys were becoming short-tempered and irritable. You just had to laugh, or you'd cry. I know from talking to guys who were with Chris at Shuga that they had the same issues. I don't recall going on a single patrol with Apache air support, and we requested it every time. The only time I saw Apaches was when the CO was on the ground, and he'd be moving around in an armoured vehicle. I guess that was courageous restraint, too.'

With the marines' hands tied, the Taliban took advantage. The IED threat had ramped up dramatically since earlier tours. Now, with more freedom of movement than they should have enjoyed, the enemy planted bombs everywhere.

'I personally never saw a sniffer dog, and I never saw any EOD people,' said Terry Holland. 'Before we'd deployed we'd been shown footage of a fabulous new piece of kit which allowed aeroplanes to identify IEDs in the ground. I never knew of that being used. All we could do was hope to identify them with the Vallon, mark them, and move on. Of course, the Taliban then came along, dug them back up, and used them somewhere else.

'You took your life in your hands every time you left the PB. We had a command post with seven or eight guys about a hundred and fifty metres away, and we struggled to get there. I believe one member of The Rifles had been killed just trying to resupply it with water. But we were told we *had* to get out. They wanted us to walk around doing what they called "reassurance patrols", though we were never quite sure who we were reassuring. So we were patrolling at least once a day, with one day off in six. It would take us up to ten hours to cover between four and six kilometres, in really hard conditions. The heat was incredible. Our hottest day was 56°C (132°F), and the only part of you that's uncovered is your mouth. You're wearing protective glasses, you've got leather gloves on… in the crop fields, particularly, the heat seemed to be trapped. You could see the air in front of you shimmering.

'Even if we had intel to say that there was a compound that we should raid, we weren't allowed to. It was scary. When we were suiting up and doing all our final checks before going out, I'd see guys vomiting because of the unknown. *Who's it going to be this time?* A lot of the time I wanted to turn around and say, "I'm not doing it any more. I'm not going." I only pressed on because I couldn't let everyone else down. When you look at the guys around you, and you know you're the only one at the PB who can do your job, you just couldn't refuse to go.'

They took two Vallons every time they left the gate, and still took casualties. In fact, a number of Vallon men were killed on the tour, as the Taliban constantly reviewed and improved their methods. Worst of all were the command wire devices, triggered by hidden killers who would often delay their strike until a section commander – a corporal – was in range. Unlike pressure plate bombs, these did not require the metal components necessary to complete a detonation circuit, and so rendered the Vallon next to useless. Other IEDs were placed in trees, with trip-wires strung at the height of a marine's radio antenna. It was morale-sapping and terrifying, even for elite soldiers such as these.

There were fifty-nine fatalities on Herrick 12. Chris Harrison was the first Royal Marine to die, but 40 Cdo lost fourteen men during the tour, including three from Terry Holland's PB Almas.[20]

'I was on every patrol when someone from Almas was killed or injured,' said Terry Holland. 'I'll never forget them. In the same incident in which we lost Cpl Stephen Walker, another guy was seriously injured. Then we lost our troop sergeant, Steven Darbyshire. He was a key personality, he'd have done sixteen or eighteen years in the Marines, and the young officer, who might only have been out of training for eighteen months, relied on him. Once the sergeant was killed, he was left to run the show with the corporals. Later we lost Adam Brown.

'Personally, I think Sgt Darbyshire's death could have been avoided. The Taliban were hiding in a river bed, and we couldn't get to them. HQ wouldn't allow us to use our mortars, and you can't engage an enemy that has cover from fire with just rifles. I was on the radio screaming that we were going to take casualties, and, lo and behold, we did. On previous tours we had been in far more serious contacts and we had got out of it okay. I'd say forty-eight times out of fifty, on those other tours, Darbs would have been fine. Even after he was killed, we had to pursue a four-hour contact with nothing but our rifles.

'The mortars were only used once at PB Almas. And that was only because the Americans had turned up and started engaging with jets, so for us *not* to use the mortars would have looked ridiculous.'

If the men at PB Shuga were suffering similar frustrations, Chris Harrison was careful not to worry his family.

'Chris went off to Afghan at the beginning of the Easter Holiday in April 2010,' said Gill Harrison, 'and we received his last bluey on April 30. I came home from work on a Friday, and there it was.'

To Mum and Dad, he wrote, on April 18. *Hello how are you both!*

> *I'm pretty sure I'll have spoken to you both before you recieve this bluey. We're just waiting for a new sat phone though so maybe not!*
>
> *The PB is an abandoned afghan compound in the middle of a small village that the unit before us took over. Its very basic but we have electricity in the ops room run by a small generator and we have made some showers from various bits. We also have a small kitchen made from rocks and ammo tins and we can boil water in an old afghan kettle on the fire and we even have a bread oven made from a mortar bomb tin sat on some coles and wood.*
>
> *Theres about 30 of us here, I share my little cave with two artillery blokes who control the spy planes overhead. My typical day so far is taken up with improving the PB defences and getting to know the local area.*
>
> *How are you dad? Still going freelance? And mum how are you, have ASDA made you man those pointy hand things yet!*
>
> [Martin is a quantity surveyor, now semi-retired; Gill works at the local supermarket.]
>
> *I am good btw and am getting a nice tan! Don't worry about me, with some good blokes and we'll all look after each other.*
>
> *Love you both so much and missing you both to*
>
> *C Harrison (Cpl Harrison Indirect Fire Specialist) XX*

'Just in case we forgot who he was!' said Gill. 'Signing it like that was just part of his sense of humour. Sometimes he even put his full name, Christopher Lewis Harrison! Later that evening, I had a phone call from him to say everything was okay. He said he'd sent that letter, and I told him I'd got it already. Nine days later, he was dead.'

Naturally, Becky received slightly more attention. 'We had thirty minutes of phone calls a week, and there were letters,' she said. 'But communications weren't that easy. I used to write him an e-bluey every night before I went to bed, and I'd send him a normal letter once a week. I'd send him parcels, too. I remember he asked for a kettle, so I sent him our old one, and then he asked for a mousetrap. I'd send him little bits of food that he liked.

'I only received three letters from him during that tour, which was pretty much one a week, if you don't count Bastion. They always seemed to be cheerful, and he was looking on the bright side, but when he phoned he sounded so tired. I think they were working very hard, and they weren't getting much sleep.

'I knew life out there was pretty basic, but they made the most of it. He'd talk about plans for when he came back on R&R, where he wanted to go, the food he'd like to eat. He'd always ask about our two dogs. And he was always telling me that he missed me. He could talk about his emotions and his feelings, but we did it in our little way. I don't think it would make sense to anyone else. His letters were always written like that, and it's really nice to read them again, even now. It's like being with him again.'

* * *

CPL CHRIS HARRISON died in an IED blast in Sangin just after six o'clock on the morning of Sunday, May 9, 2010.

ACpl Terry Holland wasn't there, but he heard the explosion at PB Almas.

'Generally, if there was an explosion at night you'd assume someone laying an IED had blown himself up,' he said. 'If it happened during the daytime you assumed it was a local, or one of us. I just crossed my fingers and hoped, like I always did. I went into the Ops room, and someone at FOB Blenheim [*where Cpl Harrison had been temporarily re-*

assigned] was sending zap numbers over the radio. These were codes to identify individual marines, using letters from your surname and digits from your service number. I remember seeing Hotel and three digits of a service number, and I knew that could have been Chris. I thought, *No it can't be.*

'Later it filtered through that three mortar guys had been involved. I got on the radio to my stripey, Sgt Matt Bentley, at Blenheim, and asked him who it was. I had that sick feeling, but I still felt it was unlikely that Chris had been killed, because he was such a big guy, and so strong. I thought he might have lost a leg or something, but he couldn't have been killed. The stripey knew that Chris and me were close. He said, "There's no easy way to tell you this. That explosion today involved Chris, and it's not good."

'I don't think I even switched my radio off. I just walked away, stunned and staggered. You have lots of close relationships as brothers-in-arms, but this was more than that. I'd go to Chris and Becky's house for meals and to watch movies. I went to his wedding. It hit me very badly. I was given a couple of days off from patrolling just to try and sort myself out.'

In a moment of seriousness earlier, Chris Harrison had asked Terry and a few other close friends to promise him that, if he was killed, they would be at Camp Bastion to carry him aboard the repatriation flight.

'They weren't sending helicopters in, even to collect the dead, so it looked like we couldn't do that,' he said. 'But Becky found out about this, and she kicked up such a fuss back home that they did send a Navy Sea King in to take me and LCpl Alex Wood, who was also very close to Chris, to Bastion. So I was able to help carry him onto the plane.'

Still reeling from the death of his friend, Terry Holland managed to touch base with a colleagues at FOB Blenheim to find out what had happened.

'The company had gone out on a patrol to achieve some mission,' he said. 'There was an area of ground that the CO wanted covered, but they didn't have the manpower so they asked for a multiple, about eight men, to stand in overwatch in this area. Because they weren't allowing us to fire the mortars the mortar guys were fairly redundant, so they were tasked to do this job as regular infantryman.

'They were good, experienced soldiers, but they went out with just one radio, and Chris was carrying it. So when he was blown up they couldn't call for help. The other guys picked Chris up, because they weren't going to leave him, and extracted on foot, under fire. I don't know how far they had to go, but in that heat, even early in the morning, with the amount of equipment everyone carried, any distance is huge. And to do it with a guy who was seventeen stone makes it even worse.

'They did amazingly well, especially because they had other casualties. One guy was blinded, although not permanently. For a small group of guys, those mortar men definitely did the business. And it was comforting to know that the guys Chris was with when he died were all mortars.'

Because she lived on a military establishment, it was a simple matter to get the awful news to Becky Harrison. The knocking on her front door started early on that Sunday morning.

'It went on for a while,' she said, 'but it was so early that I thought it must be one of my friends. When I eventually went to the door, I saw them there. I saw these officers and I just *knew*, although I didn't want to admit it. It hadn't been that long since Chris had left... It didn't feel long enough for anything to have happened.

'I said "Hi!" to these men in a cheerful way, and one of them said, "Are you Mrs Harrison?"

'I said, "Yeah, is it about Chris?"

'I didn't want them to talk, because I knew what they were going to say. So I kept on asking them the same questions, "Is he at Bastion, then? Has he been flown back?"

'In the end, they just talked over me, and said, "He has been killed."

'I hardly remember anything of the rest of the day. Next thing I knew, it was suddenly night. The day had just disappeared.'

The knock on Gill and Martin Harrison's door came at around lunchtime.

'It was a normal lazy Sunday,' said Gill. 'Martin was on the computer, and I was watching the soaps on TV. I was wearing tatty old pyjamas and a dressing gown. There was a really loud knocking on the door – a real hammering. It was so loud that it seemed to shake the house. It literally made me jump.

'I got up and walked to the door, thinking, *Who the hell is that, knocking on my door on a Sunday?* I looked through the peephole and I saw a man in a pinstripe suit with slicked-back hair. I opened the door and there, with the man in the suit, was a marine with his green beret. I knew instantly, and I backed up to the stairs, and I was screaming and screaming, "Martin! Martin! No, no, please no, no!"

'Martin started to come down the stairs in just his underpants – I always tell him to wear pyjamas, but he won't. He quickly grabbed his dressing gown. The men didn't say anything, but they didn't need to. Martin shook the soldier's hand, and I heard him say, "How bad is it?"

'The soldier said, "I'm afraid it's fatal."

'I went running through to the lounge and ripped all of Chris's pictures off the wall and sat on my chair, holding them. I just had to have my pictures.'

Martin Harrison said, 'When you see them, you just know – he's either very seriously injured, or he's been killed. It's a moment in time that you never forget. You're in shock. The first instinct was to tell Russell. Fortunately, he lived fairly locally, so he came straight over. He was very business-like and supportive, making sure we were okay. He helped notify people, and then he stayed with us. He kept his grief private, and didn't talk about Chris a lot for a long time. They were very close, like best friends. In fact, just before the funeral Russell said to me that he was in awe of what a great man Chris had become. For Russell to say something like that is almost out of character, but it was from the heart.

'The marine left and the other guy stayed with us to act as a temporary family support officer. From being in a state of shock, we went straight into a mode of telling people who are close to us as soon as possible.

'Even though there was a news blackout, Chris's old school friends all knew by that evening – thanks to Facebook, I think. One of them called to say they were all gathering that night at Chris's favourite pub, The Essex Arms in Watford, so I went to meet them. It sort of helped, because you just don't know what to do with yourself in that situation. I was very touched by the number of them who'd got together. It was a sign of how close they all were.'

The Harrisons were soon on their way down to Taunton to be with Becky. They found her in 'a terrible state', said Gill, and being comforted by other military wives.

'Being with Becky was good for both of us,' she said. 'I just wanted to wrap her up in a blanket and bring her home. I was really bad myself, but perhaps looking after someone else was good for me.

'There was an MOD press officer working with Becky on a statement. He asked us if we would like to read it, and it referred to Chris as "a Royal Marine from the West Country." I said, "No, no, no! He was from Watford. It's got to say he was from Watford." I wanted his death to be reported in our local paper.'

Within a few days, Chris's body was flown home. His funeral was held two weeks later, and his family were able to see him in his coffin beforehand, which helped them a little. Russell took the opportunity to shake his brother's hand one final time – the same hand he had shaken a month or so earlier.

'That was strange for me,' he said. 'The difference between the two was incredible, but it was almost comforting that I could do it again. I shook his hand when he went away, and I shook it again when he came back.

'As we were sitting there, I promised him that I would look after Becky. I could see the devastation in mum and dad, but they were there for each other. Becky didn't have anyone. I tried to help her as much as I could. I guess that was good for me, too, because I didn't have to focus on myself.'

Martin and Becky attended the inquest. Gill did not feel up to it, but Martin believes that the experience, though very hard, gave him 'a little closure'.

'We'd heard mixed things about coroners,' he said, 'but he was very good. He actually contributed to Chris's legend, if you like. He said he was proud to be part of the process, and to learn more about Chris. He said what a wonderful guy Chris was, and even commented on how his strange dancing style made people laugh.'

[Chris Harrison had a bizarre 'party piece' dance all of his own invention, which he called 'The Lunge'. 'He could almost clear a dance floor with it,' said Martin. 'We saw him perform it at his wedding, and it was a very strange dance that no-one else could do, or would want to do.']

Chris Harrison had been a very popular Royal Marine, with a lot of very close friends in the Corps. At the end of the tour, his family were able to see those friends and grieve together.

'They were devastated,' said Martin. 'One of his best friends said he didn't know how he went on fighting on the frontline, because when he heard about Chris, he was just numb. A number of them left the Marines after that tour because things just weren't the same anymore.'

Cpl Terry Holland was one of those friends. The explosion that killed Chris Harrison also eventually ended Holland's career in the military. He came back from the tour, had three months off, and then completed the Junior Command course to secure his second stripe. Then he was posted to Special Forces Support Group, which was a huge privilege – soldiers are hand-picked for the role – and 'a bit of a buzz' for Holland.

But that IED was always at the back of his mind.

'It was when I started to find my feet in SFSG that I realised I couldn't do it anymore,' he said. 'It wasn't because of what I'd seen; it was more because of the helplessness I felt with IEDs. You can go through every possible measure to stop it happening, but they will still get you, and the damage they do is massive. The amount of energy that courses through you when an IED explodes is indescribable. I felt that a number of times, and I couldn't go through it again.

'In Afghan, we'd lost more guys in our location than they did anywhere else, and we had our hands tied behind our backs. There were points where our inherent right of self-defence was taken away from us, and I knew I couldn't allow something like that to happen again. I also knew that I couldn't be one of the guys who tries to avoid being sent on operations, and justifies it by saying he has a wife and children, or moves around various training establishments and the like, trying to be overlooked. I couldn't do that, and I knew that Chris would have been the same. He had no respect for people who shied away from doing their job.

'But, at the same time, I didn't have the appetite for it any more. I never joined to be a camp soldier, so I left. If I'd waited six more months I'd have been given a pay-off of several thousand pounds for doing half-service, but it wasn't worth it. That said, I've really struggled since leaving. Not financially, but emotionally and professionally.

You're given quite a lot of responsibility in the Marines, and to leave and then have very little is hard. You're no longer a marine or, unbelievably, a British commando any more, and people no longer expect the same things of you. It's almost like an anti-climax. There's also an issue of self-esteem. As a marine, you feel unbelievably proud of what you are, but you have to start again in civilian life. You define yourself by your occupation, and you have to find one that's as good as being a marine, and that's not easy.

'I worked in maritime security for a couple of years, and now I'm training in telecoms. It's a good opportunity, and I'm happy about it, because it gives me security, and career progression, and I'm learning something new. But I'm not in love with my job as I was when I was a marine. We had a reputation of being able to sort things out, and we were valued. It's harder to get that sense of value in civvie street. I feel sometimes that I'm always going to be someone who once *was* something, rather than someone who *is* something.

'I look back on previous tours of Afghanistan, and I think that we had amazing success at huge cost to the insurgents. I enjoyed those two earlier tours, although they were still very dangerous. We were doing everything we'd joined up to do. A lot of it was like the war movies, and the guys enjoyed it and even thrived on it. It was almost like a drug when there were no restrictions on you. But on that last tour we were restricted and the shoe was on the other foot. It didn't feel very good.

'The guys I worked with never had political agendas. Many of us didn't even vote, because it never seemed to make a difference. The government promises to increase spending in Afghanistan, and it might happen for a while, but then it stops. It's always the same old crap. So you just go and do what you are paid to do.

'I still keep in contact with Chris's family, and I think about Chris a lot. In fact, there probably hasn't been a day when I haven't had a thought about him. A lot of things remind me of Afghan, or the person I was in Afghan. Because we were different people there. You're zoned into the place twenty-four hours a day, and you can't just switch off. A lot of things remind me of it. It could be a car backfiring, or it could be a comment from someone that takes me back.

'Or it could be an advertisement for a film on the telly that makes

205

me think particularly of Chris. If he saw a film that impressed him, he'd milk it to death by talking about it, repeating lines, and so on. He loved *The Business*, which is a film with Danny Dyer about British gangsters in Spain. It was full of 80s music, which Chris loved. He could name all the music, when a song was a hit, who sang it, and so on. I have a great memory of him in Brunei. We had a few days off, so, at his instigation, we had a night out in partying in the jungle – all dressed up like Danny Dyer in *The Business* in these tight white shorts and sunglasses, with slicked back hair. And I also have happy memories of us just sitting around in our work office. We were such a close-knit group, and I think that's why so many of us left after Afghan. Chris wasn't there, and he left a gap that couldn't be filled. It was the end of an era, and the guys knew it wouldn't be the same again.'

* * *

IF HIS FRIENDS were distraught at the death of such a charismatic and impressive man, then it's not hard to imagine the overwhelming, shattering grief which engulfed his family.

Russell Harrison struggled with it for a long time. 'I think it was six months before I realised I needed help,' he said. 'I was angry, and it didn't take much to set me off. Everything seemed small compared to Chris. I ended up going to bereavement counselling which was really good for me.

'One time, when we were down in Taunton visiting Becky, I said to her, "Whatever you want, I'll support you."

'She told me then that Chris had said, "If anything happens to me, Russ will be there for you."

'Hearing that was a real comfort, and it meant a lot to me. I feel now that I've lived up to what he expected of me.

'I still think about Chris every day. Something will remind me of him, or I'll just want to think about him. It was unbearable at first, but now I feel great pride in him, and I feel more positive. I still miss him greatly, but my feelings are much more positive now. I want people to know about him.

'I hope Afghanistan has been worth it, although I don't know enough about what was achieved by my brother and the others. What is important for me is that the guys *tried* to make a difference. I think, even if people don't believe the war was worthwhile, they should be grateful for what my brother did, and others like him. They should remind themselves that he joined the Marines not knowing what wars he'd be involved in, but ready to give whatever was asked of him. I hope they recognise that.'

For Gill, the death of her younger son has been an unbearable burden to carry.

'Losing Chris has destroyed me,' she said. 'He's left a huge void, and we're not the same. It has come between me and Martin. It's hard to explain. Martin has often spoken about selling this house and moving somewhere else, because it's a big house and there are just the two of us. But I always said we'd only move if it was to be near Becky and Chris if they had children. And, of course, that can never be. So we'll stay here, because the boys were born here. This is our family home, and Chris is buried five hundred yards up the road. You'll only get me out of this house in a box.

'In the beginning I visited Chris's grave every day. But I don't go very often now. I've been to quite a few funerals, but they've all been cremations and, to my mind, the smoke goes up and they are there in the smoke. But when I go up to the cemetery, in my mind all I can see is his body. I literally cannot bear it. So Martin and I only go on certain days: the day he died, Remembrance Sunday, and his birthday. Apart from that, no. It hurts so much.

'The first year passed in a bit of a blur, and suddenly I thought, *Oh my God, it's been a whole year!* Then it's two years, and now it's over four years. But it's not getting any better. I feel worse now than I did when Chris died.

'I know some people who have lost children through illness, but if they're ill you know where the road is going to end, and sometimes it may be a blessed relief that your child is no longer suffering. And you're there, you can care for them, and look after them. It wasn't like that for us.'

One small moment of joy, mixed with pain, came on the first birthday Gill had following Chris's death. Before leaving for Afghanistan, he had written a card for his mother and given it to Becky for safekeeping.

'It's wonderful, in a way,' said Gill. 'Becky gave it to Martin when we were visiting her after Chris died, and she asked him to decide whether or not to give it to me on my birthday.

'Chris always sent lovely, lovely cards, and on my birthday I said to Martin, "I'm never going to get another card from him." I sat down, and he disappeared out of the room. Then he reappeared and gave me this envelope. He said, "Open it." I was just about to open it, then I turned it over and saw the little safety pin that Chris always drew on the back of his envelopes. I thought, *Oh my God!* So instead of ripping it open as I would normally, I went to the kitchen, got a knife, sliced it along the top, and pulled out this card.

'It was lovely. It said on the front, *For The Best Mummy in the World.* 'Inside he wrote, *To Mum. Sorry I can't be with you for your birthday. I will try to call though! Have a great day. Loads of love, C Harrison* [in signature form] + *Becky X X*

Just in case we forgot who he was, again!

'So that was really our last letter from Chris. I don't know how I could be so happy and yet so sad at the same time, but that's how I felt.'

The Harrisons now look after Chris's playful and lively dog, Wilson. He is a constant reminder of their lost son.

'We look at Wilson differently,' said Gill. 'Martin loves to have him because he reminds him of Chris, and looking after him keeps him busy. But seeing Wilson around reminds me that we only have him *because* we haven't got Chris.

'But then, to me, Chris is here with me all the time. I still feel he is here. He was killed, but I refuse to say I've lost him. He's still our son.'

Martin Harrison is coping with his own grief by trying to look forward.

'Gill and I are an old and long-married couple,' he said. 'We try to support each other, but we mourn Chris differently. Perhaps it's a man/woman thing. The memories are enough for me, and I'm determined that he must not be everything in my life, whereas for Gill it *is* everything in her life, and she wants it to be that way. I think mothers take the loss of a son much harder.

'My feeling is that Gill thinks more of Chris as a child, whereas I tend to think more of him as an adult. I feel a huge sense of pride in what Chris achieved in life. As I said at his funeral, I want to keep on celebrating him, because it's important that he's not forgotten.

'I like to promote his memory through the charitable things I do. I organise an annual Poppy Appeal charity dog walk around about Remembrance Sunday in his memory, and it's always very well-supported. Gill is very friendly with the Chairman of the local Royal British Legion branch, and they helped us to organise a war memorial in the centre of Watford, dedicated to those servicemen killed since the Second World War. There is now a bench there with Chris's name on it. It's nice that other people think about him, and not just us.

'But you don't recover from losing someone in circumstances like that, you just hope to learn to live with it. Time stopped at the point they knocked on our door. It dominates your life and becomes part of your identity – almost as if your personality has become defined by the death of your son.

'I don't like to be obsessive about it. And I like to think we still have a life. Then again, we can't help thinking about what might have been. I know he and Becky wanted children. And it's hard, because we're constantly reminded of Chris. Especially on the anniversaries. We have his picture on our computer as a screensaver, and we have photos around us. Lots of things make us think of him, every day. Even walking Wilson reminds me of him. He's not always the most obedient dog and he's sometimes a bit rebellious, like his owner, and whenever we went to see Chris and Becky in Taunton we'd walk the dog together.

'But then, I *want* to be reminded of those things. I walk the dog through the woods at the back of the cemetery, and Chris is right on the edge of it, so I stop there from time to time.

'I like to keep the grave tidy. I quite often go up and place some flowers there. It's a military grave, and they're all supposed to be finished with plain grass, but I've bent the rules slightly and we do have sunken vases for flowers and two special vase holders given to us by 40 Cdo. And we have a bench opposite Chris's grave where we can find some peace, just sitting and thinking. Neither Gill nor I are religious, though Becky is, and Chris was a Christian in his own way. He would go to church with Becky. We thought she'd lost her faith when Chris was killed, but she's got it back again.'

209

As for the war itself, Martin is clear in his mind that it was a mistake. After talking to Chris's comrades, he is just as certain that the policy of 'courageous restraint', and of carrying out high-profile 'reassurance patrols', were foolish ideas.

'The truth is that I think the Afghanistan conflict was ill-conceived and there seems to be no cohesive long-term strategy,' he said. 'Above all, though, no cause or war could ever be worth our beloved younger son's life.

'Neither Gill nor I are ever in favour of war for any reason, and I know that our sons didn't join the military because of any influence from us. But we accept that both Chris and Russell chose to do a job that could take them to war, and we're proud of both of them for finding things in life that they were good at, and loved doing.'

The loss of her husband left Becky with a huge, aching void for a very long time.

'The military were good,' she said, 'and when it first happened I had a lot of support. I had a family support officer, WO Ceri Lewis, who was amazing. And he stayed in touch with me for about two years afterwards, which was good because I really needed the support later on. I also got a lot of support from the girls around me in the married quarters area, but that can't last forever and, after a while, I was left pretty much on my own, apart from Gill and Martin and my own family. My mum came down from Watford when she could. Initially, she stayed for a week or so before going back home, but then she came down often after that, until I moved. They were so upset. My dad in particular was really, really fond of Chris.

'Things started to get a lot worse for me, and it was quite a while before they got better. I was quite a long way from my parents and my two brothers. I think I needed to move away from Taunton. I needed to be back near my family, but at the time I just didn't understand that. I think I wanted to stay in Taunton because Chris and I had had our married life there, had planned our future there, and if I moved away I'd be stepping away from that. In fact, I did myself a lot of damage by staying there.

'But you don't always think. I just wanted to be near where Chris and I had been. I was trying to continue a life that we had known together, but alone. That's impossible, but no-one could tell me that. I got really lonely, and I just needed my family.

'I moved away from Taunton in the summer of 2012, and I've been doing a lot better since. I now have lots of support around me. When Chris and I were together I was a nurse, but I gave that up. I did go back to nursing for six months after he was killed, but I didn't enjoy it. So now I'm studying for a psychology degree and a counselling diploma and I'm planning to become a counsellor.

'I had six sessions of counselling myself after Chris was killed, paid for by the MOD. Then I had more sessions at my own cost. I didn't really benefit from it, but that wasn't their fault, it was more to do with me and where I was at that time. I saw a lady from CRUSE, the bereavement counselling charity, and they were good. Then I had more counselling, and that helped a lot more, I think because I was then ready to accept help. I think I had accepted by then that *everything* had changed in my life, and it was as if I was starting again.

'I've maintained a close relationship with Chris' parents, and that is really important to me. Chris was close to his parents. We all got on so well when Chris was alive, and I can't see why we shouldn't now.

'My favourite memory of Chris is the day we got engaged. It was a Friday – September 7, 2007, which was the third anniversary of us first going out together. Chris had finished work early and we decided we'd take a picnic and go walking in the Quantocks. Sometimes in relationships, it's about other people as well, but this day was just about the two of us. It was a lovely afternoon. He was being a bit funny, and I had a suspicion that something was going on. So he popped the question to me during that picnic. I was surprised, although I had an inkling. My immediate reaction was, "Yeah, of course!" I went back and called my mum and he called his parents and everyone was really happy. Then we went out for dinner, and we probably got a bit drunk.

'But I also remember generally just how funny he was. I remember about two months before he went to Afghan I was a bit depressed because we'd been trying for a family for a long time, without success. But after a chat with him I felt better. I don't recall exactly what he said, but after he'd talked to me for a little while, I was like, "Okay, yeah, right!" And I felt fine again. I don't know how he could do that. You could never fail to be happy around him.

'Nevertheless, the fact that we didn't have children is a huge regret. It's massive. Life is never going to be the way it should have been.'

LANCE BOMBARDIER MARK CHANDLER
D BATTERY, 3rd REGIMENT ROYAL HORSE ARTILLERY
APRIL 26, 1977 – JUNE 8, 2010

FATE IS A CRUEL and fickle mistress, and never more so than for soldiers in time of war: she makes eternal brothers of men, and then rips them apart on the merest whim.

LBdr Mark 'Bing' Chandler, Cpl 'Baz' Barrowcliff and Capt Johnny Mercer were three such brothers. Ignoring the niceties of rank, in the heat and fire of Afghanistan these men forged a bond – as a fire support team that was often danger-close with the enemy – that could never be broken. And yet it was shattered in a moment by a Taliban bullet.

For most who join the Army it is the realisation of a childhood dream. Mark Chandler was different. He had never considered a life in green until he turned twenty-five. He was perfectly content with his job as a welder in the picturesque Cotswolds town of Nailsworth, and had just bought a house with his girlfriend. A happy-ever-after ending beckoned. 'His ambition,' said his mother, Ann, 'was to be a married man with 2.4 children, a dog and a cat, and a house with an apple tree. Just like anyone else.'

But then Mark's girlfriend decided she wanted to go to Australia for a year, on her own.

'He said, "If that's all you feel about our relationship, we'll sell the house and you can go,"' said his father, Mike. 'He came back to live with us, and then one day he came home from work and said, "I know what I'm going to do, I'm joining the Army." We were amazed. We'd never seen any hint of that.'

212

The following year, Mark was a member of D Battery 3rd Regiment Royal Horse Artillery – the RHA comprising the elite regiments of the Royal Artillery – where he had acquired the nickname 'Bing', after the character Chandler Bing in the TV sitcom *Friends*, and had fitted into military life like a natural.

'He never looked back,' said Mike. 'And going into the Army changed him. I remember looking at him as we took him to the station once, and you could just *tell* he was a soldier. D Battery Royal Horse Artillery is a very professional unit and a close-knit family, and it can be difficult to become quickly accepted, but Mark was instantly popular. Everyone said he was always on top of his game. He'd needed more structure in his life,.and the Army gave it to him. He needed something to aim for, and the Army also gave him that.'

Mark had a 'best book' – a diary that recruits were encouraged to keep in training, in which he recorded his private thoughts and feelings. In one entry, read by his parents after his death, he wrote, *I think about home and my friends, but I'm not at all homesick*. In another, he talked about meeting up with his ex-girlfriend for a drink one night. *She still goes on about how great I am*, he said, *so why did we split up? I don't know. But I'm not regretting what I'm doing now. I'm still feeling good about the change of lifestyle.*

The change of lifestyle included learning winter sports – he became an excellent skier, and was the British Army luge champion two years running – and taking more pride in his appearance.

'He stopped being slouchy,' said Ann. 'I'd do his ironing for him when he was home, and he'd panic about "tramlines" – two creases in a trouser leg, instead of one. They get hauled over the coals for that. I'd say, "You can do it if you like," but he'd say, "No, mum, you do it... Just be careful."'

Their son hadn't had the easiest time at school. 'His IQ was fine,' said Mike, 'but he had a type of word blindness. It wasn't dyslexia, but, as the experts put it, they had to teach him a new language. We hadn't noticed because his older brother, Stephen, did all the talking for him. He went to a special school for a couple of terms, and at the end of that we wouldn't have been able to guess there'd been anything wrong with him. They did a very good job.'

There was a hidden silver lining to this. 'His homework took him

213

longer than it did other children,' said Ann. 'I used to say, "You can go out and play, and you'll end up being kept back a year, or you can do your homework and stay with your mates." So from the age of about six, he got used to having to work, and he never lost that work ethic.'

Mark was never clingy. Indeed, while in basic training, Ann was shocked to receive a Mother's Day card from her son – the first she could remember him sending her. Under close questioning, he confessed sheepishly that it had been posted on the orders of his instructing NCOs! And once he had arrived at 3 RHA in Hohne, Germany, months could go by without his parents hearing from him. It didn't mean he didn't care – he loved them deeply. He just didn't feel the need to say so every day.

'Now and then he'd call, and say, "I'm sorry for not ringing more often, mum,"' said Ann. 'I'd say, "As long as you're fine, that's okay." When he was based in Germany, there was a whole year when we didn't see him. He called to ask if we would mind if he stayed away over Christmas and went skiing. I said, "No, you carry on."

'Whenever we did see him, he'd mostly talk about the Army, and his mates. Like the lad who ran off with a Russian prostitute… Mark said he'd rather have the military police chasing him than the Russian mafia!'

But when it mattered, Mark was there. While he was in Hohne, his mother discovered she had cancer.

'I rang him one morning to tell him about his mum's diagnosis,' said Mike. 'He sounded a bit non-committal, but at about five that afternoon the phone rang, and it was Mark, at Cheltenham station, wanting a lift. He'd told his RSM about Ann, and they'd given him immediate compassionate leave. Within half an hour, he was heading for Hanover airport. He was a very compassionate chap. He was always good with us, and never caused us any trouble at all.'

In his early days in the RHA, he spent more than two years as driver to the-then CO, Lt Col Ian Bell. Bell, later promoted to full colonel, and now working in a senior ISTAR [*intelligence, surveillance, target acquisition, and reconnaissance*] role with UK land forces, remembers a 'very impressive' soldier.

'Mark was a quiet, mature and steady person who did what he thought was right,' said Col Bell. 'I considered him a friend. I saw him several times after I left the regiment, and it was always great to catch up. Had he still been around in ten years' time, I'm sure we would have met at reunions, had a beer, and talked about our families.

'He was my driver in Germany, but also a bit of a fixer. He would stay in the background so people didn't notice him doing anything, but he had a really excellent knack of making sure that things happened for me and the RSM. It helped that he was mature and slightly older than most of the other guys. I appreciated what he did, and I trusted him implicitly. He knew my family, too, and he was the only person that my wife trusted to drive her and the kids when they needed a lift.

'He had a great ability to engage with life to the full, and he stopped others sitting around the barracks. When he had time off, he'd often take young soldiers away to various parts of Germany to do things. I thought he was very impressive, such that, when I left the regiment, we were looking at different career paths that might better utilise his talents. We looked particularly at the fire support teams, which was in fact what he went to do. He was absolutely the sort of soldier who was required in that high-pressure environment.'

It had rapidly become clear that Mark Chandler's early educational problems were not a brainpower issue. Calling down air or artillery fire *under* fire is a demanding task, and not one for those who do not possess an agile mind which functions well under the most severe pressure.

'That job combines the ability to see the enemy and what is going on around you, while controlling a significant amount of the firepower, with the ability to strike as appropriate,' said Ian Bell. 'Forward observers are often in massively high-pressure situations. They may be under fire, while needing to understand the locations of civilians, the enemy, and our own troops. They're often speaking to aircraft, or people on the ground ten or fifteen miles away, and are making very significant decisions about the proportionality of their actions and the potential for collateral damage. They may be watching one viewing screen while pumping data into another, or sending it over voice, while lying in a wet ditch, being shot at and shooting back. And even though they may be using modern electronic equipment, they need to be able to fall back on procedures that don't rely on electronics. It is a really high pressure, difficult job, and Mark was well suited to it because he was bright, agile, worked really hard, and he got on with people. Furthermore, he could appreciate the bigger picture.'

At ease with generals and squaddies alike, Mark Chandler was offered the chance to drive General Sir David Richards, later Chief of the Defence Staff. Some would have killed for such a plum job, but he turned it down in favour of that altogether more thrilling and dangerous career – as an FST member in Afghanistan.

* * *

CAPT JOHNNY MERCER was on his third tour of Afghanistan, and it wasn't getting any easier. In large part, this was because the Taliban had changed tactics. Now, they rarely engaged the British Army in firefights – because they invariably lost, badly. Instead, they were sowing IEDs like confetti.

Mercer still didn't rate them very highly. 'If I'm honest,' he said, 'I thought the enemy could be poor. They had the local knowledge to cause great damage, but they didn't use it. I remember men engaging me and then just getting up and running without covering fire, which made it easier for me. But I often sympathised with their plight. They weren't well-trained, and they didn't seem to have a basic understanding, on a number of levels, because they had no education. If I was a young lad there, and someone offered me twenty dollars to fire a weapon at a patrol base, I'd probably do it; that's a month's earnings, and some of them were doing it so their families could survive.

'But while some of the foot soldiers were clearly amateurs, I also fought some of the people pulling the strings, the real cowards at the highest levels of the Taliban and Al Qaeda in Afghanistan, who indulge in extreme brutality; the very worst that mankind has to offer. There are and will always be some very dark people who do some very dark things. These people cannot be reconciled, and they need to be dealt with by the security forces.'

Mercer's job was to lead a small fire support team, calling down artillery fire, mortars or air assets on enemy positions in order to support infantry patrols out on the ground. Some FST officers find it easier to do this work from the relative calm of a PB, but Mercer preferred to go out with the patrols. It was better to have his own eyes-on, he felt, and better, too, for trust between his team and the infanteers. His team was small, just himself, Baz Barrowcliff and Mark Chandler. Mark was qualified to control guns and mortars, Baz to control fast jets. Capt Mercer – who was able to control all such assets – was in overall command.

'My initials are on the shell or bomb as it comes in,' he said. 'I control all the situational awareness, and make sure I'm happy with the appropriate fire support for the situation. My job was to produce the effect on the ground. If it needed to be done in haste, I'd do it myself without the other guys, but one of them would always check me. I was always chattering on the net, being as proactive as I could in lining up assets to deal with a potential contact. It also gave me a chance to be more courageous than perhaps I naturally am, as I was always busy and always thinking.'

He needed men alongside him whom he could trust utterly, and Mark Chandler was just such a one.

'Mark, Baz and I just got on very well,' he said. 'Some people join the Army for different reasons, but we were there because we wanted to be soldiers. We understood each other, and the risks we were prepared to take and the risks we were not prepared to take.

'Mark was the perfect soldier – a selfless man who would just as readily volunteer to empty the bins as go out on a patrol. Under fire, Mark would be sat in the ditch next to me smiling, seemingly without a care in the world. It was an absolute privilege to command this example of a man.'

On their return from an exhausting, twelve-hour contact, Mark would quickly clean his own kit and then – conscious that his boss had paperwork to complete – would clean Capt Mercer's, too. A rare thing to do in the heat and dust and filth of Afghanistan, but it meant the team got to knock off together.

Baz Barrowcliff and Mark Chandler were the perfect men to have out on the ground. 'There's a large technical side to our job,' said Mercer. 'You're doing arithmetic on the hoof, and it's a huge responsibility. But those guys were cool. It wasn't just running around with a gun, although there were times when we had to fight our way out with our personal weapons. We liked working together – we worked with varying standards of soldiers, and we felt that, if something was to go wrong, we were best placed to get ourselves out of it.'

Mark Chandler had earlier told his parents that he had specifically requested to work alongside Johnny Mercer.

'Everyone said, "You must be nuts! He's impossible to work for!"' said Mike Chandler. 'But they got on like a house on fire. Johnny had a bit of a reputation for being difficult, but Mark said he was the kind of man you wanted on your side in a punch-up.'

Mercer admits to having perhaps been 'quite an arrogant young man' in his early days, but believes the confidence that came with it might well have given his men that sense of security required to conduct close-quarter battle with the Taliban.

'The soldiers appreciated it, I think,' he said. 'They thought they'd be okay with me; they would enter more dangerous terrain because they thought I had the skills to extract them. It almost became an act; pretending I was braver than I was. And Mark's loyalty was absolutely unquestionable. He was prepared to do anything for me, and I for him. That is a humbling thing, and I'll be forever privileged. But it does have its responsibilities. Soldiers relying on you alone to extract them under fire, day after day, month after month… I found that quite stressful. And there is clearly some guilt when it goes wrong.'

The FST and their allied infantry, Anzio Coy, 1 Lancs, were based in PB Khaamar, in Nad-e Ali.

This is a town and wider district of some 75,000 people which forms one point of a triangle with Lashkar Gah to the south and Camp Bastion to the west. It had long been a Taliban stronghold. An old crane overlooking the main canal through the town had often been festooned with the bodies of those hanged for their failure to support the insurgents, and it was the scene of much fierce fighting. By the time British forces finally withdrew in 2013, it had a thriving bazaar, schools and health clinics, but, on the debit side of the ledger, fifty-two soldiers would have lost their lives in bringing those benefits to the locals. The governor of Nad-e Ali, Mohammad Ibrahim, would pay tribute to them, saying, 'The sacrifices that have been made by your soldiers… we appreciate that, and will never forget that.'

One of the more infamous of those sacrifices was the murder in

November 2009 of five British soldiers by a traitorous Afghan policeman, who open-fired on them at Checkpoint Blue 25 in the town without warning. Another six British soldiers and two Afghan policemen were wounded in the incident.

With incidents like that playing on their minds, the soldiers of Anzio Coy called the area 'The Jungle'.

Khaamar was 'austere', said Mercer. 'When we first got there, we washed out of a well. There were no showers. We eventually rigged up a crap shower, with shower bags. We were on rations out of a box for six or seven months, with very little fresh food. I was sleeping on a camp cot under a mosquito net. But we had an exceptional team in Bastion keeping us well supplied in all aspects. A helicopter came in every three or four days, but it was not predictable, and it was guaranteed to come under fire. The Royal Logistic Corps did CLPs [*combat logistic patrols*], and if there was someone important coming in or going out by helicopter we'd try to ensure they also brought in mail and essential kit. You plan a long time in advance, and we had three to four months' of ammunition at the base.'

Despite the obvious lack of home comforts, Johnny Mercer was not complaining. 'I didn't have a problem with it,' he said. 'I suppose, yes, there were two sides to the Afghan deployment – those of us who had to be in the FOBs and PBs, and those who were at Bastion. But even in Bastion troops and commanders were away from their families. And it was only relative comfort. Still not much fun, working incredible hours to make sure we were best-equipped and looked after to carry the fight.'

As the fighting season began, the area quickly hotted up.

'The day after the poppy harvest finished, the Taliban tried to get over the front gate and over-run the PB,' he said. 'It was a Sunday morning, and I was in bed. That's how close they were. And whenever we walked out of the gate, the action could happen at any time.

'The over-arching task was to secure areas so that others could get on with the business of bringing good governance to the place, and introduce schools and clinics, that kind of thing. Often, we were trying to take the same bits of ground day after day. It could be depressing, but you just had to get on with it.'

* * *

ON THE MORNING of June 8, 2010, the FST were out in support of another dawn patrol to reassure the locals and push enemy fighters back. They had an Afghan special forces 'Tiger Team' with them, and had pushed out into an area criss-crossed with irrigation canals and single track roads built in the 1970s by American engineers.

At first, progress was easy, and children were playing happily in the shade of a number of walls and homes dotted around. But then came a classic combat indicator: women began rounding up the children and herding them away. Simultaneously, Taliban radio chatter intensified. An attack was clearly imminent. As they pushed forward over a drainage ditch, the soldiers were able – through Mercer's overhead surveillance – to identify the compound where most of the enemy fighters were located.

Mercer busied himself in checking communications with his artillery and with a nearby helicopter.

'I needed to be sure that we were ready to call in support,' he said. 'Meanwhile, the infantry and Mark and Baz discussed a plan. Once I had finished, I said to Mark, "What's the score, mate?"'

The plan was to leave a reserve *in situ*, and to send the Tiger Team north, in a standard infantry advance-to-contact, as a small FST/1 Lancs six-man team closed in on the insurgent compound. The hope was that the Taliban would engage the Tigers; with their focus drawn, the British troops could smash their way into the compound and take them on at close quarters.

'I briefed the helicopter and the artillery, had an even briefer chat with the ground commander because I trusted him, and then we went for it,' said Mercer. 'I was in front, then came Mark, then Baz. We got to a junction on this narrow track where we were going to flick north and close with the insurgents. The first three blokes crossed the road, then me. Mark was just on my shoulder – protecting me, as always. We always remained closer than was tactically ideal, because we needed to be together to do our jobs.'

Unfortunately, they were confronted by a classic problem of fighting in Afghanistan, indeed against any insurgent force. There were men nearby in traditional garb, but there was no way of distinguishing innocent farmers from Taliban fighters with AK47s secreted in their robes or lying by their feet.

'It's not a classic, face-to-face battle,' said Mercer. 'Often, they open up from twenty metres away, and they look like civvies right up until then. As we progressed the attack, we knew there were people there, but not necessarily that they were Taliban. We thought they were in a row of buildings, but not in this particular building twenty-five metres or so away.

'I remember it as if it were yesterday. I started crossing the road. As I got to the second wheel rut, we were engaged from twenty to thirty metres away by multiple automatic weapons. Mark and myself were the only two visible to what was now the enemy.'

Amazed that he himself had not been shot, Johnny Mercer hit the ground. Then he heard Baz Barrowcliff shout, 'Man down!'

Mercer whipped around. Cpl Barrowcliff was in the ditch on the other side of the track, and Mark Chandler was lying motionless, face down, in the dirt road.

'Baz shouted again, "Boss, boss! Man down, man down!"' said Mercer. 'Mark was a matter of feet from me. He was motionless, and there was not a lot of blood, so I knew it might be an immediate fatality. I immediately jumped on the radio to engage the enemy.'

He had a battery of 105mm artillery some twelve kilometres away, and – desperate to snatch the initiative back from the Taliban, so as to create time and space to get to Mark – decided to call them in with high explosive shells to within eighty metres of his own position with his first round. This was a lot closer than normal, and the use of HE shells was also a rarity at the time – under Gen McChrystal's policy of 'courageous restraint', Mercer was firing an awful lot of fairly innocuous smoke shells that summer.

'Typically, your first round would be four hundred metres away from you,' he said. 'The idea is that you fire into an open area, and then adjust as required to creep the shells into the target. The shells should be accurate, assuming they use the same ammunition and haven't moved the artillery pieces, but it's a sensible precaution. But we were under a lot of pressure. In an ambush, most casualties are taken in the first four or five seconds. The enemy have engaged you at a time and place of their choosing, now you need to wrestle that initiative back, or take more casualties. And I had confidence in the accuracy of the guns. On my quieter days, I drove into the desert and spent lot of time zeroing them, so I knew with a high degree of certainty where the shells would land. I always made sure, whatever I was dropping, that I was closest to where it would land, to show that confidence to the blokes I was with. Additionally, on this occasion we were perpendicular to the flight of the shell [so shrapnel would splash away from them].'

The order was given and the rounds fired, giving Mercer an uncomfortable few moments.

'There's always that scary fifteen seconds when the shells are in the air,' he said. 'I can only compare it to getting an envelope containing some news you've been waiting for. It could be good news or bad news, and you won't know until you open the envelope. It's just that, with artillery, if it's bad news it's very bad news. But it goes with the territory. You can get more precise weapons than a 105mm gun, but they take time. With guns, the flash-to-bang time is so quick. That's why artillery is still the god of war.'

Unfortunately, even gods of war need comms, and Mercer nownow found he was in a dead spot, unable to talk to the battery. Frustrated beyond belief, he got through to the patrol commander on the local net, told him about the casualty, asked for covering fire to extract him, and then ran out into the Taliban bullets.

'Bing was quite a big guy,' he said. 'Baz was struggling to pull him into cover by one foot, and I could see the rounds going through the reeds above Baz's head. I thought he was about to be killed in front of me. I heard him saying, "He's dead, boss, he's fucking dead!", and just then Bing's body flipped over towards me. I could see his eyes. They were open, and I knew he'd been killed.

'I told Baz to leave him, that I would run across the road and we would pull him in together. I had a machine gunner in front of me, and I remember screaming at him to engage the enemy. But he was looking at me over his shoulder, helmet awry, eyes glazed over. He'd just gone. He'd frozen. I lost it with him. I yelled, "Get the fucking rounds down, now!" and then moved towards him to grab his weapon, which was far more powerful than mine. He faced up the track and put a burst of three rounds down. I thought, For fuck's sake, I'm just *going to have to go!* I lost it at him again to give me covering fire, and he again tried to, but this time he only got one round down before his weapon jammed. At that precise moment I'd just stepped out and couldn't return. I thought, *Shit! This is going to sting! It's all over!*

'I thought that if I got hit and wasn't killed outright, the chances were it would be in the legs, so I consciously ran across in such a way that my momentum would carry my body into the ditch with Baz, and he'd at least be able to treat me. It's like running past a winger in a game of rugby: with momentum, you might still just get across the tryline.'

Remarkably, Mercer made it unscathed to the ditch, and he and Baz managed to pull Mark Chandler down next to them. They lugged him to the cover of a nearby building, hoping against hope that they would be able to give him some kind of first aid. 'I took his helmet and body armour off,' said Mercer, 'and looked for blood. I got around the back of his neck and found the hole where bullet exited, but I couldn't identify an entry wound. Later, I did, just a small scorched wound under his left eye.

'The Taliban go ape-shit if they think they've killed someone. Everybody comes out to have a go. Within two minutes, we got engaged again from another two firing points from the east and the south. It was going to go all wrong. We were surrounded.'

As dozens of rounds zipped overhead, a young medic – LCpl Gemma Owens – risked her life to race over to Mercer's position.

'She was in a state,' he said, 'but she was a credit to her profession. In a horrific situation, she pretty much kept her cool, and went through her drills. I didn't think they would help, but she was the medic, not me. I helped her attempt CPR, but it became clear that it was doing more harm than good. *That's it*, I thought. *It's over*. I grabbed Gemma's hands, which were now soaked in Bing's blood, and shouted at her. "Enough, Corporal Owens! I'm telling you, enough!" I called her Corporal Owens so she remembered where she was. "Gather up your stuff, and we'll extract from here."

'At that point, we were engaged *again*, from closer in, to the north where we had just been. In my position, I was the senior rank on these patrols, but I always focused on Joint Fires – my primary role. I was always there for advice to the JNCOs, but I wanted them to make the

223

tactical decisions. I was more experienced, but they were infanteers and I wasn't. I always had them call me by my first name, to emphasise that fact. But there was a real threat of actually getting over-run. I told everyone there, "Right, fucking listen to me. We need to get this guy out of here now, otherwise we won't get back."'

'Everyone there' was three or four UK soldiers. The small reserve force of four or five 1 Lancs men had bravely fought their way over, but had then extracted almost immediately under the mistaken belief – in the chaos of the contact – that the party was ready to go, and was following.

'Bing wasn't even on the stretcher at that point,' said Mercer. 'Baz was heroic, as usual, but I could see the enormity of what had just happened was starting to have an emotional effect, and I needed to focus him. I said, "Look, mate, we'll be okay. I'll extract him with three others, but you need to cover my arse against this incoming fire." Without hesitation, he advanced alone ten metres towards the enemy, into their fire, and began returning fire. Massively brave, I could have cried with pride.

'Eventually the extraction party consisted of Mark, the medic, the interpreter, and me, and one other soldier. Baz was our only real covering fire. I think people sometimes think these battles involve large numbers, but often they're not like that, it's just a few young men and women fighting for their lives, hoping to live to tell the tale. I manhandled Mark onto a stretcher rather unceremoniously. The interpreter picked up Mark's weapon. He didn't even need to be there. If anyone says, "All the Afghans are terrible," that's bollocks. This guy was prepared to give up his life for Mark. He thought all his Christmases had come at once. At last, a chance to kill some of the Taliban who'd been trying to kill him. I took the safety catch off, and made him point it away from me. Then I said, "Guys we're just going to have to go!"'

They pepper-potted as best they could, struggling with the dead weight of LBdr Chandler.

'I remember seeing these fuckers engaging me from a house on the side that me and the interpreter were on,' said Mercer. 'I remember running along, carrying the stretcher, me and the interpreter both firing at the house with one arm. It's almost impossible to hit anything like that, but you've got to try. I actually wrote him a citation, but I think it got lost in the maelstrom that is the British Army's paperwork.'

During one pause for breath on the 800-metre extraction, Mercer finally managed to get through to the guns.

'I opened up with four 105mm high explosive shells into the field a hundred and fifty metres to our north,' he said. 'I couldn't drop them into the building, because I knew there were women and children in and amongst the guys shooting us. Eventually, we met up with the QRF and the Tiger Team, so we actually had numbers, about fifteen of us. I had good comms now to both artillery and air support, and I started engaging the main enemy position with artillery rounds. Again, I didn't want to hit the house directly, but I was trying to force any squirters [*Taliban who were running or 'squirting' from the target*] to another firing point where I could engage them with an Apache I was talking to on another net.

'We started running towards a main road where the armoured vehicles were, but now under the cover of large artillery explosions to our rear. The main patrol was carrying Mark, and Baz and I were at the back doing individual fire-and-manoeuvre. We had to cover the last 200 metres like this. I suppose we were under fire right up to when we got close to the armoured vehicle column. Just as we were finally getting close, still twenty or thirty yards from safety, Baz ran out of ammunition. He was screaming at me to put down covering fire so he could get in. I ran out into the field to draw the fire, seeking some cover behind what looked like a small mound of earth. But when I got there it was just dry stacked poppies from the opium harvest, so I just emptied my entire magazine into the two firing points that continued to engage. That enabled Baz to get to the vehicles, and by the time I got there the contact was broken. We had helicopters coming on target, and the insurgents were running away at the sound of the Apache.

'I wanted to lie Mark down in one of the armoured vehicles, but it wasn't long enough, so I got in – I'd had my assets taken off me by my fire co-ordination cell – picked him up like a baby, put him on my lap and cradled him, while someone shut the door on us. It was just me and Mark in there for the forty-odd minutes it took to get back to the PB. I was shaking him a little bit, and talking to him. It was pretty harrowing, really. Every soldier's death is terrible, but when it's your mate, someone you've laughed and cried with, had coffee and a smoke with every morning, and fought for your lives together, it's very, very different.

'He didn't feel as warm as he would have if he was alive, but he didn't feel cold, either. It's strange when somebody has just died. It's not black-and-white by any stretch. I kept feeling for a pulse and thinking, *Have I got this wrong?*'

* * *

UNFORTUNATELY, JOHNNY MERCER had not got it wrong.

At their Cotswolds home, Ann and Mike Chandler had risen early and were picking at a breakfast of scrambled eggs on toast.

'I said to Mike, "I don't know what's wrong with me, but I can't eat this,"' said Ann. 'I took a couple of sips of coffee and I said, "I can't drink this, either." It might have been my cancer tablets, but it was also about the time Mark was killed.'

A little while later, as Ann got started on a pile of ironing, there was a knock on the door.

'I looked out the kitchen window and saw two youngish chaps in dark suits,' said Mike. 'I thought they were Mormons, and if I ignored them they'd go away. But they carried on knocking, and Ann suddenly said, "It might be the military."

'Of course, I then shot through and opened the door, and it was these two Army chaps. I knew why they were there. It must be an awful job. The first thing they said was, could they get us a cup of tea, and was there anyone we would like them to call? I said, "No, all we want to know is, is he dead?"

'They said, "Yes, he is. He was killed at six o' clock our time."

'There was nothing to say. It was just bloody awful. It just wipes your mind blank. I guess I was telling myself this wasn't happening. I was just staring into a void. After they'd gone, Ann and I just sat and looked each other and thought, *What do we do now?* We couldn't believe he wasn't coming back. Sometimes, even now, we look at his pictures, and we think he's just gone outside and he'll be back in a minute.'

'There's no plan for this,' said Ann. 'Myriad things come to mind. The main thing was what a great loss Mark had suffered, and that we wouldn't see him again. We hadn't seen him for months, and now we weren't going to see him again, ever. You just cope with it as best you can. Each person has too much suffering to deal with. It's too much. We phoned Mark's brother, Stephen. I was concerned the news would leak out. I said to him, "Something's happened. Can you come over?" He wanted to know what it was, so I told him. I said, "You can spend time here, or we can come to you." He said, "Mum, I just want to be on my own and work it out." We're a close family, but not a cloying one. Stephen drank too much whiskey that day, and he called a few of his mates, who plied him with even more whiskey. I think he slept the sleep of the just that night. He was the big brother who taught Mark to read, to write, to walk, to skateboard, to ride a bike… For two or three days, he was inconsolable, though he eventually got out of it all right. He can talk about it now quite dispassionately. As a family, we talk about Mark quite a lot.'

Mike and Ann are still struck by the mind-numbing speed with which everything happened. Mark was killed on June 8, 2010, his body was flown home on June 10, and he was buried on June 23. At the repatriation ceremony, they were introduced by their visiting officer [WO2 Paul Corkhill] to Mark's commanding officer, the RSM, the adjutant, and one of Mark's friends.

'After about twenty minutes, it was as if we had known them all our lives,' said Ann. 'They were fascinated to find that we could actually laugh about some memories from Mark's life. Everyone was so very sombre, and I thought, *Perhaps we're wrong; perhaps we shouldn't remember the fun times?* It was a bit surreal, really.'

Hundreds attended Mark Chandler's funeral at the Garrison Church of St Michael, in Tidworth, Wilts. His family took the decision to bury Mark there so that his mates – many of whom were and are based at Tidworth – could visit his grave. The wake in the officers' mess at Larkhill was 'more like a celebration', said Mike. 'We met some amazing people. They'd come up and put their arms around us – there were so many that we couldn't talk to all of them. We've been in touch with a lot since. The experience has brought out a lot of love and friendship.

'And after the rest of Mark's team came back we met many of them, including Tom Platt, his battery sergeant major. He looked like an angry pit-bull, with tattoos all over him, but he was actually the nicest of guys. He couldn't do enough for us.'

Mike and Ann had not thought for a moment that their son would die in Afghanistan.

'I was worried that he might get injured,' said Mike. 'We knew it was very dangerous. They were in camps behind tumbledown walls, miles from medical help. Every week brought reports of soldiers being killed. If your son's a soldier in those circumstances and you're not apprehensive, you should be. But never in my worst nightmares did I think he'd be killed.'

Mark himself dealt with the risk in his own characteristically humorous way.

'I remember him hovering around me one day,' said Ann. 'I said, "What's going on, Mark?" He said he'd just worked out that if he lost a limb he'd get into the GB Paralympic Winter Sports team. "For God's sake," I said. "You're going to be fine!"'

A few days later, she said goodbye to her son for the last time, as Mike prepared to drive him to the station for his train back to camp.

'I couldn't fit in the car because of his kit,' she said. 'So I stayed at home. He saw me crying as they left, which I didn't normally do, and he said to his dad, "Why's mum crying?" Mike said, "Just work it out." And off they went. I was really looking forward to the man that this war was going to reveal. I knew it would strip anybody right down to their basics. And I know he had a great time out there. I asked Johnny Mercer if they were enjoying their war, and he laughed, and said, "Actually, we were having a super time. We were doing a difficult job, but we were doing it well, and enjoying it."'

Mercer – who has left the Army and is standing for election to parliament in 2015 – looks back with some guilt.

'I think about him and Baz every day,' he said. 'It was my responsibility. If I hadn't been there, the patrol wouldn't have attempted that engagement. Mark was with me because he never thought he'd get killed in my team. I almost feel a bit stupid for engendering that mind-set in both Mark and Baz. And I feel guilty about it. Felicity, my wife, and everyone else who loves me and has supported me, they say it's not my fault. I suppose my respective commanders have also often been quick to tell me I was saving countless lives over the years, but, you know… I didn't bring all of my men home, so I cannot have been that good.

'I don't think I'm being harsh on myself, because my primary job was to bring the team home. Over the years I've lost other friends too. But Mark was different. It was a special tour for me; one where we were presented with harder challenges than I have ever faced. But when I think of Mark, I think about *him*, rather than the nature of his passing.

'Baz still comes to my house often. He has struggled with the loss of Mark. For me, the emotions hit at odd times. Remembrance Day is difficult, but there are less obvious times, too. I almost had a little cry today. It's my daughter's fifth birthday. We were singing Happy Birthday, and I had the dog and my new four-month-old on my lap as I watched her opening her presents. She was so happy. But I was thinking, *Mark's never going to have this*. I will carry that with me as a burden. His life ended that day, and mine didn't. I always get up at dawn on June 8.

'I got back from Afghanistan having done what I wanted to do. Pushing on in the Army, perhaps being a staff officer – that always scared me. It looks horrendous. I joined the Army to be a soldier, not to be at a desk. I wanted to test myself against evil people, and I couldn't do that anymore with a young family. It's a young man's game, and I just couldn't take the risks I was previously prepared to take. My wife and I wanted to have another child. So it was time to leave.

'I don't feel that we were wrong to be in Afghanistan. If you have the capability to intervene in a state that's sponsoring terrorism, you should do so. Did we always get our doctrine right? Absolutely not. Did we set Afghanistan back when we first went there? Yes. Did we handle counter-insurgency properly? Probably not. But did we eventually make it a better place? Yes.'

That final emphatic 'yes' is shared by Col Ian Bell.

'We have achieved a level of results that means we can go and leave it to the Afghan people,' he said. 'We've made a significant difference. An argument will continue that we stayed too long, or left too early, but, if I'm honest and from a soldier's perspective, we look at what we are asked to do, we do it, we move on. We helped the Afghan Security Forces reach a standard where they now conduct the operations. The argument will run forever. People who have not yet been born will be writing essays at staff college about this.

'I'll never forget hearing about Mark's death. It was my son's fifth

229

birthday. Thankfully, my regiment, the Royal Regiment of Artillery, knew when they got the message that he had been my driver, so they tried to contact me directly. But that wasn't possible, so they told my wife, who also knew Mark really well, and she then told me. I was absolutely gutted, obviously, and hugely surprised. He was a guy I'd known really well and spent a lot of time with. I guess anyone can imagine what that feels like. Just thinking about the moment now is pretty emotional for me.

'I didn't know his parents before, but I met them at the repatriation ceremony, and we've been in touch since. I hope we'll remain in touch. They visit us sometimes when they go to Mark's grave and they have a very strong link with 3 RHA. They see us as people who were part of his life, and they know that he valued us and we valued him. I'm really impressed by Ann and Mike's attitude.

'As for Mark, there is no question in my mind that, had he lived, he would have been promoted further than most soldiers would expect. He excelled at everything he did.'

* * *

ANN AND MIKE Chandler are less convinced about the Afghanistan campaign, though they do know that their son was respected, and is remembered fondly, by a great many people.

'Johnny told us, "A lot of people looked up to Mark, so don't think he has wasted his life by being killed in Afghanistan, because he hasn't,"' said Ann. '"He's left quite a legacy of people who will never forget him. He touched a lot of people, and did an awful lot of good. He was a much-respected man." Those words came from a guy who is a really hard-bitten soldier, so they mean a lot. But I remember Mark saying that, while he quite liked the local people in Iraq, he didn't think much of the Afghans. He said they had low standards, and that they treated their animals and even their wives absolutely appallingly.

'He told me about a young woman who'd gone with her married sister and her mother to the next village to carry food back, and her brothers were so incensed [*that a single woman had gone out without a male chaperone*] that they cut off her nose and ears. If they were the good guys, who were we fighting for? I don't think Mark met them.

He said to me once, "It's a lost cause. We all know that within two years of us leaving, everything will have gone back to the way it was."'

The Chandlers are left with good memories of their son, and immense gratitude for those who were with him on the day he died, particularly his fellow FST members. 'Johnny and Baz risked their lives to get Mark back to the base,' said Mike. 'Johnny holding Mark on his lap in the armoured vehicle... That was a wonderful thing to do. It was fabulous. Two newspapers suggested that Mark had been abandoned, and when we complained about that we were awarded £2,000. We used the money to set up an award in Mark's name for his old unit. The bombardier who performs most impressively on the lance bombardier leadership course gets a rugby shirt with "Bing" written on it [*Mark was a lifelong fan of Gloucester Rugby Club*], a hundred pounds, and a beer stein. The course is tough, so they deserve it.

'When Johnny came home on R&R shortly after Mark was killed, he came straight to see us. He was concerned that we would blame him for Mark's death, but how could we? And the autopsy report said that death would have been virtually instantaneous. So Mark wouldn't have known. That was a huge relief. Johnny has become a good friend, but poor old Baz just can't come to talk to us. We would love it if he did. His wife has been in touch, but Baz just can't. We often think of him.'

They are coping with their loss, in part thanks to their other son Stephen, who works for Mencap.

'Stephen has been a great help,' said Mike. 'We can talk about what happened now, and I like talking about Mark. I hope people don't think we have forgotten him, because we haven't. Sometimes it's a bad day, and I just cry. But, generally speaking, we're pretty well up for it. Because life has to go on, doesn't it? You can't just curl up and die. We do our best.

'We like to go to Mark's grave – it has settled, at last, and the headstone's been erected, and another soldier has been buried next to him. It's nice that he has someone on both sides, now. I don't feel his presence there, but I do see him here at home sometimes. It's strange. I said to Ann the other day, "I haven't seen Mark for a long time." And then yesterday he was here, just like you are, on the settee there. It's nice to see him. I like the feeling that he's here. I might be working on my laptop, or reading, and suddenly I get this feeling that there is someone in the room. I'll just see something out of the corner of my eye, but when I turn to look at him, he goes. I said to Ann, I must not look at him.

'I don't feel he's trying to tell us anything. I just feel he may be checking we're okay. Sometimes he'll be there in the car, too. I can feel him on the back seat. I don't know why, but I just know he's there. Sometimes if I'm driving his old car, he might be there, and I feel he's telling me off for my poor driving, as he did when he was alive. Amazing, isn't it? I'm not into that sort of thing at all, and I don't believe in ghosts.'

Ann has had similar, though less vivid, experiences.

'Mike often sees enough to know what Mark's wearing, and it's often clothes he didn't have when he was alive,' she said. 'I don't see him, but sometimes I'll be sitting here doing a Sudoku, or watching the telly, and there'll be a movement of air. I will feel this presence, and I'll look up thinking there is someone there. But I don't see him. Perhaps he is there. I've dreamed about Mark sometimes, but he's just Mark in my dreams. It's comforting to know he's around.

'Mark didn't have a wife or children, or even any pets. He did have a very nice Lancia car, which he treasured, and he'd saved up quite a lot of money to get it re-sprayed and engineered from the floor up. When he died, we wanted to do something that he would have done had he lived. So we spent some money doing up his car. It's now kept somewhere nice and dry, and we take it out from time to time. We've also started raising money for Help For Heroes in a quiet way. The worst thing is hearing of his mates getting married and having children. That's what he would have been doing if he had lived.'

Mike Chandler's attitude to life has changed somewhat.

'I don't suffer fools at all,' he said. 'If someone upsets me, I just ignore them or tell them to bugger off. I'm not generally a confrontational person, but life is too short and there are too many nice people about to worry about the ones I don't like. We were up at the pub one lunchtime. I suppose I was moaning about the people who killed Mark. Someone said, "You must learn to forgive and forget." I nearly hit him. I said, "What a bloody stupid thing to say! I'll forgive that man when I shoot him between the eyes. You don't have a clue about what you're talking about. You cannot have an *inkling* of what we're going through."'

232

'Someone said to me, "Well, he was paid for it,"' said Ann. 'I said, "Actually, soldiers don't join the Army to be killed, they join to save us from being killed." But generally people are very nice. They just find it hard to know what to say. But there is nothing to say, really, is there?'

The Chandlers received a box of their son's effects from Afghanistan. Among them was his wristwatch. 'I know it will sound strange,' said Ann, 'but I'm dreading the day that watch stops. We keep it here in the living room. It's still ticking after nearly four years. He was wearing it the day he was killed, and it's our last living link, if you like, with him. I don't know what's going to happen the day it stops.'

MARINE STEVEN BIRDSALL
BRAVO COMPANY 40 COMMANDO ROYAL MARINES
OCTOBER 6, 1989 – JUNE 14, 2010

STEVEN 'BIRDY' BIRDSALL'S friends have a golden memory of him – a moment from the spring of 2010 which will linger forever.

It is a scorching hot night in a Cancún bar, and a scratch team from 40 Cdo, hastily put together by Steven, has just triumphed in the Mexican holiday resort's annual four-a-side beach football tournament. The cocktails are flowing, the music is pumping, and pretty American girls are clamouring to get to know the young bootnecks. At the centre of it all is a beaming Steven: a leading member of 'the Royal Marines sunbathing team', and a man whose boyish good looks have previously worked wonders on the female side of the Royal Navy, according to his good friend and fellow marine, Matt Baldwin.

It was all a long way from Steven's home town of Warrington, in Cheshire, and further yet from where he and his mates were headed: the dusty, deadly streets of Sangin.

In another life, Steven would not have been in Cancún, and neither would he have been about to deploy to the outskirts of perhaps the most dangerous town in the world. He had planned to join the Royal Air Force and become a physical training instructor – an altogether safer prospect. It was a natural enough ambition. He was ferociously fit, his father had been an RAF driver, and his grandfather and an uncle had been Cold War-era air traffic controllers. Steven had grown up listening to their tales of service life. But he had been turned down by the RAF careers people at seventeen as not having sufficient 'leadership

234

skills'. It was a strange verdict – bearing in mind that Steven immediately went and joined the Royal Marines, not an organisation known for taking on life's waifs and strays – and it was one that would ultimately cost the brave young man his life.

Around the same time, his close boyhood friend Tom Sephton was also joining up, though Tom went into the Army. And in 2010, not long after Steven Birdsall got back from Mexico, both men found themselves in Afghanistan.

Steven and fellow members of Bravo Coy, 40 Cdo, were sent to Patrol Base Ezeray, north of Sangin. This was not a pleasant place to spend your time. But then, you might say that about much of the country.

'There was no excitement about going to Afghan,' said Mne Baldwin, who trained with Steven. 'None of us were looking forward to it. That's why we'd gone to Cancún; just to restore morale. It definitely worked. For the entire week we were in Mexico, we completely forgot everything else.

'We took over from the Army. They'd been there in platoon strength, but a few of them had already gone by the time we got there, and those who were left looked like broken men. They couldn't wait to get out. Their officer looked like he hadn't washed or eaten properly for months. He was just a mess. One of them gestured in one direction, and said, "That's mainly where the shooting comes from." And then they left. The hand-over only took about half an hour.'

The first few weeks were 'quite surreal', he said. 'Ezeray was the pits. It was absolutely tiny, just four lookout points around the perimeter, and a small space in the middle. And we were surrounded 360 degrees by a hostile population. I don't want to use the word exciting, but in a way it was. It was so different to what we'd been used to. Our pre-deployment training had been really gruelling, but I don't feel it equipped us very well for the tour. I didn't think we were using the right kit during training, and we weren't acclimatised properly. But, despite that, something new seemed to be happening every day, and we weren't unhappy at all. The first few weeks went quite fast.'

When he wasn't part of a patrol, or on watch – or working on his tan – Steven liked to write home. In one letter, he wrote:

Mum, Dad and Liss [his younger sister, Melissa]

235

Thought I would write a quick letter whilst I have a bit of downtime…
I have no idea when you will get this as the postal system at Bastion
as you know is up it's arse, however so far I've had a letter off Natalie
[Steven's cousin] *and a parcel off Grandma, which was nice, it also*
lasted about 10 minutes… nice picture of me thinking I was The Rock
in there as well.

Anyway, things are okay this end, despite the fact on my first night
on watch some bastard tried to get in over the wall! needless to say he
got a mini flare to the face.

I also set someones compound on fire for 2 hours when I just meant
to light the sky up over the Green Zone because two blokes were
digging in the field. Oh well.

The kids here are little shits! We've been really nice to them giving
them sweets and chocolate but the minute we run out [of goodies]
we're dodging stones to the face – absolutely ruthless.

We have a lovely search dog called Molly. She's a Springer however
she's back at Bastion now cos someone threw a brick at her and
damaged her paw.

The routine here is quite hard I'm doing 3 hours on 6 off at the
minute, it's do-able but after a couple of weeks constantly plus being
on rations it starts to exhaust you, especially within the 6 hours off
were doing 4/5 hour patrols every other day. Being here makes you
realise how much you take for granted at home – i.e. I would literally
kill for a dominos pizza right now and a cold can of coke – I'd be on
cloud 9!

Anyway enough dripping [complaining] *hopefully things will kick*
off here soon and I can get some rounds down on the gun! Hope
Melissa is okay and still enjoying school. Tell everyone I said hello and
I'll ring soon as I get time.

Will write again soon!
Love Steven
x x x x

Be careful what you wish for, the old adage says. The usual May opium
poppy harvest had kept a lid on things for a while, but not long after
Steven sent that letter things did indeed kick off.

'As we reached the halfway point of the tour, the fighting season

236

began,' said Matt Baldwin. 'We were patrolling most days, and it was pretty scary. We'd be fired on pretty much every single day. Or there'd be an explosion near us, or we'd hear about another troop getting hit.

'Getting into firefights was terrifying. We'd go on patrol, come under fire, shoot back a bit and then run back to the PB every time. So, in the Taliban's eyes, they were always winning. You never really saw them. They'd just poke their rifles through a hole and point in your direction. You might see one or two scrambling about five hundred metres away. It was a constant losing battle.

'That was bad for our morale and it got to the point where the lads were fuming. They were saying, "Why should we go on patrol? We're not achieving anything." As the months passed, we got more tired, and more fed-up. We couldn't fire back when we wanted to and morale took a real hit.'

The morale of Bravo Company was further tested on the afternoon of Saturday, June 12, when Mne Richard 'Dickie' Hollington was blown up by an IED. Dickie, the son of a retired Royal Marine Major, and a former semi-pro footballer described by his sergeant as 'a big character in the troop, with big hair and a backside to match', was terribly injured but survived the initial blast and was flown back to the UK. Sadly, he succumbed eight days later, with his parents and two younger brothers at his bedside. In doing so, he became the 300th British serviceman or woman to die in the conflict, and his was a grievous loss. Maj Mark Totten, OC Bravo Coy, said of him, 'Men like Dickie are pure gold in a patrol base… His optimism was infectious, and probably best highlighted by his hundred per cent certainty that England would win the World Cup.'

Mne Karl Rickard said, 'When it was time to do the job, many couldn't do it better, and when it was time to have a laugh, still not many could do it better. Knowing Dickie has been taken from us is a very hard fact to live with.'

Mne Tom Lingley remembered 'play-fighting' with Dickie, and needing eight stitches afterwards! 'We shared a room together,' he said. 'We used to do a *Come Dine With Me* sketch, cooking for each other, and giving each other marks out of ten. Dickie always cracked stir fries and scored, on average, late sevens.'

Mne Hollington's popularity is obvious from those and many other tributes, and it was a hammer blow when he was hit. Morale was still low a week later, said Matt Baldwin, when he and others, including Steven Birdsall, had been moved to another, even smaller patrol base, Marshall's Post. Named after 6 Rifles TA soldier, and Devon and Cornwall PCSO, Rfn Mark Marshall, who had been blown up in Sangin on St Valentine's Day, it was some three hundred metres from Ezeray, though the difficulty in transiting between the two meant it might as well have been a lot further.[21]

At any given time, it was manned by only one section of eight men, and the marines took it in turns to do a week or so there. Its size and isolation meant that it was vulnerable to attack; snipers were in the area, and, on several occasions, insurgents had snuck up and thrown grenades over its walls. To counter the grenade threat, the Royal Engineers had been tasked with raising a wire guard around lower points on the wall. Steven Birdsall was told to climb a ladder and cover the engineers.

'Me and Mne Spence were told to get over the wall to help,' said Baldwin. 'The perimeter walls were about twelve feet high, and Birdy was on a ladder inside the base, watching over us and ready to give us covering fire as we put up this chicken wire. Then we heard a bang. Me and Spence knew something had happened, but we didn't know what. We had a call on the radio to come back over the wall, so we had to scramble back over, and then we found out that Birdy had been shot.'

It took the two marines and their engineer comrades a few minutes to get back in. By that time, an armoured vehicle had raced over from Ezeray – its brave crew took huge risks to do so, but they knew that every moment mattered – and had removed the mortally-wounded soldier back to Ezeray. Within the hour, he would be on a helicopter back to Bastion.

'By the time we got back in, Birdy had been taken away,' said Baldwin, 'so I didn't even get to see him. Later, we heard that he'd fallen twelve feet down from the ladder. One of the lads had gone over to help him, and was trying to hold the back of his head in place. We think the bullet had gone in under the edge of his helmet.

'It was a tough call, and it was the section commander's decision, but in my opinion he'd probably been stood there in the same position for too long. We knew there were snipers in the area. [*Earlier*]

I'd had a round whiz by so close that it popped my eardrum, and Birdy was in the same location when he got shot. So I think the same sniper shot at both of us, and I was just the lucky one. He'd only been standing there for a few minutes, but was that too long? Tough call.'

* * *

STEVEN BIRDSALL WAS a typical boy, according to his mother Jenny. 'He had the usual scrapes and breaks here and there while running or climbing,' she said. 'He joined Crosfields, the local sports club, at the age of five or six. It's really a rugby club, but they also encourage football, and from then on that was his passion for the rest of his life. He was a huge Liverpool fan.

'Steven was almost eleven when his sister Melissa was born. It was funny – I think he was disgusted and he didn't want to tell his friends that his mum was pregnant. I remember him saying, "I can't believe it!" He'd really wanted a brother to play with, but he was a very loving boy and he soon got used to having a sister. We have so many lovely photos of him holding Melissa, and playing with her.

'He took school seriously. He was neither at the top nor at the bottom, he had nice handwriting, he did his homework, and he never got into any trouble. He preferred to be in the background, and he was like that all his life. Sport was his main thing. He met his best friend Tom Sephton at high school, and they hit it off instantly. If they weren't together at our house, they were round at Tom's mum's. As they got older, they went to parties all over the place, they went to Blackpool... they did everything together. After they left school, Steven went off to sixth form college and Tom joined the Army. When Tom passed out of basic training, Steven went round to see him. He was dead chuffed about that. It was a lovely relationship.

'Steven only stayed at college for six months. Really he was just biding his time. He had a part-time job at Ikea, but he wanted to use his fitness for something.'

He considered taking a sports science degree and going into PE teaching, but the idea of being with children all the time didn't appeal, according to his father, Steve.

239

'He applied to the RAF, but they said he lacked leadership skills,' he said. 'I thought, *He's only 17! How can he have any leadership skills at that age?* He was deflated, but the next day he went straight to Manchester and applied to join the Royal Marines.'

As most do, he found the commando training hard.

'I went to see him with Melissa in week fifteen, his first weekend off,' said Jenny. 'We'd booked into a hotel so that he could get off the base and relax, but we hardly saw him. He just slept. I was shocked by the state of him. His feet and knees were full of holes. I don't how he could get his shoes on!

'He'd only reached the halfway stage, and he was exhausted. I didn't approve of what the Marines were doing to Steven, I thought they were treating him so badly, but later I realised that they needed to see if he could tolerate discomfort, and pain, and exhaustion.

'I remember his final Commando test [*the thirty-miler*]. I really wondered if he'd pass, but he did it, and I was so proud when he passed out. I'll never forget how gorgeous he looked in his green beret. That was in November 2008. He had two weeks' leave, and, on the way home, he gave me his beret. He said, "I have to give you this in case I go away and don't come back." That made me think. I hadn't been upset by him joining the Marines. It was only then, and when I read more about it, that I realised they're usually among the first troops on the front line.'

Steven and his new colleagues in 40 Cdo went to Cyprus for training, and then on to Turkey and Borneo aboard HMS *Ocean*. 'He was away for almost six months and he loved every second of it,' said his father. 'Especially when they stopped in Thailand and Mauritius on the way back. I remember him ringing home at one point and telling us to watch a TV documentary [*Channel 5's* Warship] that had been made aboard *Ocean*. Steven was in an episode called *Big Trouble in Little Thailand*. It seems they'd been having fun on jet skis, and then there had been some dispute with the owner, who'd pulled a gun on them.'

By now, Steven had really grown up, said Jenny.

'Suddenly, he was a man,' she said, 'and his whole attitude had changed. He was still very caring and loving, but in the space of a very short time they had changed everything about him. He wasn't aggressive – he never even talked aggressively – but he was tougher, and bigger, and nothing fazed him.

'He'd never tell me anything unless he had to. When he was at work, he was a marine, and when he came home, he was Steven. He'd talk to his dad about the Marines a bit more, but as long as I knew he was okay, that was all right by me. Before he came home on leave, he'd always call to ask what I was cooking. It had to be his favourite, chicken Kiev with pizza and home-made chips – they had to be home-made, he hated frozen ones. He'd come home and eat the fridge out completely.'

Before long, Herrick 12 rolled around and, with it, 40 Cdo's turn to go to Afghanistan. It was Steven Birdsall's first operational deployment.

'I'd tried to put it out of my mind,' said Jenny. 'But we were very worried. I tried to tell myself, *He's only nineteen, and they'll keep him at Bastion. He won't be doing all that really dangerous work.*'

In fact, Steven was heading for Sangin. But he showed no fear.

'I asked him once if he was afraid,' said Jenny. 'He said, "Mum, don't worry about me, I'll be fine." If he did worry, he never showed it. It was a Friday when we were last all together. He picked Melissa up from his old school. She was so proud of her brother, and she'd told her teachers and friends that Steven was going to Afghanistan, so they invited him in and he spent half an hour talking to the teachers who were still there from his time. Melissa and I were going to my mother-in-law's in Middlesbrough for the weekend, and we went to Frankie and Benny's for something to eat before Steven drove us to the station. He was very positive throughout – he knew Melissa was upset. I remember him telling her to work hard at school, and to write to him often. I knew I'd be back on the Sunday, so I'd see him before he left, but Melissa was going to be staying on with her grandmother for a bit longer. She cried all the way to Middlesbrough. There was nothing I could do to stop her. She said to me, "It's the last time I'll see him, mum."

'I said, "Don't be saying things like that!" But she just insisted she wouldn't see him again. That hurt so much. And she was right. She spoke to him on the phone, but she never did see him again.

'So that was on the Friday. I came back from Middlesbrough on the

Sunday and I said goodbye to him at home. I remember him going to the car with his dad, and he said, "No fuss, mum. I'll be all right." Just before he got into the car, I gave him a big hug, and I said, "Just make sure you come home to your mum."

'I was crying, and the girl from across the road came over and put an arm around me. I could tell from his face that he was thinking, *Oh God, mum, don't!*'

Steve Birdsall drove his son down to Norton Manor Camp at Taunton. It's a journey he remembers well.

'We were just chatting away,' he said. 'We never spoke about Afghanistan much. We got to the camp after having something to eat, and he said, "To save you messing around, dad, just drop me off at the gates." I can see him as clearly as I can see you now. I just gave him a hug and said, "Look after yourself, mate. Keep your head down."

'Then he just walked through the gates. As I turned around I glanced over my shoulder, and I saw him give me the thumbs-up. And that was the last time I saw him.'

As it happened, Steven and his schoolfriend Tom Sephton deployed at more or less the same time.

'They were in touch in the run-up to the deployment,' said Jenny. 'Tom left on April 4 and Steven a few days later. But they were in different parts of Helmand, and I don't think they were in touch out there. I know Steven wasn't able to get anywhere near Facebook, which would have been one way. There was no competition between the boys. Just the other day, Tom's mum, Ange, and I were just talking about them and the *craic* they had between them. Tom's final fitness test was eight miles over the Yorkshire Moors with thirty-six pounds of kit. We both remembered Tom telling Steven about this, and Steven laughing, and saying, "Eight miles? We do that as a warm-up!" But they knew they were both going into a messy area, and it wouldn't make any difference if they were in the Army or the Marines.'

He sent blueys back, but mostly stayed in touch by phone. He would try to ring his mother every Monday morning at about ten-thirty; his father would get calls at two o'clock or three o'clock in the morning. The Royal Marines prize good morale above almost anything, and Steven would always try to stay upbeat. But he wasn't fooling his mum and dad.

242

'It was pretty clear from our conversations that morale was not good,' said Jenny. 'I remember him saying a lot of lads were putting in to leave when they got back. "They've had enough,'" he said. "It's hard, and we're thirsty and hungry, and there's no downtime."'

His parents sent him parcels, sometimes two or three a day, crammed with magazines, soft drinks in foil cartons, packets of noodles, sweets... anything to lift their son's spirits. Occasionally, they ran into the unthinking bureaucracy. 'They'd sometimes refuse parcels if they had a liquid in them,' said Jenny, 'and Steve once had to empty a parcel at the post office because it was a few grammes overweight.'

'He was always tired and famished,' said Steve. 'He said they were often short on rations because the Chinooks were constantly being deployed elsewhere, and the road convoys were getting attacked. It sounded terrible, but we did what we could. The lads said later that Steven was known for receiving lots of boxes. He'd take what he wanted and share the rest with his mates.

'He never slated the Marines. It was just the amount of work they had to do. They'd just been dealt a poor hand of cards. I did find these conversations upsetting, but I couldn't let him know that. I just needed to keep upbeat. I'd say, "Listen mate, after tonight it's one sleep less until you come home for R&R." His leave had been due to start on the Thursday after he was killed.'

'We had our last conversation with him on the Wednesday before,' said Jenny. 'I was at home because I'd just been made redundant, and he took a chance and rang, which was really unusual. It was a strange conversation, because it was a change from his routine, and he was on the phone for a long time. In the end I felt I had to say to him, "Steven, you'll have to be going soon, surely? We've been on the phone for nearly forty-five minutes."

'I felt bad saying that, because he didn't seem to want to get off the phone. I feel now that he almost knew it was going to be the last time he'd ring home. He was telling me how much he was looking forward to his R&R the following week. I said I'd make all his favourite foods. "We can't wait to see you," I said, "and Melissa's really excited."

'He said, "I can't wait, mum."

'Then I told him I'd lost my job. He said, "Oh, mum, don't worry, it'll be fine! You'll soon get another job. I don't need the money in my bank, so you can have it if you need it."

'I said, "No, don't be silly." He was going to buy a car when he came home – he wanted a new VW Scirocco. He just didn't want to get off the phone. He was exhausted, I think. He was just longing for a pizza and a pile of chips, with a couple of chilled beers. He kept on saying, "I want to get home."

'That was on the Wednesday. The Sunday came, and it was a really nice day. We were sitting in the garden, and I remember Melissa was in the bath, and Steve's mum was with her. She was ten at the time. Steve was making some tea, when I saw two men on the doorstep in smart suits, and a priest in a long robe. I just screamed. I just knew.'

'Jenny shouted, "Get the door! Get the door!"', said Steve. 'I saw the padre, and so I knew straight away that it wasn't good. They introduced themselves, and one of them said, "Are there any children in the house?"

'The first words out of my mouth were, "Is he okay?"

'They didn't answer that straight away and just asked if we were on our own. I said that my daughter was upstairs, and I shouted up to my mother to keep her up there.'

'They sat us down and said that there had been an incident,' said Jenny. 'Steven had been shot and was very seriously injured. They said a visiting officer called Kathy was on the way, and she would help us. They said that he was being prepared to be flown back to the UK and we were to get ready to go to the Queen Elizabeth Hospital at Selly Oak. The priest had us praying for Steven.'

The Birdsalls left for Birmingham at midnight that night, in order to be at the hospital when their son arrived along with six other injured men.

'I spoke to one of the other fathers who was waiting at the hospital for his son,' said Steve. 'He said his lad had lost both of his legs and an arm. "But he's alright!" this father said. I thought, *How can that be alright?*

'Kathy, our visiting officer from the Navy, turned up late on Sunday evening, and we sat and talked. She was brilliant. She found out that Steven was being transferred to the Neurological Critical Care Department, and that we'd be able to see him shortly. The Wing

Commander surgeon who had brought Steven and the other injured lads home came in, with a flight lieutenant nurse who was in tears. She told us that he'd taken a round to the back of the head but that he wasn't in any distress or pain. They even said that at one point he'd been breathing on his own, although it was laboured. He wasn't in any distress because his heart rate was normal. One of them said, "He's got the heart of an ox."

'The Wing Commander said they'd done some tests on him at Bastion, where he'd also had surgery. He'd let it be known that he wanted to be an organ donor, so they'd got him on a ventilator. Whether that was so that he would be alive when we were there, or so that his organs could be used to help somebody who needed them, we don't know. We believe it was so he could be with us, even though nothing could be done for him.

'They took us to see Steven, but I just couldn't look at him. I just stood in the corner of the room... I was just so scared of the damage that he might have suffered. Then Jenny took my hand and said, "It's okay. Everything's there." He had a black and swollen eye, and his head was heavily bandaged, but otherwise he was perfect. He was still dusty from Afghanistan.'

The staff at the Queen Elizabeth Hospital were 'amazing', said Jenny. 'We were able to spend from six-thirty on Monday morning until about seven o'clock that night with him, and all the family and lots of his friends were able to get down to Birmingham to see him.

'After he died, his organs were used and he was able to save five lives. Somebody received his heart, and we know that lad was later able to enjoy the first holiday he'd had in three years. And two people benefited from his kidneys. One didn't survive, but the other did. Another patient received a double lung transplant. That man had been given only hours to live, but he recovered enough to be able to play football with his son.'

'Football was Steven's sport,' said Steve, 'so to know that part of him is still sometimes running around on a football pitch is wonderful. The transplant team still give us updates on the health of those who received Steven's organs, and Jenny finds that very comforting.'

Gradually, details of what had happened to Steven trickled out to his family. 'The Royal Engineers were putting zigzags of barbed wire up in the alleys near the compounds in an effort to stop the grenades,' said Steve. 'There'd been no intelligence about activity in the area, and there was no radio chatter. Steven was up a ladder with a light machine gun covering the engineers. There were just two snaps, like fingers being clicked. The first round missed, but the second one hit him. His friend Nick said when he fell off the ladder at first he thought he'd just slipped or something. But then they realised he'd been shot.

'They started treating him immediately and called for a casevac. They had to get him into a Mastiff armoured vehicle first and then drive to the landing zone. As they were trying to get him into the Mastiff, they came under heavy fire. Then when they were trying to get Steven onto the American helicopter, they came under heavy fire again. The American crew did a brilliant job, though, and they got him back to Bastion very quickly. They carried out brain surgery immediately at the hospital and then he went straight onto life support.

'The Royal Marines were really good to us. The Warrant Officer tasked to organise the military funeral was brilliant. He'd come around to the house often, and Jenny would make him bacon and egg butties. His name was Dolly, but for the life of me I can't remember his surname. He'd been a chef, now he's a visiting officer, helping other families who've lost boys.

'But after a while, when it was all over, we were left on our own. It has to be that way, but we still have an appointed contact, and we can make contact if we want to. We've been invited to a few events that the Marines organised. I went to the Royal Marines Day and to a rugby tournament. There are only 8,500 marines, so they're like a family. We still hear from his friends now and again. They'll send Facebook messages, and Dan, one of the lads who was in Afghan with Steven, always goes to the cemetery on the anniversary of his death. He'll leave a bottle of port by the grave. I didn't know it, but port is supposed to be the drink of heroes.'

As Steven had predicted, many of his comrades later left the Royal Marines, though not before they let off some steam at the Taliban. Soon after his death, PB Ezeray came under attack.

'It wasn't just a few rounds,' said Matt Baldwin. 'It was heavy, and it felt like they were saying, "We just got one of yours." Everyone in the

PB just went mental. Lads were lined up along the wall, all-firing. They were shouting and holding the triggers down for about half an hour. Our machine guns were taking mud walls down. It was like a release. Our sergeant tried shouting, "Cease fire!" but everyone just carried on. The sergeant understood, and no-one got into trouble. We found out on the radio afterwards that two or three of them had been injured or killed, so we felt a lot better.

'In the days that followed, more men were getting injured. One lad got shrapnel from a grenade and another got shot. I was just getting more and more anxious to go home. I was that nervous about stepping on something, or doing something wrong, that, in the middle of one patrol, I turned around and said, "I'm not going over there." I just lost it for two minutes. We axed that patrol and went back to base.

'I was stood at the gate once when a patrol went out. Before they'd gone very far, the point man thought he'd found an IED. It went off, but he got away with it, perhaps because it was faulty or wasn't big enough. He came running back to the gate, threw his weapon at me, and threw up on the ground.

'One of the senior NCOs had a bit of a breakdown, too. He'd be crying sometimes. But we all managed to hold it together. Then, when we left at the end of the tour, they demolished all four patrol bases in our area. You had to wonder what it had all been for. It was the most demoralising, biggest waste of time in my life. It felt like we'd achieved absolutely nothing in six months, except we'd lost some friends.

'I'd lost lots of weight, but after we moved back to Camp Bastion we stayed there for two weeks before we got shipped home. There was really good food there and there were two gyms, so when I got back to my family, I almost looked good. It must have been strange for them. I couldn't possibly explain what we'd been through. I was completely on edge. I remember sitting down in a shopping centre and a woman behind me made a noise closing her baby buggy, and I jumped out of my seat. The slightest noise would send me off. I was nervous about anything. And one night I drank too much and I had a bit of a meltdown. But I was one of the lucky ones. I got through it after only three or four weeks.

'I speak to Steve and Jenny Birdsall from time to time. The other lads and me have been to Steve's grave a few times. When I look back on that period of my life I feel as if I did everything right. I lost a couple of friends, and it was a horrible time, but I don't think I could have done anything more. I just feel that Afghanistan was a pointless experience. As I see it, the military didn't achieve anything.'

The Birdsalls would concur.

'I've come to the conclusion that we shouldn't have been there,' said Jenny. 'I'm not saying that just because we lost Steven. I'm not bitter about him being in the Marines, I just feel bitter about them going to Afghanistan. It's not our country, and we shouldn't be interfering. The politicians will say that progress has been made, and perhaps there has been some. But give it two years, and it'll be back to the way it was.

'One thing that upsets me still is that, about three weeks after Steven was killed, British forces pulled out of Sangin and the Americans moved in. They pretty much levelled the area. All the hearts-and-minds work that the Marines had done was sacrificed.

'I remember in one conversation I had with Steven, he spoke about the attitudes of the locals. He said the kids loved pens and paper, so the marines would take them on patrol and give it to the kids. They got to know the kids' faces. One day, one of the kids the marines had come to recognise was there with the two little sisters he used to bring with him, and he pulled a knife on one of the lads. He ended up with an SA80 butt in the face. Someone had persuaded this boy to try to stab one of them. It must have been brain-sapping. We're trying to improve things for them. But they seem to be living in biblical times. Perhaps we were trying to bring them into the twenty-first century too fast. Who knows? I have to wonder if they actually want it.

'But if he was alive, Steven would go back tomorrow if he was told to do so. He loved the Royal Marines, and he loved his job. One hundred per cent.'

Steve agrees. 'I think the whole thing has been a waste of 446 lives [*the death toll at the time of this interview*],' he said. 'And you could put a nought or two on the end of that figure to come up with something like the number of men who suffered serious injuries. And the injuries are not just physical; a lot of them suffer from PTSD. But if Steven was still with us today, if he'd finished college and said he wanted to join the forces, I would still say, "If that's what you want, go for it."'

They have coped with their son's death as they feel he would have wished.

'It's been really difficult, the first year particularly so, and especially Christmas and birthdays,' said Jenny. 'We're fortunate because we have a good family and good friends, and Melissa has kept us going. We've had to focus completely on her, and that helped us to forget ourselves a bit. It took a long time to get her into a good place. She was heartbroken, and we couldn't help her. She didn't want to get upset in front of mum and dad, so she bottled it up and she would have little meltdowns.

'When she was eleven, we heard about Fab Camps, which is a charity for bereaved families. We've done three of the camps now, just Melissa and me. She was able to speak to children who suffered similar experiences, and there was a sort of indirect counselling. She's now a changed little girl, and she's doing great.'

'Even as we were driving back from Selly Oak, we promised ourselves that we weren't going to mope around,' said Steve. 'We just kept thinking what Steven would tell us. We knew he would say, "You *do not* be miserable!"

'There are days when we go to the cemetery and sit for a bit before coming home. It puts things in perspective. Things that would get you down or make you angry and bitter before now seem fairly minor. Nothing could be worse than losing our son. Some of the other families have asked how we cope, and we say that Steven wouldn't want us to be miserable. If he ever heard me complaining about anything when he was alive, he'd say to me, "Stop dripping, dad, and crack on." So that's what I do.'

PRIVATE TOM SEPHTON
C COMPANY 1st BATTALION THE MERCIAN REGIMENT
MARCH 19, 1990 – JULY 5, 2010

MORTARMEN TEND TO be the heavyweights of soldiering.

Partly, it's a natural side-effect of the physical work involved in lugging their equipment and its supply of four kilogramme bombs around. Partly, it reflects the fact that theirs is a more static role, on a mortar line at a FOB, than that of the young infantryman, who spends much of his life on his feet, often dashing from one piece of cover to the next. And, partly, it's because they are older – and, they will tell you, wiser – than their counterparts in a rifle platoon. The mortars have done their days of running everywhere, thanks very much.

Twenty-year-old Tom 'Sefo' Sephton broke the mould somewhat – the young man from Cheshire was a slip of a lad, built more like a lightweight racing snake than most of his colleagues. But what he lacked in muscle he more than made up for in fitness, determination, and sheer ability. 'He smoked like Dot Cotton and drank like a fish but was still one of the fittest lads in the platoon,' one of his mortarmen mates would later say of him. 'Which isn't exactly hard!'

As soon as he arrived at 1 Mercian C Coy mortars he slotted straight in.

'From the day Sefo came to the platoon he was a top lad and a very good friend,' said one of his mates. 'He was instantly liked. He was quiet at first, but he soon came out of his shell and made an impact on everyone. We could see that he was a grafter and a mortarman.'

At his first platoon function, he was nicknamed 'Little Dolly' by way of a comparison to Pte Jamie 'Dolly' Dollery, and that reflected how his fellow soldiers saw him. 'He was small in size, but he had a big heart, and we were like his big brothers,' said one of them. 'Knowing Sefo was a pleasure.'

They spent a lot of time giving him lots of friendly advice – mainly on the tricky subject of dealing with girls.

Having grown up in Warrington, he was a natural rugby league player. He played on the wing for the company, where he had a long-running argument with the soccer fans who outnumbered him. Rugby, Tom insisted, required more skill than football, and it was also a man's game – which was why he played it. Rarely seen without a wide grin on his face, he loved to let his hair down on a night out. 'He always thought he was a John Travolta, a bit of a player,' said another of the C Company mortarmen. 'That's something we'll all miss about him.'

One of Tom Sephton's best friends outside the Army was the Royal Marine Steve Birdsall, who had been killed in June.

His closest Army mate was Pte Charlie Emina.

They met during training. At the time, Emina was nearly twenty-five. He had wanted to join up at sixteen, but his mother had forbidden it so he had read Geography and History at university and then spent two years travelling through south-east Asia and Brazil. After a spell as a landscape gardener, he finally enlisted – as a private, despite the degree which would have secured his entry to Sandhurst. Tom was seven years the younger, at eighteen, but they soon became fast friends.

'In the Army, age doesn't make any difference,' said Emina, a broad Scouser. 'We had bed spaces next to each other at training depot, and we always looked out for each other. I was always very good at ironing, whereas he was terrible at it. On the other hand, he liked to polish boots. So he'd polish our boots, and I did the ironing.

'Training was tough, at least for me. I was a bit older, and set in my ways, and Tom was young and really fit. I didn't shine the way he did. In training, they have to break you down and build you back up. He got a bit stressed over this, and I remember saying, "Tom, they're not going to beat us up. The worst they'll do is shout at us." So I'd help keep his spirits up, and he'd support me. If necessary, he'd drag me up a hill by the collar.

'Tom always stood out. He wasn't extra-loud, or annoying in any

251

way – he just stood out. He was such a nice guy. I didn't know anyone who didn't like him. He was open, friendly, and dead honest.

'We just stayed together and became the best of friends. He was like my little brother, really. I felt I was part of his family, and he was part of mine. At the weekend, when we could go home, he'd often come back to mine, or he'd take me back to his mum's house.'

Late in training, Tom Sephton stumbled and tore a ligament, which put him back a couple of weeks. As a result, Charlie Emina passed out before his 'little brother'.

'I went off to mortars in 1 Mercian,' said Emina. 'Two weeks later, I joined his family to watch him pass out. Then, incredibly, he was posted to mortars too. It was like someone was pulling the strings. It usually takes years to get into the mortars, so most of the guys were older, but everyone loved him. Even the sergeant major, who'd been in for twenty-one years. Tom looked funny in his uniform because he was so small. In fact, he looked like more like a cadet. But he was super-fit.'

A tough posting to the Falklands bonded the platoon, as did a six-week posting to Kenya, where they motivated each other through the heat and the mosquitoes. Tough as Army life could be, Tom Sephton and Charlie Emina loved almost every minute. Pre-Afghan deployment training started soon after their return from Kenya.

It was then that they were told they were to be part of the C Coy search team, whose job it was to find IEDs.

The news came as something of a shock. They had been training for work on a mortar line at a FOB somewhere – no cakewalk, with the ever-present risk of the Taliban firing their own mortars and rockets into FOBs, but not as risky as their new task. Now they would be out on the ground undertaking one of the most dangerous jobs in Afghanistan.

'We didn't tell our parents, and I didn't tell my girlfriend,' said Charlie. 'They thought we were mortarmen, firing weapons from a long way back. We were nervous, but our section – 1 Section – had done the all-arms search team course, so that was that.'

Tom Sephton and Charlie Emina were sent to FOB Rahim, on the northern bank of the Helmand river in Nahr-e Saraj. This district, sandwiched between Sangin to the north and Lashkar Gah to the south, is home to some 160,000 Afghans, and was the most consistently dangerous part of the country.

Rahim was one of a number of British bases on the northern side of the river. FOB Price was some twenty kilometres south, at the district capital, Gereshk; FOB Budwan five kilometres north. A few kilometres to the south of Rahim was a line of four smaller PBs, each a kilometre or two from the next, which extended north through the green zone from the river. PBs Spondon, Clifton, Malvern and Bridzar were linked by a dirt road which would later be named 'Route Sephton'. In the green zone on the southern side of the Helmand, five kilometres from Rahim, was FOB Khar Nikar. A kilometre or so from Khar was PB Zumbelay.

Rahim was a large, sprawling camp. It contained around fifty Afghans, a similar number of Danish troops working in a CIMIC role, and then a hundred or so British soldiers, comprising three platoons, HQ, and the FSG.

There was a sangar at each corner, a toilet area with showers – the water came from a well, and if you wanted it warm you simply left a bowlful out in the sun – and row after row of four-man accommodation tents. There was also a 'chill-out' area with a few computers and, towards the end of the tour, a TV so the soldiers could watch DVDs.

Apart from the 'phenomenal' heat, life at the FOB wasn't too bad, said Emina. 'My memory of Tom is that he was always laughing about something or other,' he said. 'We used to cook together, and sit around the fire to eat in the evening. We were lucky in that we had gas burners, so you boiled up a huge pot of water, you'd write your name on your ration pack, and then come back in twenty minutes when they were nice and hot.

'The village itself was pretty peaceful, and the locals were made-up to see us. Basically, we were there to disrupt the Taliban, to interact with the locals and let them know that we were there in strength. The Taliban hated the fact that there was a school there being supported by ISAF, and they'd blown it up a few times. So we regularly visited the school to give them a sense of security.

'I think most of us had it in our minds before we got there that every Afghan was in the Taliban, or supported them, but it's ignorant to assume that. On our first patrol we met a family, and the little boy was pointing towards the corner of a building. We called the interpreter, and it turned out he was warning us that there might be an IED there. They'd often point out the locations of IEDs.

'We used to take sweets on patrol for the kids, because they might help us further down the line, and they did. They told us a lot. Much of the time, people were so friendly. You shouldn't judge these people until you've actually met them.'

They were not mortared or rocketed at Rahim, but there were a few opportunist pot-shots.

'The threat was constant,' said Emina. 'We had to carry weapons all the time. We couldn't go to the toilet without a weapon, in case the camp was attacked. You didn't want to be lugging a machine gun and ammo around all the time, so sometimes I just carried a pistol.

'We were doing two patrols a day. You'd get up at about 5am, have a bit of brekky, then go out on an early patrol, just to show your face. Then back for lunch, a vehicle patrol might go out, and we'd go back out in the afternoon and get back just before nightfall. You'd try and get some kip, and probably get woken up in the morning at 2am to do your two hours' stag. So it was pretty tiring. I had civvie mates later on say to me, "But you must have got weekends off?" I'd be like, no, that was the routine for most days, seven days a week, for six months. It was a bit like *Groundhog Day*. The trouble was, we were the search team so we basically went out with every foot patrol.

'We didn't know what to expect when we first arrived, so I remember for our first patrol we loaded ourselves down with water, ammunition, every single bit of kit we could. We were like Michelin men, we could hardly walk. Later on, you start to work out what you can do without and it gets a bit easier.

'I think we were shot at on our second patrol. Another patrol had been out and been contacted, and they came back in. Everyone was buzzing... "What's it like, what's it like?" They wanted to experience it. Our sergeant had an old head on his shoulders, he said, "Don't wish for it, lads."'

Nevertheless, Emina found contact could be thrilling.

'You'd feel a bullet rush past your head and you'd fire back while still moving ahead,' he said. 'It was exciting. It's so sad to think about it now, but at that moment in time we were all flying really high. The funny thing is, it wasn't that scary. Now, if you told me I'd got to go out on patrol I'd be like, *No way*. But then, it was just what we did. It was like going down to the shop for a pint of milk, certainly in Rahim.'

During the early weeks of the tour, the Mercians operated under the same policy of 'courageous restraint' as Terry Holland and his Commando comrades. Like the Marines, some of them felt they were fighting with one hand tied behind their backs. Eventually, said Emina, the word from on high changed. 'We had a motto: *Shoot back, don't hold back*,' he said. 'We were soon putting down all the firepower we could if we were shot at.'

When it came to using the Vallon mine detector, Tom Sephton was a natural.

'He got picked a lot,' said Emina, 'and even if someone offered to give him a spell [*a break*], he wouldn't necessarily take them up on it. There were guys I wouldn't have trusted on the Vallon, but Sefo never got lazy or careless. I couldn't have matched his skills, and I was happy to be his cover man.

'Time after time, he'd say, "Get down lads!" and we'd all lie down, feet towards the bomb. He'd be down ten inches from an IED, knowing it could trigger any second, moving the sand to confirm that it was a bomb. He should have got some sort of recognition for finding so many IEDs. After he was killed, one of our friends got a Mention in Dispatches for it. He came to me, crying, going, "I'm embarrassed… Sefo should have got this." But our platoon commander had left about a week before Tom died, so there was no-one to write him up for a posthumous decoration. That was a shame.'

[*Tom Sephton was actually later awarded a posthumous Battalion coin for his courage and selflessness.*]

As many did, at one point Tom fell ill.

'He was confined to his tent for a few days,' said Charlie Emina. 'He was still feeling ill on my birthday. My partner had sent me some pizza ingredients, so we made this pizza and I took some over to Tom. He was down that day. He didn't moan, but I knew he was getting a bit homesick. He adored his mum and he was really missing her.'

His mates missed Tom on patrol, too.

'We were a bit worried about how good some of the point men

255

were,' said Emina, 'so when he was better and came back we were made up. It was like, "Here's your Vallon!" He slotted straight back in, and he was also cheering up again by that time.

'Then we got the news that we going to PB Malvern, which was about ten kilometres away. Each platoon would do four weeks each down there, and it had a bad reputation. As 6 Platoon [*to which Tom Sephton and Charlie Emina had been attached*], it was now our turn. We were okay about going there, but no-one was particularly looking forward to it.'

They were helicoptered in, in scenes reminiscent, Emina said, of a Hollywood Vietnam war film. His helicopter was forced to abort one landing under fire, and then came back in, still under fire. The door gunner was blazing away with his .50cal machine gun at unseen targets, and the pilot radioed back to tell the soldiers to get off fighting. As they landed, the Taliban detonated an IED on the landing zone.

'We didn't know where they were shooting from, but as soon as we got out of the chopper we formed a circle and started firing. As it lifted off again, the crew were firing the chain gun into the bushes. The guys in the base sangars were also letting rip with everything they had. We took it in turns, one by one, to run in through the gates. It was like a Vietnam movie. This was now real scary. I was just thinking, *Wow!*'

The soldiers at Malvern cheerfully confirmed that it was like that pretty much every day.

'We went from being loved at the old place, to every man, woman, and child in the area hating us. You'd wave at the locals, and they'd just give you evil looks.'

Resupply helicopters were few and far between and the Mercians started running low on rations; luckily, US troops who'd been at Malvern earlier had left plenty behind, and they were better than MOD fayre. The soldiers supplemented this with bread brought from the only person with a friendly face for miles around – a baker who lived near the base entrance, and who seemed to spend half the day carrying sacks of flour into his little bakery.

'We had to patrol every day, even though we knew it was pointless,' said Emina. 'The only way you could have brought that area under control was by bringing a thousand men in and obliterating the Taliban. We couldn't go a hundred metres from the patrol base without being fired on. We felt the whole area was closing in on us. I don't know why they didn't attack the base and try to overrun it. They'd take shots at it, but nothing more. Perhaps it was the .50cals on the walls.'

Progress outside Malvern was slow, because of the IEDs which littered the area.

'When an IED was found, we'd call an EOD team in,' said Emina. 'But sometimes we'd have to secure the area and watch over the IED for twenty hours until they could get there. We couldn't just walk away in case a kid came by and detonated it.

'After three weeks or so we started to run low on water. We were rationed to two bottles a day – if there was any left over at the end of a day, we could wash with it. We called for more water and the RAF dropped us about five hundred bottles in crates, but they missed the camp and it landed in a swampy area outside the perimeter. We had to go out at night to retrieve it via a human chain, which didn't seem right. We were running the risk of getting killed just for a load of water.

'A lot of the seals had been broken, and the swamp water must have contaminated it. We were that desperate that we couldn't be fussy, but sure enough several days later some of the guys went down with really bad diarrhoea and sickness. We had four men on drips, just to get them rehydrated.

'The RAF never let us run short of ammo, though, and they must have felt sorry for us after that bad water drop, because some days later they came back with a lot of board games and DVDs. That made us feel a bit better.'

Towards the end of their time at Malvern, the platoon commander had to leave.

'Although he'd been in the regiment less time than Tom and me, we'd developed a good relationship with him,' said Charlie Emina. 'I remember someone said, "Sir, we hated you at first but we love you now!" The new guy arrived, and of course we didn't like him. He was fresh, and he must have been terrified, too.

'The morning after he arrived, someone spotted a donkey tethered near the base. The boss went, "Right, go and have a look at it." The donkey had to go, because we couldn't have it wandering around the area. We walked right up to it – not even moving tactically – and stood in a huddle, right next to it, arguing about who was going to kill it. Then Sefo suddenly shouted, "Run! There's a bomb!" I made six or seven long steps, when *Boom!* it went off.

'They'd put a suicide vest under the poor thing's saddle, and the rope coming from it hid a command wire going to the bushes. We were all blown off our feet, and there were bits of donkey everywhere. We were ecstatic, just like big kids, and we were fighting to give Sefo a hug. "Six of us could have been dead, and you spotted it! Wow!" Only Tom had been really looking at the donkey, and saw the wire. But he was so humble about it.'

There was some disagreement between the men and their new officer, said Emina.

'We'd been there a long time and he knew nothing about the area. He was pushing us into places that we knew were too dangerous. The day after the donkey bomb, we went on patrol again and we pushed a bit further than we should have. We said, "We don't want to be disrespectful, but we're not going in there."

'He said, "No, we *are* going in there."

'So we did go into this compound, and another IED was detonated. Fortunately, it didn't go off properly, so we were fine. When we got back after that patrol, we said to him, "Stop letting your rank go to your head and listen to your troops a bit more. We know a bit better because we've been here for longer." To be fair, he did learn from that.

'The next day we were returning from another patrol, and we went by the little mill and bakery. Usually, we'd wave at the guy there, and he'd wave back. But on this occasion there was no sign of him. We thought nothing of it and just carried on into the base, tactically, like we always did, one at a time, covering each other.'

As he got near to the gate, Charlie Emina was blown off his feet by the biggest explosion he had ever experienced. Coughing and spluttering, the sun blacked out by dust and debris, and with rubble crashing down on his position, he thought they had been hit by an RPG. Tom Sephton was a few feet away, lying on a roll of barbed wire. The two friends looked at each other and winced, before staggering to their feet and back into the PB.

'It turned out that they'd been digging a tunnel for weeks from the bakery,' said Emina. 'When we'd thought they were taking in bags of flour, it was actually bags of explosives. They chose that day to set this huge underground bomb off, but they'd dug the tunnel too deep and we'd only been hit by the rubble flying up and cascading down again. The crater by the gate was still ten or eleven feet deep, so there must have been a huge amount of explosives down there. We were like, "Wow! We've escaped the donkey and now this!" We couldn't believe our luck.'

* * *

AS A YOUNGSTER, Tom Sephton was never 'Army barmy' – he only joined up after a casual perusal of some careers office pamphlets. But he was almost designed for a career in uniform.

'Tom was never still,' said his mother, Angela Horn. 'He was always falling over, banging his head, getting stitches. It was unbelievable. He loved his sports. He was playing football from around six or seven, but his father, Ian, took him to a mini-rugby league session when he was nine, he found he was very good at it, and that became his main sport. He played for Warrington Schoolboys for five years, though he supported St Helens. He was ball-boy for Warrington in a game against St Helens, and, at the end of the match, he ripped off his Warrington shirt and he had a Saints shirt underneath. Then he asked the Saints team for their autographs!

'[The Royal Marine] Steve Birdsall and he were in the same class, they both joined up, and they were both killed. It's such a tragedy. They spent a lot of time together out of school, and they'd often have sleep-overs at each other's houses. I always found it a challenge to get them to sleep. They weren't bad, but they'd get the giggles. One lovely memory of them together is a day-trip to Blackpool when they were thirteen. I wasn't brave enough to go on the big dipper, and neither was Tom, but Steven went on it.'

Tom was five years old when Angela and Tom's policeman father, Ian, split up.

'I was raising Tom and [his older sister] Sarah on my own,' said Angela. 'It wasn't easy, and money was tight, but Christmases were always lovely. I never worked on Christmas Eve; that was for the children. We'd go to the pictures, and then go for something to eat, or do something else special. Then we'd come home and they'd go to bed and I'd be wrapping presents. Christmas dinner was always just the three of us.

'We were very close. Tom would come and tell me anything and everything, and even when he was in his teens he'd come off the rugby pitch and he would give me a kiss and a big hug. He was never bothered if his friends took the mickey out of him.

'Of course, he and Sarah often had little scraps. She was five years older, which is quite a big gap, but they grew closer as they got older. She was made up when he was old enough to go partying with her. They were real party animals, those two. I used to say, "There's only you two, so look out for each other."

'Later, when Tom was fifteen, I had another boy, Reece. Tom was very good with Reece. I have pictures of him cuddling him. He was going to teach Reece how to play rugby one day.'

Sadly, that was not to be.

Tom attended Great Sankey High School with his mate, Steven Birdsall. He enjoyed school and was a popular figure, known for his practical jokes and his sense of humour, and he charmed most of his teachers with his broad, easy smile. He excelled at drama – his reports said he had 'great stage presence' – and PE. He was a member of Warrington Athletics Club, winning many club races, and he left Great Sankey in 2006 with the school hundred metres record under his belt, and having won an award for sporting excellence presented in memory of Tim Parry, a twelve-year-old pupil at the school who was murdered by the IRA in the Warrington bombing in 1993.

But he did not have much idea of what he wanted to do with his life. He didn't fancy college – academic achievement had not come easy, though he had worked hard to get reasonable grades – but while jobs for youngsters are in relatively short supply these days Tom was a natural grafter, and a likeable lad, and he had no real trouble finding work.

He took agency jobs, worked at Wynsors shoe shop in Warrington, and in the Next warehouse, and followed that with a stint at Boots. Angela had a friend who was a gardener, and Tom helped him if there was nothing else doing.

It was a shock when, one day, he came home and told his mum he wanted to join the Army.

'He was seventeen,' said Angela. 'As a young boy, he'd wanted to be a rally driver, or a rugby player, or a police diver... all sorts of exciting things. The one thing he never said was he wanted to be a soldier. So for him to actually join up and go away, then not come back... well, it's hard. I said, "Hang on a minute. Let's sit down and talk about this. There's Iraq and Afghanistan... Please stop and think about it."

'His granddad wasn't happy either. He said, "Tom, what are you on about? The infantry, in this day and age? Why not pick something different?"

'He said, "Well I'm only looking and getting information. I'm just thinking about it." So I just put it to the back of my mind. I thought he'd soon be wanting to do something else.'

On the other hand, his dad was pleased. 'I felt he'd really found something that he wanted to do,' said Ian Sephton. 'He said he felt he could make a career of it and he was very excited about joining. So I stood by him.'

Tom Sephton joined the Mercian Regiment in 2008.

As we know from Charlie Emina's account, Tom flew through training like a shooting star.

'Sometimes he'd call me and say, "Mum, we've had a real beasting today,"' said Angela, 'but he liked it, really. The camaraderie and the friendships were great. I was immensely proud when he passed out. *My Tom!* I thought. He was based at Catterick, which is only a few hours' drive away, so he often came home for weekends. He'd call me on a Friday night, and he'd say, "Mum, is it okay if the lads come round for a few beers?" I often had a houseful. But they were good. They'd have a few drinks and listen to music, and then they'd pop off into town. I woke up many a morning and came downstairs to find myself stepping over the bodies of sleeping soldiers.'

After two short tours to the Falklands – he hated the weather, he told his mum, and bemoaned his failure to see a single penguin – it was Kenya, training, and then Afghanistan. It was his mother's worst nightmare.

'I'd just put the risks and dangers out of my head until they said they were deploying,' she said. 'Christmas 2009 was his last with us. As soon as we got into the New Year I was just praying they would delay it, but they didn't. I remember kissing him goodbye before he returned to camp for the last time. It was horrendous. My mum and dad, his sister, me… We were all getting upset. I was determined that he wasn't going to see me cry. I didn't want him to be upset because I was upset. As he always did, he hugged me and kissed me, and said, "Love you loads, mum. I'll see you when I get back."

'I told him to be careful and look after himself, he said he would, and then he was gone. I stood at the bottom of the drive and waved until he was out of sight, and then I cried my eyes out. I kept telling myself he'd come home.'

Ian Sephton drove Tom and Charlie Emina to Burtonwood Services on the M62, from where further transport had been arranged to the camp. It was there that they said their final goodbyes. Ian gave them both a hug, asked Charlie to look after his son, and told them both to 'keep their heads lower than their arses, and their arses lower than their heads!'

'It was an old Army thing that my own dad used to say,' said Ian. 'In other words, stay flat on the ground! Tom said, "Course I will, dad, don't worry about me."'

And that was that.

On Easter Monday, Angela received a text from Tom at Catterick.

'It said, "Mum, we're going tonight. Love you loads and speak to you when I get back",' said Angela. 'I still have the text on my phone.'

'At least I'd been able to talk to him while he was training. But out there it was different. He'd go on Facebook when he could, but they rarely had any service. I didn't have a computer, so my sister would tell me when he'd put something up, and I'd go around to her place and send him a message. His last post was, "Been in a couple of blasts today. Somebody up there must be looking after me. THANK YOU!"' And he would phone me whenever possible. I hardly had my phone off my body all the time he was away, but one day I'd put it on charge in the hall, and I nipped outside. I'd missed him, and he had to leave me a message: "Mum, where are you? Love you and speak to you soon." I was absolutely gutted. Those phone calls were precious.'

Early letters home from the tour were full of fun. He talked of hoping to meet up with 'girls in tight tops and short skirts' on his return, and mused on the forthcoming football World Cup – 'just another reason to drink copious amounts of Tequilla lol'. In one, written to his grandparents, he said:

> *Hi Nan and Grandad, Hope ur Both well? I Am doing Fine out hear although its hard work with the heat and weight and lack of food haha but Its all good so don't worrie 2 much. THANKYOU very much for the parcels but dont send any more Baby wipes, Toothpaste or cheweing gum I get so much I could start a shop! I cud do with sum washing up power because shower gel doesnt work well on my uniform or sock and also pens pencils note pad with no lines for drawing as well please maybe sum chilli peanuts and other crazy Ideas you have I have enuff toiletries Now I just Need shower gel AND I shud B Fine. I AM realy looking forward to sum of your world famous Bacon Butties on white toast with Tommy Sauce It Sound Fantastic!*
>
> *...I hope ma sis and reece are doing ok, cant wait to C them all. I am missing everyone But I will B back Before I No It (I HOPE) any ways I am kind of running out of things to say I cant talk much about wats happening here so... and you probably dont want to no Till I am Back safeley anyway.*
>
> *I am leaving my letter as it is now so I am going to say Bye Bye love you all Tell everyone I sed HI.*
> *Love you loads*
> *Your Best Looking grandson*
> *HAHA*
> *xxx*

Tom's tone changed as the tour went on. 'The first few phone calls were dead upbeat,' said Angela. '"It's hot but we're fine, and I just want to sort out my R&R!", that sort of thing. As time went on, it seemed like he was flat-lining. He said he and Charlie had had enough, and when they came home they'd be handing in their papers. I think they were very traumatised.

'At one point, he hadn't rung for quite a while. We were all a bit worried. I got hold of Charlie's girlfriend, and, yes, she'd heard from Charlie. We didn't know why Tom hadn't contacted us. It turned out that he was feeling so homesick that he knew talking to us would upset him too much.

'I was told a lot about what had gone on by the lads after they came back. He was always the first to volunteer to be at the front with the IED detector, so he was the lead man on many patrols. They said he seemed to have a sixth sense about IEDs, and saved their lives on several occasions. One of them told me about an IED blast in which he was knocked down. He couldn't see anything at first, but when the dust cleared he saw Tom standing over him saying, "You're one lucky bastard!" Then he picked him up. There were a few near misses. Tom didn't tell me any of this, because he wouldn't have wanted me to be worried, so I always assumed he was at the back.

'What they saw out there must have been horrendous, and I think the risks must have been weighing on his mind. He was living for his R&R. I remember he said he wanted a barbecue when he got back. All he wanted to do was sit in the garden with a couple of cans of Strongbow and some fit girls. I said, "Okay, I'll see what I can do." Then he said, "Just to give you a heads-up, I've invited about fifty of the lads."

'Once he said he'd had fifty-two mosquito bites in one day. He'd had sickness and diarrhoea. He lost a stone in a matter of weeks, and he really didn't have a stone to lose. In the photos that his mates took out there, he's just skin and bones, although he had a six pack that he was quite proud of. He suffered from hay fever badly, too, so I was sending him tablets for that. The boys were often hungry, and they had those heavy packs to carry in that heat. Tom wasn't a big lad at all, although they all said he punched above his weight. It's a good thing I didn't know exactly what he was doing, because that might have tipped me over the edge. In my heart of hearts, I just think it was horrendous. The last thirteen weeks of his life were shit.'

It must be said that Ian Sephton didn't detect the same degree of unhappiness in the letters and phone calls he received from his son.

'I felt he was coping well and looking forward to finishing his tour,' said Ian. 'He was optimistic about getting promotion.'

On June 14, Steve Birdsall was killed.

'They were in totally different parts of Helmand, and they couldn't keep in touch,' said Angela. 'But word of what had happened did get through to him, and it must have been awful. It would have put the fear of God into him, too. He phoned me and said, "Mum, I know

Steve has died. Please tell his mum and dad that the moment I'm back on R&R I'll be coming around to see them." He asked me to go and see them for him. I said I would, of course, but he was insistent that I tell them that he was going to come and see them himself as soon as he could.'

Steven Birdsall's funeral had taken place on July 1, and Tom managed to call home and speak to his father shortly after it had taken place.

'We were at the British Legion Club where Steve's wake was being held,' said Ian. 'So I put him onto Steve's dad, Steven, to say a few words. Steven said, "Thanks very much for ringing, Tom, and stay safe out there." He told me it was lovely to speak to Tom.'

The following Sunday morning, at about 7.50am, there was a loud banging on Angela Horn's front door. 'We were all in bed,' she said. 'The only person who might come around at that time of the day would be Sarah's dad, so I shouted to her, "Get the door, it's your dad." I went to the bathroom, and Sarah came back upstairs.'

In fact, it was Ian Sephton and his wife Kathy at the door.

'I just froze there in the bathroom, because I knew it wasn't going to be good news. I went to the top of the stairs and I could see their body language. Ian had his back to me, facing the door, and Kathy was saying, "Can you just come down for a minute?" I stopped half way down, and I said, "No!" I could feel myself starting to shake uncontrollably.'

* * *

OVER IN AFGHANISTAN, Tom and his mates had been involved in clearing a route along the patrol base line that the troops called 'IED Road'.

'We thought, *Why would anyone want to conduct an operation down a road with that name?*' said Charlie Emina. 'They'd bought in the EOD guys, but someone had to secure the road and that was going to be 6 Platoon, with two other platoons brought in specially for the job. So basically we were company strength, with all the extras and medics. We were expected to be away for about four days.

'As soon as the first chopper came in to land at 4.30 that morning, myself, Sefo and two other lads were to go over to IED road down one

265

side. When the guys came off the helicopter, three of them were meant to come over and join us. It was pitch black and we were sitting there waiting for this chopper. I remember the sun coming up over the mountains, and it was the most amazing sight. It took twenty or thirty seconds to come up, and I just sat there looking at this spectacular sunrise, thinking, *Wow! That's amazing.* Never seen anything like it before or since.

'Anyway, the chopper came in and everyone jumped off it – and every single man ran into the camp. We're like, *Whoa, where are the guys who are supposed to be joining us?* So we had to do the dirty dash back to camp, and it was about half an hour before we were ready to head out again with the new guys.'

That meant a crucial, and perhaps deadly, delay. Back out on the track, Tom Sephton carried the Vallon, Charlie Emina was his cover man.

'I was scanning left and right and over his shoulder,' he said, 'ready to tap him on the shoulder and tell him to get down if I saw a threat. We were a little way ahead, we couldn't hear anyone behind us. We came to a massively dense bush, two gaps in it, a big field beyond it. We'd been to this spot on our second day at Malvern, and had had a firefight there. So the Taliban had seen us there before, and they must have thought, *We'll put an IED there in case they come again.*

'Maybe it would have been different if the troops had got off the chopper and deployed out straight away that morning. But because we'd messed around for half an hour or so, the Taliban had time to get into position. So, I'm on one knee and scanning the route to the left. I said to Tom, "What are we going to do?"

'He says, "Obviously we have to go through."

'I get on the radio and say, "There's only two ways through here, and we don't like it. We're going to come back."

'But the answer came that we just had to get through. I said to Tom, "We've got to do it, so let's just pick one of the gaps."

'Little did we know, but it wouldn't have made any difference because the bomb was in the middle, between the two gaps in the bushes. We picked the left gap. I was scanning left, and Tom had to jump across a little ditch. He was scanning two or three metres in front of me, and I was pulling myself up onto both feet to follow him. Then he shouted, "Wait! Shit! There's a wire!"

266

'I look up, and he's coming back towards me. I saw his face. Even though it was a split second, it was like I was seeing it in slow motion. I don't know if he'd seen the Taliban across the field, or just the wire. He jumped and landed close to me, pushing me down. He definitely did that on purpose. If he'd been any closer he would have jumped onto me to cover me.

'Then I just felt the explosion, and it was like I'd been kicked in the face so hard. I just remember lying there. I was thinking, *What the fuck?* My head was spinning. I was thinking, *What's going on? What was that?* Then I could hear, "Man down! Man down! Man down!"

'I looked up and I could see Tom lying on his back, about two feet from me. He was moaning, the bomb had blown the front of his clothes off, and I could see a gash under his armpit. I could see blood. And then I must have passed out.'

Some moments later, Charlie Emina came to again. The weight of his equipment was such that it was all he could do to lift his head.

'I heard someone shouting, "Where's Charlie?" I was thinking, *Why can't they see me? Am I dead?* A couple of seconds later, I felt someone cutting my kit off. I'd taken a bit of shrapnel to my nose and just under my lip, so blood was streaming down. It must have looked a lot more serious than it was. One of my mates told me later that he'd had a quick look at me, and moved on to Tom because he thought I was dead.

'I was helped up and given my weapon, and someone put an arm around me. But I was trying to look back and see Sefo. I remember saying, "No, let me get him. He's my brother!" A medic said, "No, Charlie, please!"

'I had no body armour by this time, and some of the lads were firing, because it looked like the Taliban were following the attack up. I was terrified, thinking, *I'm going to get shot here because I've got no body armour.* They brought Tom and put him next to me while they were working on him. I started crying. Then the sergeant said, "Move him!" and they did. But I could still see them giving him mouth-to-mouth. I could hear our medic, Heather, and another corporal talking. One said, "We're losing him!" And then the other said, "No, we've got him again."

'It was forty-five minutes of shambles. It took that long for the MERT

[*Medical Emergency Response Team*] helicopter to come in, which, with hindsight, doesn't seem reasonable. We were going on a high risk op searching for IEDs, and the MERTs should've been on standby, able to react in five or ten minutes.

'I had a bit of a pain in the stomach and it felt like someone had kicked me in the balls. They cut my pants off and found I had a lot of shrapnel to my legs, and shrapnel in the testicles. They were really swollen, but I knew I was going to be okay. They put us on the chopper, me on first and then Sefo. I was lying on my back trying to look behind me, and I could see them trying to squeeze bags of blood into Tom as fast as they could. At Bastion, they wheeled him off and took him straight to the theatre.

'I was put in the hospital, too, and a couple of officers came to see me later that night. They said Tom would be okay. They went through my injuries and said they couldn't operate on me for another twenty-four hours because I had food and water in my stomach. I remember slipping in and out of consciousness that night. Next day, they operated on me to remove some of the shrapnel, and when I came to again it was as though I was right back in the same place, immediately after the blast. I know I was screaming, wanting to know about Sefo. They had to hold me down.

'Eventually, they put me in a wheelchair and took me to sit with him. I held his hand. He was heavily bandaged but he was all clean, compared to when I last saw him. He just looked so peaceful. I was crying my eyes out, and saying I was sorry and grateful for what he'd done for me. As I was sitting there, the shrapnel was pushing itself out from my groin. I tried to stand up, and a big splat of blood went onto the floor and I was haemorrhaging. I went into shock and passed out. They removed the shrapnel and then took me back to bed. When I woke up again it was the same again, I was screaming, "Where is he?", and they had to hold me down again.

'Someone said they thought he was going to be okay, but that they were sending him home. I thought, *I don't care if he's lost his legs or an arm. I don't care. He's alive. He's going home and if I have to push him around in a wheelchair forever, I will. I don't care. He's alive.*

'I was saying to everyone, "He's going to be fine because they're sending him home." I was so happy. It wasn't until a day or so later, when I hobbled down to see one of my bosses… He sat me down and he said, "You know what I'm going to say, don't you?" I just thought, *No*, because I didn't. He said, "Young Tom's died. He wasn't too well, and they knew he wasn't going to make it so they wanted to get him home to his parents. I just wanted to let you know that he passed away."

'I just stood up and said, "Okay, sir. Thank you."

'As I was walking back to the tent, I saw our old officer. He was still at Bastion because he hadn't got a flight home yet. Obviously he'd heard about Tom. I just burst out crying and collapsed. I remember him picking me up and he was crying his eyes out as well. I couldn't believe it. It was like it wasn't real. I was just so ill in the head. I stayed in Bastion for two weeks before going home, and most of that time, I felt like I was flying around the place. I was on lots of medications including really heavy sleepers. But when I was awake it was hard.'

* * *

BACK IN WARRINGTON, Angela Horn remembers slumping to the floor as someone said, 'He's alright. He's been injured but he's alive. He was caught in a bomb blast and has lower leg injuries and shrapnel to his tummy and chest, but he's alive.'

'The Army visiting officer [*Capt Joe Dodd*] kept me in the picture as best he could,' she said. 'I was told Tom would be okay, and he'd be coming home soon, but that night Joe was called again and told he'd taken a turn for the worse. Joe told me this, but I was not going to accept it. I said, "What are you telling me?"

'He said, "Ange, he's not going to…"

'I said, "Don't you tell me he's not going to make it home!"

'Next thing I was beating shit out of Joe, apparently. I went to the floor and dragged him to the floor too, and I wet myself with shock. I was screaming at a picture of Tom. I was saying, "Don't you dare leave me! Don't you dare die in that Godforsaken place! You get home to your mother now!"

'Our Sarah ran to get the neighbour to help drag me off poor Joe. I was shouting, "No, he's not going to leave me! Don't you dare leave your mother!" I was just hysterical. But within half-an-hour, Joe had received another phone call saying that they'd managed to stabilise him, and they'd be flying him back to the UK immediately. I had to believe that Tom felt he needed to get home to his mum.'

With Tom being brought back to the Queen Elizabeth hospital in Birmingham, arrangements were made for Angela, Ian and Kathy to visit him, first thing next morning.

'I ran around getting things I thought he'd like,' said Angela. 'I even wrote cards out. I've still got them. I didn't realise how bad the situation was, obviously. We arrived at the hospital on Monday morning, before the aircraft carrying Tom had landed, and we had to wait what seemed like a long time while they brought him to the hospital and settled him in a bed.'

Then the medical staff who'd brought Tom back from Afghanistan updated Angela and Ian as to their son's condition.

'They were very friendly,' said Ian, 'but they were also very professional. He'd been stable during the journey, and we'd be able to see him, but his injuries were worse than we'd first thought. I was prepared for the worst.'

Angela remembers one of them taking her hand and telling her that Tom was 'failing'.

'Apparently, when the medics got to him, immediately after the bomb went off, he was conscious but unresponsive. I didn't know what that meant. I wanted to know if he was in pain. Did he know what had happened to him? The worst thing was that I wasn't there. As a mother, you are always there when your children hurt themselves. But he was so far away. I was told his body would have gone into shock very quickly, so he wouldn't have felt anything. We only had a couple of hours with Tom at the hospital. We all talked to him and told him to open his eyes. Every now and again there was a tear in his eye, and I would wipe it away. I'm thinking, *Can he hear us? Does he know we're here?* But he never regained consciousness.

'It was all so quick. I wanted my mum and dad with me, but we didn't have time to get the rest of the family down there.'

Those who were there were able to spend some private time with Tom. Angela kissed him – she 'couldn't leave him alone', she said – but eventually they were approached by the doctor in charge.

'He said Tom's condition was getting worse and he couldn't breathe on his own,' said Ian. 'I asked if we had any options, but the doctor said he wasn't responding to any of the medication and treatment they were giving him. I said, "Please do what you think is best."

'We all stood there while the machine was switched off, and we watched as he passed away slowly. But we knew he was in no pain, and that helped a little. He wasn't suffering.

'Then we were taken into a family room and the organ donor advisor said to me, "I'm awfully sorry, because I know Tom was a registered donor, but we can't use his organs because of the nature of his injuries."'

As if all that had happened was not enough, this was another level of distress for Angela.

'That was like a kick in the teeth,' she said, 'Even though I had lost Tom, I wanted somebody else to gain from his death.

'We left him there at the hospital and went home. I assumed that I was going to see him again. But it was ten days before he was released to the funeral director, and it then had to be a closed casket funeral because of the time that had passed. To be told that I couldn't see him again was awful. I look back now, and I think, *Why did I leave him there?* I could have picked him up out of that bed and brought him home in the car. He was my child, and I left him in Birmingham where he didn't know anybody. In my head, he was still my child, and he should have been at home with us.'

Angela's thoughts turned to Charlie Emina, too.

'He was very traumatised,' she said. 'His injuries weren't that bad – he had shrapnel in his arm and down below. But mentally he wasn't fit. He just kept shouting, "Sefo! Sefo!" He kept on saying, "I've got to get home to mum!" One of the doctors told me later that Charlie wasn't talking about his own mum; he was on about me. I begged them to get Charlie out for the funeral, and they did.'

Ian Sephton could not think more highly of the Army officer tasked to support the family.

'Joe Dodd handled all the funeral arrangements,' he said. 'The cortege was led by police motorcycle outriders, and all the roads to the church were closed. When we passed the local police station, there were hundreds of officers lined up on the street saluting. It wasn't my station, but they were paying their respects anyway. That was very emotional for me, because I wasn't expecting it.

'Outside the church were thousands more well-wishers – including firemen, St John ambulance, more police, all of whom saluted as we passed them. The Royal British Legion standard-bearers were outside the church. It was awesome. I looked at Kathy, and I said, "My God! This is all for Tom!"'

The young soldier's coffin was draped in a Union Flag, and his younger step-brother Dan placed Tom's Army cap on top of the coffin. In recent years, Tom had been living with Dan, Ian and step-mum Kathy, and the two boys had become the best of friends. Tom's uncle, Anthony Gibson, read a eulogy, which talked about family games of chess, days spent building go-karts, and trips to theme parks, his nephew's enjoyment of bacon sandwiches, Haribo sweets, and Christmas dinners. Tom's great loves, family apart, he said, had been convertible Audis, blondes and brunettes, and his 'favourite lucky orange shorts'. In fact, many of his family and friends wore orange ties, ribbons or dresses in his memory.

'Regardless of your beliefs,' said Anthony, 'I have never met a soldier more deserving of eternal life than Tom.'

'He made everyone in the church laugh and cry, almost at the same time,' said Ian Sephton. 'Some of the brigadiers and generals who were there said it was the best eulogy they'd ever heard.'

The funeral was a traumatic affair for Angela, and her memory of it is vague.

'I just had my head down all the time,' she said. 'My heart was broken and I never stopped crying. People told me I was almost carried in and carried out of that church by my visiting officer. He held me up.'

Charlie Emina's memory of his time in hospital at Bastion is similarly cloudy.

'They carried on with the operation, and a couple of the other lads were injured so they came to the hospital at Bastion, too,' he said. 'We got together, and we cried. I really can't remember those two weeks clearly. I just remember hovering across the ground. It sounds weird, but that's what it was like. Tom's mum and dad said that they wanted two things, a photo album that they had made for him, and they wanted me to go back for the funeral. So they sent me back on July 18, and the funeral was on July 22.'

Not long afterwards, Emina's girlfriend gave birth to his daughter. 'She was born on August 10,' he said. 'She was like a miracle baby. I wouldn't have been there to see her if it hadn't been for Tom, so we thought about calling her Tom. We decided to call her "Isabella Tom" instead. We figured that when she got older and went to school, the kids would ask her why she had a boy's middle name, and she'd be able to say, "Well, my Uncle Tom saved my dad's life in Afghanistan." We feel that his name will live on through our little girl. Tom would have been Isabella's Godfather if he'd lived. Instead, Tom's mum is her Godmother. She'll be four in August. It's gone quick.'

Charlie Emina ended up being medically discharged: the explosion had left him deaf in his right ear, and partly deaf in his left.

'I was okay about leaving,' he said. 'I did love the Army, but it wasn't the same without Tom. I think of him every day. I love him with all my heart, and I'm lost without him. We have a couple of pictures of him and me in the hall at home, and Isabella has a picture of her Uncle Tom in her room. She sometimes asks what happened to him. I have to say, "He's in heaven, but he saved daddy's life."'

* * *

TOM SEPHTON'S LOSS left a huge hole in his family.

'Life is never going to be the same for us,' said Angela. 'Sarah feels lost. She's suffered really bad depression. Her fiancé helps her a lot. She can talk about Tom now, which is good. She can even have a smile and a giggle about some of the memories of Tom. But she misses him so much. She misses their banter, and I miss them talking about what they'd been up to when they went out together. Reece has missed out on a fantastic big brother, and Tom has missed out on the joys of seeing Reece grow older and perhaps teaching him rugby. He was four when Tom died and he's eight now. He remembers Tom, vaguely, and he knows who he is, because we have photos all over the house. Recently we were talking about Tom, and he just turned to me and said, "But mummy, you've still got me and Sarah."

'It broke my heart. I couldn't say to him, "Yes, but it's not enough."

'I tried counselling in the early days, but it doesn't help. All I did was sit there and sob my heart out. I just gave up in the end. I know they're trained, but counsellors can't understand what I've been through. My doctor then wanted to put me on anti-depressants. But I said I wasn't depressed. I was grieving, and sad. So I haven't taken any tablets.

'Jenny [*Steven Birdsall's mother*] and I didn't know each other very well before. Usually we were busy, so we'd just say, "Hi, how are you?" or something like that when one or the other of us was picking up the boys or dropping them off. But after our two boys were killed, the relationship between Jenny and me became very strong, and very important. No-one else could understand what we had been through, and we bonded very strongly. We still have a great friendship, and we support each other. We meet up quite often, and have lunch and a glass of wine or two. We talk about the boys, and we watch videos and DVDs of them together. That's our own form of counselling. We always contact each other on anniversaries and birthdays, but we don't even need to ask each other how we are feeling, because we know. We go to the cemetery together, too. The boys are buried near to each other here in Warrington. It's a nice, peaceful place.

'I still feel I'm a member of the regimental family. Every year on the anniversary of Tom's death, the Mercians send me a bouquet of flowers, and they send me a card at Christmas. If the regiment has organised any kind of event, they ask me if I'd like to come along. They've been very good like that. Tom spoke to me once about his sergeant major. He said, "He's tough, mum. He's got scars, and he's been in loads of fights, and he's done this and that. I think me and Charlie Emina are his favourites, because he told us to go and get McDonalds for all the lads the other day." That sergeant-major came around to see me when the battalion got back from Afghanistan. He said that, out of all the lads, Tom was the one he never had to raise his voice to, and he never had to tell him to do something twice. No matter how awful the job he had been given, Tom would just do it without complaining.

'Then that big, tough man just sat in my chair, and cried. They'd lost nearly a dozen men on that tour, and the poor man had to visit all the families. He put his papers in and left the Army after that.'

[*The Mercian Regiment lost eleven men, including two reservists, on Herrick 12.*]

274

Cpl Chris Harrison during a brief rest on patrol somewhere near PB Shuga, Sangin. Inset, Chris with Becky on their wedding day.

Cpl Baz Barrowcliff (left), Capt Johnny Mercer (centre) and LBdr Mark Chandler, suited and booted.

Mark, Baz and Johnny enjoy a little downtime.

Mne Steven Birdsall in a picture believed to have been taken the day before he died. Inset, Steven with his soldier mate Tom Sephton on a night out together before deploying to Afghanistan.

The young marine gets to work on one of his many blueys home.

Tom and Charlie Emina prepare to cross a canal bridge – just the sort of place the Taliban might lay an IED.
Inset, a proud day: Pte Tom Sephton with his mother Angela.

Tom and Charlie strike a pose during a quiet moment at the FOB.

Rgr Aaron McCormick with his beloved 'ma' and with a comrade on the deadly streets of Afghanistan.

LCpl Jon McKinlay in a selfie with his daughter, Megan. 'I think about dad all the time,' she said. 'He is my hero.'

Kevin relaxing at home with his wife Nia and his mother Sue.

CSjt Kevin Fortuna on patrol in Afghanistan: he was 'one of the very, very best'.

An adrenaline junkie, Jon McKinlay was a born soldier who died trying to help his ANA colleagues to pray.
Inset, Jon and his wife Lisa on their wedding day.

LCpl Peter Eustace, the 'Big Scouse Bear' as a tiny lad.

Peter and his family – mum Carol (centre), brother Ryan (right) and sister Kirsty – in a precious, home-printed photo.

LCpl Eustace gets some rounds down with the GPMG.

Lt Dan Clack – a natural leader of men and an excellent soldier – meets a local elder while on patrol.

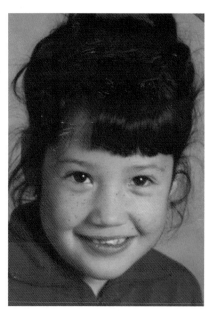

Pte Channing Day as a little girl; her ferocious will-to-win drove her on to become a brave young combat medic.

Channing about to go out on patrol – cheerful as ever.

'Tom is remembered in our area through his love of rugby league. Every year, we have a one-day rugby tournament, the Tom Sephton Memorial Trophy [*played between Army teams and Crosfields ARLFC*]. It raises money for military charities, and it's just got bigger and more important every year. We sell programmes, and there's a bar and loads of stall and entertainments. One of the guys in the regiment said to me, "It's a fantastic legacy that your son has left. The Army now is playing more rugby league than rugby union!"

'Those are good thoughts, but it's horrible to see other kids getting married and having babies. I feel bitter sometimes. I just feel robbed. Christmases are very difficult. I wake up on Christmas morning, and I cry. It's like… He's not going to be here again, *ever*.

'There are times like birthdays when it's just too tough, and I cry. Of course, that doesn't make me feel better. I say to people, "I can't Skype him, I can't write to him, I can't phone him, and I can't see him."

'It's changed me. My patience is so thin, and I get very angry with people who complain about small things. I feel like saying to them, "Excuse me, would you like to step into the shoes I've been wearing for the last few years? You've got nothing to complain about." Unless you have lost a child, you have *nothing* to complain about.

'I don't think we should have been in Afghanistan at all. The politicians made the decisions that took Tom and his friends there, but you know it wasn't their children who had to go out there and fight. People have asked me if I think it's been worth it, and my answer is, No, I don't think it has been worth it. Nothing is worth losing your child for. No progress has been made in Afghanistan. So many countries have gone to war there, but no-one ever wins.'

Ian shares Angela's opinion about the war, and was obviously hit just as hard by Tom's death.

'I do feel bitter about Afghanistan,' he said. 'I don't think we should have been there. I took three months off from my job. Work put me through counselling, and they arranged a phased return. My colleagues were all brilliant, but I just couldn't settle back into the job with the same enthusiasm I had before we lost Tom. So in March of 2013 I retired.'

Dan, Tom's stepbrother, was also deeply affected. The two boys had become the closest of friends and had agreed that, if Tom died in Afghanistan, Dan would join the Army in his place.

'Dan was heartbroken when Tom died,' said Ian. 'And it was especially awful because it happened on his eighteenth birthday. Since then, Dan's never celebrated his birthday.

'He did as he'd promised and joined Tom's old battalion, 1 Mercian. Since then he's served in Afghanistan himself, and he's currently in Cyprus on a United Nations peacekeeping tour. Of course, I now worry every time Dan goes away.

'There isn't one day that goes by when I don't think of Tom. I know I'm going to miss him getting married, becoming a father, and doing all the other things that children would normally do.

'Every day is a struggle, because Tom wasn't only my son, he was my best friend. People say it gets easier, but it doesn't. The only thing you get used to is talking about it.' To do so brings this heartbroken father a small measure of consolation. 'In another forty years no-one will have heard of me,' he said. 'But they will certainly have heard of Tom.'

RANGER AARON MCCORMICK
A COMPANY 1st BATTALION THE ROYAL IRISH REGIMENT
FEBRUARY 2, 1988 – NOVEMBER 14, 2010

THERE WERE PLENTY of difficult and dangerous jobs on offer to British infantrymen in Afghanistan, but – as we have seen – one stood out above the rest: Vallon man.

The Vallon man was his mates' first line of defence in the war-within-a-war between the soldiers and the Taliban's pernicious IED gangs.

He walked ahead of everyone else on patrol, exposed to enemy fire, sniffing out the buried devices using his wits and his gut, his experience of ground-sign like disturbed earth, and a 4kg 'Vallon', which looked a little like a metal detector but also had ground-penetrating radar.

If the electronic alarm sounded in his headset, he would hold up a hand to signal to his comrades to back off, get down low, and go into all-round defence. Then he would lie down on the ground to investigate the find, head towards the bomb, probing the soil, sometimes flicking material away with a paint brush. If the warning beeps were right – and if all went well – the spot would be marked and EOD experts called in to defuse it.

But the risks are obvious. Mentally and physically taxing, and with a terrible attrition rate, it was a volunteer role only for men of extraordinary courage and nerve.

Dane Elson of the Welsh Guards was one such, Tom Sephton another. Ranger Aaron McCormick was so uncannily skilled at the job

277

that his comrades nicknamed the keen *Stars Wars* fan 'The Jedi'. He literally embodied his regiment's Gaelic motto, *Faugh a Ballagh* – Clear the Way – and in doing so he saved dozens of lives.

Until one Remembrance Sunday, when the Taliban got lucky.

Rgr McCormick – a whip-smart, twenty-two-year-old, who was an excellent clarinettist and a regular winner of jive and rock 'n' roll dancing competitions back home – was on his second tour of Afghanistan. Things had changed since his first visit, to the mean streets of Sangin in 2008. Since then, the insurgents had all-but given up trying to take on British troops in firefights. With their inferior weapons, tactics and shooting, they lost every significant contact, badly.

The resultant casualties had forced them to fall back on a standard guerrilla tactic – the planting of IEDs.

These were put together by experienced bomb-makers working in 'factories' hidden in residential compounds – many of the ISAF patrols were dedicated to uncovering these workshops of death. The bombs could cost as little as five dollars to make, and varied from small, home-made affairs, packed with fertiliser explosive, to more sophisticated bombs made from old Soviet tank shells. They might be planted singly, or in 'daisy chains' of multiple devices. They were hidden in ditches, or alongside tracks, or in walls, or disguised as rocks. As discussed in earlier chapters, they had initially contained lots of metal. But that had made them relatively easy to locate, so by 2010 the Taliban were using more plastic and wood in their construction. Because of this, some twenty per cent of IEDs were next-to-impossible to find. They could be triggered by simple pressure plate – often two rusty saw blades, separated only by a small piece of wood, which came together to complete an electric circuit when an unlucky man or woman stood or drove over them. Or they were set off remotely, by hidden command wire, radio or mobile phone signal, with the killers watching and waiting for the right moment to initiate their bombs.

The worst of them had caused multiple deaths, as in the incident that killed young Will Aldridge and four of his fellow members of 2 Rifles. Many more soldiers had lost limbs after setting off an explosion.

Apache helicopters and special forces troops spent long nights hunting the enemy teams which were laying these deadly traps. But it was a numbers game, and inevitably many got through the net.

For the soldiers who then had to go out on patrol through Helmand, the Vallon man was like their goalkeeper, perhaps even their guardian angel.

Rgr McCormick's friend and comrade Ian McKergan said Aaron was the best operator he'd seen. 'I wouldn't say he necessarily liked operating the Vallon,' said Rgr McKergan. 'But he knew he was good at it, and that everyone else was safe when he was at the front. I did it only once and I couldn't do it again. It wrecked my nerves. I'd rather carry the electronic counter-measures equipment, extra ammo, anything, despite the weight and the heat. I don't know how Aaron did it time after time. He didn't have to volunteer, and he earned a lot of respect from me and the other boys for doing it. He was an amazing guy.'

* * *

AARON MCCORMICK WAS born in Coleraine, County Londonderry, the third child of Maggie and Lesley, and a brother to Michael, Tammy, and Callie.

It was 'a brilliant pregnancy', said Maggie. 'He was no problem at all. We were celebrating Michael's birthday on February 1 when I went into labour. But I just carried on with the party, and Lesley took me to the hospital later that night. Aaron was nearly three weeks overdue, but when he decided to come, he came just like that, so he did.

'He was a near-perfect child, too. Don't get me wrong, he had his bad points, but he was full of life, and he was the wee joker of the family. If there was any carrying-on around the house, you'd know who would have started it.

'The only thing was, he had chronic asthma. As a young boy, he used two different types of inhalers three or four times a day. He had his own nebuliser at home, and he was sometimes on that four times a day. And he had to take steroids. Because he couldn't go out and play as much as the other children, he always had his head stuck in a book, so he could read, write, and count before he even started school. I remember his first day at school so clearly. I took him there, settled him in, and walked out a little while later crying my eyes out. It felt like I'd lost my left arm, because – thanks to his asthma – Aaron was always in the house with me, even when the others were outside playing. Leaving him at school broke my heart.

'But he loved it. He wasn't the greatest sportsman, because of his condition, but he just loved learning, and he was usually top of his class in every subject. He had brains to die for, and was so quick at everything.

'He was a very kind wee boy. One memory I cherish is when he was six and he went on a school trip. He bought me back this wee ring with a stone set into it out of one of those vending machines. We'd given him some pocket money, and he'd spent fifty pence on it. He came home pleased as punch. He said to me, "Here, ma, this is for you! Look at the diamond I got you!" And then he said, "If you keep that diamond, ma, I'll buy you the real thing one day." And, do you know, when he was about eighteen he *did* buy me a ring with a real diamond. I was in floods of tears. He asked me for the cheap one back, but I wouldn't give it to him. That fifty pence ring was worth more to me than any diamonds.'

From the age of about four, Aaron wanted to join the Royal Air Force.

'He was obsessed with it,' said Maggie. 'He loved making model aircraft, and watching films and documentaries about planes and pilots. Then, at sixteen, he suddenly changed his mind and decided he wanted to join the Army. Lesley had done three years in the Royal Irish Rangers, now the Royal Irish Regiment, and he had heard his dad's stories about life as a soldier, so it was probably that.

'By then, he was this strapping, six-foot-two bloke. The asthma had started to leave him when he got to about thirteen or fourteen, and he didn't need the steroids any more. They'd made him a bit tubby, and he wasn't very big. But from being this wee, chubby thing, he just suddenly shot straight up like a sunflower. It seemed to happen over the nine weeks of the school holidays.'

Aaron's plan was to join up at eighteen, complete his full twenty-two years' service, and then retrain as a primary school teacher. He went with his father to an Army Open Day to discuss the options. The recruiters took one look at his exam qualifications – nine GCSEs, three A levels, and a place at university waiting if he wanted it – and suggested he think about Sandhurst. But he was determined to start out as a 'tom'.

'He said, "No, I'll work my way up,"' said Maggie. 'He wanted to go in on the ground, so that if he was ever giving orders he'd know what he was talking about. In fact, before he went to Afghanistan the second time, he said that when he came back – if he came back – he was going to apply to Sandhurst.'

Aaron went to Catterick for his six months of basic training. Taking him to the airport for the flight to England broke his mother's heart a second time, she said – it was the longest period she'd been separated from her son. She was worried as to how he'd cope with the physical side of the course, as a recovering asthmatic, but he did well and in no time was passing out. His family flew over for the big day.

'Oh God!' said Maggie. 'He was so embarrassed by me. I was so proud of him that I was knocking generals over as I moved around to make sure I was getting the best view. I was like, "Get out of my way! I want to see my son!" I'm sure some people were saying, "Mind your woman there, she's mental!" But we were so proud. It was January 26, 2008, and it was freezing and blowing a gale. Berets were blowing everywhere across the parade ground, but Aaron's never moved. All the instructors and officers had brilliant words to say about him, every single one, so they had.'

Within a few weeks of passing out, Aaron McCormick was on his way to Afghanistan for the first time on Op Herrick 8.

Maggie remembers his mood as nervous but excited.

'I know it worried him,' she said, 'but he wasn't the kind of boy to let you see that. And he was looking forward to going. We had a few weeks of partying and generally having a great time, but there were some really serious moments, too. There's nothing as hard as your teenaged son sitting down and telling you that he's written his will and thought about what songs he wants played at his funeral. I told him not to be stupid, but he said, "No, ma, we've got to have this conversation… These are the songs I want. And I want to be brought home and buried here."'

Those songs were The Foundations' *Build Me Up Buttercup*, Journey's *Don't Stop Believing* and *Open Arms*, the X-Factor Finalists singing *Hero*, David Bowie's *Heroes* and Lynyrd Skynyrd's *Sweet Home Alabama*. They were indeed played at his funeral.

'Horrible didn't begin to describe that conversation,' said Maggie, 'but I had to sit and be strong for him. I needed to reassure him, and say, "You're going to be alright."'

A few days after that chat, she took Aaron to Belfast Airport for a flight to rejoin his regiment prior to departure.

'Lesley couldn't come with us because he was working,' she said. 'I didn't let Aaron see how upset I was, because I didn't want him to worry about me. I gave him a big hug before he went through to the departure lounge, and then I went back to the car. Then I sat in the car, and I cried for about two hours.

'Aaron wasn't a great letter writer, but he'd promised to phone me as often as he could. They'd often be hour-long calls. Aaron could have talked the hind leg off a horse, sure he could've. He even called from Brize Norton, just before he got onto the plane to Afghanistan. I just kept saying to him, "Now, don't you go and do anything stupid. You keep your head down, and do not volunteer for anything!"

'He said, "Ma, I'm going to save the world." Sure enough, that was his motto. "I'm going to save the world." He genuinely believed they were doing good out there. My honest opinion was that they shouldn't have been there. But he'd say, "How would *you* like it if it was so dangerous that you couldn't go out your door and go shopping, or if you were having to watch who you talk to all the time? We're there to give these people their rights."'

Rgr Ian McKergan had trained alongside Aaron McCormick at Harrogate. He remembers 'a really good bloke, good craic when you were out'.

'I remember clearly when I met Aaron,' said McKergan. 'It was July 15, 2007, and we'd just started training together. We were in a six-man team and sharing accommodation. We didn't see eye-to-eye for a while, but we eventually became good friends, and that friendship was firmed up when we deployed. Afghan makes you close.

'He was over-educated for a normal soldier. You could tell he was a lot smarter than the rest of us – we used to call him "the Rupert" because we reckoned he should have been an officer. He only had to be told something once and he'd pick it up, so he was well-respected among the instructors. I remember he was particularly good at map-reading. He was a lot better than me at taking orders, too. Too often, in those days, I'd argue, but Aaron would just go and do what he was told to do, like a soldier should.

'But he was a real nice guy. He'd never turn you away if you had a

282

problem. He always had a sympathetic ear. When you're living on top of each other like that, you help each other out. I was better at ironing than he was, and he was better at polishing boots, so I did the ironing and Aaron polished my boots.

'Off duty, he was one of the best fellers I'd ever gone out with. Obviously, the drunken times are hard to remember, but generally Aaron didn't drink too much. He was always up for chatting with the girls, and he was always quite forward with them. He was good fun.'

The two men served together on Herrick 8 – a tough six months, which ended with eighteen members of the regiment receiving awards, including three Conspicuous Gallantry Crosses and three Military Crosses. They were based in Sangin, which they took over from the Royal Marines. Initially, they were tasked with simply ground-holding; later, they were reinforced by the US Marines and a large contingent of ANA men, and took part in a number of deliberate operations. McKergan fired more rounds than he could hope to count. The first firefight came in late April, after a patrol involving himself and Aaron McCormick, which was hit by a suicide bomber.

'We were coming up a canal path and heading back to camp,' said McKergan. 'I passed a compound on my left, and a man stepped out. Immediately, there was a huge explosion. It was a few seconds before we realised it was a suicide bomber. Then they attacked us from the rooftops about a hundred and fifty metres away. We went on the offensive and they withdrew, allowing us to take the compound and clear it. That engagement lasted for six or seven hours, but we were very lucky – apart from one guy with heat exhaustion, there were no injuries.

'After that, we had to see about the suicide bomber. Regardless of what they were trying to do to us at the time, we couldn't leave his body parts lying everywhere. The ANA soldiers lifted the parts, which were scattered all over the place... there were pieces of him at my feet. They were placed on a stretcher and brought back to the District Centre, so they could be buried within twenty-four hours, in line with Muslim tradition. It was really shocking. I was nineteen and Aaron had just turned twenty; we'd trained hard to handle people shooting at us, but not blowing themselves up.

'There seemed to be IEDs everywhere. A few went off near us, but although one member of another Royal Irish company was killed[22], no-one from our platoon died on that tour. Mostly, that was down to Aaron. He found so many IEDs with the Vallon. A lot of guys owe him their lives. He was outstanding with it.

'We spent most of our time at Sangin, but from time to time we'd deploy to smaller patrol bases that were not usually occupied. We'd move into these and build all the defences and sangars, cutting down trees to make better arcs of fire so that we could defend ourselves if necessary. I used to worry about being at these PBs – there'd only be about thirty of us, and we'd be there with just the bare essentials for anything between three nights and three weeks. We'd have ammo, food and water, but no comforts and certainly no phones to call home.

'Towards the end of the tour, we were rotated frequently through PB Cupples [*named for Justin*] quite frequently. The Sangin canal ran through the centre of the base, so after a hard patrol or a firefight we'd just jump into the canal to cool off and have a swim. When we did that, it was as if we weren't even in a war zone.

'The insurgents really hit us hard at Cupples, almost on a daily basis. I think we fired close to ten thousand rounds, mainly by the machine guns. Fortunately, there was more ammo at Cupples than I've ever seen in one place.'

While Aaron McCormick made lots of calls home, he was careful not to let on about the fight he and his mates were in.

'I only found out later that he was the Vallon man,' said Maggie. 'He'd asked me to send him some paintbrushes, and I said, "What are you painting?"

'He said, "Oh, we're just doing up the base." Little did I know. I only found later, when he came home and showed me a video on his laptop. I said, "Who's that, lying on his belly? What's he doing with that paintbrush?"

'He said, "That's *me*, ma. I'm using the brush to uncover an IED."

'I think that was the only time in his life that I hit him. It literally scared me so much that I got up and I hit him. We knew he was going back to Afghan soon, so I said, "Don't you *ever* do that again! *Promise* me you'll never do that again!" I kept begging and begging, and in the end he did promise. But of course, he did it again.'

It was tough for his family while he was away. Maggie, a cleaning supervisor at Coleraine University, found it very hard to keep her mind on the job.

'We would get occasional text messages from the regiment telling us someone had been injured,' she said. 'But they didn't give us the name until the families had been informed. So I was going into work not knowing if it was my son or someone else's son who'd been hurt. I wasn't sleeping or eating properly. It was a sheer, bloody, six-month nightmare.

'But he came back home okay, and we went to the airport to pick him up. There was another Army boy with him, and I literally sent him reeling in my rush to get to Aaron. I jumped onto him and wrapped my legs and arms around him, and I'm sure I must have looked like a mad woman. I was *so* happy to have him home, and it was like a huge weight had been lifted off my shoulders.'

But Aaron was a changed man.

'I knew things weren't right,' said Maggie. 'There was the physical side – he'd lost so much weight that he looked like a concentration camp survivor. He'd gone from somewhere around twelve stone down to nine stone. They were burning off so many calories with so much weight to carry, and I don't think they were being fed properly. That was despite us sending out parcels with high-calorie food, sweets, Pot Noodles...

'But it was the mental side. We didn't get our wee boy Aaron back. We got the man Aaron back. I'm not saying there was a great difference, because he still had the cheeky sense of humour. But there was something different about him. You could see something different in his eyes. His brother worded it right: he said, "You knew he'd been to hell."

'One of his friends had been killed, and another had been blown up but survived. He likely talked about it to his friends, but he didn't talk about it to Lesley and me. But still, you could see it in him. I wouldn't be surprised if he was suffering from PTSD, to some extent. He was at a nightclub with his friends one night, and there was a loud bang. It wasn't anything serious, but the boys said that Aaron freaked out. He was drinking a lot more than he had in the past, and he had nightmares. We'd hear him screaming, and we'd go in to his room and wake him up. "You're all right, son, you're all right!" I'd say. As soon as he realised what was going on, the brave Aaron would come out: "Oh, I'm fine, ma. It's all right. You go back to bed."'

Around that time, Aaron had met and fallen in love with a young woman, Becky. They were together until he died, and Maggie McCormick believes it would have ended in marriage and children.

'He was a very good-looking boy,' she said, 'and he'd always been a bit of a ladies' man. They flocked to him but, for about two years before he was killed, he'd been seeing Becky, and they were in a steady relationship. That two years was a good period, because he seemed to be home nearly every other weekend, and I knew he was safe. Becky said he still had nightmares, although probably not as often as he once had. I think he got better at hiding it. As the second Afghan tour approached, I believe he was dwelling on it more. Becky and Aaron came to stay with us for a while, shortly before he left. I remember him repeatedly saying to me and Becky, "I'm not coming back this time."

'That upset me a lot. I said "You'll be fine. You're coming home so don't get that in your head. You're coming home."

'But it got that bad that I had to ask Becky to tell him to stop it. Of course, she was worried sick, too. Eventually, he did stop talking about it to us, but that didn't stop him thinking those thoughts. We found out after his death that he'd taken his friends Dave, Tom and Gordy to the pub next door to the church, and said to them, "I won't be home again. I won't be walking in my own front door again. So look after me ma and dad."

'It was as if he had a premonition; as if he knew. But, strange as it may seem, he was still cheerful, and he didn't want to leave the Army. Lesley sat in the kitchen with him one night and said, "Let us buy you out, son. We'll get a bank loan or whatever it takes, and buy you out." But Aaron wouldn't hear of it. He just loved the Army.

'He said goodbye to his brother and sisters, as he would normally – just, "Bye, see you later." But I never said goodbye to him. We went to the airport – me, him and his dad. Lesley and I watched him check in, and then we went to the departure gate. I hugged him and kissed him, and I told him, "Don't you ever say goodbye to me." So he never did.

'Tearful wasn't the word to describe me that day. I cried all the way from Belfast International Airport home, and then I went to my bed and I cried for the rest of the day. Lesley felt the same. I knew there was something different when he left that time. I know it sounds stupid, but something told me I *wouldn't* see him again.'

* * *

A COY WAS SENT to Nad-e Ali, north-west of Lashkar Gah.

In February 2010, ISAF forces had launched Operation Moshtarak. A lightning quick early-morning helicopter insertion of more than a thousand British and Afghan troops into the area (and US forces into Marjah, to the south), it had left the Taliban in disarray. Many fighters had fled – a significant number having been killed by special forces ahead of the operation – and a large amount of weapons and bomb-making equipment had been seized, along with significant quantities of drugs. [*The* Daily Telegraph *reported that '27 tons of ammonium nitrate, along with detonators, blasting caps, pressure plates, mortars and several jugs packed with explosives ready for detonation' had been found, along with '17 tons of black tar opium, 74 tons of opium poppy seeds, 400 pounds of hashish and 443 pounds of heroin'.*]

As a result of Moshtarak, the Dari word for 'Together', the number of violent incidents had dropped dramatically, and freedom of movement for civilians and security forces in the district had improved. In May, around three thousand people had voted in elections for the local council – an unthinkable turnout had the Taliban been watching. But as ever, while it was possible to kick the insurgents out of a given area, holding the ground permanently was a different matter. Over the summer, they had slowly filtered back and, as Herrick 8 began, it was still very much disputed territory, and one frontline in the ongoing war.

The men of the Royal Irish were spread over several bases laid out in a rough circle. Aaron McCormick was sent to Checkpoint Tanoor. His good friend Rgr Vaughan White was located at the nearby PB Kalang, a bigger compound with a small ANA detachment. The two positions were virtually within shouting distance of each other, but moving from one to the other was a major operation.

'Aaron was a good mate of mine,' said Rgr White. 'He always had a smile on his face, never had a bad word to say about anyone. He talked about his family a lot, and had lots of pictures of them up in his room. He was a really outgoing bloke, too. It was hectic being on a night out with him. He loved his Jägermeister, and we'd always have a great laugh. I remember taking coffee to his room at Tern Hill [*barracks in Shropshire*] one morning after a night out. I went into his room and jumped on him to wake him up. Just as I did, he pulled back the blankets and he was bollock naked! It was the only time I've been in bed with a naked man. That was typical of his sense of humour.

'At the start of the tour, we were still trying to get a hold on the area and gain some trust among the locals, but the Taliban were dominating it, and our patrols were engaging with them almost every day.

'The adrenaline rush was huge. You'd often feel the wind from rounds passing you. But I never thought I was going to get shot – I just thought if it was your time, it was your time. Back at the PB you'd have cigarette and a can of coke or a cup of tea and just have a laugh about it.

'Gradually, over the months, we gained control. Life was easier at Kalang than it was on the checkpoints because we had more people, enough to have a QRF and to take the pressure off guard duty – there were more of us, so we had to do less time on stag. Life was generally a bit more chilled. We had ten-man ration packs and plenty of water, and there were enough people there to have conversations with and so the time passed a little quicker.

'The checkpoints were different. I spent time at one with the US Marines. There was no shelter from the sun and we slept under the stars. We made it more bearable by buying goats and chickens and fresh vegetables and fruit locally, but it was far from comfortable.'

Rgr Ian McKergan was also based at PB Kalang.

'Morale wasn't too bad,' he said, 'but the tension was a lot worse than on the first tour. There was no canal to jump into this time, and nowhere to have a bit of fun. There was a lot of arguing and bickering at Kalang.

'Tanoor was only a kilometre or two away, but it might as well have been a hundred klicks at first. The place was riddled with Taliban – there was a compound about a hundred and fifty metres away, but it took us two weeks or so just to clear that. We had contact every day, from when we arrived in September until just before Christmas. I lost count of the engagements, but on some days we had two or three. You'd see the Taliban running, and occasionally you'd see them firing, but they tended to put the rifle above the wall and fire. Only occasionally would you see those who were better-trained or braver getting up to aim at you.

'It was so bad that we had to fly between us and Tanoor. Obviously, partly that was because our priority was to build up our bases, but it shows how the insurgents dominated the ground early on. Towards the end of the tour, we had a massive push from both sides, and by the end we were walking between Kalang and Tanoor every day, and the enemy had been pushed back far to the east.'

By mid-November, the Royal Irish had suffered a number of gunshot casualties, though no deaths, and had yet to suffer any IED hits. Partly this was down to the skill and bravery of Vallon men like Aaron McCormick, and partly because the troops were trying to avoid the tracks and roads where the devices were often laid.

But on November 13, Rgr McKergan and another soldier were blown up by an IED as they cleared a compound. McKergan was dumped on his backside but otherwise unhurt; the other man lost part of his heel and calf.

'It was a massive shock,' he said. 'The heat and noise and pressure… But training kicks in, and you get on with it. Get your mate patched up and get him medical attention, that's what matters. From the time of the explosion to him being on a helicopter and out of there was less than seventeen minutes, which was pretty good.

'I think that was the first IED that hit us on that tour. The second was the one that killed Aaron. At least, that's how I remember it.'

The following day, November 14, was Remembrance Sunday. Prince William had flown into Camp Bastion for a wreath-laying ceremony but, out in the sticks, day-to-day soldiering had to go on.

A suspected IED had been spotted close to CP Tanoor the day before by the soldiers. Nearby locals had also used stones to mark its location for the British troops, but it still had to be assessed, and Aaron McCormick went out early in the morning with a number of others to take on this dangerous task. It meant getting up close and personal with the device, and, as Aaron approached it, he must have known that he was putting his life on the line. Tragically, the young ranger somehow activated the pressure plate linked to the bomb, and it exploded.

The force blew patrol leader Sgt Peter Keogh and others off their feet, but it killed Rgr McCormick instantly.

[*Aaron McCormick's family believes firmly that neither the Army incident report nor the inquest gave a complete account of the events leading up to Aaron's death. The family is seeking further information from the Ministry of Defence and the Army.*]

Rgr Vaughan White was over at PB Kalang, not long back from an early morning patrol.

'It started off like any other day,' he said. 'We'd been out, we'd come back safely, and it was still warming up after a freezing cold night. Of course, it was winter. I was often responsible for the camera surveillance system at Kalang. We used it to keep an eye on what was going on around Kalang, and to follow guys on patrol in case they had a contact.

'I was on the camera system, checking to see if there were any insurgents about, when I heard, and felt, a huge explosion. I turned the camera around and saw this massive dust cloud over towards Tanoor. Then it all started to unfold before me. There was no firefight, but I watched the other guys trying to revive someone. At that point, I didn't know who the casualty was, even though the optical system was so powerful that I could see some of the faces of the men. It was clear they were trying their best, but about ten minutes later we were told over the radio that Aaron had been killed in action. The doctor said later that he died very quickly.

'As usual, he'd been the lead Vallon man, so he was at the front of the patrol. He had gone down to investigate the IED when it was detonated. Routine drills meant everyone else had backed off into 360 degree protection, so that's why Aaron was the only one killed.

'Aaron was also the first man we lost on the tour. It was very hard to get to grips with it. We were all fond of him, and a lot of us were very angry. The first instinctive feeling was to get some payback. We wanted to get the insurgents and kill them. But I guess the senior NCOs and officers were aware of this, because over the next couple of days we were briefed before going out on patrol not to do anything stupid. Don't get me wrong, we are trained to be professional in the field, and the last thing we wanted to do was shoot random persons. That would have jeopardised all the progress we'd made. But it was hard. We weren't really in the right state of mind to go on patrol.'

Rgr Ian McKergan had also been out on a late night patrol.

'I was knackered and got into bed about four in the morning,' he said. 'I woke up at about six feeling something was wrong. I was lying there, but I couldn't sleep. It was a weird feeling, and something I can never describe. It could have just been coincidence; perhaps it was a bit cold that morning. But I remember being awake and lying there feeling something was wrong. So I was fully awake when I heard the explosion. I remember the whole place shaking from the explosion. It was so powerful that I thought it was right outside the gates of the patrol base. I can only imagine how big it must have been.

'I jumped up and had my full kit on and my weapon in hand by the time news came that someone had been killed. Within the hour, they named him as Ranger McCormick. I remember just going out the back and crying. I don't know why, because I hadn't cried before. We were friends, I guess.

'Guys came up wanting to put an arm around me, but I just wanted to be left alone. There was an empty sangar and I sat in it with a bottle of water for about half of the day. It was all over. I felt I should have done something to help, even though there was nothing I could do. It was a strange feeling. The lowest point in my Army career.'

* * *

BACK AT HOME in Northern Ireland, Maggie and Lesley McCormick were hoping and praying that their son would come home unscathed a second time.

'He couldn't get to a satellite phone often, and they didn't have great reception anyway, but we'd made the most of it,' said Maggie. 'There were days he would phone and you could hardly make him out. The next day he'd ring and he could have been sitting next to me here. I didn't care – we got one or two calls a week and it was always wonderful to hear him and speak to him.

291

'He never told us anything about Afghanistan, but he wanted to know about everything that was going on at home. What were his sisters doing, what was his brother doing, what was his little niece Tamara doing? They were particularly close. Tamara's birthday is October 6, and he phoned me about a week before her fourth birthday while she and her mum were here. He asked me to put Tamara on the phone and he said, "What do you want for your birthday, darling?" She said she wanted one of those Kodak kiddies' cameras, so he said, "Right, give the phone back to granny." He said to me, "You've my bank card, ma, so you go and draw the money out and get her that wee camera."

'So Tamara got what she wanted for her birthday the following week. We had a party for her at a place called Cheeky Chimps, and Aaron actually phoned during the party. She thought that was brilliant. But she never knew he was in Afghanistan, and we never spoke about it in front of her. If the news came on and she was in the room, we changed the channel. She didn't know what Afghanistan was.

'Lesley and I were constantly petrified, thinking about Aaron and his friends. We sent out over 250 boxes to Afghanistan during that two months. That wasn't just to Aaron, it was to all the boys in the battalion. Our spare bedroom had more stuff in it than the local shop. We were sending five parcels a week to Aaron alone. And then Becky and her family were sending him parcels, too. Apparently Aaron's nickname was Del Boy because if you needed something, he had it. All thanks to those boxes.

'We know he appreciated them. He called us once and said he'd just got back in from a patrol and there were ten boxes waiting for him. He said it was like Christmas, sure it was. I also sent him a lot of letters. In fact, the last thing I did before I went to bed every night was to write to him, sending our love.

'Aaron only wrote to us once, and that letter was to his sister Callie who was twenty-one on November 1 that year. She got it a couple of days before her birthday, and Aaron said he was sorry that he couldn't buy her a birthday card. *There's no shops round here*, he wrote. *But when I come home in February for me R&R, I'll take you out and teach you how to drink. We'll make up for it then*. That was the last thing he sent home. He never made it to his R&R.

292

'I remember everything about the day we were told he'd died. Absolutely everything. We'd had a holiday in Tunisia booked long before we knew Aaron's tour dates, so Lesley and me were there. It was Remembrance Sunday, and we'd got up early because we'd booked an excursion. We got back to the hotel at about 12.30, and the girl on reception said to us, "Someone called Tammy has been on the phone. She keeps phoning and phoning."

'We knew then. We never even waited for the lift. We ran up the three flights of stairs, got into the room and picked up our mobiles. I had around fifty missed phone calls from Tammy on my phone, and the same on Lesley's. I phoned home immediately and Tammy answered. I never gave her the chance to speak. I just said, "I know, but I've got to hear you say it."

'She just said, "Mammy, he's been killed."

'I threw the phone to Lesley and I ran out the room. I actually ran to reception and I was screaming at them behind the desk, "Get me Thomas Cook! Get me Thomas Cook! I've got to get home!"

'They kept saying, "Why, why, why?"

'I screamed at them, "My son's been killed!"'

A call was made to the British Embassy, and 'a wee woman called Julia Smyth' took control of the situation, in that unflappable Foreign Office way. Ms Smyth – who would later say that the McCormicks, and Aaron's death, had made an indelible impression on her – organised a taxi to take the distraught couple to the airport, having managed to get them onto the last plane to Stansted that night. She also arranged an easyJet connection to Belfast the next morning, which meant an overnight stay at Stansted.

'We found out that the captain of the plane had radioed ahead and booked us a room at the Radisson Stansted, and had even paid for that hotel room himself,' said Maggie. 'It was incredibly kind. Afterwards, I wanted to meet and thank him, but I don't even know his name. I couldn't get over that kindness.

'We spoke to Tammy and found out that the visiting officers were with Callie. She'd just turned twenty-one, and she'd been lying in bed at eight o'clock that morning when the knock came at the door. She told me later, "Ma, I knew who it was even before I got out of bed."

293

'They didn't want to tell her because she was on her own. Callie kept saying. "But my mammy and daddy are on holiday. I know why you're here. I'm not stupid." It was an hour before they actually told her. Callie then phoned Tammy, our eldest daughter, she came straight home. The neighbours were very good, and they helped the children a lot until we got home the next day.

'We caught the first easyJet to Belfast the next morning. It was incredible. I was sitting next to this woman whose son was getting ready to go to Afghanistan. She was crying her eyes out, and I says to her, "What's wrong, love?" She said, "I've just said goodbye to my son because he's with the Army, and he's getting ready to go to Afghanistan."

'I sat and listened to that woman crying, telling me about her son, about going to Afghanistan, for an hour, and I never told her who I was. About a week later, I got a letter saying, *Maggie, I'm the woman that was sitting next to you in the plane. It was only when I picked my car up at the airport, and turned on the radio, that I realised who you were. How the hell did you sit and listen to me?*

'I wrote back and said, *Because you took my mind off what I was having to face. That's why I sat and listened to you.*

'Of course the children were glad to see us. *Mammy and daddy are home*, I suppose they thought. *They'll sort things out. We don't have to be the big, brave ones anymore.*

'Our visiting officer was Capt Mick Butler, and he was brilliant, a tower of strength and a real gentleman. He was in touch with The Royal Irish Regiment, and, on November 19, they took us to RAF Brize Norton for Aaron's repatriation ceremony. Before the plane landed, we were sitting having coffee with some senior Army officers. Callie was telling one of the Royal Irish officers that she'd always wanted to join the Army herself, but because she had a wee girl she couldn't do it. He said, "We do take one-parent families." I just snapped and said, "You've had one of mine and you couldn't look after him. You're getting no bloody more." I didn't even say it as politely as that, believe me. The whole room went silent. You could have heard a pin drop. But I was angry, and I just exploded.

'With that, we were told that the plane was about to arrive. We were taken outside to see it land. I swore I wouldn't cry. I refused to cry, because Aaron wouldn't want me to. Lesley cried his eyes out. But I stood there and I never dropped one tear, sure I didn't. My head was held high.

'They took him to the John Radcliffe Hospital in Oxford and he came home about a week later. We had his funeral on the Saturday. We couldn't bring Aaron to the house because of the media attention we were getting. Awful wasn't the word for it. The press attention was relentless, and we couldn't even answer the phone. The visiting officer tried his hardest to keep them away, because we just didn't want to talk to them. We just wanted to be with our family.

'Aaron was in a closed casket and we weren't able to see him. He'd been dealing with an IED when it went off. He'd detected it and he was actually down on the ground uncovering it when it went off. Aaron was blown to pieces. It was instant. He would have felt nothing, so I suppose that is some consolation. I've double-, triple- and quadruple-checked for my own peace of mind, so I know that's the truth. But I still find it hard to accept. From what I have heard since, I know that some local people had told the Army about the IED about twenty-four hours beforehand, so they had plenty of time to get a bomb disposal expert in to defuse it. But instead it was Aaron who was sent down that road ahead of his friends looking for danger.

'During the inquest, some of the guys who were with him said that, just as Aaron was getting down onto the ground to deal with it, they heard a blast somewhere in the distance. Aaron turned round to the guys and said, "Holy fuck!" and then he started laughing. Believe it or not, it helps to know that one of the last things he did was laugh.

'Aaron had a military funeral. I knew all the music he wanted, because he'd told me. I held myself together, and I never cried one tear. Callie, Tammy and Michael got up to read words that they'd written about Aaron. And his best friend, James, got up and read that soldier's poem, the one that goes, *Stand easy now, soldier. You've walked the streets of Hell…*

'There were hundreds of people in the wee church, and we had to have speakers outside for those who couldn't find space inside. There were people there I'd never set eyes on before, but – and I know this sounds stupid – I didn't see them. I blanked everything out.

'It didn't hit me until that night, when all the strangers had left and it was just us family and his friends. We had a couple of drinks in the pub. I don't normally drink, but I had four double brandies that night, so I ended up a bit drunk and having to be put to bed. I slept from seven o'clock that night until nine o'clock the next morning, and I needed it because I hadn't slept properly for about three weeks. I'd hardly eaten in that time, either.

'The lads from Aaron's company started coming home on R&R, and visiting us, and they came after the tour was over. They'd lost three of their number out there, not to mention the seriously wounded, and I think the whole battalion was in pieces.'

Rgrs Vaughan White and Ian McKergan certainly recognise that sentiment. White had to be flown back to the UK after suffering a back injury in contact, and was medically discharged from the Army in 2014. He suffered PTSD as well as his physical injuries, and is still taking medication though is 'making progress'.

'The regiment hasn't been in touch to see how I am since I left, which is disappointing,' he said. 'If there's anything on TV about Afghanistan, I tend to turn it off, because it brings back all the memories, especially memories of Aaron. He was a cracking lad, it's such a shame he had to go.'

Ian McKergan was able to go back to Camp Bastion for Aaron's repatriation.

'Being in the room with his coffin with the Union flag over it was eerie,' he said. 'I just stared at it for ten minutes. A few of the boys shed some tears, but I couldn't cry. I was in too much shock. When we'd put him on the plane and the tailgate had closed, I looked back at the massive plane with the tiny coffin in it containing my mate. That's when I really broke down. We had a brew in the camp, and then those of us who'd come up for the repatriation ceremony started getting ready to go back out onto the ground. We had to get on with it. You have to do it when you are out there.

'It's not until you get home that you can start thinking about things properly. We were kept so busy that, in a way, it was easier. We thought on a day-to-basis. We didn't think outside the perimeter of the patrol base.

'We lost two more men, Rgr David Dalzell, and LCpl Stephen McKee. Morale did suffer towards the end. When we had time to think, we realised that there were three boys not coming home with us. That's when it started to sink in.'

Rgr Dalzell, twenty, and from Bangor in County Down, was one of seven children. He was killed by a gunshot wound inflicted by a fellow Ranger in a tragic accident, having proven himself a brave and resourceful soldier in a series of heavy firefights. His mates remembered a soldier who regularly had them in stitches with his wry and witty observations, was always first to the bar, and who enjoyed his dance music.

LCpl McKee was killed by an IED, aged twenty-seven. He left behind his wife, Carley. To compound the tragedy, the couple's baby daughter had died suddenly the previous year. His wife said in tribute, 'You will always be my hero and, every step I take in life, I will have my two angels looking after me. You truly are the best husband, father, son and brother anyone could ask for. Till we meet again. Love you always.'

His friend Cpl William Haighton, of Javelin Platoon, D Company, 1 R Irish, said, 'You were a true hero and a loyal friend – reunited with your daughter. RIP mate. Gone too soon!'

'It was weird after we returned and went back to barracks,' said McKergan. 'I didn't feel comfortable there anymore, because from my door I could see what used to be Aaron's room just across the corridor. I don't know if it was survivor's guilt, or just that my mates weren't there anymore, but I suffered from PTSD. There were five or six hundred people in that camp, and I felt like I was the only one there. I just wanted to be with my family, and so I left the Army. I was sent to specialists, and I got better. That's the best I can ask for, isn't it? Part of it will never go away, though. Aaron's buried near his family home and, although I live fifty miles away, I visit his grave and visit Maggie and her family as often as I can. I've been there eight or nine times. It helps me a lot, because it's good sharing memories of Aaron. I think it's helped her a bit as well.

'I have a lot of great memories of Aaron, but the best are probably from training. He loved taking pictures and videos. We were all on the range one day with GPMGs and rifles, and he wouldn't shut up until he got a shot of us all posing as if we were in [the SAS TV show] Ultimate Force. He eventually got a shot of us all walking away with our weapons over our shoulders. I look at it from time to time and it reminds me of him. I miss him.'

Maggie McCormick and her family are dealing with the loss of Aaron as best they can.

'We were always a very close family,' she said, 'but we're even closer than we were, which I would have said was impossible. We all live within a couple of doors of each other, and we're in and out of each other's houses constantly. We go on holiday together, and we'll all stay in the same hotel, usually with connecting rooms.

'Aaron's involved in our everyday lives. We think about him when we plan anything. Pingu, the little toy penguin we gave him and which used to travel with him, now comes with us wherever we go. Pingu went to Kenya training with Aaron, and had his photo taken on top of a machine gun. And we have pictures of him in the Valley of the Kings in Egypt, and sailing down the Nile. No amount of money would buy that penguin. I know it's only a wee stuffed toy, but Aaron loved it.

'Somehow, it's as if there's a bit of our body missing. But then, in a strange way, we're always conscious that he's here. We can feel him sometimes. We might be sitting here, and we'll feel hugs – literally, someone hugging you, but there's nobody there. A friend was sitting in my kitchen once, and she said, "Oh my God! I can feel somebody hugging me." I said, "Oh, that's only Aaron." That friend will tell you that there is something freaky about this house.

'Sometimes the smell of midnight jasmine, which is one of my favourite smells, gets so strong that it would sicken you, but we can't see where it's coming from. These things comfort me, because it's Aaron being the joker and trying to wind us up.

'I don't believe in God, but I do believe there's an afterlife when we will all be together again, sure we will. I know I'll see him again. That's what keeps me going. I know that, when my time comes, my son will come for me. I'll be buried right beside him. I will be with my son.

'I hate Afghanistan now. Quite truthfully, I couldn't even be in the company of somebody from the place. I couldn't. I'll never forgive them. We shouldn't have been there. It wasn't our war. The Taliban have said that they'll be back in power six months after the last of our soldiers pull out. So what did Aaron go out there for? I won't say what did Aaron give his life for, because Aaron didn't give his life. He was murdered. His life was taken from him.

'I don't accept it when people say time's a healer. It doesn't heal. It gets harder, sure it does. I often think that someday I'll wake up and find all of this has been a nightmare. That door will open and I'll hear someone saying, "Ma, get the frying pan on." Or I'll wake up at three o'clock some morning to go to the toilet and he'll be standing in the kitchen eating my dinner, just as he used to.

'To this day I haven't said goodbye to Aaron, because he's not gone. I'll never say goodbye to him as long as I live. He's still my baby, and he's still at home. What makes it worse is that I can see his grave in the churchyard from my window. We could never leave this place because of that, and because we feel he is with us all the time. I go down and I sit with Aaron and talk to him often. Maybe it's in my head, but I can hear him answering me back saying, "Wise up, woman! Come on, pull yourself together. Keep going. You're a Royal Irish mother, so you get up, and you fight!"

'I see Aaron in little Tamara. I see him in the way she behaves and the way she looks. His blood is here, so he's still here.'

COLOUR SERJEANT KEVIN FORTUNA
A COMPANY 1st BATTALION THE RIFLES
JUNE 18, 1974 – MAY 23, 2011

KEVIN FORTUNA was perhaps the ultimate soldier's soldier. He had joined the Army at sixteen, and had served for nineteen years. He had wanted to see the world, and he'd certainly done that, through sunshine tours to Cyprus, Italy and Australia, and deployments to altogether hotter trouble-spots, including Iraq – both with his regiment and as a volunteer attached to other regiments – and Afghanistan. He'd risked his life to bring peace to the Balkans, and had undertaken dangerous undercover work in Northern Ireland.

It had taken him some time to reach Colour Serjeant – he told his wife Nia that some officers felt he was not dominant and 'shouty' enough to be a senior NCO – but whatever doubters there might once have been had long been silenced. As he prepared for his second visit to Helmand, he had been told that he would be promoted to WO2 on his return.

The news surprised no-one who knew him. There was nothing flash about Kevin Fortuna – unless you counted his prized BMW Z4. He was just extraordinarily good at what he did.

Dave Hill met him way back in December 1992, and the pair were good friends for the rest of Kevin's life.

'Kev was clever,' said Hill, 'and he could have stayed on at school and got a commission, or done anything he wanted in the Army, but he wanted to be a foot soldier so he chose the infantry. We spent five years sharing accommodation, at Catterick and in Cyprus. We were a

300

two-man team in the machine gun platoon, and we did that for a good four years.

'Kevin was completely professional, and incredibly thorough. If we returned from an exercise, most of the blokes would just sit around relaxing, but not Kev. Even if we were dog tired, the first thing he'd do was strip down the weapons and clean them and all his kit. I picked up that good habit from him. And he had a great ability to think and solve problems. I remember him in the early days taking a look at something that had been done a certain way for ages, and saying, "Why don't we do it like this?" Of course, as the newcomer he'd be ignored, but it often worked out that, a little while later, everyone would be doing things Kev's way.'

Rfn Dan Meally was another very close friend, and a member of the Machine Gun Platoon of Support Company, 1 Rifles, which Kev Fortuna would lead. 'We were both keen on history,' said Meally, 'so we got on straight away. I was just a rifleman, but the rank difference didn't matter. We were on first name terms – just not in public – and he was a considerate guy, too. A few months before we deployed, my mum became very ill. The first person I went to was Kev. He offered to drive me home immediately. Later, and because mum was still ill, he gave me the opportunity to not go to Afghanistan. But I was adamant that I wanted to go with my friends. I'd been in Iraq and I'd deployed to Afghanistan before, so when some new guys were brought in to bump up the numbers, I worked closely with Kev on the training side.

'I considered myself fairly knowledgeable until I met him… What he didn't know about machine guns and other heavy infantry weapons wasn't worth knowing. The ranges are normally a static form of training, but for Kev range work was about speed and manoeuvrability. He drilled us in using the.50cal gun accurately in single-shot mode and taught us how to load it quicker, using a method none of us had ever heard of before. That enabled us to have the gun out of action for less time in a firefight. The things he taught me basically improved the odds on my surviving.'

WO2 John Greening, second-in-command of the 1 Rifles Mortar Platoon, echoed all of the above. 'Kev was one of the very, very best,' he said. 'There are no words that will ever describe just how good he was.'

His friends knew him affectionately as 'Meerkat', because of his fondness for the little creatures, some of which he had 'adopted' at a local zoo. But Cpl John Wheatley, a member of the 1 Rifles Machine Gun Platoon, said the teenaged riflemen under CSjt Fortuna's command had nicknamed him 'The Laser' because of his scary attention to detail. 'I have never known a platoon run so well,' he said. 'I was proud to call him my boss and my friend.'

* * *

SUE FORTUNA NEVER wanted her son to join the Army.

'Like Nia [*Kevin's wife*], I'm a nurse, and of course we don't like the idea of killing people,' she said. 'So it broke my heart. I worried about both the moral aspect of soldiering and whether he'd be safe, and his dad felt the same way. [*Kevin's father died in 2001.*] But that was his chosen path in life. Kev was a very intelligent boy who could have gone on to university and done anything, but he wanted to join the Army as quickly as possible. He took his last GCSE on his sixteenth birthday, and the following week he enrolled with the Army's Junior Leaders course at Shorncliffe. We weren't able to see him for a few weeks, but eventually we were able to visit Shorncliffe and take him out for an afternoon. Back at the camp later that day, I noticed all these other mothers crying their eyes out, and the boys trying to keep back their tears, too. I looked at Kev and saw a look of horror on his face. I thought, *Whatever you do, girl, don't cry now*. I cried all the way home, though.'

Despite her misgivings, Sue was very proud of her son when he passed out, as a junior sergeant, still too young to join his regiment as a fully-fledged soldier. 'They put him into the drums platoon,' she said. 'He was incandescent with rage, but he passed out from the drums course as the most-improved soldier, so even though he wasn't happy he did his best.'

And it worked out well for the young Kevin, too. 'His first trip away was an exercise to Italy, and when he got back to Catterick he phoned and said, "I'm going around the world tomorrow!" There was an exercise in Australia, and they wanted a qualified drummer, so off he went Down Under at the age of seventeen. He had a wonderful time.

I thought, *Well, whatever the future holds, the Army has given him that great experience.*

'Kevin was a lovely child and, even as a young man, he was a cuddler. If I was sitting on the sofa, he'd come along and snuggle up to me. That changed once he met Nia, which was quite right, because he transferred all his affections to her.'

Nia Fortuna met her future husband in Colchester in 1997. 'He was twenty-two and I was eighteen,' she said. 'My friend Heather and I were in town on a girlies' night out and ended up at a nightclub called The Hippodrome. We were just standing near the dance floor when I was suddenly aware of this tall bloke... He had blond hair, he was tanned, and very attractive. I said to Heather, "I quite like him!" Heather said, "No, come on, this is a bloke-free night!" so we went onto the dance floor, but before long Kev was there, too. We sort of caught each other's eye, and that was it. Soldiers didn't have a particularly good reputation in town, so if you were in the Army you didn't necessarily declare the fact. Kev told me he was a geography teacher. I thought, *Brilliant!* Later on that night, after a few more beers, he did confess that he was a soldier.'

The two were soon an item. 'When we first met, he said, "Of course, you do realise we're not going to get married,"' said Nia. 'He saw so many of his friends getting divorced. But five years down the line, he admitted defeat.'

They were married on April 6, 2002, just after Kevin returned from a lengthy posting to Northern Ireland, and a couple of years after Nia qualified as a nurse. They had a two-week honeymoon in Cancún, Mexico, but even then Kevin's mind was on the Army. 'His company was training in Jamaica,' said Nia, 'and he was actually tempted to go on from Mexico to Jamaica to join them, to which I unreservedly said that was not an option. So we flew back to the UK together. But within a couple of days he was back on an aeroplane on his way to rejoin the company.

'Neither of us wanted to have children. We were both career people, so there was never any disagreement over that. For Kev, I think, his Army career came first, I came second, and if you introduced a child into that mix it would just make things way more complicated. But that was fine. I don't regret not having children. It wasn't part of my life plan.'

After Kevin was posted to London, the couple lived on an Army estate in Hounslow for a while, but it wasn't to Nia's liking. 'For the last few years of his life, I lived here in Colchester while Kev was based with the regiment in Chepstow,' she said. 'I could be sure I wouldn't see him Monday to Friday, but with a bit of luck I would see him on the weekend. But even that wasn't guaranteed, because if he had work duties he would stay at the camp. Even when he was home, he'd often be working on some spreadsheet or another. It used to drive me insane. Very rarely did he truly relax. The Army always came first. Some days I accepted that; other days I couldn't. I might say, "Come on! Let's go somewhere together." And he'd say, "No, I can't. I'm working." Sometimes I'd say, "Oh, for heaven's sake! Just do something with me for once!"'

Nia had another, more unusual frustration. 'He was exceptionally organised and tidy,' she said. 'Everything had its place. If he was home on leave, or for the weekend, I'd come in from work, shove my coat over the bannister, leave my bag in the hallway and my shoes wherever I stepped out of them. I'd go upstairs to the loo, and by the time I'd got back a minute or two later everything would have been put away. "Things don't belong there," he'd say. Or I'd have a drink, and put my empty glass on a coaster. I'd blink, and it would've been taken away. "It's empty, you don't need it anymore." I like my shoes, and would buy quite a lot, but he'd say, "One out, one in. You don't need more than five pairs of shoes." So things got hidden. My friends would say, "Oh, you're so lucky! Your husband washes, does the ironing, cooks and cleans..." I'd say, "Yes, it is good but it can be a little annoying at times!" I could never find anything!'

He was told he was being promoted from colour serjeant to warrant officer just before his final tour. 'It took him a while to make serjeant,' said Nia. 'Kev wasn't a shouty person, and some of his reports said he wasn't dominant enough as an NCO. He still got what he wanted from people, just not by shouting. One afternoon when he was home, he kept stepping out of the room to take mobile phone calls. I kept hearing, "Thanks, mate... thanks, mate." I asked him what was going on, and he said, "Oh, I've been promoted."

'I said, "Wow! That's amazing!"

'He said, "I didn't want to mention anything until it was a hundred

304

per cent certain." Secretive is the wrong word, but he was protective. He didn't want me to be disappointed if it didn't happen. And because he wasn't a shouty person, he wasn't going to brag about it.'

Sue Fortuna hated it every time her son was deployed. 'I was terrified,' she said. 'In his first week in Bosnia there were two accidents involving Saxon vehicles, and I think four men were killed, two of them Kev's friends. He brought back photos of the accident sites, and I could see that the roads were so dangerous. But he enjoyed the excitement. On New Year's Eve, everyone was shooting and sending up flares. They could hear the Serbs just behind them cheering, and they joked about people shooting at them. They were young men, full of adventure. But I always felt every deployment might be his last, and the final time was no different. Kev came round, we had a chat and then off he went, the same as he'd always done. I just said, "Take care of yourself and keep your head down."'

Kevin had first gone to Afghanistan in 2006. He left for the second tour on the day Nia ran the London Marathon in aid of the charity Help for Heroes. 'It was on April 17,' she said. 'It was a shame he couldn't be there to support me, but he did ring me. I think he was calling from a field phone, because it was a terrible line. He kept on saying, "Did you do it? Did you finish?"

'I remember saying, "Yes, I actually did it!" I sent him photos of my medal in a bluey. I'd driven him back to Chepstow about a week earlier, to give him time to get his stuff sorted out. I stayed overnight, then drove back to Colchester. It just felt weird. It was usually him leaving me. I didn't tell Kev how I felt, because I didn't want him to be worried about me worrying about him. I remember just saying, "Alright, see you later." But, driving out of the camp, I felt horrible. I had a terrible feeling that I wasn't going to see him again. I couldn't put my finger on it, and I can't say there was any particular reason, but it was such a bad feeling. He'd been away on operations so many times, and I wondered what had protected him so far, and if that could continue. I thought, *You've been in the Army for nineteen years, and nothing bad has happened to you. But I think your luck's running out.* It was a very uneasy feeling. At that time, soldiers were dying and being seriously injured pretty much on a weekly basis. I went out for lunch later with one of my best friends, whose husband is also in the Army, and I said to her, "I have got such a bad feeling about this tour." She said, "He'll be absolutely fine. We worry about them, but he'll be fine."'

* * *

KEVIN AND HIS comrades had been tasked to support the 'Black Knights' of Kilo Company, 42 Cdo Royal Marines, in Sayedabad Kalay, Nahr-e Saraj.

'We amalgamated with 1 Rifles Anti-tank Platoon to form a large platoon of about forty guys in vehicles,' said Rfn Dan Meally. 'Or we were *supposed* to be in vehicles. But, shortly before leaving, we were broken down into multiples of twelve, and then farmed out to various other rifle companies. Kev took over as a multiple commander and asked me to go with him as his GPMG gunner. Things were quite disjointed when we deployed. We were given all the information about the Patrol Base 4 area, where we were supposed to be going – essential information, like areas where IEDs were more likely to be planted. But three days before we left Bastion we were told we were not going to be based at PB4, but at a checkpoint [*CP Sarhad*] in Sayedabad. It was bad enough that we'd spent months training as one group, and then we were split into multiples. But then to be deploying in support of a completely different group, in a place we knew very little about… That was a blow. The basic complications, such as mail being misdirected, were a pain in the arse, but my main concern was that I'd been comfortable with the people I was working with, and I just didn't know the new people.

'We left Camp Bastion and went to PB4, got everything we'd need for the rest of the tour, and moved on to where Kilo Coy were and got briefed again. That, at least, was a great six hours of briefing. Then we patrolled out that night on foot for the first time.'

The riflemen were not overly impressed with their new home.

'Living conditions were absolutely basic, and so were the defences,' said Meally. 'The Marines had just taken over from 3 Para, and they'd only built some very basic defences. Given the risk of a breach into camp, it was unfit for purpose. So, for the first few weeks, when we weren't patrolling we concentrated on the defences. Kev took to that

306

like a duck to water, organising things like that was his bread and butter.

'We were seeing very little action at this time. The uncomfortable truth is that the Taliban are totally mixed up with the locals, in fact there is very little difference. So they were busy gathering lots of information about us as they went about their everyday lives. What we had to do was let them know that we were the new sheriff in town. We'd go out with night vision kit while it was still dark, and go into the poppy fields – they were very unlikely to IED their own crops. They'd start harvesting the opium, and we'd pop up and scare the bejesus out of them. We hoped they'd assume that we'd been out all night keeping an eye on them. That bit of deception was Kev's idea.

'We'd listen in to the Taliban radios to see what we could learn. They tried to use a code, but they never changed it so we could understand a lot of their conversations. Like they always called an IED a "watermelon". But we also knew that there were some quite clever games going on. The Taliban knew we were monitoring their radios, so they would sometimes try to plant disinformation that would lead us into an ambush. They watched us so carefully, and from so close, that often we'd hear one of them telling his mates that a patrol was leaving the base. We identified a guy who'd been hanging around with a radio, and we were convinced he was setting up an ambush. So we got permission to kill him. The sharpshooter took him out, we got an Apache in to have a look at what happened next, and they saw the body being taken away on a motorcycle. Later we heard the Taliban talking about one of their scouts being killed.'

Not much of this was filtering back home to Nia Fortuna or her mother-in-law.

'Communications were particularly bad,' said Nia. 'There seemed to be problems sending blueys to and from the base, there was a lack of satellite phones, and internet access was atrocious. On the rare occasion he was able to get access to the internet, he'd be almost randomly pressing the keys.'

In one e-bluey, in April, he wrote that everything was very basic and requested she send him 'bobbins' like 'soap (dove/simple), toothpaste (any), razors (Gillette Sensor)… as i already mentioned i do have a fair bit of wash kit here, but this should keep me topped up.'

We do have computers for e.blueys and sat-phones for calling back, but everything is very worn out (the computers are missing keys through near constant use). If i start missing letters out or having poor spelling then this will be my excuse!

I did some laundry today, using a cement mixer. I poured some water in, added some detergent and my clothes and then let it 'do its business'. It worked a treat, but i think i will stick with the Miele brand when i come home!

He also sent Nia many hand-written letters. On May 20, he wrote of a parcel he'd received from her parents – it had included a photograph of a meerkat which he found 'very morale-boosting'.

Could you thank them for me (apologising once again for lack of communications).

I had a bag of the jellybeans you sent to me... Possibly the best 'food' I have had here, with maybe an exception of a 'nice chilled apple' I had today (possibly my first piece of fresh fruit so far – scurvy here I come!!!). I'm not fed up with rations just yet – I'm trying to be fairly creative, but there are some limits. I may give bread making a go soon. I have some flour, sugar and yeast – plus a recipe. I just don't have an oven – but plan to build/improvise one – we shall see!!!

My suntan is coming along slowly. I reckon I could turn/burn really easily, but I keep myself covered up head to toe. My face is particularly tanned, but I have plenty of pasty parts as well! Squeak soon
lots of love
Kev
x x x

The following day, he wrote again with an update on the stray dog that he and his mates were 'adopting'.

Hey there Nia
How are you keeping? I have just received a couple of letters from you (in fact they were printed twice – double the fun). In the letters you said that you were incredibly tired when coming in from work – just having a glass of wine and then snoozing. I have felt the same, but

*unfortunately no wine for poor little me! When I come home on R&R,
and at the end of the tour I reckon one small glass of beer will knock
me out!*

*Our dog is getting fatter. She gets hidden every now and then when
we have visitors just in case they go along the official 'no pets at our
locations' policy. Technically she isn't a pet and is free to leave
whenever she likes, but currently she decides to live with us (plenty of
food + water, and only occasionaly being trodden on!)*

*It's nearly 1000 am, but I've been up since 0500, after only a couple
of hours sleep I've already managed to do a few 'bits and pieces' today,
so I may try for a mid-morning snooze to try and recharge my
batteries.*

Lots of love and snuggles

Kev

x x x

'He had the ability to fill a whole letter full of nothing,' said Nia. 'I'd
get no blueys for a week, and then I'd get five or six together. I have a
large box packed, crammed full with letters and cards that he wrote
over the years. And there is another box full of all the letters and cards
I wrote. Our life is in those boxes. But the letters he wrote to me on
that final tour are especially precious, and I keep them in my safe. The
other day I read some of them again for the first time in about eighteen
months.

'I spoke to him five times, but invariably the phone line would cut
out. I just got used to communications being bad, but I think it
contributed to my conviction that this deployment didn't feel right.
But Kev played things down. He didn't want to alarm me by saying,
"It's horrible out here at the moment, and people are being killed and
injured left, right and centre." He wanted to protect me.

'I hadn't spoken to him for some weeks, and I was at work one day
when a call came through. I had my mobile in the pocket of my
nurse's uniform, which I shouldn't have. It rang, I answered it and I
just heard this crackling on the line and distant voice: "Hello! It's me!"
I asked one of my colleagues to look after the patients until I could
get back, then I found a store cupboard where I could speak to him. I
can't remember what we talked about, but it was just brilliant.

Afterwards, I went into the matron's office and said, "It's brilliant! I just heard from him!"

'She knew I shouldn't have had my phone with me, but she said, "That's great!"

'That was the last time I spoke to him. He was killed a week later.'

* * *

ON THE DAY of CSjt Fortuna's death, the men of the Rifles and their Commando comrades were mounting a patrol in Sayedabad.

'Most of the buildings were unoccupied,' said Rfn Dan Meally, 'which was a dead giveaway for IEDs and ambushes. Movement had been seen in the area and we were to meet a marines patrol and then jointly check the village out. We'd had a good briefing the evening before, and we did all the usual checks of weapons, comms and GPS. Then we moved out. We always tried to use the tracks that could be seen from the sangars, but as we started to get around the other side of the village, heading east, we entered the dead ground that we couldn't observe so well, around the poppy fields.

'There were some migrant workers there, which was a concern, because the Taliban were known to conceal themselves among them. We spoke to the locals a couple of times and indicated where we were going to some extent, because we knew that some of them would advise us if it was safe, so long as no-one was watching. We pretty much got the nod from these people, so we continued to an area that was flat and had a stream running through it.'

At the front of the patrol was a Vallon operator, Rfn Gareth Yates, but the Taliban's low-metal-content IEDs, built out of cloth, bits of old flip-flop, and wood from chopped-up fruit crates, were hard to locate. The British soldiers unknowingly walked straight over a 5kg bomb buried just below the surface of the farm track. Three men stepped on or around it without triggering the pressure plate; Kev Fortuna was not so fortunate.

The explosion knocked Yates and others to the ground, and caused devastating injuries to the colour serjeant.

'I was at the rear of the patrol with the GPMG,' said Dan Meally. 'My first thought was that it could be a rocket, but then we realised what it was and we hit the ground. Everyone shouted to everyone else to check we were all okay, and then we started looking for more devices. Then we got news from the front of the patrol that Kev had been badly injured. The two guys at the front were giving him first aid. The patrol of marines was nearby by this time, and they came running across to help. We had to clear a helicopter landing site so Kev could be evacuated.

'I was still at the rear of the patrol with the sharpshooter, and we noticed that more people were active in the field we'd come through just a little while earlier. We thought, *This is the ambush!* I fired some rounds from the GPMG over their heads but they carried on coming. The sharpshooter tried to get one of them but wasn't able to. But we must have spooked them, because the ambush didn't happen.

'The guys were working hard to help Kevin, and I have to be honest and say I'm glad that others did the first aid, so that I can remember him how he was before the attack, not how he was after. The MERT Chinook was with us within eight minutes, but they never managed to stabilise him for long enough, and he died that night. I found it hard to believe that Kev didn't survive. On my first tour in Afghanistan, I'd been involved in force protection for the MERTS and I'd seen people go on those helicopters apparently dead but still survive.

'Later that night, the RSM, the CO and the Padre drove to the checkpoint to give us the news personally. It was a long night. A flask of whisky got passed around from somewhere, and that helped slightly. I wasn't new to this sort of thing, but when you lose friends it's a million times worse than losing people you don't really know that well. It was the day before my birthday. I remember calling home and finding that news had already got around that our call sign had been hit, and someone had died. That's not supposed to happen, of course, until the next-of-kin have been informed.'

Earlier that day, Kev Fortuna had written a last letter to his wife – rendered especially poignant for its chatty and relaxed tone.

Hey Nia
I have just finished writing you a letter, but decided that as I had a few minutes spare, plus another bluey available I would write again. I haven't really anything extra to say, but hopefully just getting another letter is an 'unexpected' bonus.

311

The temperatures are really starting to soar, every day is in the high 40s and I can't help but get a tan, even though I try to stay as covered up as possible. I am drinking loads of fluids (no alcohol – unfortunately) along with some very basic 'squash' powders – mmm!!

I'm currently eating some chilli-puff lap-snacks which you sent to me, which are very good – yum. I may even start on some sweets as well – have a real gorging (snout in trough) session. Unfortunately that is about it for now, but I will keep putting pen (or pencil/crayon) to paper.

Squeak soon, lots of love
Kev
x x x

Not long after he had handed it over to be posted and left on that fateful final patrol, Nia Fortuna was at home, preparing to go in for a night shift at the hospital. It was about five o'clock in the afternoon, and two women turned up at her door.

'They were wearing suits and holding some paperwork,' she said, 'and my first thought was, *Oh, someone's trying to sell me something*. I opened to the door, and they said, "Are you the wife of Colour Serjeant Fortuna?"

'I said, "He's dead, isn't he? He's been killed."

'They said, "We need to come in and speak to you."

'I said, "You've got to tell me now. He's been killed, hasn't he?"

'I just walked into the lounge, and they followed me. I can't remember what they said then. I know it was something very formal, and I think they were reading from a script. I don't remember what I said, other than, "Oh my God! What can I do? What am I going to do?" I just felt complete shock and devastation. How could this have happened? I phoned my mum and dad, because they just lived around the corner. My mum picked up the phone, and I said, "Mum, you have to come around, now." She got my dad, and within five minutes they were here. I opened the door, and I just said, "Kev's been killed."

'I can't remember too much about what happened after that. I knew I needed to make sure as many family and friends as possible knew before the news became public. My dad offered to go around with the military people to Sue's house and tell her. The military people stayed for a couple of hours and then – not in a horrible way – I said, "If you're not going to give me any more information, can you just go?" 'I think they were a bit taken back by people crying, and they knew that nothing they could say would make us feel any better. The following day I had a visiting officer allocated to me.'

Sue Fortuna's first reaction to the news of her son's death was to be angry with the military visitors. 'I felt like saying, "How dare you come into my house and tell me that?"' she said. 'It was as if they had watched a television programme involving a similar situation, in which there are all those terrible pauses. One of them said, "I've got some bad news for you, I think you should sit down." I said, "No, just say what you've got to say now." But they were just doing their job. And they only had the most basic information.'

'You want to know everything,' said Nia, 'but they don't have the details. Just the basic fact that Kev had been killed was not enough. Gradually, I learned more. Kev was the only one seriously injured in the explosion. I believe the interpreter suffered minor injuries, and the other guys were knocked off their feet, but they were able to get up again. Even though there were guys in front with IED detectors, Kev actually stood on the device. Perhaps some of the men in front weighed a few stone less and they didn't set it off. Or maybe they walked just to the left or to the right of the pressure plate. To say he was unlucky is an understatement.'

The grief that Kevin's mother and wife felt is hard for them to put into words.

'Over the first few days, I couldn't cry,' said Sue Fortuna. 'I could howl but I couldn't cry. And the worst thing of all was that I couldn't comfort Nia. When my husband died, I had phoned Nia, and although I was in Sheffield and she was in Colchester, the first thing that she said was, "Do you want me to come up to see you?" But when Kev died, I couldn't face her. I didn't even see Nia until we had to go to RAF Lyneham to bring Kev home. I think I was trying to deal with my own grief and I just couldn't cope with hers as well, which was very cowardly.'

'People grieve in different ways,' said Nia. 'Equally, I could have gone to see Sue. But there was so much going on here. There were so many people coming over. I was the focus of it all, and you couldn't see the

313

floor of the lounge because it was covered in flowers. I didn't know where we were going to put them all. But they did help. It was really nice to know that people were thinking of us.'

When CSjt Fortuna's body was flown home, his widow and mother had the chance to see him in the coffin.

'I *needed* to see him, too,' said Nia. 'Thankfully, there were no injuries to his face or upper body, so that was possible. I needed to see him just so that I knew it was him, and to know that I would not have a knock on the door in two years' time, and find somebody telling me, "There's been a mistake, he's been in Afghanistan all this time," or something like that. I spent about two minutes in the room with Kev. *God, it is actually you*, I thought. I had asked my visiting officer to tell me everything about the circumstances of Kev's death, no matter how gory or how horrific things were, so I knew about the injuries he'd suffered. And they had disguised them very well. Everything I could see looked fine, but I wanted to shift things and look. I didn't do that, because once you have seen things you can't erase them from your mind. I wanted to touch him, too, but I didn't because I knew he'd be cold, and that would just leave a horrible memory. Then I just needed to get out of the room.'

Sue also took the opportunity to see her son for the final time. 'I went in on my own,' she said. 'It was him, but it didn't really look like him. He still had his beautiful nose, though. The make-up artists had done a very good job, but I thought, *What have you done to his hair?*'

The funeral followed a few days later.

'Because Kev hadn't specified what he wanted, I had freedom to do what I thought was right,' said Nia. 'The only thing he might have been a bit peeved about was his military funeral, and the fact that he was wearing uniform. He refused to be married in uniform. But because he was killed on active service, I thought, *Right, you're having a military funeral*. I felt quite strongly about that. I didn't want him buried, but I didn't want his ashes scattered, either. I wanted to think he was tidily in one place. So we had his ashes placed in the military cemetery where he has a gravestone.'

The music was suggested by Kev himself, after he had chosen it for his own father's funeral a few years earlier. 'He particularly liked one piece,' said Sue, 'the Adagio in G minor for Strings and Organ, by

Tomaso Albinoli. He said to me later, "If I die, that's the music I'd like for my funeral. I'd like to be carried away to that piece of music." It was quite a long piece and it was perfect for Kev's service in a big church that was absolutely packed. It took twenty minutes to walk to the front of the church with the coffin.

'I looked at the coffin and I thought, *That's Nia's wedding bouquet.* I didn't know that she had arranged for the flowers on his coffin to be like those she carried at her wedding.'

* * *

AN INQUEST FOUND that CSjt Fortuna was unlawfully killed. For his widow, there were nagging questions. 'I'm a nurse,' she said, 'so I wanted to know whether mistakes had been made, what led up to the situation and what happened afterwards. I learned about his immediate injuries, the time of his death and that he had still been alive when he was evacuated in the helicopter, although he didn't make it to Camp Bastion. I'm still uneasy about one or two things that happened before the arrival of the medical helicopter. But you have to understand that the guys who were with him at the time were very young, and probably in shock and panic themselves. Later on, I had a copy of the post mortem and all the witness statements. Going through the post mortem report helped me. I could be clearer in my own mind that, considering the injuries he had, it was not possible to save his life. I have to accept that his injuries were not survivable, or, if they were, I don't know how he would have coped with life.'

For the men he left behind, the pain was less intense; nevertheless, as Maj Carl Boswell, OC A Coy 1 Rifles put it, they felt they had lost 'a brother'.

'We had to put the grief to one side and get on with the job,' said Rfn Dan Meally. 'In the days that followed, things began to escalate. For instance, while me and some of the others were still in Bastion for Kev's repatriation, there was a major op to the north of our operating area. The guys literally landed in the middle of Taliban city, and, in retaliation, they attacked every PB. So we came under attack from machine gun and RPG fire.

'The threat was now very real. We became much more aware of

315

where we put our feet. The patrols went very slowly. Then, two weeks later, we were hit by another IED, and three guys were seriously injured – Andy Searle, who was one of the guys who gave first aid to Kev, lost his left leg and most of his right leg. After that, we were lifted out as combat ineffective. We'd just lost too many guys. So we were moved back to a patrol base. We asked if we could re-join our friends in A Company, and they arranged that. I found it very hard, because this compounded the feeling of wanting to hit back at them hard.'

For Meally, despite the loss of Kevin and others, the war was justified.

'I always thought the Taliban needed to go, and I still do. But fighting them is like playing a game of poker when you're the only person not cheating. We don't use IEDs, and I'll always consider them a coward's weapon, especially so because more local people are killed by them than troops. Camp Bastion's hospital used to have more local patients in it than NATO troops.

'Fighting the Taliban is like fighting the Nazis. Someone needs to get their boots on their necks, but it won't be easy for the ANA. To me, they were deluded about their own capability. They seemed to believe that when we left, there would be warehouses of artillery and aircraft left behind for them. I don't think they understand the challenge they face. When the Taliban begins its summer offensive in 2015, there are going to be a lot of naïve people in the Afghan military dying in large numbers.'

Dave Hill left the Army long before Afghanistan, but stayed close to Kev Fortuna. He last saw his friend just before the tour, when they met up for a few beers. 'We chatted about the coming Serjeants' mess open day,' he said. 'There'd be a chance to get out on the ranges again, and I was really looking forward to that. We didn't make a big thing about him going. I just said, "See you when you get back."

'It was a Monday night when I received an email from Nia asking me to call her. I immediately thought something bad had happened. Nia told me what had happened, and she asked me to contact as many of his friends as possible so they would know before it appeared in the papers. I used social media to send messages around, asking our friends to call me, and they all got back to me quickly. Telling them was awful.

'After I'd done that, I started to wonder if it was someone's sick joke. I couldn't sleep, my mind was playing tricks. It was bizarre, but I started wondering if he really had been killed. It really, really upset me and it took me a long time to get over it. He'd played such an important part in my life. It was the only time in my life that I've been completely hit for six. Of all the people who this could happen to, I didn't expect it to be Kev. I should have seen more of him in those last couple of years, but of course there's nothing I can do to change that. We'd speak often on the phone, but that wasn't the same as seeing him.

'Rebecca and I travelled down to Colchester for the funeral. It was horrible and I remember going into the church and seeing a book of condolence. Physically, I just couldn't write in it, because it was impossible to find the words. I've even felt a bit guilty that I left the Army and am still here.'

For Nia and Sue Fortuna, life moves on, inching slowly forwards.

'During the first year, contact with the regiment was pretty intense,' said Nia. 'Towards the end of the first year, contact dulled down slightly, and I thought, *They've forgotten him and about me!* Then the first anniversary of his death came around, and they were in contact again. Then I thought, *They're raking all of this up again.* It was a bizarre way of thinking, but I was still going through turmoil of emotions. I wanted to get on with things, but equally I didn't want people to forget about him.

'Now, two-and-a-half years on, I haven't heard anything from The Rifles for a while. That's fine. I have numbers if I need to speak to somebody, and I know there will be people there. But you have to understand that there comes a point when they have to let you get on with your life.

'On Remembrance Sunday this year, a soldier came to lay a wreath on Kev's grave on behalf of The Rifles, and one of Kev's good friends from 1 Rifles also came from Chepstow to lay a wreath. He's now doing the job that Kev should have been doing. And the Colchester Garrison Sergeant Major has been great. If I'm in town and he sees me he'll always stop me for a chat.'

Sue deals with the sorrow in her own way. 'A lot of the time, I almost think Kev is just away on a long deployment,' she said. 'It's not as if I'd been living with him, and have to remember not to cook for two people. My house was no longer full of his things anyway. I don't sleep really well, and very often before it gets light I get up and make myself a cup of coffee, and I light a candle. In the early days, I would feel I was having a cup of coffee with Kev. Then I'd blow the candle out and I would watch the smoke from the candle as it went away. It was as if that was Kev going away. Sometimes the candle would go straight out and sometimes it would take ages.'

Kevin and Nia had a longstanding plan to get themselves a dog – a retired greyhound, to be specific – when he finally left the Army. After his death, she went ahead and got Bailey. 'Some days have been incredibly difficult,' she said. 'But Bailey keeps me occupied, which is a good thing. He gets me out and about, and stops me feeling sorry for myself.'

'That's the best thing Nia did,' said Sue. 'We share him. If Nia's at work I look after Bailey.'

'Even now, if something really funny, or exciting, or even tragic happens, I think, *I must remember to tell Kev about that*,' said Nia. 'When he was away on deployment, I would jot things down so that I could tell him about them in a letter. I don't know if things get easier to deal with, or if you just get used to coping and managing. I think the legacy that Kev has left me is a message to live my life and enjoy it. But it can be hard, especially when friends are getting married, having babies, or having a lovely old time, and they keep going on about how wonderful their lives are.

'I used to love Christmas, and when Kev was home he would make such a fuss of me. He'd get me loads of presents. And he never forgot my birthdays. Even if he was away, he'd arrange to have flowers delivered. And of course there are our wedding anniversaries. There are certain days. If I've had a bad day at work, I think, *I want a hug!* But obviously that doesn't happen.'

Was it all worth it? 'I just feel so incredibly lucky, because he was my son,' said Sue. 'I feel sorry for people who never got the chance to meet him. And I hope I'm right in believing that Kev and all the others *have* made a difference in Afghanistan. There are children being educated, especially young girls, and I'm hoping that will go on after we leave.'

'I don't feel particularly bitter about Afghanistan,' said Nia. 'Kev chose to join the Army, and he was aware of the risks. If he'd been very opposed to what he was doing he wouldn't have gone to Afghanistan twice. He could have left the Army. I think that he believed in what he was doing. I have to accept that he died doing a job that he wanted to do. I'm sad and disappointed, but not bitter. That just makes you angry, which is a waste of time. We've had to accept what has happened, and try to build our lives back up. I wouldn't be without my years with Kev for anything. If somebody had told me when I met him that, fourteen years later, this would happen, I would still have chosen to be with him and experience the pain. Better that than never to have known him. It was a good fourteen years.'

LIEUTENANT DANIEL CLACK
C COMPANY 1st BATTALION THE RIFLES
MARCH 25, 1987 – AUGUST 12, 2011

ANOTHER DUSTY DAY had dawned at Checkpoint Shaparak, and Daniel Clack was going through his orders for the day.

Shaparak – Pashtun for 'butterfly' – was a spartan British Army outpost on the edge of the village of Tasikan, in Nahr-e Saraj. Dan, a twenty-four-year-old lieutenant on his first tour of Afghanistan, had taken over there from 2 Para some weeks earlier. The Paras had been 'awesome', he wrote, in a letter home from 'the hot place' to his mother, Sue, and his younger brother, James. The 'great job' they had done over the preceding six months would make his six 'much easier and safer'.

> [The] *check point is cool, it is a big old Afghan house/compound that used to be owned (and was built) by an Opium and heroin dealer! It is a lot nicer than a lot of other CPs but is still basic (a well in the middle, no power except for our generator, all our resupply is dropped in by helicopter).*
>
> *The area is surprisingly beautiful, it is poppy harvest time so the fields are filled with bright pink and white flowers and the rest of the area is really lush and green.*
>
> *It has been getting hotter every day and broke 40° for the first time today... which is seriously hot. But I feel I have definately started to aclimatise and am not as affected by the heat as most people seem to be. And yes, I am using plenty of sun cream!*

I hope all is well at home, James' work and revision is going well and Mum the census job is as easy as it was before! Please send my best to Grandad and let him know that everything is going well.
Speak soon, love DAN

Shaparak was 'a bit of a dive', according to Cpl Hayley Reading, the base's RAMC medic, but at least it had solid floors and holes for windows. And Dan Clack and his men had made the best of it, installing a makeshift gym and sunshades, and improving washing and toilet facilities. They had also worked tirelessly to build up both the outpost's defences, and their relationship with the locals.

Tasikan was one of three villages under the protection of 8 Platoon, and the day's mission called for them to travel to neighbouring Dactran, to prepare for a *shura* the following day. A couple of Army vets would be available to help farmers with any sick livestock, as part of the hearts-and-minds process at which the young officer was proving so adept. His company commander, Major Bill Eden, would later talk of the 'great gratitude and warm affection' for Dan and his men among the locals.

Still, patrols were challenging and dangerous, and today's would be no different. Dactran was not far away, but the soldiers would need to proceed with extreme caution, along rutted verges and roads which were perfect for IED traps, and through fields of tall young maize which offered thick cover for a Taliban ambush. And some form of attack was almost certain.

Earlier in the tour, Dan had written home to his parents to say that all was quiet – too quiet, for some of the men. When they were not carrying out routine patrols, they found plenty of time for weight-training, Army banter and board games. It was a matter of some dispute, but Dan Clack saw himself as the platoon's Monopoly king; he always chose the Top Hat piece as his counter, and some of his men would later have that symbol tattooed on their arms in his memory and honour.

But with the onset of the scorching summer heat, and the harvest of the local opium crop, the situation had rapidly deteriorated. Leaving the checkpoint was dangerous, and small arms and mortar attacks on the base itself were commonplace. On July 21, a young rifleman had been flown home after losing both of his legs and suffering other major injuries – among the worst survived by a British soldier during the war – after triggering an IED while out on patrol. Dan Clack had travelled with his gravely-wounded comrade to Camp Bastion, not merely to complete the necessary reports and seemingly endless paperwork but also to keep him company and ensure that he got the best treatment possible. It was typical of the love he felt for his men – a love which was unashamedly returned, almost from the moment of his arrival in the regiment after completing his Platoon Commanders' Battle Course in July 2010. The 1 Rifles CO, Lt Col James de Labillière, later said, 'His men adored him, and they showed him a loyalty and respect reserved for only the very few and the very best.'

His former platoon serjeant, Darren Gornall – who counted himself a friend of Lt Clack – said simply, 'He was the best young officer I have worked with. I know when tragic events happen they always say that the person was outstanding, but in Dan's case it really is the truth.'

'Dan was quite happy to take account of the experience that others had,' said Hayley Reading. 'That was a brilliant quality, and not all officers are like that. He was really approachable, too. I liked him from the first day I met him. I had a hundred per cent confidence in him. He knew what needed to be done, but he made sure it was done right. If he wasn't happy about a situation, he'd radio HQ for aerial reconnaissance, or to tell them that he was changing the plan. He wouldn't expose us to unnecessary risks.'

At least Dan's visit to Bastion meant he had access to the internet, and could update his Facebook page. It gave him a rare opportunity to contact his family, and his long-term girlfriend Amy, who was Parliamentary Assistant to the then Defence Secretary Liam Fox. Dan and Amy had met at Exeter University, and he had dropped hints to his parents that, on his return from the tour, he would be asking Amy to marry him.

His final Facebook message, posted during that visit to Camp Bastion on July 26, read, 'Internet for the first time in two months. Living the dream. Thanks to anyone who has sent parcels. If you haven't yet, then you should feel bad. Get on it!'

It was a message most readers would have taken at face value. Only a few close friends and family members could read between the lines: if Dan Clack was back at Bastion the reason was not good.

Back at CP Shaparak, after a final run-through of his plans, and a last equipment check, Lt Clack was ready to lead his men, and their RAMC medic, out from the relative safety of their base. It was late afternoon and would be the last patrol of the day.

* * *

IN A WAY, it was inevitable that Dan Clack – known to family members as 'Army Dan' – would find himself in that situation. Although there was no great tradition of military service on either side of his family, he had dreamed of an Army career since his early teens, and the dream only grew with his involvement in the CCF at his school, Bancroft's in Woodford Green, Essex, and then his university Officer Training Corps [OTC].

'Dan never had any doubts,' said his mother, Sue. 'I remember one of the other mums from school telling me that Dan and his mates had been at her house, and they were discussing which branch of the Cadets they would enter, the Army or the Air Corps. He had said, "Well, there's no question about it. You wouldn't want to do anything else but join the Army." I don't recall him talking about any other kind of career from the age of about fifteen.

'He was born in March 1987, and was just an ordinary boy. He was always well-behaved, he never suffered from any childhood illnesses, and he went everywhere and did everything with Martin [Dan's father], James and me.

'His brother James came along about two-and-a-half years later. They were the best of friends while they were growing up. I just loved to watch them having fun together. They were both keen on rugby but, because they were different ages, they wouldn't normally play in the same matches. I know that one of James' favourite memories is of the one occasion that he and Dan played together in the same team. [A feisty, talented scrum-half, Dan Clack would go on to represent Bancroft's, Woodford Rugby Club, RMAS and his Battalion.]

'James was every bit as involved in the Cadets as Dan, but he didn't think seriously about joining the Army. In fact, once Dan got to Sandhurst and started telling James a bit more about what training was like, he decided more than ever to do something else! He's now a qualified diving instructor and spends much of his time overseas.'

Even Dan's choice of Exeter – where he read geography – was made in large part because of the university's reputation for having a very strong OTC.

'That was very good preparation for Sandhurst,' said Sue. 'He seemed to spend most weekends training in the Brecon Beacons and places like that. The day that the letter with his [*Sandhurst*] offer arrived was one of the most exciting of his life. It was 2008, and Dan was actually away in France with the Exeter OTC. I knew the letter was coming, and Dan had asked me to open it and then text him. It dropped through the letter box, and I remember just standing holding it in my hands. I knew how important the contents were to him; this made A level results pale into insignificance. I opened it, and the news was good. He had a place! I was so relieved that I just sat and cried for a bit, and then found my mobile to text him.

'I kept it brief – *All okay, you're in* – and sent it off. It was a few hours before he rang me back. He had been out on manoeuvres with no phone signal. He made me read the whole letter out to him, just to make sure I hadn't got it wrong. He was so excited, and couldn't wait to find out which other of his friends at Exeter had got in, too. There were actually about ten of them altogether, although they didn't all take up their offers at the same time. One of Dan's closest friends, David Boyce, joined six months after Dan. David commissioned into The Queen's Dragoon Guards, deployed on Herrick 15, and was killed in action three weeks into the tour. [*Lt Boyce died alongside LCpl Richard Scanlon when their armoured vehicle struck an IED while on patrol in Nahr-e Saraj on November 17, 2011.*] To lose him and Dan was a terrible blow for Exeter University, the OTC, RMAS and their combined close group of friends.'

After graduation, and before going to Sandhurst, Dan Clack spent three months driving around America with three friends from Exeter. Already a keen adventure sportsman, he went sky-diving, and even played rugby with students at Princeton University. On their return to the UK, two of his friends had organised ski season jobs in Verbier, Switzerland. Not to be outdone, Dan flew out to join them and found a job driving for an upmarket ski chalet rental company, which fortunately gave him plenty of time to ski – his other great passion. Having survived Verbier without serious injury, he returned home just in time to get his things together for RMAS, which he eventually joined in May 2009.

By then, his girlfriend Amy had graduated. Her family lived in Maidenhead, much closer to RMAS at Camberley than Dan's family home, so there 'were a lot of Sunday afternoon visits to see Amy and get some washing done', said Sue. 'Amy had started at Exeter a year after Dan,' she said. 'They actually met, I believe, outside the local chip shop during Amy's first week. They then met up again when Amy enrolled in the OTC. Also, one of Dan's close friends from school, Eleanor, ended up sharing a house with Amy, and still claims to have introduced them!

'As the eldest of six close cousins, Dan was leading the way with girlfriend/boyfriend relationships. Amy came to a number of Clack family events, and was under close scrutiny from all. And it wasn't long before Dan's aunts were talking about hats for weddings!'

For now, though, Dan Clack was focusing on becoming the best young officer he could be. Lt Michael Evans, of 2 Royal Gurkha Rifles, was an Afghanistan veteran who counted himself 'fortunate' to have gone through infantry training with Dan Clack.

'He was a youngster amongst a platoon of relative old men through training,' said Lt Evans, 'but you would not have known it. He was an easy man to admire. I have many lasting memories of him, from stolen minutes during training, drinking tea and having a healthy gripe at the system, to skiing in France that saw me walk away with broken ribs and Dan a guilty look.'

Lt Tom Francis, a fellow 1 Rifles platoon commander, fondly recalled the 'scrapes' the two got into during training.

'Despite his capabilities as a soldier,' he said, 'I will never forget the look of absolute misery on his face sitting in two feet of snow whilst on a Sandhurst exercise!'

The Afghanistan War was years old by the time Dan Clack joined up, and he knew exactly what he was getting into. He relished the challenge. His father, Martin, said, 'He told me once, "When we have training sessions about tactics, I pay so much attention. Because I know that sometime, maybe in a year or so, men's lives will depend on my decisions." But he never spoke to me about fear. He knew he was going to a dangerous place, but he wanted to go. Before he deployed, he went back to Bancroft's School to meet the master who had run the Cadets. Dan told him that his only real fear about Afghanistan was that he might not live up to the expectations of his men. In the end, of course, that was what he did best. But I wasn't that worried about him going, because I *knew* he was going to come back. I don't know why, but I was completely confident of that.'

Sue Clack was more worried about the motorbike her son was planning to buy on his return from deployment, the quicker to get home along the busy M4/M25 from his Chepstow barracks to Essex.

'I can honestly say that I never tried to persuade him not to go,' she said. 'But I did talk to him about the possibility of him not coming back. I remember sitting with him in his room the week before he left, and he was writing eulogies for all of the men in his platoon, in case any of them were killed. He turned around to me and said, "You know that someone somewhere is writing mine?"'

If that was a sobering moment for any mother, it was a reflection of Dan Clack's mature attitude. As part of his GCSE history coursework, he had visited the British war graves in France.

'He saw a gravestone there inscribed with the words, "Duty called, he answered",' said Sue. 'He was quite young then, but he said to me, "If anything happens to me, and it's suitable, those are the words I would like." I carried them in my diary, and they are now on Dan's headstone, and a number of other memorials to him.'

Towards the end of his time at RMAS, he took part in the selection interviews which are held to allocate the commissioning officers to regiments.

'Dan was so happy to be accepted by The Rifles,' said Sue. 'I can remember him saying to me that he couldn't understand anyone going through all of that training and then not wanting to go into an infantry regiment.'

After Sandhurst, he went through platoon commander training and then straight into the regiment for pre-deployment training for Afghanistan. Sue Clack's brother had been seriously ill, and she had taken early retirement to spend time with him. There was one happy side-effect to this sad situation.

'Looking back,' she said, 'I'm so glad I wasn't working. It meant I was able to spend time with Dan at home when he was on leave. We had a big family farewell dinner, including all of Dan's aunts, uncles and cousins, about three weeks before he left, and for the next few weeks he came and went between home, Chepstow and Amy's home in London.

'Then, on the Friday before he deployed, Dan, James, Amy and myself went out for meal at Roast in Borough Market. We met at a pub first – it was only April, but it was a glorious evening, and lots of people were standing outside enjoying the evening sun.'

It's a moment – her handsome young son, laughing, drink in hand – which is frozen in time.

'It was quite a jolly evening,' said Sue. 'We wanted to make it that way, rather than think too much about what might lie ahead. Dan had to report back to Chepstow on the Sunday night, and I remember him getting ready to leave on the Saturday afternoon. He was wearing his usual uniform of chinos, deck shoes and a striped shirt, and was going to see Amy before heading back to barracks.

'I gave him a long letter I'd written that he was to open when he got to Afghanistan. That letter came back to me after he was killed, so I still have it. I told him how proud we all were of him. I said that I'd wished him on his way when he went to university, and done the same when he went to Sandhurst, and then to Chepstow. Each time he was getting a little further away, and it was getting harder for a mum to keep a watchful eye on him. Now he was going to Afghanistan, and a mum's ability to keep an eye on her son was being pushed to the limit. But I said we would all cope. I ended by saying that when it got really hot in Helmand, he should remember that he'd soon be home and then a little while later he'd be going off for a skiing holiday with Amy.

'I don't really remember what I said to him as he left. I think it was probably just, "See you in August." I do remember him waving out of the car window as he drove down the road, and then I came in and went and sat in his room, surrounded by his stuff, for a while. The whole thing was very upbeat. We were aware of what could happen, but I couldn't give him a hug and say, "This is in case I never see you again." I suppose I was trying to be strong for him.

'Then, on the Sunday at about 7pm, I had a text message from him to say he was ready to go. I still have that text: *Hi how are you? I'm all packed now heading over* [to Brize Norton] *at about 8. Have had a few ideas of stuff you could send me A rugby ball (deflated) and a pump, a featherlite smock size med, grey, and a tub of multivitamins that won't melt, Hope you are doing ok.'*

After arrival at Camp Bastion, and the usual week-long training package, it was time for Lt Clack to head out into the badlands. His father Martin remembers one of the occasional satellite phone calls home that his son was able to make, during which he said he was 'really chuffed' with his new base at Shaparak.

'Later he managed to send home some photos of it,' said Martin. 'My God! It was the kind of place you wouldn't want to keep farm animals in.'

Those phone calls helped the family deal with his absence.

'I remember the very first time he called me from Camp Bastion,' said Sue. 'I wasn't expecting to hear from him. He said, "Hi Mum, it's Dan," which was how he started all his conversations with me. He sounded so clear and close... It was so unexpected. It was uncanny to think that he was so far away.'

As most soldiers do, Lt Clack was careful to play down the danger of his position when talking to his family. 'He'd say things like, "Don't worry about me. It's poppy harvest, and the Taliban are too busy at the moment,"' said Martin.

That changed a little as the situation darkened, especially after the July incident in which one of his men was so badly injured.

'That really knocked Daniel,' Martin recalled. 'When he spoke to me shortly afterwards, he did let his feelings show. He was saying, "It's not all fun out here." It really did hit him hard, because he genuinely cared so much about his men. He continued to play it down, and maybe I went along with the pretence that it was all okay, but we now know that he was right on the front line, in what became really heavy Taliban country. He was in a very dangerous place. It had gone from being too quiet for the men's liking to becoming a nightmare. The Taliban were using the three villages, the safety of which was Dan's responsibility. He knew the locals were intimidated by the Taliban, but he also knew they had little choice.

'When the young rifleman had his legs blown off, which was only a couple of weeks before Dan was killed, everyone at Shaparak took a raincheck. Dealing with an IED when it goes off almost on top of you is something no-one wants to experience. I think it was remarkable that the next day, or perhaps even that afternoon, the guys in that patrol had to resume patrolling. They would have just seen their colleague's legs shredded, and Dan would have had to say, "Come on, we're going out again."'

The incident provided the young officer with a special challenge. 'Dan told us there were some guys saying they weren't paid enough to go through that again,' said Sue, 'and there were others who just wanted to get out there and kill anything that moved. He had to manage both extremes.'

* * *

CPL HAYLEY READING recalled the fateful day. 'We had two sections of troops at the checkpoint,' she said. 'Numbers would vary, but there'd be between twenty and thirty of us on the base. One section would stay at the checkpoint while the other went out. But I was the only medic, and that meant I had to go on every patrol. There could be three to four patrols a day, so I was knackered most of the time, but the guys would help by allowing me to do fewer stags than everyone else.

'On the day of the incident, we had a third section with us at the checkpoint temporarily, so our normal two sections went out on the same mission but slightly apart, while the new section stayed behind to defend the base.

'I was with the boss's patrol. We set off about five minutes before the other one, in single file, the Vallon man in front, Dan in the middle. About 150 metres out, we were crossing a small bridge when someone pulled a control wire and set off a remote IED, hitting six of us, including the interpreter. Only two were uninjured.'

The explosion ripped through the patrol, shattering and numbing them. For a moment, they lay dazed and deafened on the sandy ground, as debris rained down all around. Cpl Reading, herself badly wounded, had been blown off her feet. Slowly, through the chaos, some semblance of order began to be restored. With it came the shouts and screams of the injured.

'I heard one of the guys, Joe Collinson, shouting for me,' she said. 'I stood up and went running over to him. He was holding the boss,

329

who was on the ground, unconscious. He had a lot of injuries. We later found out that the device had been packed with ball bearings, and a lot of these had hit him. He was losing blood fast from a leg wound, so I put a tourniquet on that. I also put a special device called a FAST into his sternum, which enabled me to get fluids into his body via intraosseous infusion.

'Then I heard Rfn Lowe shouting for help. He'd been seriously injured, too. I asked Joe Collinson to carry on helping the boss, while I ran to find Lowey. He was in a similar state to the boss, though he was conscious. I picked a few ball bearings out of his neck to help him breathe and gave him some morphine.'

All the while, there was the obvious risk that the Taliban would mount a follow-up assault on the crippled section. This was a classic tactic: injure as many men as possible, leaving them static and vulnerable, and then attempt to destroy the helicopter – a prized target – which arrives to collect the casualties. Fortunately, while a follow-up attack did come, it was only after the casualties had been carried back to the checkpoint and after the medevac helicopter had arrived.

'I remember thinking, *Shit! We need to get out of here!*' said Cpl Reading. 'Fortunately, we were very near the base. By this time, our sister patrol had got to us with a quad-bike and they were able to carry Dan and Lowey back to the base. Rfn Singh and me ran behind the quad, and the other injured lads were able to make it back on foot.

'When we got back, the third section was already on the walls defending the place. I assigned a couple of people to treat each of the less seriously-injured casualties, and myself and few others, including the vets, treated the boss and Lowey.

'I was well aware that Dan might not make it. His heart stopped several times and we had to give him CPR. He was in and out of consciousness, but he'd come back so many times that I honestly thought he'd be okay. He'd squeeze my hand when I asked him to, and he'd bite down on the airway when I asked him to do that. But still, in case the worst happened, I wanted him to know that he was with all of us, and not on his own. I lined the guys up to speak to him as we worked on him. They were saying things like, "Come on, boss! You can have a sleep later." That was a bit of a joke with us because Dan used to nap a lot. The guys just let him know who they were and they said whatever they thought would help him. I think now that telling them to talk to him was probably the most important thing I did for Dan.

'The helicopter arrived after about an hour, a US one because our MERT Chinook had already been tasked elsewhere. When that arrived, I felt we had him. As they took him and four of the others onto the helicopter, we shouted at Dan, and he opened his eyes. I remember shouting, "We'll see you later, boss!" But we didn't. Unfortunately, he died on the flight to Bastion.'

It was only after the medevac chopper left that Cpl Reading thought to check her own injuries – which were significant.

'I didn't realise that they were as bad as they were,' she said. 'I had ball bearings and shrapnel in my legs, and my left kneecap was particularly damaged. So later I was also taken to hospital in Bastion.'

She had surgery herself, and when she came round the doctor who had received Dan Clack's body was waiting to talk to her.

'He told me that Dan was never going to survive,' she said. 'His carotid artery was severed, and he wouldn't have lived if it had happened on an operating table. Technically, he shouldn't even have been awake with us in the checkpoint, although I know he was.

'I struggled a lot with it afterwards. I wracked my brains wondering if there was anything else I could have done. Also, I felt bad that I wasn't going back to the checkpoint to support the other guys.'

Back at Shaparak, Dan Clack's grieving men had to pick themselves up and go back out on patrol over the following days and weeks, with their fallen boss's words of encouragement and advice in their minds. One minor comfort was to be had in the small campaign of disinformation they were able to spread. The locals were merely told that Lt Clack had gone away on his planned R&R and was then being posted to a different area; this at least denied the Taliban the knowledge that they had killed an officer, and meant that someone missed out on the reward money he would have expected to receive for carrying out such an act.

* * *

SUE AND MARTIN Clack were away on separate holidays at the time, and counting the days before their son's return home for ten days' R&R, due to start on August 25.

'Dan was killed on the Friday,' said Sue. 'I was on holiday in Norway, staying at the home of a girl called Pia who had been the boys' first *au pair*. I'd had to keep 1 Rifles up to date with my contact details, and I remember emailing them my address in Norway, and thinking that they would never find me as it was so strange. On the Saturday morning, two officers, one a NATO officer and another from the Royal Air Force, knocked on the door of Pia's house. I answered the door, and this guy just said, "Do you speak English?" As soon as he said that, I knew. I said, "You're from the Army, aren't you?"

'They had been contacted by the MOD in London and had travelled from Oslo to find me, right in the south of Norway. They had identified Pia's house in the early hours of the morning, but waited until 8am to wake us. They had to be careful as they only had Facebook photos of Pia and myself and we were both blonde, hence the opening question.

'That moment changed my life forever. All I wanted to do was get home. They were all brilliant. I was driven to the airport and flew home via Amsterdam. I had sunglasses on, and every time I went through security, they asked me to take them off, exposing my red-rimmed eyes. I had to wait for quite a while in Amsterdam, and when they called the flight I just couldn't stand up. It was horrendous. I got onto the plane somehow, and two guys who were about Dan's age sat down beside me. I couldn't even look at them. They must have thought I was completely mad.

'I was met off the plane and whisked through Customs. The Army had laid on a car for me, and the driver, who was ex-military, took me to tell Amy. She had already anticipated there was a problem as she hadn't heard from Dan for a few days, and she knew that things had been bad out there. She wasn't at home so I rang and said I was back in UK and at her flat. We drove on to meet her. She was hoping I was going to say that he was severely injured, but I just ended up saying nothing… Luckily she had some of her closest friends with her. We then set off for my house with the task of breaking the news to others.

'Our Army-appointed visiting officer, Barry, had arrived at home a few minutes before me, and had had the awful task of telling my younger son, James. Martin was on holiday, so I had to call him on his mobile to tell him what had happened.

'He came home that night, and, for the next two weeks, people were continually coming to the door, writing or phoning. I'd open the door or lift the phone, and there would be silence because, having got that far, people just did not know what to say. There were a lot of hugs and a lot of tears. The press and TV were good to us. And everything I have read and heard about Dan has been very respectful.'

Martin Clack, numb with grief, found the worst moment was his son's repatriation at RAF Lyneham – the last before all repatriations were moved to Brize Norton.

'It was just Dan coming back,' he said, 'so only our family, seven of us, was in attendance, along with senior members of the military. We waited in a lounge, trying to deal with coffee and sandwiches. Then a call came saying the plane was fifteen minutes away, and we all went outside. It was mid-August, but the weather was atrocious, pouring with rain. They had said that they were not sure if they could do the official flypast because of the low cloud, but they did.

'We walked out onto the tarmac and everyone was standing there under a marquee. It was a surreal moment, as the clouds seemed to be touching the tops of the trees. Then suddenly, out of the gloom, came these bright lights and this massive RAF C17 seemed to be almost coming through the trees. I just couldn't take it. I left everyone else and walked to the white line at the edge of the taxiway and just watched that plane coming over the horizon with Dan on board. That was a real moment of acceptance.'

'I just kept saying to James and Amy that he was home,' said Sue. 'We went back inside. There was quite a wait before they brought the plane round in front of us, for the ceremony of bringing the coffin from the plane to the hearse. There was a little chapel at RAF Lyneham and they put the union flag-draped coffin in there for us to pay our respects. We were able to go in and spend some time with Dan. I remember telling him that I was not impressed, and that this was not part of the plan. We were then taken to Royal Wootton Bassett, and we watched as the cortege came through. I found it helpful that I had seen the coffin earlier, but, for others in the family, that was the first time they saw it. There were hundreds of people there, and along the route to the John Radcliffe hospital. There was a lot of media coverage of his return home, as he was the last to go through the town.'

Dan Clack left letters for his parents, his brother James and for Amy, and, unusually, one for his fellow Riflemen, all to be opened only in the event of his death.

'He had been sitting in his bedroom writing them when he was home shortly before he deployed,' said Sue, 'and it was clear he didn't want to be disturbed. He didn't say anything to me about them. He just gave them to James to look after. The family were all here at home on the Monday after Dan died, when James brought the letters down. We sat with Dan's granddad, uncles, aunts and cousins and, of course, Amy. As we read them out loud the tears were flowing. Our shopping that weekend had been tea bags and boxes of tissues, and we needed them all.'

In his letter to his men, Dan Clack wrote:

BROTHER RIFLEMEN
I REALISE THAT LEAVING THIS NOTE MAY BE A LITTLE UNCONVENTIONAL OR EMOTIONAL, BUT HERE IT IS ANYWAY.

I JUST WANTED TO SAY THAT IT WAS AN HONOUR TO SERVE ALONGSIDE EVERY ONE OF YOU. IT SOUNDS VERY CLICHÉD BUT COMMANDING RIFLEMEN ON OPERATIONS IS THE GREATEST HONOUR THAT I CAN IMAGINE. TO A MAN BRAVE AND COMMITTED, I ONLY HOPE AT THE TIME OF WRITING THAT I WAS ABLE TO LIVE UP TO THIS FOR HOWEVER MUCH OF THE DEPLOYMENT THAT I SURVIVED!

TO THE RIFLEMEN AND CHAIN OF COMMAND OF C COMPANY: I COUNT MYSELF AS PRIVILEGED TO HAVE BEEN WELCOMED INTO THE COMPANY AND YOUR TRUST AND RESPECT IS THE GREATEST THING I COULD EVER HOPE TO HAVE EARNED.

TO THE OFFICER'S MESS: IT WAS AN HONOUR TO CALL YOU MY FRIENDS, AND (AS OFTEN AS WE SAY IT TO OURSELVES) YOU ARE A BLOODY GOOD BUNCH OF BLOKES!

334

I HAD THOUGHT ABOUT CONCLUDING WITH SOME ROUSING PASSAGE FROM HENRY V OR I VOW TO THEE MY COUNTRY, BUT WILL SPARE YOU ALL THIS BY SIMPLY SAYING IT WAS A PLEASURE TO HAVE KNOWN YOU, AND BEST OF LUCK.
SWIFT AND BOLD, DAN CLACK

In the letter to his mother, he wrote:

DEAR MUM
The fact that you are reading this means that I must start by apologising for the pain that you are going through now. I know that there is not much I can say that will make you feel better, but I hope that you take some comfort in knowing that I loved my job, was incredibly proud of what I was doing and fully accepted the risks and was always prepared to make this sacrifice.

Thank you for giving me an amazing life and for the sacrifices that you made for James and I. We have had every opportunity that a young man could want and we were incredibly lucky to have your support every step of the way. Not only a great mother but you are also a great friend to me.

This letter will never do justice to the lifetime of support and love that you have given me, but I want you to know that I always appreciated it and I apologise if I ever seemed to take you for granted.

Thank you once again,
Always your loving son,
DAN

Lt Clack's funeral was held at St Paul's Church, Woodford Green, on August 25 – the day he should have been flying home for his R&R. Hundreds of people packed the pews and filled the church green outside, listening to the service via loudspeakers. In his eulogy, Lt Col James de Labillière, CO 1 Rifles, said Lt Clack was 'engaged in the war of our generation, one he was so proud to be part of' and had conducted himself with 'complete integrity.'

A display of white chrysanthemums, spelling the word 'Boss', was placed next to Lt Clack's coffin. From his men, it was accompanied by

335

a large, handwritten tribute reading, 'It has been an honour and a privilege to serve under and alongside you, and to call you Sir. We never wanted to say goodbye, so it's just farewell until we meet again and laugh at the memories we have shared together over the past year. Stand down and sleep easy, Sir.'

Lt Clack's younger cousin, Adam Clack, told the mourners, 'He was boss to his men but Army Dan to us. We can't begin to explain the hole that's been left in our family by the loss of Dan. Every time we gather around the piano to sing, he'll be there with us. Dan, we'll always love you and always miss you. You'll always be in our hearts.'

* * *

ONCE THE FUNERAL was over, the friends and wider family had departed, and the media had left for the next big story, Sue and Martin Clack and their remaining son, James, were left to grieve alone.

'Out of all of us, I know that I'm the strongest,' said Sue. 'I've gone through things first, and I have copies of things that Martin has not looked at. I have archived everything. My attitude has been that, when anything comes in, I will look at it or read it, because it tells me more about my son. I then store it for posterity.

'The impact on James was huge. He's had no choice but to get on with his life, but the loss of his brother changed his outlook completely. I think James was influenced by Dan's last wish for him. He said his brother should do what he wanted to do, and not settle for second best. James was a beneficiary of insurance policies that Dan took out, so he has been able to afford to develop a career as a diver.

'I've coped by getting on with things. We organised much of Dan's funeral ourselves, and Dan had left ideas about what he wanted. So we were quite busy over that first couple of weeks. And then it was only three months before Dan's men came back from Afghanistan. We interred Dan's ashes the following March on what would have been his twenty-fifth birthday, and a lot of the Rifles guys who had been deployed with him in Afghanistan came to that, as they'd been unable to attend his funeral. I'd written to them beforehand, and I still keep in touch with many of them on Facebook. I worried that people might not remember, but everybody does. On the second anniversary of

Dan's death, I put a picture of him up on Facebook and 112 people responded to it.'

His father was hit very hard by Dan's death.

'I struggled for about six months,' said Martin. 'I don't think I coped very well. But I slowly started to get better. Occasionally, if I see a photo I haven't seen before, or someone says something that reminds me of Dan, I will have a little tear. Certain things still get to me. For example, since Dan's death I have been to two young people's weddings, and I sobbed at both of them, because I'll never see Dan get married. But time does help, and generally I cope. Just to have known Dan for twenty-four years was a privilege. I have to look at it like that.

'Dan's death came at the time of the riots in London and other cities, and it received a lot of attention because there was such a contrast between his life and the attitude of the rioters. The *Daily Mail* wrote a brilliant piece comparing Dan and the rioters. It was a very nice thing that they did. I like to talk about Dan, because I don't want to feel that he is forgotten, or that he didn't exist. He was so special. I suppose all parents believe their child is special, but it's true.'

Sue has stayed in touch with many of Dan's men and his military friends, including Hayley Reading – who went on to marry one of the men of C Coy after the tour, and who was Mentioned in Dispatches for her brave and determined efforts on the day of Lt Clack's death. And she is still close to Amy, which is 'lovely'.

'Amy considers James a kid brother,' said Sue, 'and I know he feels she's like a sister to him. We marked the anniversary of Dan's death with a big party at the Cavalry and Guards Club in London. In his speech, James said then how much he had relied on Amy during the previous year, and I know she felt the same way.

'Amy and I see each other, and we talk about Dan a lot. It doesn't matter if we get emotional. If Dan had lived, they would have been married by now.'

'Hayley is an exceptional person,' said Martin, 'and the family have got to know her and her husband Scott well. Because she was the medic rather than a rifleman, I think Dan felt he could open up more to her. She was the "mother hen" of Shaparak. He always wanted her out on the patrols, so she ended up doing more patrols than any of the men, poor thing, and she's only five-foot-nothing!'

'I miss the boss every single day,' said Hayley Reading. 'But Lowey is alive when technically he should've died, so that's a good thing. And if Dan had to go, then it was brilliant that he spent that time with us. It was right that he knew he was with his guys. All the blokes spoke to Dan, and I know he heard them. If it were me who was going, knowing they were there would have made me feel a thousand times better. I felt safe with those guys, because I loved them all. They were my brothers, and the boss would also have felt they were his brothers. Although his actual family couldn't be there, we were the next best thing.

'I saw his letter that he wrote to us. Reading it made me extremely emotional, but what he wrote didn't surprise me. That was the sort of thing he would have told us. What a top bloke he was.'

Sue Clack carries a poem with her in her handbag.

'The last two lines read, "You can cry and close your mind, be empty and turn back, or you can do what he'd want; open your eyes, love and go on,"' she said. 'That's what we try and do.'

LANCE CORPORAL JON MCKINLAY
B COMPANY 1st BATTALION THE RIFLES
NOVEMBER 7, 1977 – SEPTEMBER 14, 2011

JON 'JJ' MCKINLAY WAS in some ways an unusual junior NCO – the slightly wayward, public-school educated son of a lieutenant-colonel, he had turned up on his first day at basic training oozing charm and 'talking like Prince Charles', said one man who joined with him.

But in other, sadder ways, he was just like many others who served in Afghanistan, in that he knew only too well the extreme pain of losing close friends.

The first man in his circle of 1 Rifles mates to die was Cpl Steve 'Tommo' Thompson, a thirty-one-year-old father-of-one, who was killed by an IED in Sangin in March 2010. Cpl Thompson had left a training role at Catterick to volunteer to join 3 Rifles as a battlefield casualty replacement near the end of Herrick 11. He was quickly and warmly accepted – it's not always easy coming to a new battalion – and had proved himself a superb section commander.

The following year, when 1 Rifles were themselves in theatre on Herrick 14, another very good friend of Jon McKinlay – Cpl Mark Palin – lost his life in an explosion in Nahr-e Saraj, where the men of B Coy 1 Rifles were based. Cpl Palin – 'Maldoon' – was a popular and self-deprecating NCO, known for his enthusiastic late-night dancing, his love of Tottenham Hotspur FC, and an infectious level of banter which kept up his men's morale in the toughest of situations. He was also a brave and committed soldier who had volunteered for the mission on which he lost his life. A large haul of IED components had been

339

discovered hidden in a ditch. EOD experts were called, and the thirty-two-year-old corporal undertook to lead them to the spot. Approaching the cache, he took out a map to double-check his position. As he put the map back into his pocket, he rocked back on his heels and triggered a hidden device. He died instantly, leaving a pregnant wife and a toddler son.

Jon McKinlay was in Afghanistan with B Coy at the time. It was his second visit to the country – he had been a 1 Rifles section commander during Herrick 9. His close mate Sjt Gavin Sharrock was with him on that tour, and remembers a highly professional soldier who acquitted himself well.

'Life was hard,' said Sharrock. 'We did a lot of patrolling, often at night, often in company strength, and we got into a lot of contact with the enemy.'

In one firefight, with the fog of war lying thick on the battlefield, Jon McKinlay shot what he thought was a Taliban fighter sneaking through the undergrowth – only to realise later that he had in fact hit an unfortunate stray camel which had been minding its own business.

'He laughed about that,' said Sharrock. 'But Jon was always up for a laugh, or doing something to make conditions a bit better. When we weren't on patrol, or on stag, he always seemed to be building things – gym equipment, that sort of thing. He'd often do the cooking, he enjoyed that. Our rations were okay, but a bit basic, so we'd give the ANA guys who were with us some money, and they'd go to the local bazaar and buy us luxuries, like bread.

'You did feel very remote and lonely sometimes, and among hostile people. But if you were feeling a bit vulnerable, you'd think of the other units nearby, the heavy weapons systems we had, the QRFs, the air assets, the MERTs, and you'd realise you were okay.'

On Herrick 16, LCpl Jon McKinlay had come out as a mortar fire controller – and, like Steve Thompson the year before, a battlefield casualty replacement. He was grief-stricken at Mark Palin's death, on July 18 – as was Lisa, to whom Jon had been married for just ten months.

'I was just leaving the clinic where I worked,' said Lisa, a nurse. 'As I often did, I checked my phone to see if Jon had called, or if I had any messages from him. I had about five missed calls, and I recognised the code for Afghan so I knew it was Jon. But, then again, Jon would text me a thousand times a day if he could, so I wasn't particularly worried.

'When I got home I logged onto Facebook, and I saw all the messages to Carla, Mark's wife. I called a really good mutual friend, and she told me that Mark had been killed. I can't describe my emotions. I was in bits. Mark and Carla and Jon and I were really good friends. We saw a lot of each other. I felt awful for Carla. She had a baby, and another on the way. What was she going through? And of course I then starting thinking of Jon. He and Mark were in the same battalion, they'd worked together. It just really hit home what could happen to Jon.'

She put the phone down and it rang almost immediately. On the other end was her husband, phoning from his patrol base.

'I can't remember how the conversation went in detail,' said Lisa, 'but I know it was hysterical. I was just beside myself. Jon hadn't been with Mark when he was killed, but it was still horrendous. I said, "Poor Carla. I've had enough now. I don't want this. I don't want that to happen to you." He said, "I'm going to be fine, don't be stupid, get a grip of yourself."'

It was the sort of conversation too many wives, husbands, mothers and fathers had with soldiers serving in Afghanistan.

Jon McKinlay's first Afghan tour had been challenging – several members of the battalion were killed and many more injured – but he had come home safe. Lisa knew that she would hear of any incident involving him before the media, so that helped her to deal with the stress a little. 'Thinking about what might happen can be all-consuming,' she said. 'You just can't spend all your time doing that. Whenever I heard of a death on the news, I felt awful for the family of the person who'd died but at least I knew it wasn't Jon. So I was able to just get on with life while he was away on that first tour, and it seemed like before I knew it he was home again.

'He didn't really show any signs of being concerned about going away the second time. He hadn't really been expecting to go, at least not so soon, and he didn't have much notice of the posting. He was called on to replace one of the men who'd been injured. He told me – the bugger! – that it would probably be easier than the first tour, because it was winter and they wouldn't have to put up with those awful summer temperatures. I was worried, of course, but he didn't want to talk about the risks. If I raised the subject, he just said, "I'll be fine, babe! It won't be as dangerous this time." So in the end I just had to say, okay. But, of course, it was every bit as dangerous.'

* * *

LCPL MCKINLAY CAME from an Army family – his late father Malcolm had retired as a lieutenant-colonel in the Royal Corps of Signals – and he had been born in Germany, in a British military hospital.

'He was a noisy baby,' said his mother, Valerie. 'In fact, he was noisy to the end. He wasn't a very good sleeper to start with, but then his dad went away to Northern Ireland and I thought, *Right, we'll get that cracked.* And I did get him sleeping, and sleeping really well. He loved his food as a baby, and I don't think he stopped eating all his life. You could always tell when he came back off leave if he hadn't done a lot of "phys", as they called it. "It'll be alright," he'd say. "When I get back to work and start running again, it'll fall off me!"

'He wasn't a naughty child, but he was always up to mischief, and he never learned the meaning of the world "no". He would badger you into exhaustion. And if he was ever told off, and put in his room, within ten minutes this little face would appear around the corner, grinning. He was incorrigible.

'When he was about three-and-a-half, his sister, Rebecca, was born. He was a really good brother – always very gentle and very tender with her. I remember when we moved to Germany and Becca must have been about three or four months old. She was in her crib and I could hear her beginning to grizzle, because it was almost time for her feed. I thought, *It's all right, she's not having a full-on tantrum, I'll just finish what I'm doing here.* But suddenly it went up about five gears. I rushed into the bedroom and there was Jonathan. He'd taken her out of the crib and had put her on the bed, and was stroking her head.

'Trying not to sound panicky, I said, "What are you doing?"

'He said, "She was crying. I didn't know what to do."

'I said, "Well, I'd rather you didn't get her out of the crib again, Jonathan!"

342

'But he meant well. He always meant well. He and Rebecca were much easier to handle if they *weren't* getting on with each other. When they were pals they were an absolutely immoveable force. There was a great deal of affection between them.'

There was never much doubt as to the career that Jon McKinlay would follow.

'He was an adrenaline junkie,' said Valerie, 'and he never had any fear. He ran full pelt at everything. He walked at ten months, and the pushchair was more or less redundant. He was never one of those children who sat down and coloured, or played quietly. He went to Bembridge, a boarding school on the Isle of Wight. We chose Bembridge partly because it was quite an outdoorsy school on the coast, and they did sports every afternoon. This was ideal for someone who was never going to set the academic world on fire, but who had a huge amount of excess energy. He was quite sporty, but he had a bit of a butterfly attitude to life. He'd try lots of different things, but not stick with them. He did horse riding for a while. And then he was into golf. He only ever did things to a minimal level.

'When he was about ten, the teachers realised that he was dyslexic. For a long time, he wouldn't read for pleasure. Ironically enough, it was the *Sharpe* series by Bernard Cornwell that did it. We recorded the TV programmes for him so that he could watch them when he came home on holiday. Then he twigged that they were based on the books, and he started to devour those. I always say that it was Sean Bean who got Jonathan reading.

'His maths wasn't that great, either, but the summer he died he had been on a mortars course at Warminster. I was working with the lady who had been the special needs teacher at his school, and I told her that Jonathan was doing this course that involved lots of maths. Her eyes opened in amazement. I said he was using a computer, but he had to be able to do it with a protractor and graph paper, too. She just said, "Oh my God!" But he got through that course with distinction, I think because it had a relevance to what he was doing. He perhaps hadn't seen the relevance of maths in his life until then. He'd done his GCSEs, but his results were very poor. I think he got one grade C in English. It wasn't a hideous surprise for us, but he was a bit devastated.

'He came home to Blandford Forum, where we were then living, and got a job working in a shop where they sold TVs and radios. He also used to deliver and install the TVs. I remember him coming home one day and saying, "I'm going to have to go back out. I had to fit a TV for a little old lady today, and she wasn't feeling very well, so I think I'd better just go and check on her." At times he could be an absolute bugger. You were lucky if you got a birthday card. But he could be very, very kind.

'After about eighteen months, he went into the Army. I think it was inevitable, though he wasn't going to get into Sandhurst because of his poor exam results. I wasn't against it. He was never going to sit in an office for any length of time and it was pretty much the family job. And it can be a good career. But I did have a conversation with him, in which I said, "It's not all running up and down mountains and having a very exciting time, you know. You have to face the fact that somewhere down the line there could be a bullet with your name on it."'

* * *

LISA AND JON McKinlay met online in 2007, via a chat website. By then, he was a divorced father-of-two, and Lisa might have been forgiven for not having seen him as the greatest catch in the world – not least because he held his cards close to his chest.

'He hounded me with messages for weeks,' she said, 'but he hadn't posted a profile picture, so I didn't engage with him. But he still kept on sending me messages. One day I sent one back saying, "You're clearly ugly, and if you can't put a picture up I'm not really interested, so stop bothering me."

'So then he *did* send me a picture. But he looked horrible in it – like a munchkin with cam-cream on.

'I said, "You're not really my type, but I enjoy your banter so keep on talking." Eventually, we exchanged numbers, and we started chatting by text. That digital relationship went on for about six weeks, and then one night I'd had too much wine, and he said he'd come around and introduce himself. Catterick was only half an hour away from where I lived. I said, "No you will *not*!" but then, after some more wine, I said, "Oh, all right then. But bring a bottle of wine and some flowers!"

'He came around that evening and we just chatted non-stop for about four hours. He was lovely. Just lovely! He told me once that his first memory of me was when I bent over to get him a can of beer from the cupboard, and he saw the small tattoo on my back, and he liked it. We sat for hours that night, just chatting. And that was it. He never left – well, he left that night, but he came back every day after that. Eight months down the line, we bought a house together in Darlington, which was convenient for Catterick, and also for the hospital where I was working.

'I had a daughter, Piper, from an earlier relationship, and Jon knew that, if he took me on, he was going to be taking Piper on, too. And they got on beautifully from the beginning. She was only five when he came into her life, which is a good age to meet new people, and we became a family very quickly. He'd been married before and he had a daughter, Megan, and a stepson, Ollie, from that relationship. They lived mainly with his first wife, although they spent time with us, too.'

At the time, Jon McKinlay was a full corporal. But his Army career meandered slightly – he would be promoted a rank, and then busted back down for some misdemeanour or other. Sure enough, he was soon back at lance-jack.

'Jon was a vibrant character,' said Lisa, 'and that didn't always work well for him in the Army. He was perhaps a little too prepared to speak his mind, and he could lose his temper. His colleagues and bosses often said that he was dedicated, but that didn't stop him getting into trouble. So promotion didn't come easily. He was probably the most over-qualified lance-corporal in the regiment. It didn't worry me, because rank didn't matter to me. I felt that, as long as we were all right as a family, then it was fine.

'He was frustrated, because all his friends had been promoted above him, but at the same time he didn't help himself. I did say to him once, "When are you going to stop bloody messing around, for Christ's sake? You keep on moaning that you're not being promoted, so you just need to rein yourself in a bit." But if you have a personality like Jon's, it's hard to rein yourself in.'

Despite this, he was respected enough to be posted to ITC Catterick as a trainer, along with his great friend Gavin Sharrock.

'One of my best memories of Jon is from that time,' said Sharrock. 'The recruits were learning camouflage and concealment, I was taking the lesson, and Jon was one of my demonstration troops. The point that we were making to the lads was that you have to have just the right amount of camouflage – not too little, but also not too much. As I gave the cue for one of the guys to demonstrate the art, Jon emerged from the undergrowth and ran across in front of the recruits – totally naked except for a small tree on his back. The recruits loved it. That was typical of him. He was a bit of a joker, and he always lived life to the full.'

Sjt Nick Howe was another good friend.

'Jon had qualifications coming out of his ears,' he said. 'The problem was that he would just do something wrong and set himself back. Before that final Afghan tour, he went on pre-deployment training, and the CO went to see them in this simulated Afghan village. While he was there, they came under simulated attack, and called up mortar support. Jon was in charge of the mortar line, but it was Friday and he'd packed the mortars up so they could get an early start home! That didn't go down well. I could always get away with things, but mud stuck to Jon somehow.'

By 2011, though, with that earlier Afghan tour under his belt, as well as a 2006 visit to Iraq and postings to Northern Ireland and elsewhere, he had become a highly-experienced junior NCO, and was finally gaining the respect his service demanded. Even those who had found him an acquired taste had come round.

Dan Cartwright, a rifleman on the 2011 tour, was one of those.

'I'd first met Jon when I joined the Devonshire and Dorset Regiment in 1999,' he said. 'I'll be honest, he wasn't my favourite bloke in battalion before Afghanistan. He had his own ways of doing things which not everyone liked, but I saw a different side to him in Afghan, the real Jon, which changed my opinion of him.

'We were based at CP Chaabak in Nahr-e Saraj, a fairly remote spot about seven kilometres north of B Coy HQ at CP Jeker. It was a fairly quiet area, but out to the west of us it was rife with Taliban and insurgent activity.

'Jon joined us about three months into the tour as our MFC. He would often cook pizza and fresh bread for us from the ration pack, and the lads loved it – it was a welcome rest from the ten-man ration packs we were living on. He made an oven from an H83 container [*a foot-long steel ammunition box*] which was very effective. He just thrived off it. My memory of him now is of a bloke who, hand on heart, was as good as any. He was always good for banter, most of it aimed at himself. He would always help the younger lads in the platoon, and would pass on his wealth of knowledge and experience.

'And his love for Lisa and his kids was unbelievable – that's all he talked about.'

Sjt Nick Howe agrees.

'The general view of Jon had changed,' he said. 'His stature just grew massively. He'd gained a massively good reputation after [Herrick 9 in 2008/9], and a lot of people had a good impression of him. He got really close to all the lads, and he was getting invited out all the time, and we were bonding a lot more. He had a lot of good friends and a lot of people had a lot of good things to say about him. And his personal life was getting squared away because of Lisa. Jon lost his life just at the point when he was most happy and most respected.'

* * *

JON MCKINLAY DIED on a joint patrol with Afghan policemen.

The circumstances of his death are somehow particularly poignant. At around 6pm, ninety minutes after leaving CP Chaabak, the Afghans needed to pray, so the patrol halted in a small garden. Since Muslims must pray to the east, LCpl McKinlay had taken out his compass to point his comrades in the right direction. At that moment, and with his attention distracted, a hidden Taliban gunman opened fire, spraying the static group of men with AK47 rounds. Jon was hit in the neck and the leg, and collapsed into a ditch with what was later described as an 'unsurvivable' injury.

After a brief but fierce contact, lasting some seven minutes, the Taliban were driven off, and a Royal Navy doctor who was with the party as medic was able to get across to the ditch. He found that the thirty-three-year-old soldier was dead.

Back home, Lisa McKinlay had been 'in panic mode' since the death of Cpl Mark Palin, two months earlier. Jon had at least been able to get back on R&R, and they'd had 'an amazing time'.

'He only had one week,' she said, 'but we fitted in so much. We went to Garstang, where my family is from, and we visited his mum down south, and his sister and her boyfriend. When it was time for him to go back to Afghan, I dropped him off at Brize Norton for his flight.

'Jon was quite an emotional little thing, and he was very loving. As we said goodbye at Brize, he was really tearful, bless him. He didn't want to go back. Then he did something that surprised me. He gave me his wedding ring, which he hadn't done before. He said, "Here, have this until I get back." I was like, "What for?" But he didn't explain any further. Anyway, I took it, we said an emotional goodbye, and then he was gone.

'It was just horrible. I tried to get on with life and focus at least a bit on things other than Jon in Afghan. I had to do that, if only for Piper. I know I didn't do it very well, but I had to try, somehow.

'We kept up our stream of e-blueys, calls and texts. I was knackered from receiving so many texts! Every minute he had free, he'd be sending me messages. And if I didn't text back straight away, he'd be back on minutes later saying, "Why haven't you replied? I haven't got much time." I'd reply, saying, "I'm at bloody work!" The phone would be vibrating in my pocket as another text arrived, and I'd be thinking, *For God's sake, do your job!* I couldn't just say to my boss or my patients, "Oh, I'm sorry, my husband's on the phone so I'm just going to drop everything and answer him." He was constant with his messages. Of course, in hindsight, that was nice.

'Most of them were mundane and loving, and usually avoiding the realities of Afghan. I received a lovely text from him on the day he was killed. He wrote, "Morning, baby. Hope you have a good day. I'll speak to you in a bit."

'I sent him back some news about Gary, one of our friends. Gary had been planning to go to Germany on his motorbike, but now he couldn't because someone had rammed it. Jon never replied to that message, but I didn't think anything of it. I knew he went on patrols, and that the system sometimes went down, so I got on with my day.'

In fact, the reason for his failure to reply was more sinister.

'I'd had a long day at work, and I'd just got home,' said Lisa. 'It was my mum's birthday, and I was planning to call her. My hair was plaited for work, so I remember letting it out and roughing it up to be more comfortable. I didn't plan on going anywhere that evening. I was getting tea ready when there was a knock at the door, and there were two men in suits. For a fleeting moment, I knew. But then I wondered briefly if they were Jehovah's Witnesses.

'I opened the door, and they just said, "Mrs Lisa McKinlay?"

'I said, "Yes?" and they flashed their identity cards and asked if they could come in.

'At that point, I realised something was badly wrong. I thought, *He's been shot, and it'll be his leg, and now all I'm going to hear for the rest of his days is "I was shot in Afghanistan!"* That was the sort of thing I could imagine Jon doing, because he could be a drama queen. They said, "Unfortunately, your husband was shot an hour-and-a-half ago."

'I was like, "Is he dead? What's going on?"

'They said he was dead. I said, "No, you've got it wrong!" but they were adamant that he had been identified. I just went numb, which was how I remained for a long time. I couldn't take it in at all. But I began convincing myself that, for some reason, he'd swapped uniforms with someone, and they therefore assumed it was Jon, whereas another man had been killed. I know it sounds unlikely, but that was just the sort of thing he would do when he was mucking around.

'They kept asking me if there was anyone I wanted them to contact. I said, "No, I'm on my own, so leave me on my own." But they wouldn't leave until I had someone else here. In the end, I told them to get a friend, Andrea, from across the road, who had a brother in the Army. She came over, and soon after that Piper came in and saw me with two men in black suits and Andrea. I'd been crying, but I'd stopped by that time. I couldn't explain at that moment, so Piper went back out to play, but then she panicked and went around to another neighbour and said I was in the house with two strange men and had been crying.

'She came back, and at that point I told her that Jon had been killed. She was beyond heartbroken; she was devastated. But a little while later, her friend knocked at the door and asked if she could come out to play again, and she looked at me, and I said, "Okay!" She went out and played for another two hours. I was pleased, because I just wanted to be her age at that point, rather than be forced to process this terrible information that, even an adult, was almost impossible to handle.

'My mum rang to ask why I hadn't called her on her birthday. I just couldn't tell her about Jon. I suppose I wished her a happy birthday, but then I sat up all night. I was half-crying and half-telling myself that they had made a terrible mistake. I didn't go to pieces. I was on my own, but that's how I like it, because I am very independent. But I knew I couldn't keep myself in a bubble, I had to tell other people, and things needed to be done. So at about quarter to five in the morning, I called my mum and dad and told them.'

Jon McKinlay's mother Valerie had had a similar knock at the door; she, too, thought that the Jehovah's Witnesses had come calling.

'It had been one of those days when I was bobbing in and out of the house,' she said. 'I learned later that they'd been looking for me for about three hours. I came in at about 8.45 that night and the phone was going. It was Rebecca. We were laughing and chatting on the phone, and I literally still had my bag on my arm. Then the doorbell rang, and I said to Becca, "I'll ring you back." It didn't occur to me to wonder why anyone would be ringing my bell at that time of the night.

'I opened the door and there were two guys in suits, at least one of whom was carrying a document case. One said, "Are you Mrs Valerie McKinlay?"

'I thought, *That's odd*. He held out his ID card, and said, "I'm from the MOD." Then it all just fell into place.

'I just said, "Is he dead?" They wouldn't tell me, and they had to physically bring me through to the living room and sit me down. I kept on asking, "Is he dead?" They were so young. I couldn't believe it.

'One of them said, "Is your son Jonathan McKinlay?"

'I said, "Yes."

'He said, "It's my very sad duty to inform you that your son was killed this afternoon."

'I just didn't know what to say. Eventually, I said, "I must ring my daughter."

'She picked up the phone and said, very cheerily, "Hi, mum!"

'I just said, "Becca, Jonathan was killed this afternoon."

'She just said, "We'll be right up."

350

'When I'm distressed I pace up and down the room, and I remember doing that. I rang my brother who lives in Ireland. He just said, "I know." Becca had called him. I could hear my sister-in-law crying in the background.

'It was the wrong time of day to be told, and no sleep was had. Becca and Dan, who is now her husband, were on their way up to be with me, and I asked these young men to stay until they got here. They said that someone would be in contact in the morning.

'The next day, we visited an elderly relative whom we didn't feel we could just tell over the phone. Then, when we came home, the house just seemed to fill with people. The chaplain from the camp was there, and the guy who was going to be my support officer, and a couple of others, I think. On the Friday I took myself off to the doctor. I wasn't sleeping because my brain was in over-drive.'

For Lisa McKinlay, the early days passed in a haze of tears, phone calls and funeral arrangements.

'Normally, when someone dies, you go to the funeral, you lay them to rest, and that's it. But with the Army there's so much more. You're officially informed, you have the repatriation ceremony, then the funeral, and then there's the inquest, and later still a memorial dedication. It was really awful dragging the children through everything that followed.

'Jon was the second soldier to be repatriated through Brize Norton.[23]

'On the day he came home, I think I had more diazepam flowing around my body than I had blood. Not that I would display my emotions much anyway, but it helped me to stay calm and get through it all. Jon's friends carried him off the plane, which was a lovely thing to do. The Army looked after us very well, and they were as supportive as possible, but nevertheless I felt the repatriation process was very invasive, especially when we were taken by car to the area where hundreds of people pay their respects. We were lined up on one side of the road and the other side was packed with press. They didn't know who I was, and I wasn't about to be outed. So when the hearse drove past, I just stood there with Piper and Megan. I found all of this very alien, and so invasive. It was just awful.'

Valerie McKinlay shares that memory of her son's repatriation.

'It was a very strange day,' she said. 'The night before, we were taken

351

to a hotel just outside Oxford. The guys who were going to be Jonathan's honour party all knew him well, and they came and had a drink and supper with us, which was rather nice. And then the next day we were given a very impersonal military briefing about it all. There were a whole load of people sitting on these chairs facing us, and to this day I can't remember who they were or what they were there for. It was almost like too much Army bullshit.

'We waited for the plane to arrive, and all they could do was pour tea and coffee down us. I couldn't stand it any longer, so I went and stood outside. I was chatting to someone when I looked up and saw the plane. All I can really remember of that day is snapshots, and the sight of that plane coming in to land is one of them.

'It was so sad to see this huge plane and know that there were just two bodies in it. It's the saddest, saddest thing ever. We saw the coffin in the chapel of rest at Brize Norton. There was just one bit of wood between me and my son. And I just knew that, behind it, he was all dirty and dusty and bloody and shot about. It was unbearably painful.

'I'd said I didn't want any photographs of the children to be published, because it wasn't fair on them. But long-lensed cameras were focused on us in the car on the journey between Brize Norton and Carterton, and at Carterton there was a scaffold construction with press photographers. All you could hear was the clicking of the cameras. We were so vulnerable. It was like a Roman circus. I do feel a little bit angry that we more or less sleep-walked into this.'

With all of that going on, it was several days before Lisa remembered that Jon had given her his wedding ring.

'I don't think I took it very seriously when he gave it to me to look after,' she said. 'Or perhaps subconsciously I didn't *want* to take it seriously. Anyway, I'd just left it in the car. But as soon as I remembered it, I ran out to get it. I've got it upstairs now, and I always wear it on my thumb when I'm in bed at night.'

She decided to hold his funeral at St George's Church, Bulford Camp. His coffin, draped in the Union flag, was carried by six of his comrades, to the sound of *High on a Hill*, with its haunting, moving trumpet solo.

Hundreds of mourners watched Sjt Gavin Sharrock read a eulogy. He ended by saying, 'Jon, I cannot believe I'm standing here doing

352

this, when it's only eleven months ago that I was doing your best man's speech. I was proud of you then and I am proud of you now. You served your country with honour, and you were an asset to the Rifles. Mate, it's never going to be the same without you. You've done your job, stand down.'

The coffin was taken from the church to the sound of Pink's *Who Knew*; in the churchyard, the 1 Rifles Honour Guard saluted their fallen comrade with a volley of fire.

'It was a military ceremony because that's what Jon would have wanted,' said Lisa McKinlay. 'He loved the glory and tradition of the Army, so I was glad that we could do that. Gavin was absolutely invaluable when we were organising it all. So often, I just couldn't think clearly. Gavin would just say, "Right, Jon would want this, or Jon would want that." I trusted Gavin completely, so I let him crack on with it. And he would liaise with my visiting officer, Stuart Cochrane, so that the military could deal with their side. Stuart Cochrane was amazing. In the days and weeks that followed Jon's death, he came round every day. I'd make him a cup of tea and offer him some cake, and we would chat. He'd always have his little notebook, and I'd say, "Right, what are we cracking on with today? Come on, let's get it out of the way and then we can have another brew." He'd often laugh at me.'

Valerie McKinlay had been able to take some time off from her job as secretary in the estates department of a school in Dorset, in order to go through the early stages of her grief. 'I'm lucky to have a good boss,' she said. 'He told me to go away and come back when I was ready. So I took about a month off. I was still absolutely shattered when I went back, but life goes on. What was I going to do at home? Just sit and stare at the four walls? I just don't see any point in being at home and dwelling on it. I'm better off at work where I have distractions.

'How do I cope with it now? You have to. You just have to, although I have my bad days. I have a daughter who became engaged about six months after Jonathan died. They got married quickly and when I asked why, Becca said, "What's the point of waiting? We don't know how much time we have left. We want to get married and have a family, and that's what we are going to do."

'Then, nine months later, along came their little girl, Izzy. That was good for me. I'd been feeling very down, but then I thought, *I have to get well for my daughter, because she's going to need me. I don't want to be the grandmother who is always sad.* So I went off and had some bereavement counselling, which helped.

'I might not have Jonathan any more, but I still have Rebecca, and she does not deserve to have someone who is constantly grieving. We still talk about Jonathan and sometimes we have a little cry. And then there are my grandchildren. I need to help them because two of them went through things that they shouldn't have had to go through until mid-life. Jonathan wouldn't have wanted us to sit around weeping all day.'

Jon's daughter Megan was twelve when her dad was killed. Three years on, she is doing her best to hold on to his memory, and finding her own way through the pain.

'My dad was always very kind and he was very funny,' she said. 'He made a lot of jokes, and he was fun to be around. Some of our best times were when dad took us rock climbing. Olly [*her brother*] and me both loved that. And we'd go swimming sometimes. Every Boxing Day we'd all go to the cinema. These memories are all very precious to me.

'We went to Alton Towers once, and he tried to get me to go on this really big ride. But I was so scared that I wouldn't do it. But two years later I went there again, and that time I did go on the ride. I did it for him.

'He was very into his cars and motorbikes. We still laugh when we remember going out for a drive in the new car that mum and dad had just bought. It had been raining really heavily, and dad thought we'd be able to drive through a deep dip in the road that was filled with water. We were half way through when the engine stopped. We couldn't even reverse out, so we all had to climb out and wade through the water. We'd only had the car for about an hour! Me and Olly found it very funny and we were laughing. But I think mum was a bit angry.

'In those days, we lived on an Army camp about an hour away from where dad worked, so he drove there every morning in his uniform. After my mum and dad divorced, I didn't really see him in his uniform again, but recently I found a picture of him packing his uniform, getting ready to go to Iraq. I'm in the photo with him. I'd just got back from school when it was taken. In a way, it's difficult to look at that photo, but it also helps me to cope.

'All the pictures we have are of memories. If we went out to dinner or we went rock climbing, or if we went to a play area, someone would always take a picture. So when I see these pictures now, they bring back happy memories.

'It was a big shame that he had to spend so long away with the Army. It was just horrible saying goodbye to him every time he left. If he was away on exercise, we'd get a phone call every day, or every other day. But when he was in Afghanistan he'd only phone or write when he could. We sent him little parcels when he was there. Mostly we'd send him food to make life a bit better. We always sent him Tabasco sauce, because the Army food was very dull and he loved spicy food. He liked to cook for his friends out there, and as a bit of a joke he made a kitchen and he put up a sign saying, "JJs Bar and Grill". My grandma has the sign on the wall in her kitchen now.

'It did upset me when he went off on a tour, because we worried that he wouldn't come home, and I knew he'd lost friends. I was so young when he went to Afghanistan for the last time, and I was such a daddy's girl. It was very hard. I don't really remember what he told me before he left, but knowing him he would have said something like, "Do really well at school!" and then a little joke about something.

'In his letters, he told me how he was doing, that he had an amazing tan, and he joked a lot. I remember a letter he sent me when he was out there the first time. He said he'd shot a camel by mistake. We laughed about that. He really did love Afghanistan, even though it was a bad place.

'My mum and dad had been divorced for four years when dad died. I was happy for them both when they married again. They stayed really good friends, and that made me happy. I think they were better as friends than they'd been when they were married.

'Olly turns eighteen in December. He's hoping to join the forces. He wants to join the Marines, but if he doesn't manage that he'll join the Army. In a way, he'll be joining daddy and Uncle Luke [*the brother of Jon McKinlay's first wife, and an Army mate from his early days*]. They were very close. Mum and dad met because daddy used to share a room with Uncle Luke.

'My mum knew that dad had been killed a couple of hours before she told me. It felt like a very odd day, because my step-mum had phoned the house to tell mum, and although I didn't know what they'd said I just felt something was wrong. Mum was so upset. She didn't want to tell me before grandma had been told. She then sat us down and told us. At first it didn't feel real. We cried for days and couldn't sleep.

'I like to remember him teaching us to ride our bikes, and our rock-climbing trips. I remember the names daddy called me and Olly. I was Chikeroo and Baby Girl. Olly was Beaky Boo. One memory that makes me smile still is the time, when I was seven, when I swallowed a ring. Dad rushed me to the hospital, and they said that if it didn't pass through me, they'd have to operate. Dad had the job of checking to see if I'd passed it! He found it the day before they were due to operate on me. Dad always laughed about that and said it was an example of true love. Then there was the time that he took our dog Pelham out for a walk late one evening after work. He came back crying and holding Pelham. Dad had thrown a ball for him and he'd been knocked out when he ran into a lamp-post as he chased it. Pelham was fine, but it was hilarious.

'In a way, now, after three years, it's a lot easier to cope with, because I've got used to knowing that he was killed. But only in a way. I think about dad all the time. I have lots of pictures of him in my room, so I see him every day. I feel sad when I think about him, but I have memories and pictures. I wish I had more. I'm very proud of my dad. He is my hero.

'I'll worry about Olly if he joins the Marines or the Army, especially after what happened to dad. But it is Olly's choice. It's what he wants to do.'

Jon's comrades miss him almost as much.

'His banter was absolutely shocking,' said Sjt Nick Howe, fondly. 'His one-liners could kill a room of politicians just like that. It was so shit it was good. I think it was because he came from a very posh background. His dad was a lieutenant-colonel, and Jon turned up talking like Prince Charles, even though he'd joined as a private. So because of this posh background, he'd get ripped for just about anything. But he gave it back even better.

'We were on Herrick 9 together. We were stationed south of Garmsir District Centre, about 70km from the Pakistan border. No-one was deployed further south than us. We'd engage with the Taliban on a regular basis. Jon was ideal. He was a good lad, and good in the firefights. He was a good soldier to have by your side.

'My best friend in the world was killed in the war. Mark Palin – or Maldoon, as we called him – died just two months before Jon. We'd already lost Tommo, and then Jon was killed. It was just a body blow to everyone, and life has never been the same since. But you've just got to crack on. It's the Army mentality.

'I was on exercise with the recruits when I heard about Jon's death. I had a phone call from one of the other boys. Gav Sharrock had been speaking to Lisa and he asked me if I would help to carry the coffin at Jon's repatriation. I said yes, of course, and we went to Brize Norton a few days before he came home. That year had been just funeral after funeral, but we just cracked on and got it squared. The night before Jon's funeral, we went out and got absolutely rat-arsed to try to numb the pain.

'My favourite memory of Jon is at Butlin's during 'Orse's [*Gavin Sharrock's*] stag do. It was day three of a three-day bender and Chesney Hawks was live on stage. He broke into *The One and Only*, and Jon picked me up on his shoulders. Every time I hear that song now I think of him. I still miss him. He was a top man.'

Gavin Sharrock was also back in England, in a training role at ITC Catterick, when he heard the news. 'I was in my office when someone phoned and said, "I've got bad news. Jon's been killed,"' he said. 'I didn't really believe it. We'd only just lost Mark Palin. It was hard to take it in, and it was hard to believe. It was pretty full on then with Lisa. She got in touch with my wife very quickly. I was very upset but I felt I had to hold it together for Lisa so that I could help her as much as possible.'

Of course, Lisa McKinlay's suffering – and that of Jon's step-daughter, Piper – was immense.

'I had three months off work on special leave,' she said. 'I went back to work in January 2013. After that, I just threw myself into nursing. I told myself that Jon was working away. That self-deception is still the easiest way around it for me. Rationally, I know he's not here, but at the same time I can believe that he's working away.

'I tried counselling, and although I did start to open up and talk about my feelings, after a while I just shut down again. My counsellor said we couldn't make progress until I could open up and talk freely.

But I won't let myself explore my feelings beyond a certain point. If I was to let myself accept what has happened, I think I would go down, and I don't think I'd come up for air again. Until I can handle it, I'll just have to bimble along in my own way. But that way is very difficult. I'm a mess a lot of the time when I'm on my own.

'I don't show my emotions very well in front of other people. I've shed very few tears in public. It's not me. In a way, that has served me well, but I know I'm supressing my emotions and that isn't good in the long run. But Piper was only ten years old then, and I needed to show her that life goes on. There was also Megan, and although I don't see her often, she also needs to know that we move forward. I have to confess, though, that it's a bit of an act.

'The inquest was held eight months later. It was up to me whether I read the autopsy report but I'm a nurse, and I wanted to understand all the circumstances around Jon's death. When they told me that he had been shot in the neck, I knew that it would have been instant. That was all I needed to know. If he'd been shot in the leg and had been bleeding from an artery, that would have been a long and painful death, and I'd always have wondered, *What was going through his mind, and how long was he lying there alive?* So I consider it a very tiny mercy that he wasn't aware of what had happened. But still, the details were very vivid, and, even now, I can see him in my mind's eye, lying in a field in Afghanistan.

'It has been made clear to me that I am part of the Rifles family for life. I haven't particularly felt it recently, but then I haven't needed them either. It's only recently that I put my hand up and rang someone in The Rifles, because I was struggling with a number of issues. I felt I was drowning in difficulties, and I said, "Honestly, someone needs to help me here before I do something desperate." They pulled out all the stops and did their best for me.

'Jon and I were planning to sell up in Yorkshire and move back to be near my family and friends in Garstang. Jon liked being part of our little community there. He fitted into my close group of family and friends very well, and that group became very important in our lives together.

'Not all that long before he died we had discussed him leaving the Army. But, at the end of the day, he absolutely loved it and we had to consider the pension. There aren't that many alternative careers in civilian life for blokes who've done sixteen or seventeen years in the Army. He wasn't that far off his full twenty-two years, and we decided between us that he'd stay in. That way, he'd have his full Army pension, and if he could find work part-time somewhere we'd be fine. He always joked about working for B&Q, but I think he'd have been a skydiving instructor. He was so passionate about skydiving that he even got me into it. I skydived once with him, and I loved it.

'After he died, Piper and I went ahead with the plans Jon and I had made. We sold up in Yorkshire and moved to Garstang. It's great being near my family, especially knowing that Jon was so happy here. But since we've moved, I've taken ten steps back in the way I function. In Darlington, I was managing really quite well. Sometimes it seems so bad that I don't know how we have got to this point, almost three years since he left us.

'Jon is literally there all the time, from the minute I wake up until I go to sleep, and then he's in my dreams. There is not a second when I do not think of him. Everyone thinks I'm coping fine because I'm very independent – perhaps too independent. But I won't be carried, and I will go my own way. The hurt doesn't get any less, but perhaps I don't feel it so often now. I put on a brave face, even though I'm broken inside. Fingers crossed I'm going to be okay. I'll get there in the end.

'Piper has been doing really well. Children adapt and are resilient. But she has emotional outbursts every now and again. That's harder to deal with, because they come out of nowhere, and I feel awful because what can I do? At least when I'm dealing with my own unhappiness, I can shut myself off from the world. But I can't help her. I tell her all the right things: that it's normal to feel the way that she does, and, if she can't talk to me, then she needs to talk to other people. I know she doesn't always tell me everything, but I also know that she talks to her friends, and to the mother of one of her friends. I do worry about her a lot.

'There's no rulebook on grief, so I don't know what is right and what is wrong about the way I handle life. I still need Jon around. He's *got* to be here. I have all his pictures around the house and I've had his medals framed.

'I don't want to be seen as living in the past, but in a lot of ways I'm quite happy there. His clothes are still in the wardrobe. And I'm doing all the things he'd have loved to do, even sky diving to raise money for military charities. Some days I'm broken, and some days I'm numb. I swing between the two. When I have no choice but to get on with things, my body just does what it needs to do.

'Recently, I've become quite heavily involved in the Army Widows' Association. We meet up quite often, and I've now got a lot of widow friends. I have a close network of family and friends, but they don't really understand what I've been through in the same way that other widows do.

'Jon's a bit all over the place – literally. As he was in life, he is in death. He was cremated, so part of him is in the military cemetery at Tidworth, so that his mum and his sister can visit him. I brought the rest of his ashes home. I've had some incorporated in a ring so I get to take him everywhere I go. I did a tandem sky dive in Netheravon last year. Jon used to skydive there, so I managed to spread part of him over the place as we descended. But the largest part of him is near me in Garstang cemetery.

'I like having him all over because that's where he was in life. He was all over the bloody place. With Jon, you rarely knew what you were going to be doing, where you were going, or why. I often have a little chat with him and tell him about what is going on in my life. I wonder if he's watching. But only once did I feel anything. I went for a long walk in the country, and I don't know if it was because I was in a particularly low mood, but I felt his presence. This particular walk is nice and lonely. It goes through lots of hills for about three hours and ends at a place called Nicky-nook. I had my headphones on and had probably cried my way around the entire circuit. I think I was going through all the memories. I sometimes think that I don't want to be here anymore, and I think I was having those thoughts as I sat by a stone marker. I was crying my eyes out and it was odd. I don't know how to describe it but I felt he was there. Maybe it was his way of telling me, "Come on, Lisa! For God's sake. You've been through worse moments. You can do it again." It was a nice, enveloping feeling, and I felt like, *Wow!* I had a chat with him for a few minutes, and then I realised that actually I was still on my own, so I started off home again. I'd like to have more experiences like that, but I make the best of what I have.

'I know there's masses of debate about Afghanistan, and I've never really understood it all. In my mind, Jon had his job and he loved doing it. They join the Army and put the uniform on to fight if necessary. And for Jon that meant going to Afghanistan. I hear people banging on about wasted lives, and that we should never have sent our people to fight in Afghanistan because it's not our territory. My response to that is that they chose to go. They knew the risks. Yes, they thought it might not happen to them, but it was their choice. And it was my choice to stand by my husband. I knew the risks as much as he did.

'I loved the way we moulded together. We loved holidays and short breaks away, eating out and stuff like that. Recently, I've found some little videos of those times. Looking at them makes me sad, but also happy. We were just good in each other's company. There are some lovely videos of him playing with Piper, too. They were great together. We socialised a lot, but we could also just party on our own in the front room. We were always happy in our own company. Jon could be quite extravagant, and he'd sometimes go out and buy a bottle of champagne on a whim. We'd sit by the fire in the garden enjoying it. Or we'd have little cocktail nights to ourselves.

'We'd been married just ten months when he left us. But we'd had five great years before that. In fact, it felt more like thirty because we packed so much into a short time. Jon was always fun, full of banter, and so passionate.'

LANCE CORPORAL PETER EUSTACE
MORTAR PLATOON 2nd BATTALION THE RIFLES
AUGUST 13, 1986 – NOVEMBER 16, 2011

SHORTLY BEFORE HE left for his second tour of Afghanistan, LCpl Peter Eustace sat down to write a letter to his mother, Carol Horan.

It was to be opened only in the event of his death.

On the outside, 'Eust' was a tough, seasoned soldier. A classic mortarman from inner city Liverpool, he was, at 6ft 4in tall and 17st, 'a big Scouse bear', according to one mate from the regiment. He'd joined the Army seven years earlier and planned to do the full twenty-two.

But the note to his mother, full of love for his family and regret for whatever small troubles he might have caused them during his life, hinted at the thoughtful and sensitive man beneath the wisecracking twenty-five-year-old's imposing exterior.

DEAR MUM, he wrote.

> *AM SORRY FOR WRITING THIS, BUT IF YOU'VE GOT IT IT MEANS AM GONE.*
>
> *I JUST WANTED TO LET YOU KNOW AM SORRY FOR ALL THE TROUBLE, SCARES, + GRIEF I'VE EVER GIVEN YOU. I KNOW MOST OF THE TIME I'VE BEEN A BIG SHIT, WHETHER ITS BEEN WHERE AM PISSED OR DRUNK BUT I REALLY AM SORRY!*
>
> *I LOVE YOU AN AM GREATFUL FOR THE BOSS LIFE YOU'VE GIVEN ME AN THE WAY YOU BROUGHT ME UP. I'LL*

NEVER BE ABLE TO PROPERLY SAY AM SORRY AN THANK YOU.

TELL KIRSTY [his younger sister] *SHE CAN DO ANYTHINK SHE WANTS TO IF SHE PUTS HER MIND TO IT. AN TELL HER AM SORRY FOR ALL THE THINGS I EVER DONE TO HER WHEN I WAS PISSED AN THAT AM REALLY SORRY + I LOVE HER.*

TELL RYAN [his younger brother] *TO STAY OUT OF TROUBLE, HOPEFULLY HE'LL DO WHAT I DID AND HE'LL CALM DOWN. TELL HIM I LIKED THE WAY HE SAID GOODBYE IT MEANT A LOT TO ME.*

LOVE YOU ALL LOADS

LOVE

PETER

It was a letter he fully expected Carol to have to read.

Peter arranged a leaving party in Dingle before he deployed. It was one of the best this close and gregarious family had ever had, said his nan, with a lot of Peter's school friends there. The drink flowed, silly hats were worn, and the place was buzzing. But there was an emotional undertone to the night.

'He couldn't wait to go back to Afghan,' said Carol, 'but he was also scared. He'd convinced himself that he wasn't coming back home. He liked Cuban cigars, and I remember at the leaving party he was smoking one, and he put it back in its case unfinished. For some reason he said, "That's a memory you'll have, because I won't be coming back."'

If he was scared, it wasn't altogether surprising. Peter Eustace had been in Sangin in 2009, on what had been a very hard tour for 2 Rifles. They had lost thirteen men – including five on that fateful day which claimed young William Aldridge's life – and a quarter of those who deployed had come back injured. Peter had returned physically unscathed, but he was in some ways a changed man. His irrepressible sense of humour – and what his sister, Kirsty, described as 'the happy, silly Peter, always teasing me, always singing if he'd had a bit too much to drink' – seemed to have disappeared. Now he was a more serious, troubled individual.

'He would never say what it had been like,' said Carol, 'but then I'd be the last person he would talk to about it. But we knew there was a risk that he'd have been disturbed by the experience. The regiment tried to warn us about it. They said we might want to disconnect the doorbell before he came home, and generally avoid making any sudden, loud noises. Because if he was suffering from stress, that could trigger something. And we *did* feel that he'd been affected.

'He started drinking a lot, and he'd get angry very quickly. When he was home on leave, he'd sit here drinking and looking at pictures and videos on his laptop. A lot of it was put together by the Americans… It was gunfire from planes and helicopters and tanks. I saw some of it, and I thought it was unbelievable that he'd actually witnessed things like this.

'He'd sit there drinking, and looking at these pictures and videos, and sometimes even shouting at the laptop. I didn't know how to approach him about it, so I just kept back. They don't get anyone to counsel them when they come home. They're just left to look after themselves. Soldiers only get help if they ask for it. I don't think what he was going through was as extreme as PTSD, but he was definitely suffering from what he'd seen.

'I was so worried about his drinking and going out at night that I couldn't sleep. I would wait up for him to come home, whatever time it was, expecting there to be trouble. One night he got his nose broken in a fight with the bouncers at a club. Another time he got stabbed. He couldn't remember anything, he was that paralytic, but he was in hospital for a week.'

But whatever fears and other demons he might have been battling, Peter Eustace was able to face them down. A career soldier, he had recently signed on for another four years, and had told his grandfather, John Horan, that he planned to work his way up through the ranks, 'though he was only really interested in going as far as sergeant… He said if you go higher than sergeant, you're no longer one of the boys, and that was important to him.'

Once he reached Afghanistan, too, his innate bravery showed itself. 2 Rifles Intelligence Officer Capt Rob Hilliard would later say of him that he was 'always one of the first to step up and volunteer' to go on patrol through the dangerous, IED-trap alleys of the villages around his base. The battalion CO, Lt Col Bill Wright, said simply, 'He had nothing left to prove as a warrior. He was one of those men you can completely rely on when things get tough.'

Carol and her father have a clear memory of seeing Peter for the last time. He was heading off to the 2 Rifles base at Ballykinler in Northern Ireland prior to flying to Germany and then Afghanistan.

'It was so hard,' said Carol. 'He gave us all wristbands saying *2 Rifles, Op Herrick 15* and *Swift and Bold*, their motto, and when he said goodbye to me he made sure no-one could see us. He was hugging me and we were both sobbing. I said, "Look after yourself, son, take care, and you'll be back. You *will* be back, and we'll see you in a few months on your R&R." I'd never seen him sobbing like this before. In fact, he'd been crying a lot during the weeks and months before he left.'

Aimi, Peter's girlfriend of eighteen months and a district nurse from Mountain Ash in South Wales, was there, too. The attraction had been 'instant' when they'd met.

'We fell in love quickly,' she later said. 'We were infatuated with each other. My parents and sister adored him, everybody did. He'd always say, "Well, babe, what's not to love?" There was no drama, no arguments, just pure happiness and contentment with one another.'

As Peter kissed Aimi goodbye, telling her he loved her, she didn't know that he was planning to propose to her if he returned from the tour.

Carol, aware that Aimi was nervous and agitated about the farewell, tried to reassure the two of them – and herself.

'I was feeling very bad for her,' she said, 'so I said to him, "You'll be okay. You've been on two tours before and you've always been okay."

'He said, "Yeah. Look after yourself, mum, and take care." He asked his brother Ryan to drive him to the airport for the flight back to Northern Ireland. They'd never really got on very well, but for the two or three months before Peter went to Afghan they couldn't be separated. They were often hugging each other, like best mates.'

'When they got to the airport,' said John Horan, 'Peter said to him, "Take care, I love you, look after me mum." And then he was gone. We knew it was dangerous, but he swore to us that where he was going was reasonably safe. Of course, it was one of the worst parts. Maybe that was why he believed he wasn't coming home.'

* * *

CAROL HORAN WAS a young single mum – 'only seventeen and just out of school' – when her first son was born.

'He was a big baby,' she said. 'He weighed 9lb 3oz and he was twenty-one-and-a-half inches long. I was in labour for forty-eight hours, and I ended up having a C-section. Unfortunately, it was the same with the other two children [*Kirsty, now twenty-five, and Ryan, twenty-two*].

'When he reached the terrible twos, he could be terribly moody. When he got a cob-on, he'd hit the walls or floor in frustration. Fortunately, I was a full-time mum, because you had to have eyes in the back of your head with him. I was involved with the local parent support programme, so when Peter was six months old I would put him in the crèche at the local junior school and I'd then do cooking, needlework, and woodwork classes. The staff were very supportive, and I met lots of other mums there. Peter started nursery when he was nearly three, and he had a bottle and was still in nappies until a week before that.

'He was a loveable, loving child. He was always wanting cuddles, and was always giving me kisses. He didn't push his luck with me, but he did sometimes lead Kirsty astray. Her favourite memory is of the two of them getting into sleeping bags and sliding down the stairs in them, from the top to the bottom!

'He'd play happily with his Mutant Ninja Turtles and his Power Rangers, but he always seemed to have scrapes and bruises. When he was seven, he broke a leg falling off a climbing frame. And I remember when he was nine, he came home from fishing in the local park in an ambulance. Someone had caught him in the nose with their fishhook, and he'd had butterfly stitches in his nose. He liked fishing a lot, despite that.'

Peter was 'Liverpudlian through and through', said Carol. The family has lived in the Dingle area of the city for a century, and like most lads from the city Peter loved football. Unlike most of them – and perhaps demonstrating his independence of mind – he was a firm Chelsea supporter from the age of eleven.

'He used to get ribbed a lot for that,' said Carol. 'Obviously, most of his mates were Everton or Liverpool supporters. But it was never serious. He had loads of mates. He enjoyed school, and it probably helped that he was in the same class as his cousin, Danielle. He was a bit lazy, but, even so, he was in the top learning groups. He was particularly good at art, and used to spend a lot of time drawing. He had his own little logo, a tag with his name. He took after his dad in art. But all of his teachers always gave him good reports. They said he was a pleasure to work with, and they liked having him in class. His good reports continued right through until his final year, but then something went wrong and he got expelled for fighting. Another kid had been baiting him, and, in the end, Peter threw a chair at him. But it hit the teacher.

'He could have gone to another school, but from the age of nine, he'd known that he wanted to join the Army, so he forgot about school and started planning for that. I was very upset by that. He was doing GCSEs at the time, and now he wasn't going to sit any of his exams. Instead, he became a painter and decorator for about a year.'

'We really don't know why Peter was so interested in the Army,' said his grandfather, John Horan. 'But he wanted to see the world, so perhaps that had something to do with it. When he was a teenager, he and some other youngsters were invited to spend a week with the Army to get a taste of life as a soldier. They had to go over assault courses and that kind of thing, so it was really quite tough. He was the only one to last the week. He certainly had grit and determination.

'He was a big lad, 6ft 4in and 17st – actually, that really came home to me when he died, because I remember his coffin was 6ft 10in long – but he wasn't that fit immediately after leaving school. So while he carried on with his painting and decorating work, he really set about getting fit enough for the Army. He'd been given a date for his fitness test, and he had six months to knuckle down. He was a bit stressed about it, but he was keen and absolutely adamant that he was going to pass. He'd put bricks in his backpack and run around the park, and up and down the garden. He wore a hole in the garden that's only just grown back.

'It worked, he got in fine and then he did basic training at Catterick for six months. We went to see him at half-term, and they showed us what they did. He'd bulked out a bit, and it seemed like he'd transformed into a man. Later, we all went to see him pass out. We were so proud of him, and there was a lot of crying. He joined the Royal Green Jackets [*one of a number of regiments which were amalgamated into The Rifles in 2007*] and they did this fast march. Peter stood out above the crowd because he was so tall, and it looked quite funny to see them marching around at such a speed. It was a bit of a giggle, but still, we were so proud.

'After he died, we found Peter's training record among the things that were returned to us. Among all the records of the courses he did was his disciplinary record. Apparently, his section commander had warned him about not shaving on a daily basis. If that's all he did wrong, then I think he did pretty well!'

Peter joined 1 RGJ, aged eighteen in late 2004, and 'took to soldiering like a duck to water' said, Carol.

'He loved every minute, and thrived on it,' she said. 'He became quite domesticated, and when he shared accommodation with a couple of lads he taught them how to cook, how to iron clothes, even how to use the washing machine. He'd have meetings with them every now and again where he'd go through all their domestic issues, as if it was a lesson. He really was like the boss of the house. I certainly noticed a change for the better when he came home. He'd changed from teenager to a man, basically. If he was there while I was at work, I'd often come home to find he'd mopped the floors and brushed the yard. And he always said, "Don't do my ironing, I'll do it myself!" I think he felt he could do it better than me.'

Not long after joining his regiment, Peter was deployed to Iraq, on Operation Telic 9, as part of 19 Light Brigade. It was a difficult tour, which saw twenty-six soldiers killed in action and more than 130 wounded. Carol Horan had been relaxed about her son's deployment, until the dead and injured began coming home.

'Going to Iraq didn't seem to bother him at all,' she said. 'He was happy, he had a good career ahead of him, he was getting paid and he was doing something he'd always wanted to do. And I was happy for him, and I didn't start worrying until he was actually posted to Iraq. Then my nerves went, because there were so many young lads dying. I felt nervous and agitated, and remember thinking to myself, *Make sure you stay safe, get through the tour and come home.*'

Peter's sister Kirsty was then just fifteen, and not really too aware of the danger her brother was in. She remembers being 'proud' of his service.

'I didn't know exactly what his job was,' she said, 'so I used to tell all my friends he was a front-line gunman!'

Granddad John Horan was more concerned. 'I can't explain the feeling exactly,' he said, 'but I was very worried every time he went away. But Iraq was more of an open war, the Iraqis didn't fight like those slimy buggers in Afghanistan. Anyway, he came back safe, had a good leave, and then went to Cyprus on a posting. Later, he went to Kosovo to help keep the peace while elections were held. That was the cushiest thing he had had to do. I think he was sunbathing much of the time. He passed his junior NCO's selection cadre in March 2009 and got his first stripe, though he didn't tell us until after he got it, which was typical of Peter. I think that was because he didn't want us going to the parade, making a show of him and embarrassing him by cheering him on. We were very proud of him, though.

'He deployed to Afghanistan the first time that year, on Herrick 10, and then came back for a while. He wasn't very happy and used to say Army life back in the UK was boring. "I'm waiting to go out somewhere," he'd say. And then, in 2011, he went to Afghan again.'

* * *

PETER EUSTACE HAD been posted to FOB Khar Nikah, north of Gereshk in Nahr-e Saraj, in the green zone on the south side of the Helmand river.

He was a mortar fire controller, and part of a mortar line of three 81mm barrels and three 60mm barrels at Khar, which covered the area around the FOB and FOB Rahim, a few kilometres away on the north side of the river. They were there to support patrols by the men of Delhi Coy, 1 Yorks, which was reinforced with Gurkha troops and designated a ground-holding company, and their counterparts from the ANA's 3 Coy 3 Bn 3215 Brigade. The ANA were being mentored by Capt Neil Watson and Bugle Major Sjt James Davies of 2 Rifles.

Capt Watson was happy with the arrangement: in his view, LCpl Eustace and his fellow mortarmen were about as good as it got.

'The 2 Rifles mortar platoon was a close-knit bunch,' said Watson. 'These teams tend to be made up of experienced soldiers, and they need a passion for what they do. Traditionally, the mortar guys might not be the fittest in the battalion, but they're much more robust than most of us. They need to be, because an 81mm mortar is not a light piece of kit. They were mobilised for Afghanistan at short notice, and the real feather in their caps was that they didn't have a platoon commander at the time, so they planned their own training and went away and got themselves validated ready for deployment. They were all desperate to go.

'Among the nine of them at Khar were three MFCs [*mortar fire controllers*], and Eust was one of those. Everyone knew him. He was very much a larger-than-life character, always smiling and always cheerful – you couldn't have been in the same battalion and not know him. There was, for example, an incident in camp in which someone – and we don't know who it was – crashed LCpl Eustace's car inside the camp and actually left it hanging from a lamp post. No-one could prove anything, but LCpl Eustace had a smile on his face… But when it came to work, he was exemplary. Eust was only a lance-jack but he was very qualified and skilled. He would have got a glowing report after this deployment and been promoted. That was a no brainer to me.'

Of the three MFCs at the FOB, one would go out on each patrol so that he had 'eyes-on' if mortars were needed. He would then transmit co-ordinates to the other MFCs who would do the necessary calculations, check them, and then issue the command to fire.

'The whole process can be done in a matter of seconds,' said Capt Watson. "We did have some 105mm artillery support, but it was only used once because the guns were a long way away, and firing at such a range that they'd lose accuracy. The effect we wanted could be much more easily achieved with mortars. The time-of-flight for the mortar rounds was really short, and the forward controller with us would have been calculating ranges and so on all the time as we went along, so we could bring mortar rounds in really quickly. A good MFC out on the ground is constantly moving his targets – rather than waiting for an engagement before sending the coordinates back to the mortar line. The job is made a little easier by pre-existing calculations for a number of known targets, locations that the mortars have fired on before, but in practice the men are moving the barrels nearly all the time. In addition, the mortarmen will be handling different ammunition: they might fire smoke rounds first and then high explosive, or illumination at night. It really is an art, and they were incredibly skilled at it.

'We could really count on them, and Khar and Rahim were the busiest mortar lines in Helmand during Herrick 15. In excess of 3,000 rounds came out of Khar in six months. The day that Eust was killed, they fired in excess of 200 rounds – probably 260 – to support his extraction.'

Capt Watson and Sjt Davies spent a lot of their time with the ANA in on-the-job training, on patrols and deliberate operations. 'We would routinely be out five or six times a week, on foot patrols that would last for between three and eight hours, sometimes more,' said Watson. 'The patrols were about dominating the ground and supplying and providing security for a number of outlying PBs, of which there were five in our area. These small bases were a minimum of eight hundred metres and a maximum of 2.5km away from Khar Nikah.'

On November 16, 2011, Neil Watson, James Davies and their ANA men were involved in an offensive operation, supported by US Cobra attack helicopters. Peter Eustace would be on the patrol as MFC, and a Royal Artillery Fire Support Team commander was back at the FOB, prepared to call on the 105mm guns if necessary.

'We had identified an area where we wanted to expand our influence,' said Watson, 'and we intended to push four or five hundred metres beyond where we had been before. It was an early morning patrol, and it was just starting to get light as we left the FOB. We wanted to get off the road before it was light and operate more covertly in the fields. We came out of the base heading south, towards the fields, and then started heading east-northeast. The first 400m or 500m were quiet, just us and a few people working in the fields, but we made slow progress. The fields were really wet, because the farmers had recently opened the sluice gates and were filling the irrigation ditches, and that made it relatively tough going. Every ditch was a vulnerable point that had to be cleared. It took us about an hour and forty minutes to cover about 1.8km.

'We got to an area of compounds, which was an area of interest for us, and stopped to get an understanding of our surroundings. We had a compound straight in front of us, which was occupied by what we presumed to be a family. A man and his children came outside, and the ANA and I were talking to them. We knew we were beyond the forward line of the enemy troops, but that was deliberate. We were pushing into that area to generate a reaction so the Cobras could come in and strike. It's a standard tactic – you're taking the enemy on at a time and place of your choosing. You know where you're probing their lines, who you'll do it with, and you have the helicopter support ready. The odds are stacked in your favour.

'It became clear that the people in the compound were quite uncomfortable with us being there. They were nervous and, seeing this and being aware of previous enemy firing points in the area, I left the ANA guys talking to the locals and walked back to have a chat with LCpl Eustace. I wanted his opinion about where he would lay his mortars. My concern was that we might be about to receive small arms fire, and if that happened I wanted to be able to respond quickly. I remember he smiled and said, "That's already done, boss. Don't worry about it." He was completely relaxed.

'We received some intelligence suggesting that the Taliban were setting us up for small arms. We'd stopped for long enough. We weren't going to go any further, and we were ready to head back to the base. The insurgents' *modus operandi* was to attack when we're turning back. They watch you, and play their hand when they think they have the best chance of getting away. They probably assume that's when we're ready to head back.

'So we moved off back into the fields. Rfn Suman, a Gurkha, was in front with the Vallon, the section commander was in front of me and then came LCpl Eustace in fourth place. Initially, we tried to force a route through some really dense scrub but that wasn't passable, so we turned north towards a ditch. We stopped for a very short time while I went forward to brief the Vallon man about the point at which we wanted to cross the ditch. This was clearly a vulnerable point. It was about four foot deep with about six inches of water. The metal detector guy went forward, he cleared one bank, then he cleared the ditch, then the other bank. Then he was out in the opposite field, and going back towards the FOB.

'The section commander was next to cross. The distance between us was just four or five feet. I stepped onto the near bank of the ditch, then stepped across. I don't remember putting my foot down on the other side. There was a massive ringing in my ears and I was thrown forward into the field. I found out later that I'd been blown at least fifteen feet, maybe twenty.'

Just behind Capt Watson, Peter Eustace had triggered a large, hidden IED.

'It was huge,' said Watson. 'I'm quite a small guy, and the Gurkhas are pretty small, but Cpl Eustace was a big chap, probably twenty-five stone with his kit. We determined afterwards that it was a 40kg-plus IED, pressure-pad operated, and probably designed to immobilise the Danish armoured vehicles that had previously been deployed in the area. We think that the Vallon didn't pick it up because of the depth it was buried to. Some of us had successfully walked over it, but Eust was the first big guy to walk across it and he initiated it.

'The irrigation ditch at the point we had tried to cross was now a crater at least six feet, if not seven feet, deep and eight feet across. He would have been killed absolutely instantly. The one thing that you hope for in a situation like this is that no one suffers, and he absolutely did not suffer. He wouldn't have known anything about it.

'I started to come around – I don't think I lost consciousness – with my ears still ringing. I looked around and there was a scene of absolute devastation. I saw my weapon about eight feet away from me. It was in three pieces and the barrel was embedded in the ground. There was stuff scattered absolutely everywhere. I had my daysack over my head, my right leg somehow up under my chest, and I was unable to feel my left arm. By this point the guys in the patrol behind me were shouting. The bugle major was trying to shout to me. I heard him talking to the rest of the multiple, and he was saying, "It's the boss. He's dead." At that point, I shouted back at him to say I was okay. And, in fact, my injuries were pretty minimal. I had some shrapnel in my hand and was knocked about a bit, but I was incredibly lucky. To be four feet from a guy who didn't make it… Well, whatever you believe in, it wasn't my day to go.

'I was still trying to work out what had happened. The two in front of me had also been blown off their feet – the section commander was struggling quite a lot, the blast had burst both his eardrums – and, as I looked up, we were engaged by small arms fire from two points. One weapon was a light machine gun, a PKM, which is a variant of the AK47.

'Having realised I was alive, BMaj Davies was now taking control of the situation and the patrol was starting to engage back. I reported what was happening to the ops room at the FOB, and while I was doing that we were engaged from third and fourth firing points. BMaj Davies then did something remarkable. He came through the crater, spoke to us, then got up and started firing, fully exposing himself to the multiple enemy firing points. He made himself a target so that we could crawl back to the other side of the ditch. And he didn't do it once. He did it twice. I have no idea how he did not get shot, because as I was crawling back, the ground was exploding with gunfire around me. He was standing up there talking to us and firing at the same time.'

Bugle Major Davies was later awarded the Military Cross for his extraordinary bravery that day; the Vallon operator was Mentioned in Dispatches. The surviving men had by now scrambled down into the bomb crater, and Capt Watson got on the net to the ops room back at the FOB to discuss options.

'This was at 08.03,' he said, 'and we didn't break contact until 09.50. There was a suggestion that Brimstone, the EOD people, would come out, but had they done so they wouldn't have been able to do anything without serious risk to life. There in the crater, it seemed like the entire world had opened up on us. So between myself and the company commander back in the FOB, we decided we would extract. Meanwhile, the FOB was sending out a QRF to help us.

'There were other call signs trying to get to us, but really importantly, as soon as we reported the incident to the FOB, the mortar line there began firing. They knew one of their own had been killed, but all they were concerned about was helping us. And without their help, I think we would have lost more men. They brought eight to twelve rounds into the treeline where the attackers were, using the coordinates Eust had pre-selected for them shortly before he was killed. This was remarkable: it really seemed that LCpl Eustace was helping us from beyond the grave. It wasn't easy, but thereafter, by using the company net, BMaj Davies and myself, and Sjt Nicholls in the observation tower at the FOB, were able to adjust the fire.

'The two US Cobra gunships also came in to assist, but they couldn't put down any fire because the smoke being generated by the mortar rounds was obscuring the targets. The pilots did, however, hover low over us, acting as a deterrent, and that was hugely risky, because if the insurgents had had an RPG it could have gone very, very wrong.

'I crawled out of the crater and gave the orders to the guys. I was thinking, *We've had a difficult day, but we're going to get back.* We placed LCpl Eustace into a bivvie bag – I wanted people to be able to concentrate on the task in hand, rather than on the gore of his injuries – put him onto a stretcher, and off we went. We did a classic fire-and-manoeuvre extraction over a distance of about 600m until we were able to link up with the QRF that had been sent out from the FOB. At that point, we were able to place LCpl Eustace on a quad.'

They made it back to the FOB with no further mishap. The mortar line was still working, their barrels almost red hot as they laid down a carpet of fire to assist the withdrawal of Capt Watson's flanking call sign. They, too, made it back safely. Peter Eustace's body was flown to Bastion, and thence repatriated to the UK with the bodies of Lt David Boyce and LCpl Richard Scanlon, of The Queen's Dragoon Guards, and Private Thomas Lake of 1 Princess of Wales's Royal Regiment, who were also killed by IEDs at around the same time.[24]

* * *

PETER HAD RUNG home as often as he could – he jokingly complained that it was hard to get onto the satellite phones because the Gurkhas were always hogging them – and wrote when he got chance, too. His letters were necessarily free of news of the fighting, and concentrated instead on the trivialities of everyday life back home, and on alleviating the harshness of FOB life. He asked Carol to send him out some malt Horlicks ('the just-add-water one!'), laughed at her having sent him a bluey addressed care of 'DELHI CITY', rather than 'DELHI COY', and asked her to send roll-on deodorant, as aerosols would not be accepted at the post office.

His girlfriend Aimi had set up a special Facebook page in which friends back home could write messages of support or chat with Peter. His popularity was evident from the fact that he would mention that he'd quite like some instant noodles to supplement his rations and, in the next RAF delivery, seventy packets of noodles would arrive. At one point, he had twenty shower gels, and had to beg people not to send any more. But they were a close bunch at the FOB, so any excess got shared round the less fortunate men.

In a letter to his 'nan and grandad', written four days before his death, he talked about the cut-off date for Christmas parcels and a £600 veterinary bill for his beloved dog Macey. 'Ok, am off I'll phone soon!' he ended. 'Lots of love, Peter xxxxxx.'

His final Facebook messages, sent on the eve of his death, saw him bantering with his sister, Kirsty. She had just passed her driving test, at the second attempt. 'About bloody time!' posted Peter – 'forgetting' that he had himself failed his test eight times.

In some strange way, the humdrum and everyday nature of these communications helped to reassure friends and family that all was well. But then two men arrived at the school where Carol Horan works as a special needs teaching assistant.

'It was going on ten-thirty,' she said, 'and I'd just finished my break. My boss come and said to me, "There's two Army guys here." I just screamed and started crying. I was shaking with fear.

'My boss said, "He might just be injured," but I said, "No. They don't send Army guys to see you if they're just injured. It means he's dead."

'She made me sit down in the meeting room. I was sitting there crying, and shaking, and shouting, "Hurry up! Where are they? Hurry up!" My partner came in with one of the guys who'd gone to the house. He just said, "Carol Horan?" and I said, "Yeah. He's dead isn't he?" I started screaming and sobbing.'

Peter's grandfather had been out and about, and when he got home he found his brother waiting, with his wife's cousin. 'My brother says to me, "Sit down, John,"' he said. 'I said, "This doesn't sound good." He said, "It's Peter. He's been killed in Afghan. He stood on a mine and he's been killed."

'The emptiness, shock, horror, the state of disbelief… All these things come to mind.'

For Carol, 'everything had become a blur'.

'I know that loads of people were coming to see us,' she said, 'and the house was full, day and night. And I remember you could hardly see the floor; there were flowers and cards all round. But it was like time had stopped.'

LCpl Peter Eustace was repatriated on November 24, more than a week after his death. 'During that time, I think we were living in a daze,' said John Horan. 'We didn't even know what day it was. The waiting was just terrible. I felt empty, and I don't think any of us knew what to do. I'm only his granddad and Ann's only his grandmother, but we had over 120 cards from people. The main thing, though, was that [*CSgt*] Peter Reid, the liaison officer, was guiding us all through it. He was absolutely fantastic. He nurtured us through the whole procedure, from when Peter died till after his funeral. He was with us much of the time… He wouldn't go home until the last one of us had gone to bed. One hell of a man.

'About two days after Peter was killed, Peter Reid said to me, "Do you want to know the details?" and I said, "Yeah, I really want to know." It emerged that, unfortunately, he had lost both of his legs, one of his arms and part of his lower abdomen. I was thinking to myself, *Jesus Christ!* I really wanted to see him, and if I hadn't been able to I don't think I'd be the same now. Bugle Major James Davies, who was on the patrol with Peter when he was killed, said later on Facebook, "I kissed him and gave him a hug. I said the Lord's Prayer and closed his eyes." Knowing that lad had written that gave me hope, because if he'd kissed our Peter then his face must have been okay. And when I saw him he looked fine. I know they'd put a bit of makeup on him, but considering he'd been blown up like that, I was absolutely delighted. I was able to see him and kiss him.

'It was some consolation to know he died quickly. He wouldn't have wanted to live if he'd lost his legs. I think he'd have gone off the rails. He's better off where he is. I admire other soldiers you see on the telly who get on with life after losing limbs, but that definitely wouldn't be Peter.'

For Carol, the repatriation was worse than his funeral.

'I think it was because he was actually home again, on British soil,' she said. 'Eight of us went to Brize Norton. A lot of the senior Rifles officers were there, and they looked after us very well all day long. There was hot food, coffee, and everything was served on the best china. We went outside to see the plane coming in. There were four men coming home, and Peter was the last one off. There was a bugler playing *The Last Post*, and I was just crying from beginning to end. From the minute I'd woken up that morning, the tears were just non-stop. Peter Reid warned some people to grab Kirsty if necessary, because he thought she was going to run onto the airfield towards Peter's coffin. It was just horrible.

'After that, I just wanted him home. He was at the undertakers' around the corner at first, but on December 2 we brought him home to our house, and he stayed here until the day of his funeral, which was on the twelfth. The lid was off his coffin most of the time, but on the eighth day I had to ring the funeral directors because the body was starting to smell. They came and put the lid on. We'd put all sorts of things in with him, box sets of DVDs, clothes, a little bottle of Jack Daniels, teddies, cigars and sealed letters. The Rifles lads said to us after the funeral, "What on earth did you put in that coffin? He weighed even heavier than he did at the repatriation!"

The family were very moved by the funeral – Peter's aunt Margy recorded a TV broadcast of the events and still watches it twice a week or more. 'The hearse came to the close, and he was escorted by two police officers on horses,' said John. 'There were also eight police motorcyclists, and they stopped the traffic when necessary on the way to Liverpool Cathedral. I remember people coming out of the shops, clapping, and paying their respects. It was a military funeral, but we had a lot to do with the planning. We chose the hymns, and our Kirsty chose a record by Adele, *Someone Like You*, because it was Peter and Aimi's favourite song. Peter is buried just ten minutes up the road at Allerton cemetery.'

Three years on, Aimi herself is struggling to deal with Peter's death. 'I wake up every morning and for the first two minutes everything is fine,' she said. 'Then it hits me like a bullet to the chest, that he's gone. His last words to me were, "I love you Aims", and I take some comfort from that.

'I don't miss just one thing about Peter, I miss the million tiny little things that made him who he was. He was a loving, gentle, caring boyfriend, so funny and laid back. He made me feel so safe and loved.

'Although he has been taken away from me and our families, I am so grateful I had my time with him. He made me a better person. He was my missing half, and I'd cut my right arm off for two more minutes with him. I still feel that he'll walk through the door one day, as if he's been on exercise.

'I miss every hair on his head. The beautiful blue of his eyes, his infectious giggle, his singing. I miss him every minute and I will love Peter until the day I die.'

Peter's mother still finds it 'unreal'.

'I couldn't accept Peter was dead, and even until recently, I kept thinking he was on deployment,' she said. 'Sometimes I think he's come home and he's knocking on the door, and then I wake up and look out the window and realise I've been dreaming. We miss him loads, and I can still see him bouncing through the door, saying, "It's only me!"

'We're very proud of Peter. I was especially proud that there were so many of his Army colleagues and friends at his funeral. It proved that he was very well thought-of. People didn't have to go, but the Cathedral was packed. It took them fifteen minutes to carry his coffin in. And he's left us lots and lots of memories. We were always a close family, but now we're even closer. We don't do anything without each other. We often have parties, and we invite Peter's friends and comrades, and we have a good time. Peter was a party animal, so we're doing what he loved. He liked Jack Daniels, so we always raise our shots of JD to him. At times like that, most of us can't speak, so my dad normally says something like, "Thank you very much for coming and, as you know, we're here because of my grandson and he'd be very proud to know that we are all here, and he's looking down upon us now and we should give him a toast, God bless you, mate."

'We go to the cemetery as a family at Christmas, on his birthday, and on the anniversary of his death. The first Christmas without him was one of the worst times, but now we put a bottle of Jack Daniels on his grave at Christmas. And on his anniversary we go to the cemetery and set fireworks off. That's not really approved of, so we set them off just before we leave, and then we run.'

Capt Neil Watson thinks often of the big Scouse bear who didn't come home.

'I will never forgive myself that one of my riflemen died and I didn't,' he said. 'It's a commander's responsibility to look after his men, and if you don't feel like that then you don't have the moral mandate to command.

'But I feel the tour as a whole was successful. It showed that the ANA were able to stand on their own as a credible force. It went from us leading them by the hand to them standing up for themselves. The offensive operations that we conducted together proved that. By the end of our tour, the ANA were issued with some mortars and they were starting to develop their own capability, although that is an art.

'Unfortunately, four of the guys we'd been mentoring were killed while trying to defuse an IED, and our advisor company also lost Capt Rupert Bowers. [*Capt Bowers, a 24-year-old married man, was killed by an IED on March 2012. His wife Vicky had given birth to their first son Hugo the previous month. While on R&R, shortly before his death, the young officer did at least see and hold his son.*] In the end we had a 50% casualty rate among the guys who were leading the teams.

'Nothing can justify the loss of one of your soldiers. He's someone's son, someone's brother, someone's loved-one. But when we went there, we all understood the risks. The important thing was that we did the best job we could to keep each other safe, bring some security to the area, and let the ANA do their job. We wouldn't have achieved that if we'd wrapped ourselves up in cotton wool and stayed in the FOB. We can look back and say we achieved something. And we can all be proud of LCpl Eustace's contribution.'

LANCE SERGEANT DANIEL COLLINS
FIRE SUPPORT GROUP 3 1st BATTALION THE WELSH GUARDS
AUGUST 13, 1982 – JANUARY 1, 2012

DANIEL COLLINS WAS a strong, tough soldier, and the kind of man upon whom the British Army has been founded since the days of Wellington. He had spent more than a decade in the Welsh Guards, where he was an outstanding NCO. He was a member of the elite Fire Support Group, had worked undercover in Northern Ireland, and had special forces potential. He was a 'bullet magnet' who had been blown up twice and shot twice in Afghanistan, and had laughed about it.

And he was a close friend of Dane Elson: he had taken it upon himself to collect up his friend's body parts, after Dane's grisly death in an IED blast in July 2009. He never recovered from that experience.

On New Year's Eve 2011, Daniel left home and drove into the Preseli Mountains in northern Pembrokeshire. There, haunted by the memories of lost friends, and of Afghans he had killed, he hanged himself.

He left behind a video message to his mother, Deana Collins, in which he sobbed as he said:

> 'Hey mum, just a video, just to say I'm sorry, okay? Ever since I've come back from hell, I've turned into a horrible person, and I don't like who I am anymore. This is why I'm doing what I'm doing, okay? I know it's selfish but it's what I want and what I need. I can't live like this anymore. One thing I'd like to ask is could I have a full military funeral, if that's possible? That's how I'd like to go. Mum,

381

please don't get too upset. You've got to understand this is what I want. I've tried all the help. There's nothing seems to be working, okay? I love you, okay, and I'll see you, I'll see you up there in a few years – well, hopefully not a few years, but you know what I mean. I love you. Bye bye.'

He was twenty-nine, one of a significant number of veterans of the campaign who have died by their own hand, and as much a casualty of the war in Afghanistan as Dane Elson and the other men and women who died in action.

'The second Daniel was born, I had an overwhelming feeling of love for him,' said Deana. 'I was a single mum, and the pregnancy was a shock. But my mum was great, and she was there when Daniel was born. He was a remarkably good baby. I actually took him to the doctor when he was about three weeks old because I was worried he didn't cry. The doctor said, "What are you complaining about?"

'We lived in St Albans, and most of my friends didn't have children. They'd often say, "Can I have Daniel for the day?" and off they'd go. They spoiled him rotten. Then he hit the terrible twos, and it was like, *Whoa! What's happened here?* But he got through that, and when he started at school he settled down. He got up to mischief, as boys always do. One day he came home but knocked on the door rather than running inside, as he normally would. He was standing there in floods of tears, covered from head to foot in red gloss paint. It turned out that he and his friend had built a den in the woods, and someone had given them a tin of paint to decorate it. Apparently his friend accidentally kicked it, and Daniel was covered in the stuff. It had started drying, and I had to scrub him in the bath to get it off. He was often getting into scrapes like that.

'As he got a little older he became very outgoing, and always wanted to be the centre of attention. But he was very polite. I remember one of the teachers saying, "You should be so proud of Daniel." That surprised me, because his school reports weren't great. But she said, "I've never met a little boy with such wonderful manners." He carried that through life. I knew that he'd know how to behave properly wherever he went, and I was so proud of him for that.'

The military fires were lit at an early age. 'He was such an outdoors boy, and when he was about eight he saw a military uniform for sale in the market. He said, "Can I have that, mum? Please, *please!*" So I bought it, and altered it to more or less fit. The first time he put it on he said, "I'm going to join the Army." And from then on until he grew out of it, I could not get that uniform off his back. The minute he came back from school he'd get changed into his little Army uniform.'

By the time Daniel was twelve, Deana had married his stepfather Dave. They had a toddler daughter, Megan, and the family had moved to Wales. 'At first Daniel wasn't happy,' said Deana, 'because he'd had to leave his school friends behind in England. But he went on to learn some Welsh, and he developed a Welsh accent. In fact, he really thought he was Welsh.

'He wasn't all that keen on schoolwork. The staff all liked him, because he was cheeky and always telling jokes, but only his PE teacher had anything good to say about his work. I'd do my best to encourage him, but all he focused on was the Army. My father and mother and my brother had all been in the Navy. He was very close to his grandma, and she said to him, "Daniel, why don't you join the Navy? It's far better." But even she couldn't change his mind.'

At sixteen, he sat the exam for the Army Foundation College in Harrogate; he failed by two points and was 'devastated', but the Harrogate staff, seeing his determination, gave him a second chance, and he passed. 'There were only seven boys in the whole of Wales who got accepted that term, and he was one of them,' said Deana. 'I was so proud. I wanted to take him there, but he wanted to go on his own so I dropped him at the train station. It was absolutely heart-breaking. To me, he was still a baby. But he said if I didn't let him go, he'd join up at eighteen anyway. It's what he wanted to do.

'I know boys pretend to be men, but deep down it's different. I think he was petrified. After about a month, he phoned me in floods of tears: "I want to come home, mum, I'm homesick and I don't like it here." I phoned the college, and the man I spoke to said he'd have a chat with Daniel. A little while later, the man phoned back and said, "He's fine! It was just a little bout of homesickness. He's doing well." And he was right, because after that Daniel seemed to be fine and he made it to the rank of sergeant at the college.'

Daniel came home often during his two years at Harrogate. 'He'd walk straight in the door, dump his stuff, say, "See you later, mum!" and off he'd go with his mates. Or he'd go down to Cardigan Rugby Club, where he'd played before going to Harrogate, and join them for training. He loved his rugby, but I didn't like to watch. It seemed like every time I went to I went see him, he'd be injured.'

In 2000, Daniel's stepfather Dave was killed in a car accident. A little while after that, his grandmother had a series of strokes and died. 'It was a very difficult time,' said Deana. 'Megan was only eight years old, and trying to explain to her what had happened to her father was very hard. Daniel understood, of course, but it was a very tough period for us all. But he left Harrogate with an excellent record, and joined the Welsh Guards, did his basic training and then, at eighteen, he was a real soldier. And he absolutely loved military life. He always wanted to lead and never be a follower. This is a typical example of his attitude: his unit stood in for the striking firemen, and he received a police commendation for rescuing a person with learning difficulties from a burning building.'

Much of the young Gdsm Collins' early career was taken up with ceremonial duties. 'He was at Buckingham Palace, and took part in the Queen's Birthday Parade,' said Deana. 'I went to watch, and I was so immensely proud of him. *That's my boy!* I thought – even though they all looked the same, and I couldn't really figure out where he was on the parade ground!

'In 2002, they went to Bosnia. There were still landmines in places, but on the whole it was peaceful, and I remember Daniel loved the landscape. When they could, they'd go off for a bit of exploration. But they also had to help excavate mass graves, and he found that harrowing. I remember him telling me of one old man standing nearby waiting patiently for them to uncover the remains of somebody from his family.

'Then it was Belize for jungle training, which he loved. He said it was like another world out there. Prince William was in Belize at the same time – Daniel said he was just like everybody else, and was making jokes about his grandma.'

After brief spell in the Falklands, Daniel went to Northern Ireland, where he spent much of the time in plain clothes working with anti-terrorist officers. Then, in 2005, he deployed to Iraq.

'He was based in Basra,' said Deana. 'I was worried about him, because it was still dangerous, but it was nothing like the dread I felt when he was in Afghanistan. He had some photos and videos from Iraq, and when he came back he showed me some of them. But they were horrible... children playing among dead donkeys, a body which had been severely burned... I said, "Sorry, but I don't want to see any more of these." But he seemed to be tough enough to handle it.

'He enjoyed Iraq, despite all that. He used to mention the children a lot. They'd follow the soldiers everywhere, asking for sweets and money. I didn't pretend to understand the politics, but I didn't agree with certain aspects of what we were doing out there. He'd try to explain, but I just felt so sorry for the people who were suffering, and when I thought of the children, in particular, I couldn't handle it.'

* * *

BY NOW, DANIEL had been promoted to lance-sergeant – the foot guards' equivalent of a corporal – and was thought by many in his regiment to be a man for the future. And then came Afghanistan – the perfect place to put into action all the training and experience he now had.

'I had this horrible feeling of dread about him going out there,' said Deana. 'At that time, we were hearing frequent reports of soldiers being killed. I knew that, when Daniel went, he would be facing very intensive fighting. He came home for some leave before deploying, and spent some time with his mates, who used to call him Taliban Dan. We enjoyed our time together, and the day of his departure arrived much too soon. He was dressed in his deserts that day, and I remember saying, "My God, you look so smart." Of course I started blubbing, and said I didn't want him to go.

'He said, "Well, tough. This is my job and I'm going. And I *want* to go."

'He was driving down to his barracks, and I'd thought I'd go with him to see them board the bus. But when it came to it, I just couldn't do it. I apologised, but he said, "Don't worry, mum, it's fine."

'When the door closed, and he walked off, it broke my heart. I remember saying to my friend, "I don't know if I can deal with this. I don't know *how* to deal with it." I'm one of these people who can only handle things if I pretend they're not happening, but that was hard because I was always waiting for a phone call. We mainly kept in touch by phone. On the odd occasion when I wrote a letter, I felt that what I was writing about was insignificant compared to what he was going through. Here, everyday life was going on as normal, out there they were putting their lives at risk.

'I might go two days and he'd phone, and then I'd not hear from him for two or three weeks. He called once and said, "Mum, my socks are rock solid."

'I said, "Well, wash them then!"

'He said, "I ain't got time to sit and wash my socks."

'So I used to send him new socks, and packets of biscuits, and he always wanted Pot Noodles and instant rice things. His mates from home would send parcels to keep his spirits up. I remember one phone call, he said, "Mum, the bastards! They've sent me a gay magazine!" They were a bit cruel, his mates, but it did amuse him. They also sent him a cookbook with all these lovely recipes that they knew he couldn't have.

'It's quite a small community here and lots of people knew Daniel and where he was, so they would come up to me and ask me if I'd heard how he was. I'd just say, "He's fine." But I was brushing it under the carpet. I tried to think he was just away on a tour somewhere nice, but I couldn't avoid hearing about casualties on the news. I'd have that feeling in the pit of my stomach, and I'd be thinking, *Oh my God! Some poor family has got to deal with this.* I wondered how they could possibly cope. I wondered how *I* would cope.

'He'd been out there some time when he called sounding really happy. He said, "I don't want you to panic. Don't worry, but I've been shot."

'I said, "What the hell do you mean, you've been shot?"

'He said, "Oh, it's nothing to worry about. I was shot in the back, but my body armour saved me."

'He said it was like being smashed in the back with a hammer, but he was otherwise okay. That was great, but then reality really hit me. I knew he was patrolling almost daily, and that the Taliban were doing their best to kill him and his mates. I was thinking, *Thank God he's fine, but if that can happen to him...*'

386

As many soldiers do, Daniel had developed little superstitions to help keep him safe. He'd been unshaven on the day he survived that AK47 round; thereafter he never shaved before patrols. Next to his skin he wore a wooden cross blessed in Bangor Cathedral before the tour by the padre. Perhaps these things worked, for Dan did not fall victim to the main threat at that time – the Taliban's insidious IEDs.

Others were less fortunate. After he returned from Afghanistan, Dan would meet up with Toby Harnden, author of the bestselling book *Dead Men Risen*, about the Welsh Guards' tour. In a later *Daily Mail* article, Harnden wrote: '[LSgt Collins] described to me how during Operation Panther's Claw he had already carried the body of one dead comrade to a Pedro medical helicopter when there was another blast. A Light Dragoons lance corporal had stepped on an IED... The company sergeant major had gone into battle shock – wide-eyed and falling over as he barked out orders. It took more than five minutes for Collins to find the lance corporal, who was lying in an irrigation ditch and had lost both legs and an arm. For nearly fifteen minutes, Collins and others fought to save the lance corporal's life. Collins told me: "He was unconscious, but one thing that stuck in my mind and I'll never forget it. As I was doing compressions, I looked at his face and I could see his eyes opening. I don't think he knew anything about what was going on but it was like he was looking at me."'

The lance corporal was pronounced dead on the helicopter; even worse, Daniel lost two close friends to IEDS. The first was LSgt Tobie Fasfous; the second was Dane Elson.

'Daniel and Dane had been great friends since they joined the Welsh Guards,' said Deana. 'Dane's family live not far from us, so the two spent a lot of time together when they were on leave. He phoned to tell me about Dane. I could hear him trying to hold his tears in. He said, "One of my chums has gone, mum."

'I said, "Daniel, I'm so sorry. I don't know what to say."

'He said, "Mum, there's nothing you *can* say."

'He was a little way away from Dane when the IED went off. Daniel told me, he kept shouting into the radio, "Dane, Dane! Answer me! Answer me!" Then he went over to where he thought Dane was, and found him. He'd been killed instantly. They called in a helicopter to evacuate his body, but Daniel refused to let Dane be put on the helicopter until he had picked up all his body parts, so that he was whole. He never told me about that – Dane's mum, Debby, told me. I look back now and I think, no wonder the poor boy suffered so much. Having to do that! I just can't imagine it.

'When Daniel was happy he used to call me "Mother Hen". I'd hear this voice on the phone saying, "You alright, Mother Hen?" But I never got another "Mother Hen" after Dane was killed.'

In fact, the effect of Dane Elson's death on Daniel Collins' morale had been severe. Deana recalled one particularly distressing conversation.

'He phoned me one day, and said, "Mum, this place is hell on Earth." He'd been pinned down in a ditch, under fire from all angles, for an hour or so. He said he and his mate were just hugging each other. They thought this was it. They thought their life was over. He said to me, "I just want to get out of this hell hole."

'I remember saying, "Can't you pretend you're not well?"

'He said, "No, I can't. I've got my boys here. I can't leave my boys. I've got to stick it out."

'He looked tough on the exterior, and being in the Army he had to pretend to be a tough cookie. But deep down he was sensitive. He was very upset by one of their Afghan interpreters. He told me how this young lad had told him, with tears in his eyes, that he could never go back to see his mother because she might be killed if he did. Daniel really felt for this boy, who had given up his family and everything to be an interpreter.'

* * *

AS PART OF FSG3, Daniel stayed out in Afghanistan after the rest of the battalion came home. It was a tough period, during which he was again shot – the bullet grazed his ankle – and blown off his feet by another IED, but was again unscathed.

'Losing his friends was devastating,' said Deana. 'He sounded so low, and there was nothing I could say to lift his spirits. I'd come out with things that seemed really stupid. Afterwards, I'd think, *Why did I say that? My poor boy is out there, I can tell he's not happy, and I'm saying something insignificant.* I felt terribly guilty. When he finally came home I went to pick him up from Catterick. The first thing I thought was,

God! Look at the tan on him! I went up and gave him a hug. And then I saw his eyes. There was nothing behind his eyes. He looked dead behind them. That still haunts me. He gave me a big hug and said he loved me. I said, "I love you too, boy! It's so, so good to see you!"'

That night, Daniel Collins went out with his old mates from home and got roaring drunk. And in the weeks that followed, people who didn't know him well might have assumed all was well. But he wasn't fooling his mother. 'I knew,' she said. 'His eyes were telling me. And he was drinking too much. His mates continued taking the mick, in a friendly way, calling him Taliban Dan and wanting to see his injury, and things like that. He said to me one day, "Why am I going out drinking with that bunch of prats? All they keep on going on about is Taliban Dan and things like that." It wasn't his friends' fault. They didn't know what he'd experienced. It was just their way of welcoming him back. But it became a struggle for him, and after a while he stopped seeing them.

'I started to notice that I'd be talking to him, and he'd suddenly go completely blank, off in a world of his own. I'd say, "Daniel, are you okay?" and he'd come back: "Oh, right! Sorry, mum. Yeah, I'm fine." But soon he was completely shutting off from the world. It was as if he wasn't there. At first, he didn't talk much about Afghanistan. Then snippets came out. I tried to talk to him, but it was very difficult. He said once, "I actually shot someone, and I saw his face explode. It was the enemy, but he must've had a wife and children. I killed somebody. How would you feel?" I didn't know what to say. A lot of the time he would just sit and rock like a baby. Just sitting there, rocking. I think survivors' guilt was a big part of it. He often said, "Why am I still here when the others are gone? I should have gone while I was out there."

'He returned to barracks after his leave, but he couldn't handle it. The Army signed him off sick, and he came home to wait for a referral to a specialist. He was deteriorating badly, and I was in a state of shock myself, seeing my son going through so much pain.'

To complicate matters, Daniel had met and fallen for a girl, Vicky, not long after his return, and had moved in with her.

'He loved the idea of being in love,' said Deana. 'As a lad, he'd always been falling in and out of love. But he started arguing with Vicky. He would come back to me often and say, "I can't handle this, I can't handle this." Then he started finding it hard to leave their house. Sudden noises alarmed him. Vicky told me that they were in a store once, and a door banged. Suddenly, Daniel was down on the floor. He'd have nightmares – he saw the face of the dead lance-corporal, or Dane's body, and he'd wake up screaming Dane's name, or yelling "Medic!"

'Vicky went away for the weekend, and I knew Daniel was in a bad place and couldn't leave the house. So I called him and asked him if he'd like me to go round and make him a roast. He loved his roast dinners. He said, "Oh, yes please!" So I went over there. I cooked roast lamb and he seemed to be enjoying it. But all of a sudden he threw the plate across the floor. He went down on his knees, and started shouting, "Burning flesh! Burning flesh!"

'I got down onto the floor with him and cuddled him. We must have been on the kitchen floor for about an hour. All the time I was holding him.'

In the two years following his return from Afghanistan, Daniel went through peaks and troughs. A major turning point was when he took an overdose and ended up in hospital.

'I got in touch with the Army, because medically he was their responsibility and they were not treating his case with any urgency,' said Deana. 'I said, "This boy needs help!" Some toffee-nosed twit said, "Well, what do you expect us to do, Mrs Collins?" I said, "I expect you to help my son. There's a military base near us in Haverfordwest. Can you get someone from there to go and see him?" This man didn't even realise there *was* a base in Haverfordwest. Anyway, it was agreed that they'd send someone from Welfare over to see him, but it wasn't followed up with any action that might help Daniel.'

Things came to a head after Daniel and Vicky went to a wedding. 'Vicky said they were having a good time,' said Deana. 'But Daniel had had a fair bit to drink, and suddenly he got up and left. Vicky pleaded with him not to go, but he got in his car and drove off. We found out later that he'd tried to drive his car into a brick wall, but, thank God, he chickened out at the last moment. Eventually, the police found him – he'd spent the night in a field. He was sectioned then and taken to a mental health unit. That didn't help. I've worked with people with learning difficulties and mental health problems, and I knew that wasn't the right environment for him. They just pumped him full of medication for four weeks, and then sent him home. They arranged for people to go in to see him at home. They said that he'd get priority treatment because he was employed by the MOD, but that didn't happen. I kept on urging the MOD and the Army to do more, but no single person was allocated to deal with me. The amount of paperwork that the MOD produced was huge, but I couldn't get on the phone to anyone in particular and say, "Right! What happens now?"

'Vicky phoned up MOD Welfare to talk about Daniel, and they said she was being a drama queen. That was so wrong. Daniel wanted help! I phoned [the charities] Combat Stress and Healing the Wounds, but neither of them could help because technically Daniel was still serving, even though he was on sick leave. The MOD did diagnose him with PTSD, but their help was slow and inconsistent. He would drive all the way to Birmingham for treatment, and end up seeing different people. He said to me once, "Mum, I've just driven three hours, filled in a form and then come home again."

'I know from my own work in mental health that you have to build a rapport with a patient before he will open up. It's a slow process, but it works. But that wasn't happening. He should have had that consistency of treatment with one person.'

On Boxing Day 2011, Deana went to visit her son.

'He and Vicky had had a barney, which I can fully understand because Daniel wasn't easy to live with. But he was on his own on Christmas Day, and that worried me. I phoned him. He wanted to be alone, but I persuaded him to let me see him the next day. And we had a lovely day together. I asked him if he wanted me to cook, but he said no, he'd rather I treated him to a McDonalds. I am so, so grateful for that day. He wasn't cheerful, but the bond between us was good. I was sad he wasn't calling me Mother Hen, though. It seems really trivial, but that's what Daniel called me when he was happy. I only ever wanted him to be happy.'

Deana felt more optimistic after that Boxing Day, but at about two o'clock in the morning on New Year's Day, she received a phone call from the police. 'They asked for a description of Daniel,' she said. 'They said he'd phoned them to say he was in Preseli, up in the mountains, and he was going to take his own life. They hadn't found him at that

391

stage. The strangest thing was that I didn't pick up the phone to call him. I just didn't know what I was doing. I was walking around like a headless chicken. But I should have picked up that phone. I started cleaning the oven, just to keep myself occupied. I can't remember how much time passed. A few hours, I suppose. There was a knock at the door, and it was the police. They told me they'd found him. I couldn't take it in and I just said to them, "I've got to finish cleaning my oven." The police phoned my friend Mandy, and suddenly the place was full of people. I don't remember much at all of the next three, four or five days. It's just a blank.'

Daniel's body was taken to a local crematorium, and a police officer asked Deana if she wanted to see him. She was unsure, but the officer persuaded her that it might be good for her to see her son at peace. 'It didn't seem real,' she said. 'He was so cold. The Army came with a uniform for him, and they dressed him in it and I went to see him again. He looked so smart. He was a good-looking boy, and he loved the women... He used to call himself a babe magnet. But seeing him didn't make me feel any better. I don't like reality, but I couldn't avoid this reality. I can't get rid of that last image of Daniel, although I try to block it out as much as I can. I don't want it to be the last thing I remember about him.

'The coroner was fantastic. I got the verdict that I was hoping for, a narrative verdict which meant they couldn't be sure that he really meant to take his own life. I believe it was a cry for help. He wouldn't have phoned the police otherwise, and given them his name, rank and number. It was a cry for help that went wrong. I don't care what anybody says, that is the truth.

'The Welsh Guards did as he asked, and organised a military funeral. They also said they were going to have a military ceremony to dedicate the headstone, but I never heard from them again. Dane's mum and I talk often, and I know that she's had fantastic support from the Guards. I'm not after their support, but it would have been nice to have a phone call occasionally. "Hi Deana. How are you doing? Is there anything we can do for you?" And I'd like some recognition that my son served with them. He joined the Welsh Guards as a boy, and they had all of his adult life. It's too late now, though. I don't want them to call me about it.

'They and the MOD know that it was Afghanistan that killed Daniel, and that they did not do enough for him. I'd like them to say they will learn from his death. But then they'll be admitting fault, and they won't do that. My son wasn't killed in action, and, although it sounds awful, I wish he had been. If he'd been hit by an IED, it would have been instant and he wouldn't have felt any pain. But to see him suffer mentally, knowing there was nothing I could do to help him, was terrible. I still try to deny things. *Daniel's away on tour*, that's what I tell myself. I've only been to his graveside once since his funeral, because if I saw his headstone it would be real. And I don't want it to be real. I'm very clever at putting up a brave front. People often say to me, "You're doing really well." I say, "Yeah, I'm doing fine." But I come home from work, and the minute I close that door, it's totally different. I keep the scarf that he took on tours under my pillow, just to be close to him. I talk to him a lot. I just ask him why, and I tell him I'm sorry that I couldn't help him.

'I go to work, because I have to, because I have bills to pay, and I have to live. I don't really want to see people, but I make the effort. I have friends, and I have to see them and socialise with them. But in truth I don't want to. I know that denying what has happened is wrong, and one day it will just explode. But until that time comes… The doctor gave me anti-depressants, and I took them for a few weeks, but then I thought, *What's the point of dulling this pain? I've got to go through it*. So I came off them.

'Megan's twenty-one now, and she has a little daughter, so I'm a grandma, which is very nice. Megan doesn't like to talk about Daniel. If I mention him, she changes the subject. I think that she's lost a lot in her short life. But she's got the baby, little Honey, and I think that's what she's wanted. Maybe it's her way of coping with things. She's got something she can care for, and that can't be taken away from her. She's a fantastic mother. And Honey has given me another purpose in life. She's ten months old now, and crawling and getting into everything. I always had Megan, of course, but Honey has brought us a little bit of joy. She is so adorable.

'I worry constantly that something will happen to them. If I phone my daughter and she doesn't answer the phone, I go into panic mode. I wish I could get over that. But I'm a tough cookie. I can cope. I think things are thrown at you for a reason. I just don't know what those reasons are yet. A friend of mine said to me, "Him up above only makes life tough for people he knows can handle it."

'A little old man of ninety-four who fought in the Second World War came to see me at work one day. He'd heard about Daniel, and that I was raising funds for Healing the Wounds. He said to me, "I'm so, so sorry about your son. I've suffered myself for years and years. You should be so proud of yourself to get it out there and make people aware of this." He told me about the number of friends he'd lost, and what he'd experienced. Then he handed me a cheque for a thousand pounds for Healing the Wounds.

'I do feel it's been a tough life, but I'm not after sympathy. It's what life throws at you. I really believe that things happen for a reason, and I'm hoping that Daniel's story will draw attention to PTSD among soldiers, and force the military and the MOD to take it more seriously. I think that must be why this happened to him. He was a jack-the-lad, and he could be a pain in the backside, but he was a good boy and he doesn't deserve to be where he is. It upsets me that his name will never be carved anywhere, like it is for all the other fallen soldiers. His name will never be remembered like that.

'My brother said to me once, "You have to remember, Deana, that you were dealing with Whitehall and senior people in the Army. That's not the Army Daniel loved. It was the boys on the ground that Daniel loved." He was right about that. And those bonds are still strong. I recently met one of Daniel's friends who was badly injured and spent a long time fighting with the Army to get a diagnosis of PTSD. He'd also been raising money in Daniel's name for Healing the Wounds. He said to me, "Daniel's made it easier for me to talk about PTSD." I was so pleased to hear that. I hope that will be his legacy. I don't want his death to be in vain.'

The friends and colleague of Dane Elson and Dan Collins took their deaths very hard.

'When we eventually got home from Afghan, we had a two-day FSG3 piss-up in Cardiff,' said former Guardsman Paul Liddy. 'That helped us to get back to normal. But we knew there was something that wasn't right with Dan. He had a lot of issues, and things were just getting on top of him. And then all the emotions that we'd pushed to the backs of our minds started to come out. Dan had tried to commit suicide once before. Maj Durham asked me to get hold of him and have a chat with him because he was worried that Dan would do something. I said to Dan, "Don't do anything stupid. We're all brothers and we need you. Remember, Dane died for us."

'They signed Dan off work for some months. Meanwhile, I was starting to slip a little too. I was going out and getting drunk all the time. The strange thing was that *Dan* was trying to advise *me*. "All that drinking's not good for you," he'd say. After he crashed his car, he didn't come back to the regiment at all.

'I spoke to him a couple of times, because we needed to meet up for an anniversary, but he was in the hospital. Then I had a phone call in the early hours of New Year's Day 2012 to tell me that Dan had gone into the mountains and committed suicide. My New Year's resolution had been to stop drinking, but I immediately started drinking heavily again, and I didn't stop for about a week.

'The remaining guys of FSG3 still keep in contact, and we still support each other. Dan used to sort out the FSG3 flowers for Dane's anniversary. We'd all put the money up, and he'd get really nice flowers. Then we'd all meet up and have a bit of a cry before we joined Dane's mates from back home and went to his graveside. Everyone who wanted to would say a few words, and then Mac would sing a few Fijian songs and we'd all join in. We still get together on Dane's anniversary, but now Dan's gone I organise the flowers. The trouble is, I can't find the big, chunky white ones that Dan used to get, which is disappointing.'

As often happens in such cases, many of Dan's friends were at first angry with him for having done what he did. But with the passing of time, they came to realise that their comrade had been in mental agony. As Paul Liddy puts it, 'I know now that he must have been going through so much, and in the end he was very brave to do what he did. Now we understand. Lately, I've been reliving it all over again. It has been tough. But I'm slowly sorting things out, and I'm a lot better than I was two months ago. Debby [*Dane Elson's mother*] has been looking after me, and I've got family in Cardiff who help.

'It's not really my place to say what I think about Afghan. But I can't understand why we're pulling out now, because what did the people who died out there die for? We all put so much into making it a safer place for the locals, and when we pull out, the country's going to go back to square one.'

CORPORAL CHANNING DAY
3rd MEDICAL REGIMENT ROYAL ARMY MEDICAL CORPS
MARCH 12, 1987 – OCTOBER 24, 2012

CORPORAL CHANNING DAY was a rare thing in a company of elite Royal Marines on a combat mission: a woman.

But the pretty and diminutive medic had been specially picked for her skills and courage – both well-proven during a previous tour of Afghanistan. In 2009, under fire, she had saved the life of a young soldier who had had a leg blown off by an IED. Scots Guards LCpl Jack Ritchie had been blown ten feet in the air and peppered with shrapnel. He would certainly have died without prompt medical attention, and Channing Day gave him that attention, despite the grave threat to her own life. As a result, the young guardsman not only lived but was back walking on a prosthetic limb inside three months, and was soon asking to go back to the front line.

It was that sort of fearless and decisive action which made Channing, a Combat Medical Technician Class One, a popular member of the C Coy 40 Cdo Transition Support Unit at Nahr-e Saraj.

'She gave us the confidence to go out on patrol,' said one of the marines. 'You knew that if things got a bit cheeky Channing would be straight there. You can't overstate the importance of that, it's a tremendous comfort to the lads.'

They loved her cheerful attitude and willingness to muck in in the insalubrious surroundings of the patrol base, too. That was no surprise to those who knew her – Channing was a tremendously gutsy and determined young woman, whose broad smile seemed almost permanent.

Sgt Jody Mardling met Channing in 2011, when they were both attached to 21 Engineer Regiment. 'Channing had a room on the base,' said Sgt Mardling, 'and I had a married quarter outside. I'd got to know her a little bit when we'd been out for a few drinks, and I liked her, so I asked her if she'd like to come to my place for tea. So she came around, and I never got rid of her after that! She arrived in my life at just the right moment. I'd been going through a bad time in a relationship, and Channing helped me through it. She gave me a new lease on life by helping me to feel better about myself.

'Like most people, I remember her smile and her laugh and her little Irish accent. Channing had just passed her driving test – although I don't know how she did it – and we'd go off for adventures together. She was a nightmare behind the wheel. She had the smallest car in the world, and she *still* couldn't park it. She didn't like overtaking, and I remember once that she was so scared as she overtook a car in the fast lane that she actually closed her eyes. I remember shouting at her, "For goodness' sake, open your eyes, Channing!"

'But she was wonderful. She used to look after my little girl, Megan, and Megan adored her. She was just full of life, and so joyful. She never had a bad word to say about anybody, and everyone loved her. She was a true friend, bless her.'

The two women deployed to Afghanistan a few weeks apart. Sgt Mardling was based at Camp Bastion, and when the young medic flew in they spent what time they could catching up in the NAAFI. 'She was very busy with training,' said Mardling. 'We chatted about going off on a little holiday together when we both got back, and we were going over to see her family in Northern Ireland. We had lots of plans. But we never spoke about the risks. Now I look back and think, *Why didn't we talk about that?* The only thing she was worried about was not being as fit as the marines. There was no danger of that.'

* * *

CHANNING WAS THE SECOND of four children born to Rosemary and Leslie Day.

Lauren, twenty-nine, is a geography teacher in Liverpool; Laken is twenty-five, and works in a nursing home; Aaron is twenty-four and a car valeter.

'Leslie and I met when he was in the Army, based at Kinnegar, near here,' said Rosemary, a part-time school cleaner who lives in Comber, County Down. 'We met at a party on December 28, 1985, and we got married six months later. My mum nearly had a fit, right enough. Leslie liked a drink in those days, and she thought we should have waited longer. "It'll never last a year," she said. But we're still together. We wanted to have our children close together, and I'm glad we did. It made us all close as a family. Channing emerged after sixteen-and-a-half hours of labour, and from the day she was born she sucked her index finger on her left hand. It was always in her mouth, and she never truly lost this habit. Even when she was grown-up I would sometimes see her with her finger in her mouth, particularly if she was sleeping or a bit stressed.

'Unlike her big sister, she was reluctant to start crawling and doing all the other things infants get up to. In fact, we thought something might be wrong with her, because all she did was sleep and eat. She was no bother at all, but she was stuck to me permanently. She was very shy and didn't talk much for a long time. And when she did, only Lauren could understand her, though I had no idea how. It was almost as if they had their own language. I'd say, "Lauren, why is she crying?" Back would come the reply, "She wants a drink and a biscuit, mum."

'Channing went to school when she was just four. She was still very quiet, and very shy. She took a while to adjust. For quite a long time, I had to take her to the door and make sure she had her coat and bag off. As she walked in, she'd turn and wave at me and say goodbye, and then, just before she disappeared, she'd turn around, wave again and shout "Bye!" She was that type of child. She never pushed herself forward, she felt better at the back of a crowd.

'She was never cheeky at school, and never used bad language. I wouldn't have allowed any of the children to say even mildly bad words, and they certainly wouldn't have been able to take the Lord's name in vain. One day, Channing came home from school and said to me, "I must be the only one at school who isn't allowed to say B.I.T.C.H." In fact, I never heard her swear until she came home on leave from the Army in the early days. We were shopping in Belfast, and she tripped over a paving stone. I heard her say, "Sh…!" and she just stopped before she said it. I said to her, "I beg your pardon! Just because you're in the Army it doesn't mean you can swear when you're at home, young lady!"

'She was always smiling, and was she was very loveable, but as she got a wee bit bigger she developed a temper. Channing liked to win at everything. She had to be first, and if she wasn't she got very upset. We used to laugh because she'd stamp her little feet on the ground like a rabbit. We couldn't stop laughing when she did that, which of course just made her angrier.

'The other thing about her was she slept as much as she could, and she could snore for Northern Ireland. The three girls had a big attic room and Aaron was below them in another room. The other girls would say, "You have to get to bed before Channing does, and then get to sleep, because otherwise you'll never get any peace." When she joined the Girls' Brigade and went camping, the others wouldn't share a tent with her because of her snoring. It was the same in the Army. They were on exercise somewhere and a load of girls were sharing a room. They all went to bed, but the next morning Channing awoke with a start and found the room empty. She assumed she'd slept through the alarm, but when she opened the door the corridor was full of all the other girls, lying in their sleeping bags. None of them could sleep thanks to her snoring, so they'd left her to it. She had her adenoids and tonsils out but it didn't help.'

Channing channelled her will-to-win into sport from a very early age, becoming Northern Ireland gymnastics pairs champion. As a youngster, she played alongside boys in her school football team, and then she discovered ice hockey.

'She came to that through Aaron,' said Rosemary. 'He had an attention deficit problem when he was a little boy, so sport was a way to burn off his energy. He got involved in ice hockey and we went to watch him playing one evening. Channing was impressed, and afterwards she said, "Mum, can I have a go?"

'Of course, she loved it, so we ended up having to buy another set of ice hockey kit, which was really expensive. But she was so good that she ended up playing with the boys, and represented Northern Ireland. She played in defence and always got stuck in. This is despite being a tiny girl – when she went to her secondary school, Strangford College, we had to have a blazer specially made for her because we couldn't find one to fit.'

Channing had mapped out her career path early on. Her father Leslie had been in the Royal Pioneer Corps, and had transferred to the Ulster Defence Regiment so that Rosemary could be near her family in Northern Ireland. Channing grew up with her dad's kit hanging around the house in Comber.

'She wanted to be in the Army almost from the moment she could walk,' said Rosemary. 'She'd often put on her dad's beret and march around the house. I'd say to Leslie, "Look at your woman there!" There was a May Fair every year at school, and the Cadets were always looking for recruits. She was absolutely desperate to join. Every year, she'd pester the guy representing the cadets. "Am I old enough to join, yet? Am I?" And he'd say, "No, not yet. You have to be at least thirteen."

'This went on for a few years, and by the time she got to twelve he was fed up listening to her. "Can I not, can I *not* go to Cadets yet?" He gave in and let her join, but he said she couldn't wear a uniform or go on exercises until she was thirteen. That was good enough, though.'

While she was in the Cadets, Channing had the chance to travel to England to compete in a triathlon.

'She phoned me when she got there,' said Rosemary. 'She told me that one of the adults hosting the Cadets had said she didn't have much of a chance, what with her height. I thought, *Mate, you've just waved a red rag at a bull.* And, sure enough, Channing phoned me later to say that she had won the gold medal.'

At that stage, her dream was to join the Royal Engineers. But nature was against her. 'As soon as she was sixteen, she went to Palace Barracks to talk about joining up, but they said she was two centimetres too short for the Royal Engineers. She came home in floods of tears. "I'm going to wait a while," she said, "and see if I can grow a bit more." She spent the next year working hard at a hairdressers' and helping in the kitchen at a care home, saving every penny she could. In her free time, she worked out at the gym, stretched, and ran. She did everything possible to grow that bit more. But when she went back to Palace Barracks, seventeen by this time, they measured her and she hadn't grown at all.

'She came home and stomped upstairs, and I knew it hadn't gone well. I went up to see her and found her lying sobbing on her bed. I said, "Look, it's not the end of the world. Let's see what other units you can join." She had a list of them, and one was the Royal Army Medical Corps. She said, "I hadn't thought about that. But I don't want to be stuck in a hospital." I said, "You don't need to be stuck in a hospital. You could be a medic."

'"Well," she said. "That would be okay." So she went back to the recruiters, told them she was interested in becoming battlefield medic and they accepted her.'

* * *

THAT WAS IN 2005. Channing was hugely enthusiastic about starting her training, her mum less so.

'I was nearly frantic with worry,' said Rosemary. 'How was she going to get onto the plane in Belfast and then find her way to the training camp in England? I asked Leslie to fly over with her and see her onto the bus taking the recruits to Winchester. Of course, when it came to getting on the bus, Channing didn't want the others to know her daddy had come with her, so she said, "Right, dad. You stay here out of the way."

'So he watched from a distance, giving me a running commentary on the phone. He said, "She's all right. She's standing there and another couple of kids have arrived." And then he said, "Oh, I've had the nod from Channing. She's okay. I can go now." So then he flew all the way back home.'

Channing sailed through training, and passed out before her family knew it. 'She was delighted,' said Rosemary. 'In fact, we were all so happy that she'd got through it. We went over to England for her passing out parade and it was a very, very emotional day for me. Channing was a tiny figure among all these other young soldiers on the parade ground. The pride was just bursting out of me.

'She had this great smile on her face, and I knew it was what she wanted. I had to say, "Well done, Channing! We're so proud of you." And I was. We all were. But part of me was scared. This was my wee Channing, in the Army now. I remember standing there with my mother after the rest of the family had gone off to get some refreshments at the NAAFI. I said, "Mummy, it's not what I want, but it's what she wants."

'I looked around, and there was another mother in tears. The two of us looked at each other and we started laughing. Somebody said, "This is supposed to be a happy day, not one for tears!"'

The other mother was Sally Veck. Her daughter, Pte Eleanor Dlugosz, had become Channing's best friend in training. Tragically, Eleanor would be killed by an IED in Iraq in 2007. She was nineteen.

'I can remember Channing phoning me and screaming down the phone telling me that Eleanor had been killed,' said Rosemary. 'She was in an awful state. I felt terrible because she was hundreds of miles away in Germany, and I couldn't comfort her.'

Channing Day came back to the UK to go to Eleanor Dlugosz's funeral; five years later, Sally Veck would attend Channing Day's repatriation ceremony.

As always, the hard work started after basic training. 'She had course after course,' said Rosemary. 'After she died, they sent us all of these boxes, which were full of notes and textbooks. She must have worked so hard. She took to the Medical Corps well, but she had her doubts about some aspects of it. She was once asked to help in an operating theatre, but she didn't really enjoy that. Nevertheless, she knew that she would need to improve her medical qualifications if she wanted a similar career one day in civilian life. So she told us she was starting to think about training to be a nurse. I said, "Channing, that's entirely up to you." But in the back of my mind I was thinking, *I don't think you want to go to university, which you'd need to do, because that's not who you are. But I'll let make your own decisions and we'll see where it goes.*

'She didn't have good enough GCSE maths to take up nursing, so she decided to take night classes and then sit the GCSE again. She did that for a year and sat the exam but was still just one point away from the grade that she needed. Had she passed, she'd probably have started nursing training in the Army, and then she wouldn't have gone to Afghanistan.'

Instead, Channing changed tack and decided to train as a paramedic. It meant not only better training for the battlefield, but also that she might find a position in the civilian world – not that she was planning to leave the Army any time soon. She was loving both the service and the camaraderie, and was now playing football and rugby for the Army women's teams, and had qualified as an Army ski instructor.

When she was twenty, she was deployed to Iraq. Leslie and Rosemary Day had discussed the likelihood of their precious daughter travelling to some very dangerous places, but it still came as a blow.

'She had a boyfriend in the Medical Corps at that time and I thought, *He'll be with her and he'll look after her,'* said Rosemary. 'That made me feel a little better. She just couldn't wait to get to Iraq. She said, "What's the point of all the training if you can't use it?" She didn't worry about it at all.

'She had leave before her deployment to Iraq, and both deployments to Afghan, and it was always lovely to have her home. But when it was time for her to go, I could never go with her to the airport, because I'd get too upset. Channing preferred to say goodbye at the house. She said, "If you start crying, then I will too, and I don't want to be getting on the plane with my mascara running down my face." So we would always say goodbye here at home, and her dad would take to the airport.

'Channing didn't write many blueys. She wrote once to us from Iraq, but she preferred to phone us, and later she kept in touch using Facebook. We would talk a lot, and she played down the dangers and the challenges. If I told her I was worried, she'd say, "Oh mum! I'm fine, I'm fine!"

'Anyway, Iraq passed safely enough, but soon she was off again, this time to Afghan. I didn't know what to expect, but I remember being worried about the flight from Brize Norton to Afghan, and what I imagined to be this long and dangerous road trip to Camp Bastion. When I told her this she laughed, and said, "Mum, the plane lands *at* Bastion!"'

It was on that first deployment to Afghanistan that Channing Day saw serious action – including the incident involving LCpl Ritchie.

'She rarely talked about her work at home,' said Rosemary. 'When she was on leave, she was fun Channing, the shopping and the dressing-up Channing, the going-out-and-dancing-into-the-early-hours Channing. She was very like her dad, in that she seemed able to put unpleasant things in a little compartment. But I knew there was something worrying her after that first Afghan tour. She'd go out clubbing with her mates, and would have a wee bit more drink then was normal for her, and there'd be a few tears through the drink.

'I asked her once if there was anything worrying her. She said, "When people say I'm lucky going over there and doing what I do, they don't understand that the guys who've been killed or wounded are your mates. Sometimes you have to pick pieces of your mates up off the ground." I think she may have suffered from a wee bit of PTSD, but she'd concentrate on the next course she had to do, or on her sports.'

An odd fact of life for soldiers on deployment to Afghanistan was that the prosaic and humdrum real world back home carried on just as it ever had. One moment, you're literally fighting for your life; the next, you're chatting to your mum about something funny the next door neighbour has said. In Channing Day's case, on her first tour, she was coming back from huge contacts with the Taliban, wiping the blood, sweat and dust off her face, and then getting on the internet to buy her first house.

'To be more accurate, we did it for her,' said Rosemary. 'I'm not sure I agreed to do it, but somehow off we went to have a look at a few places. She made an offer on one and it was accepted. "Happy days!" she said. "Now, I'm sure you can deal with it, mum."

'So she gave me power of attorney, and off she tootled to Afghan, leaving me to deal with the estate agents, and the bank, and the solicitor. The impressive thing was that she had the deposit in place. Channing was smart with money. She had no problem getting a mortgage. Just before she came home from Afghan, she phoned us and said, "Mum, the house needs painting and I'm going to have a house-warming party when I get back. Could you do it for me? You send me the paint charts, I'll pick what colours I like, then you and dad can paint it."

'So, like two idiots, Leslie and I worked on this, and we were still working at it at two o'clock in the morning the night before her party. I was thinking, *How did we manage to get into this situation?*

'She took a look, and said, "Doesn't my wee place look lovely! But I think the kitchen needs a coat of paint, too. I'll help you, it won't take us long."

'So we did that, and on the night of the house-warming it was looking really nice. After a while, though, Channing was well on her way to being steaming. I heard her say to Leslie, "Dad, give me that bottle of champagne."

'I said, "I know what you're going to do."

'"No mum, I'm not!" she said.

'But she took the bottle, shook it and opened it. Of course, champagne went all over the newly-painted walls! It was a great night though, and a lovely way to celebrate her return from that first tour of Afghan.'

Sadly, Channing never really got the chance to live in her own little house.

'She used it when she was on leave, to have her friends around for a drink or for a DVD night,' said Rosemary. 'She stayed in it one night, but at one o'clock in the morning her dad's mobile rang. "Dad, would you come and pick me up and bring me home, please?" So Leslie had to go and pick her up. All Channing ever had to do was say, "Daaad!" in that voice of hers, and she'd get anything she wanted from Leslie.'

The months ticked by, and then it was time for Channing to return to Afghanistan. The fast-moving, kinetic shooting war had long since given way to the terrifying unpredictability of IEDs, and Leslie and Rosemary Day were more worried than ever about their little girl.

'I had a sick feeling in the pit of my stomach that last time,' said Rosemary. 'For some reason, I don't remember much about her leaving for the other deployments. Perhaps it was because in those days I didn't know how much danger she'd be facing. But this time, it was different and I remember it very clearly. I'm sure that when she left us before I would have hugged and kissed her, and told her I loved her, but there was something more about it this time. That last hug and kiss, and her final look going out the door, will stay with me forever.

'We had a joke between the kids and me about which one of them was my "Number One". Of course, I loved them all exactly the same, but there was a particular closeness with Channing, just something special, and I wanted her to go away knowing that. So I said to her, "Channing, you're my Number One."

'She looked at me and said, "I know I'm your Number One, mum."

'She wasn't in tears. She's more like my husband, Leslie, than me, and she'd have been thinking about the job she had to do. She wanted to put her training into practice and she couldn't wait to get to get to

Afghan again. I was an emotional wreck. We spent our final half hour or so on the sofa, and Aaron took some photos of us. Channing knew that I hated having my photo taken, so she kidded me about it. "Now I'm going to put your pictures on Facebook." Of course, I would have hated that and we laughed about it. We watched the clock and when it came to two o'clock she said, "Mum, I'll have to go now."

'"I know," I said. We went into the hall and I hugged and kissed her, and I said, "No heroics, please. Just do your job and come home."

'I can still see her face at the door. We just looked at each other, and then she turned away and got into the car with Leslie to go to Belfast Airport. The door closed, and I waved through the glass. She waved back, and they left. Then Aaron came out with something I cannot forget. "Mum, you'll never see her again."

'I said, "Aaron, please don't say that."

'"Mum, I'm telling you. You shouldn't have let her go."

'I said, "Darling, I can't stop her. It's her job, and if she didn't go back to camp she would be considered AWOL. I can't keep her here. She's twenty-five years old and she's a grown-up."

'There *was* nothing I could do to stop her going. I have to remember that she wanted to go.'

It was a while after she arrived in Afghanistan before Channing got in touch with her family.

'We didn't hear very much from her at first,' said Rosemary, 'and I suppose no news was good news. Her first call was mainly to ask us to send her things for Christmas, like a Christmas hat and some fairy lights. So I did all that for her, and then she called me again to say that she was being moved to a new patrol base with the Marines, which I think was Patrol Base One. She was only there twenty-two days before she was killed.

'We kept in touch mainly by Facebook, and I have to say that the conversations were often about the guys. She'd frequently ring me around bedtime out there. She'd be relaxing, and I'd say to her, "Any nice eye-candy out there, Channing?" We'd have a laugh about which of them was nice and who she got on with well. She got on particularly well with a guy called Liam. They used to play Jenga at night.

'I'd been a bit worried about her fitting in with the Marines, but by now she was much less timid and she was quite confident. She said they were all very nice, and she just mucked in with them. I know, on the first tour of Afghan, conditions were really bad, so I assume it was more or less the same this time. On that first tour, there were no showers, so modesty went out the window and she had to go down to the river to wash.

'She didn't have a boyfriend when she was killed, but she'd had one for three years in Germany. He was a soldier, too, but they'd split up. They still had an off-on sort of relationship, and I believe she still loved him at the time she was killed. He came over for her funeral and bought pink roses for her grave. Then he went off to Afghan himself. I think he was her true love.'

Channing Day's death came during a patrol with seven men of C Coy 40 Cdo to conduct first aid and counter-IED training with the Afghan police. As they neared the village of Char Kutsa, they were fired on by two men. Cpl Day sustained a fatal wound to the chest and died, along with Royal Marine Cpl David O'Connor, twenty-seven, and a single man from Havant, Hants.

The Royal Marines returned fire, killing one of their assailants. The dead man was a drug-using Afghan policeman called Naqib, who was later said to have felt angry and slighted at having been disarmed the previous day by British troops.

* * *

'CHANNING WAS KILLED on the Wednesday,' said Rosemary Day. 'I'd heard from her the last time on the Monday. She'd phoned me, but the line was so crackly that I couldn't hear her. So I said, "Go onto Facebook and we'll chat there. At least that way we'll be able to understand each other." So we exchanged messages for a while on Facebook.

'She said she'd been on night stag. "It was a bit cold but it was brill," she said. We chatted on, and then I had to see to dinner so I put her onto Rees, her cousin, who happened to be here. He said, "I can't wait until you're home in February." Channing replied, "I can't wait to get home to see you all." Then I said dinner was nearly ready. So she said, "Okay, I'll let you go."

'I said, "Okay. Love you. Take care."

'She said, "Love you too."

'And those were the last words we said to each other.'

On the Tuesday, having heard nothing, Rosemary logged on to Facebook and waited.

'I was hoping she would come up and say "Hey mum!" as she often did. But she didn't. On Wednesday morning, I got up and wrote on her Facebook wall, "Love you Channing." But there was nothing back. I had a funeral to go to that morning, but throughout the service I was sitting there thinking about her. I came home, hoping she would have left me a message or at least "liked" my comment on Facebook. But there was nothing.

'I went to my cleaning job at the school in the afternoon, and I remember going through one set of doors and seeing two huge white feathers on the floor. We're into signs and omens and things like that, and I remember wondering if this meant anything. I've worked at the school for years but never seen anything like that. A little while later, I saw another large white feather on the floor. This bothered me, and I was still thinking about these feathers when I got home that evening. The first thing I did was go online to see if she had left me a message. There was nothing, but I left her a message saying, "Hope you're okay. It doesn't matter what time but contact me and let me know you're okay."

'I think it must have been about 6pm that evening. We'd just eaten dinner. Leslie and Aaron and I were here. Someone knocked on the door, and Leslie got up to answer it. I didn't hear the front door open, but then Leslie came back into the living room, looking as if something was going on in his mind. I said, "Leslie, what's wrong?" He didn't say anything, but went back out and opened the door. Then in came these two men. Nobody spoke. My first thought was, *Are these two policemen? Has Aaron done something wrong?*

'Nobody spoke. The two of them stood in front of the television, and Leslie stood with his hands on his head and he looked at me. I looked at him, and I thought, *Is anyone going to speak, here?*

'What I didn't realise was that Leslie knew these men from his work at the Army base [*where, having left the Army, Leslie now worked as a security guard*]. So when he saw them through the front door window, he knew why they were there, and he didn't want to open the door. They didn't have to tell him why they were here, he knew.

'I said to these men, "Are you police?" They just shook their heads. I sat for a second. The penny hadn't dropped at all. And then it did. I looked at Leslie, and I saw that his eyes had filled up, and I realised it was nothing to do with Aaron. I said, "Are you from the Army?"

'One of them said, "Yes." I said, "But she's okay? She's just been injured?" He said, "No."

'I don't remember too much after that. The shock was just too much, it was more than I could handle. Aaron was hysterical, and Leslie just stood there. What do you do in those circumstances? I was just sitting there thinking, *Is this true? Maybe they got it wrong.*

'I do remember that after the men had left Aaron said, "I told you that day not to let her go." But an hour or so later he was sitting on the stairs, crying his eyes out, and he said, "Mum, I didn't mean that." And he hugged me. He just wanted someone to blame.

'It's all a blur, but I know I thought about the other two girls and my mum. They had to know before it was on the news or Facebook. Laken was living just down the road, so getting in touch with her was not too difficult. But Lauren was teaching in Liverpool, and she was on her own. I wanted so badly to put my arms around her and tell her face-to-face, but it couldn't be. We had to tell her over the phone. And mum was in Bangor, but I persuaded her to come here.'

The Army released tributes from colleagues, obviously devastated by the terrible news.

Sgt Karl Hinton RAMC said Channing was 'a quirky Northern Irish girl who loved to play mother hen to the younger medics.' 'In my eyes she is a true hero,' he said, 'giving her own life to help injured comrades; I will never forget her, nor will any of her colleagues. Channing Day, a true legend, we will never forget.'

Corporal Kelly Pope RAMC said, 'For once I am lost for words. The loss that we are all feeling is unbearable. I am proud to have served with you, my fellow Corporal, my friend, my confidante. *In arduis fidelis.*' [*Faithful in adversity, the regimental motto.*]

Pte Bethany Gilford RAMC said, 'Meeting Channing has set the bar for any friendship I will ever have.'

LCpl Grace McLeod RAMC, said, 'Words cannot begin to describe how we are feeling right now. We have lost a dear friend and colleague, and what I would call a family member. Going to have to find a new gym and cinema buddy now, and I miss our little nights in my room drinking my famous cups of tea! We are having a massive party when we get back to the UK but gutted it's in such devastating circumstances. I am missing you so much right now and I love you to pieces. Rest in peace, Gorgeous.'

The following day, WO2 Gaz Knott, the family's Army visitor, arrived, and was able to pass on more details. For Rosemary Day, there was some small comfort in the fact that her daughter had been shot, and not killed by an IED.

'I don't know how parents cope if they know their kids have been blown to pieces,' she said. 'Her being shot was bad enough but the thought that my wee Channing had been blown up would have been terrible. Gaz and the people from 3 Medical Regiment who'd been assigned to help us were wonderful. We probably couldn't have got through it without them.'

Over in Afghanistan, Channing's friend Sgt Jody Mardling had gone out for a coffee and a chat at Camp Bastion. News had filtered back that a medic had been killed, but the ID had not yet been released and she felt sure it would not be Channing.

'Things seemed fairly normal,' she said. 'We both had access to the internet, and we'd been keeping in touch via Facebook. We heard a lot about the lads being in the thick of it, of course, but somehow I didn't think she'd be in it as well. Next morning my boss came to see me and told me she had some bad news. I thought it was about my daughter. But then she told me. I just sank to the floor in tears. I really struggled to cope. I rang my mum and rang Channing's mum, and we had a vigil service for her. The padre let us play one of Channing's favourite songs, *Take Care*, by Drake and Rihanna. I spoke about how we'd met and I said how much she meant to me. And I'd written a poem, which I put on a little cross. "In memory of my dear friend," it said. Channing was always worried that people didn't like her, but it was obvious how many people loved her and cared about her.'

In Comber, Channing's family were struggling to deal with the catastrophic news.

'It was as if a fog had come down,' said Rosemary. 'I felt above it, somehow. I kept on wondering if it was real. I couldn't sleep, eat or think properly. All I could think about was Channing, lying in a morgue on her own. This was the one time that I really needed to be with her, and it was impossible because she was in Afghan. I just wanted to get her home. The thought of my wee Channing on her own was just too hard to bear.

'The repatriation was horrendous. It was heart-breaking to stand on the tarmac and see the plane land. We all broke down. The coffins were bought off the plane, and we were able to have a little time privately with Channing. A strange thing happened at that point. My four kids have always called themselves my "ducks". When one of them came back after being away for a while, we'd always have a group cuddle and say, "The ducks are all back together again." We were standing in a room waiting for Channing's coffin, when the kids started nudging me. I said, "What's wrong?"

'One of them said, "Look at the walls."

'I looked and noticed that the wallpaper had pictures of ducks among reeds on a river. And there were three ducks on the ground, and another in flight. We all saw the significance, and we hugged. I went into that room with a heavy heart, but I left it feeling better because it seemed like Channing was there with us, saying, "It's going to be okay." I felt that all my ducks were home.'

Channing arrived back in Northern Ireland five days later. Laken, Aaron and Leslie couldn't bear to see her in the funeral home – her father telling his wife, 'Rosie, I can't, I want to remember Channing the way she was.'

'But I had to see her,' said Rosemary. 'Partly because I still didn't believe a hundred per cent that she was in that coffin. Only when I saw her could I really accept it. Lauren came in with me. Channing looked peaceful and beautiful, as if she was sleeping. I was able to hold her hand, to kiss her, to touch and to look at her and say goodbye before she was buried. To be able to spend time with her, and place things in her coffin, was so important.'

Cpl Day's funeral was held at First Comber Presbyterian Church on Thursday, November 8. It was attended by a truly staggering crowd which soared well into four figures. Rosemary Day was 'in shock', and just went through the motions.

'I don't remember who was there or who spoke to me afterwards,' she said. 'But I do know the church was full, and so was the hall. They put speakers outside for those who couldn't come inside and the streets were lined by the British Legion, the Cadets and so many ordinary well-wishers.

'We were amazed by the number of people who contacted us. We received nearly a thousand sympathy cards, from all over the world. Channing looked so pretty and young in the picture that was published in the newspapers, and I think that must have touched people. It was nice to know how much people thought of her, and how much people admired her. It gave us a good feeling.'

One of the many people who loved Channing Day was Jody Mardling. 'I'd lost my best friend,' she said, 'but it was hard to grieve out there. I worked hard to take my mind off it, and after I returned from Afghan I went over to Northern Ireland to spend a long weekend with her family. While she was alive, we'd planned that I'd do that, and I wanted to do it even if she couldn't be there. It was good to be with people who understood the way I felt. I met Channing's other friends who she'd spoken about, and I learned that she'd talked about me to them too, which was lovely.

'On the anniversary of Channing's death, I did a tandem sky dive in her memory, raising money for Combat Stress. I felt, all that way up in the air, that I was close to Channing again, and she was with me as we descended. That day, I felt she'd helped me to accept what had happened.

'I would always be reluctant to take chances on things before, but now I'm more likely to do that, because I know life is short. I don't want to think about any what-ifs when I'm older. Channing left me that message. I have so many memories of her, and all of them are good. Everything about her was fun and laughter. I'd talk about everything to her and she wouldn't judge me. There's so many things I still want to talk to her about. In my house I've got this picture board with lots of pictures of me and her. I set up a Facebook page in her honour, and I express myself a lot on that. But still, sometimes I get a little down and I miss her. I just want to pick up the phone and speak to her.'

Of course, a friend's grief, no matter how profound, is a fraction of a mother's. For Rosemary Day, two years on, the fog has only just begun to lift a little.

'I cry at the drop of a hat,' she said. 'Sometimes at work, I'll go into an empty room to get away from people and cry. I always said that if anything happened to any of my kids, I would not be able to go on living, so now I feel guilty that I *am* going on with life. But I'm doing it for my other children, and my mother and Leslie. I have to try to go on for them.

'I just feel dead inside. I used to be a really happy-go-lucky person. I liked to sing and dance and go out and have a few drinks with my friends. But now I come home from work, and all I want to do is go to bed. I get up in the mornings, and I do what I have to do. I'm only existing. I don't know if I'll ever be right again.

'I think some people are bound to see me crying and think, *Rosie, it's eighteen months or more down the line, now*. Of course, no-one would say that. But who wants to be looking at somebody who cries all the time? I'm not the only person who's lost a child, I suppose.

'I just wish we'd never had to go to Afghanistan. I don't think it was our fight, really. But they went, and Channing had to do her job. Did she do any good there? Who knows? I hope she did some good. She taught the Afghan police about first aid, so I like to think that some lives might have been saved through the knowledge that she shared.

'People loved Channing. She had a great outlook on life. The pallbearers from her regiment who were at the repatriation and the funeral were all her soldiers, and they said Channing was a great boss. When they went out on the weekend, she taught them how to dance, and when they went back to work she was back to being their corporal.

'It's hard for the family to talk about Channing together. Leslie, Lauren and Laken have different ways of coping. Aaron and I, though, like to talk to each other about Channing. I get a lot of comfort from Aaron, because his emotions are quite like my own. We can talk and laugh, and then we both cry.

'She was just a good person. I'm proud that I had such a lovely daughter.'

GLOSSARY OF TERMS

AFC: Army Foundation College (at Harrogate).

AK47: The main assault rifle employed by Taliban fighters. Backed up by the **RPK**, a light machine gun based on the same principles.

ANA: Afghan National Army. Some 250,000 men, equipped largely by the USA and trained by British and other NATO forces operating as OMLTs (see below). Basic unit is the kandak, a battalion consisting of six hundred soldiers. Vary widely in capability, from extremely courageous and well-drilled troops to near-rabble plagued by desertion, insubordination and criminality.

ANP: Afghan National Police. Nationwide police force of Afghanistan, some 160,000 strong. Equipped largely by the USA and trained by civilian and military police from Britain and other allied nations. Plagued early on by allegations of corruption and drug abuse, and believed to contain significant numbers of Taliban 'double agents'.

Apache: Boeing AH-64, the world's leading attack helicopter. Operated by US and British forces. Features sophisticated target acquisition and night vision systems, and carries 30mm chain gun and mixture of Hellfire missiles and Hydra rockets. Used to support troops-in-contact or as a stand-alone weapon to destroy IED gangs or other Taliban fighters.

AT/ATO: Ammunition Technician/Ammunition Technical Officer. Bomb disposal soldier or officer.

Battalion: British Army infantry regiments are divided into numbered battalions, 'Bn', (eg 3 Para, the third battalion of the Parachute Regiment) numbering around 650 soldiers. Battalions are commanded by a lieutenant-colonel, and are further divided into **companies** (Coy) – usually a headquarters company, a support company, and three rifle companies. Companies generally contain some 120 soldiers, are commanded by a major, and are named A Coy, B Coy and C Coy. Companies are further divided into **platoons** of approximately thirty soldiers, under the command of a captain or lieutenant, made up of several **sections** generally of eight, under the command of a corporal. Some will be specialists in signals, mortar fire, fire support, or anti-tank warfare. These bring heavier firepower or other skills and expertise to the battlefield, in support of the general infantry soldier.

Bdr: Bombardier – rank equivalent to corporal in the Royal Artillery and Royal Horse Artillery. (Lance-Bombardier, or LBdr, is equivalent to lance-corporal.)

415

Bergen: British military rucksack.

Black Hawk: Sikorsky UH-60 Black Hawk medium-lift utility helicopter operated by US forces. Used for casualty evacuation, and movement of small numbers of troops (up to eleven) or supplies.

Boomerang: A device which uses passive acoustic detection and computer software to process and announce in under one second the location from which incoming small arms rounds are fired.

Casevac: Casualty evacuation.

Catterick: Infantry Training Centre (ITC), where the Army's infantry recruits undergo initial training.

CCF: Combined Cadet Force. A school-based cadet programme.

Chinook: Boeing CH-47 twin-engine, two rotor heavy-lift helicopter. Used for troop movement, artillery placement, battlefield resupply, and casualty evacuation. Maximum take-off weight twenty-two tonnes. Top speed of 170 kts (almost 200mph).

CIMIC: Troops engaged in civilian and military co-operation – they report to the military commander of a given area, but liaise closely with the civilian population and non-military actors to expedite humanitarian assistance and the development of civilian infrastructure, winning 'hearts and minds' in the process.

CLP: Combat Logistic Patrol. A patrol undertaken to deliver ammunition, food and other supplies to an outlying base.

CMT: Combat Medical Technician. Army medic attached to fighting patrols. Undergoes thirty weeks of specialist medical training.

CO: Commanding officer of a battalion or above. Below that unit size, **OC** (officer commanding) is used.

Cobra: Bell AH-1 single engine attack helicopter. Largely phased out and replaced by Apache, though some still in operation in Afghanistan. Remains the US Marine Corps' main attack helicopter.

Dicker: A term derived from British military involvement in Northern Ireland which describes unarmed and ostensibly non-combatant enemy observers who pass on details of troop locations, strengths and movements to enemy forces.

EOD: Explosive Ordnance Disposal (bomb disposal).

FOB: Forward Operating Base, a secured forward military position used to support patrolling and ground-holding operations. Large FOBs may cover many square miles, but most are much smaller. Often sited in existing residential compounds, with additional 'sangars' (watch towers) and HESCO Bastion (mesh bags filled with earth and rubble) walls. Distinct from Patrol Bases (**PBs**) and Observation Posts (**OPs**) At height of Operation **Herrick**, British forces operated well over a hundred FOBs and PBs.

Full screw: British Army slang for corporal.

Fus: Fusilier – a private soldier in the Royal Regiment of Fusiliers.

GPMG: General-purpose machine gun. A medium weapon which fires the 7.62mm calibre standard NATO round. Distinct from **Minimi,** a light machine gun manufactured by Fabrique Nationale (FN) in Belgium which fires belt-fed 5.56mm standard NATO rounds, and the.50 cal, NATO's main heavy machine gun, designed during WWI by Browning and still in service. It fires the 12.7×99mm (or 0.5 inch calibre) NATO round and offers devastating firepower.

Herrick: Operation Herrick is the codename under which British operations in Afghanistan have been conducted since 2002. The US equivalent is Operation Enduring Freedom.

IED: Improvised Explosive Device. Home-made bombs buried just under the surface of roads and tracks, triggered by remote control or pressure plate.

ISAF: The multi-national International Security Assistance Force established by the UN Security Council in 2001 to train the Afghan forces and help fight insurgents.

Jackal: An open-top armoured light patrol vehicle, designed as the successor to the **WMIK**. It weighs seven tonnes, is over five metres in length, and can reach 49mph off-road and 80mph on the road. It carries a three-man crew and a.**50 cal** heavy machine gun, or a grenade launcher, and a 7.62 mm **GPMG**.

Lance-jack: British Army slang for lance-corporal.

Leopard: A sixty-two tonne German-built main battle tank operated in Afghanistan by Danish forces.

Lt: Lieutenant – the second-lowest officer rank in the British Army, above **2nd Lt** (second-lieutenant) and below **Capt** (captain). Next rank up is **Maj** (major).

Mentioned in Dispatches: A soldier who has shown particular gallantry in the face of the enemy may be mentioned in dispatches sent by his superior officer to the high command.

MERT: Medical Emergency Response Team. Usually based on a Chinook, this medical team flies into the heart of a battle zone to collect casualties and evacuate them. Significant equipment aboard to enable treatment in-flight.

NCO: Non-commissioned officer. Above private soldiers but below officers, these are the backbone of the British Army. **Cpl** Corporals usually have six years' experience. Command a section, with **LCpl** (lance-corporal) as 2IC (second-in-command). **Sgt/Sjt** Sergeants – in some regiments serjeants – usually have at least twelve years' service and are 2IC of a platoon. Responsible for advising and assisting junior officers who may have far less experience. **CSgt** Colour Sergeant or **SSgt** Staff Sergeant is a senior man-management role at the company level. **CSM/WO2** Company or Squadron Sergeant Major/ Warrant Officer Class 2 – the eyes and ears of their company commander. **RSM/WO1** Regimental Sergeant Major/Warrant Officer Class 1 – performs the same role at a regimental level. The most senior NCOs in the Army.

NVG: Night vision goggles. Gave British troops a major edge while fighting after dark.

OMLT: Operational Mentoring and Liaison Team. Small unit of British soldiers, often no more than six or seven-strong, living and working alongside much bigger Afghan National Army force to train them. Known colloquially as an 'Omelette'.

OTC: Officer Training Corps at university.

Pinzgauer: High-mobility, lightly-armoured, all-terrain utility vehicle manufactured by BAE Systems in 4x4 and 6x6 wheel-drive variants. Capable of carrying section-plus, but criticised for vulnerability to IEDs and heavy weapons.

Pte: Private, or 'Tom' (for 'Tommy Atkins', nickname for soldiers in use since 1700s).

QRF: Quick Reaction Force. Reserve force held back at FOB or PB in order to respond to support or rescue troops out on the ground, should the need arise.

RLC: Royal Logistic Corps.

RPG: Rocket-propelled grenade.

Scimitar: An elderly tracked armoured vehicle, weighing nearly eight tonnes and having a top speed of 50mph. Introduced in 1971, it was originally intended for use in reconnaissance, but was sometimes employed in a fire support role in Afghanistan, where its 30mm RARDEN cannon proved very effective.

'Snatch' Land Rover: A lightly-armoured patrol vehicle based on the Land

Rover Defender. Developed for use in Northern Ireland in the 1990s, it provides some protection from small arms fire but has been criticised for its vulnerability to more powerful weapons, particularly IEDs.

Stag: British military slang for sentry duty.

T1: One of four triage categories applied by the British military to assess casualties. T1 refers to a soldier with life-threatening injuries, likely to die without rapid intervention, and requiring immediate casevac. **T2** ('urgent') are casualties whose injuries may be life-threatening if treatment is delayed. **T3** ('delayed') are those who can wait for casevac without serious risk. **T4** ('expectant') are soldiers who are dead or likely to die even with optimal treatment.

Task Force Helmand: The military arm of ISAF in Helmand. Established in April 2006, with Operation Herrick 4, and disbanded in 2014, its responsibilities devolved to Regional Command Southwest, an international ISAF group mainly comprising units of the US Marine Corps.

UAV: Unmanned Aerial Vehicle – a surveillance drone.

Vallon man: Operator of the Vallon mine-detector.

Warrior: A British armoured fighting vehicle weighing twenty-five tonnes and armed with a 30mm RARDEN cannon, armour piercing rockets and a 7.62mm chain gun. Carries a crew of three and seven infantrymen at off-road speeds of 30mph.

WMIK: Weapons Mounted Installation Kit Land Rover. Based on WWII SAS vehicles, and designed for reconnaissance missions or hit-and-run attacks on enemy forces, the WMIK is a stripped-down Defender XD 'Wolf' equipped with a roll bar and mountings for machine guns and other weapons.

Zap number: An identification code, made up of the first two letters of a serviceman or woman's surname and the last four digits of their service number, used to identify personnel via insecure channels.

NOTES

[1] Martha is a board member of The Captain James Philippson Trust Fund, a charity set up in his name. On the charity's website, at http://www.captainjim.org/, she thanks James for showing her 'how to live life to the full, to get off the sofa and not waste a minute of the day'. 'I feel privileged that I had the chance to be with him and get to know his family,' she says. 'Positivity, a glass-half-full attitude was James' outlook on life and I try to live by that day-to-day.'

[2] Camp Bastion, Britain's largest military base in Afghanistan, was built north west of Lashkar Gah, the capital of Helmand, in 2006. A supply and logistics hub which supported the troops dispersed at various Forward Operating Bases around the country, it was originally intended to accommodate 2,000 personnel. In a graphic demonstration of the way in which Operation Herrick grew, it would eventually house 28,000, and a perimeter fence some forty kilometres long would encircle an area the size of Reading. In many ways it resembled a small English town, too, with its own fire station, hospital, Pizza Hut and police force (police officers with speed cameras lurked behind tents and shipping containers, enforcing the 15mph limit – three tickets meant a ban, much as it does back home). But the hundreds of aircraft movements, and the heavily-armed convoys which trundled in and out of the main gates on most days, left little room for doubt as to its essential purpose.

[3] The Kajaki Dam also provided, and continues to provide, a powerful example of the difficulty involved in developing the infrastructure of a country like Afghanistan. The Soviet invasion in 1979, and the subsequent occupation, brought the project to a premature end, with only two of three intended turbines installed. In 2008, an ambitious plan was conceived to transport the remaining turbine to the site to increase its generating capacity, and this task was duly completed, at vast expense. Thousands of British soldiers shepherded the giant machinery through the foothills, and a large number of insurgents were killed attempting to disrupt the operation. Since then, the turbine has been left sitting in its packaging, unassembled and unused, coalition forces being unwilling or unable to transport the estimated 1,000 tonnes of cement needed to bed it in place.

[4] Adjutant Joël Gazeau and Senior Corporal David Poulain were members of the elite Premiere Régiment de Parachutistes d'Infanterie de Marine. On May 20, their twenty-vehicle convoy was ambushed on Route 611, which links Gereshk in the south of Helmand to Musa Qala in the north, and

which passes through Sangin. The two soldiers were captured and tortured to death – tied up and gutted alive, their genitals and noses sliced off.

Route 611 was considered by many to be the most dangerous and blood-spattered road in the whole country; over the years that followed, it would be littered with the rusting wrecks of civilian vehicles whose drivers had fallen victim to IEDs.

[5] Task Force Helmand was the name given to the ISAF command operation in Helmand. It was established in April 2006 for Op Herrick 4.

[6] Two months after this incident, Lt Illingworth would find himself charging a Taliban machine gun position at Garmsir, as people fell all around him. It was an action for which he would be awarded the Conspicuous Gallantry Cross, Britain's second highest award for bravery. He tells his story in the Monday Books title *In Foreign Fields*, which focuses on the stories of twenty medal-winning soldiers, Royal Marines and RAF men from Iraq and Afghanistan.

He arrived late to the incident in which James Philippson was killed, after his vehicle's axle became entangled in the wire as they raced out of the FOB Robinson. He helped extract Capt Philippson's body, and later reflected on his friend's death. 'Obviously, once you get a moment, you think about Jim,' he said. 'He was only twenty-nine years old, a really great guy in the absolute prime of his life, and his death was a tragedy. I think for me, it was mostly the shock of how quickly everything had happened. It brought home the fragility of life. He was buried while we were still in Afghanistan, and we had a memorial service up in Sangin on the day of his funeral. We all got together, had some whisky and said a prayer, which was our way of saying farewell. The Afghans who'd worked with Jim... they see death very differently to us, but they were clearly very sorry that he had died, and they consoled us, but they also saw it as a matter of pride that he had died for their country. Mixed in with that, I think there was some guilt, the sense that it should have been one of them.'

[7] The Paras were also fighting hard in Now Zad, Musa Qala, and Gereshk. During the tour they would be involved in more than five hundred contacts, and would fire some 13,000 rounds of mortar and artillery shells. Soldiers sometimes found themselves under fire for twenty-four hours at a time; when they could snatch sleep it was for an hour or two at the most, and it was taken in body armour and helmets. One company was involved in firefights on thirty-one of thirty-five days, in combat of an intensity unseen since Korea.

[8] LCpl Hartley was later awarded the George Medal for his astonishing and selfless actions. Fus Andy Barlow received the same medal. Cpl Stu Pearson was awarded the Queen's Gallantry Medal.

[9] Pte O'Donnell was twenty-four, and originally from Clydebank, Dunbartonshire. A fan of Celtic FC and the rock band Queen, and a very popular soldier, his girlfriend was expecting their first child that coming Christmas. He was killed by a suicide bomber in Kabul.

LCpl Muirhead was twenty-eight and a single man from Bearley, in Warwickshire. He was injured in a mortar attack on the hotly-contested DC at Musa Qala, though he lived on for five days, long enough to die in his mother's arms after she flew out to Afghanistan to be with him.

Rgr Draiva was hit by the same bomb, but died immediately. He was twenty-seven, and one of many Fijians in the British Army. He was both the first Royal Irish Ranger to die in Helmand, and the first Fijian; deaths among his countrymen on Operation Herrick would eventually enter double figures.

LCpl McCulloch, originally from Cape Town, was just twenty-one, but had already served with distinction in Northern Ireland and Iraq. Known for his beaming smile and ability to laugh at himself, he also died in a mortar attack on the DC.

[10] *Monty And Tyler Take The High Road*, by Des Feely, is published by Margon Press. Proceeds from the sale of the book are donated to several charities supporting war veteran casualties and their families.

[11] This was a classic Taliban tactic. When an IED was detonated, gunmen would appear and, in the ensuing chaos, attempt to pick off the injured and their rescuers, particularly any MERT helicopter which might appear.

Cleverly, some British troops used this predictability against the enemy. For instance, in 2010, a section of Grenadier Guards deliberately set off their own explosives, to give the impression that they had been struck by an IED. As expected, a group of Taliban, including a two-man sniper team, quickly appeared on the scene, eager to take advantage.

Unfortunately for them, the Guards were waiting with their own snipers, and a heavily armed FSG team. As the insurgents came forward, they were cut down and ten were killed.

[12] Some forty or fifty thousand people live in Gereshk, perhaps the key strategic location in all Helmand. The town sits astride the River Helmand, and is at the junction of Route 611 and Highway One.

Route 611 – the scene of the ambush near Sangin in May 2006 which led to the gruesome deaths of two French special forces soldiers, and many other horrific incidents – takes the brave or unwary traveller north from Gereshk, through Sangin, to Musa Qala.

Highway One is a circular, two-lane, asphalt motorway of some 2,200km which links many of Afghanistan's major cities, including Kabul, Kandahar and Lashkar Gah, and cuts through Gereshk going east to west.

Gereshk itself has seen much bitter fighting between the British and the Afghans over the years – its fort was first captured by British soldiers in the First Anglo-Afghan War (1839–1842), and taken again during the Second Anglo-Afghan War forty years later – and many British soldiers were killed or injured there during the recent conflict.

While the Taliban were repeatedly kicked out of the town, as in most areas of Helmand there were never enough ISAF troops to hold it. But not everyone was hostile, and there were periods of relative calm. In 2012, for instance, it was safe enough for British troops to take on Gereshk Cricket Club, the provincial champions, in a match at Main Operating Base Price, the ISAF base in the town. MOB Price won by seven wickets, and afterwards presented the delighted local side with two full sets of kit, including pads, bats and gloves.

[13] The Osprey Mark IV body armour is a modular system which contains a number of pouches for Kevlar plates. The ever-increasing amount of body armour worn by British troops was, to some extent, the result of the political and media fallout after the deaths in Iraq of troops who were not supplied with body armour. But some soldiers felt that it was a step too far – it was extremely heavy, it restricted mobility, and it made aiming a rifle next to impossible in some positions. 'We always felt it had been designed by someone behind a desk who had no idea of what we do,' said one soldier. 'To be honest, I thought we'd have been better off in flip-flops and pyjamas, because every time I shot at a bloke dressed like that he just seem to leg it without a scratch!'

[14] Sgt Ben Ross and Cpl Kumar Pun were killed by a suicide bomber while on patrol in Gereshk with Afghan police whom they were mentoring.

Sgt Ross, a thirty-four-year-old Royal Military Policeman, was originally from Bangor, in Wales, but grew up in Dubai. His wife, who served alongside him, said he was 'a very loving husband and a gentleman... A genuine, quiet, selfless man, who was the centre of my world.'

Cpl Pun, thirty-one, and married with two young daughters, was the son of a Gurkha. One comrade, LCpl Deepak Thapa, said, 'When I heard the shocking news that my best friend Kumar was no more in this world, I did not believe it. But it dawned on me later that I had lost my best friend forever. I was in shock, and could not control my tears. Kumar, you are my best friend, I can never forget you and you will be missed forever.'

Rfn Adrian Sheldon was twenty-five, and from Kirkby-in-Ashfield, Notts. A fan of Mansfield Town FC and a keen student of darts, he'd served on operations in Sierra Leone and Iraq, had then left the Army and worked in IT recruitment, but had rejoined. An expert machine gunner, he was killed when his Jackal vehicle was hit by an IED. He left behind his parents and a younger sister. His OC, Maj Iain Moodie, said he was a 'hugely competent' soldier. 'It was always great fun to be in his presence,' said Maj Moodie. 'No matter what the rank, a quick-fire ribbing and a big grin was always the approach from him.'

[15] Tragically, one of the men involved in that effort – Captain Mark Hale – would die that summer after being caught in an explosion. Capt Hale, a married man with two daughters, was forty-two and from Bournemouth, and 'a man of true Christian faith', said his CO, Lt Col Rob Thompson. 'Mark wasn't a fifth gear man,' he said, 'he was a sixth-gear merchant. Us mortals could rarely keep up.'

Capt Hale, who had been promoted through the ranks, died near Sangin on August 13, while on a patrol tasked with searching for IEDs. Another soldier, LBdr Matthew Hatton, was himself mortally wounded by an IED which had detonated in his face; Capt Hale and Rfn Daniel Wild rushed to help their stricken comrade, but as they helped him from the building a second device went off and all three died.

LBdr Hatton was twenty-three, and from Yorkshire. He had 'grinned like a Cheshire cat' at the news that he was going to Sangin, said his good friend, Bdr Ryan Brown. 'He was having the time of his life,' he added. 'Hatts, you will be missed but never forgotten.'

Rfn Wild – who had just celebrated his nineteenth birthday, and was from Easington in County Durham – was 'smaller than most (smaller than everyone, if I'm being honest)', said Lt Col Thompson, but he was 'a metaphorical giant... always the lead man in his patrol, facing that risk every day without complaint.'

Rfn Steve Glover was one of many who paid tribute to him. 'Rfn Wild was my best friend and my little brother,' he said. 'Wildy was one of the strongest men I've ever worked with and I feel so proud to have served alongside him. A brilliant soldier... Rest in peace, Wildy, you'll never be forgotten.'

[16] Pte Robert Laws, just eighteen, and from Bromsgrove, died when his vehicle was hit by an RPG. He had only completed his Combat Infantryman's Course in March, deploying straight to the front line near Garmsir from Catterick. Known for his mischievous sense of humour and his 'random taste in music', he was also an excellent marksman – 'Best Shot' on the light machine gun during training – and an Army swimmer. He had been planning to take his girlfriend on a romantic trip to Paris after the tour. Tpr Curtis Clifton, a childhood friend serving with The Light Dragoons,

remembered Robert as a seven-year-old. 'He was stood in the school playground by himself,' said Tpr Clifton, 'a small, shy lad reading a book. We became very good friends and did everything together.'

LCpl David Dennis of The Light Dragoons was killed as he watched the departure of the casevac Chinook carrying away Pte Laws' body and a number of injured soldiers. LCpl Dennis – who was engaged to be married – had helped to clear the landing site for the helicopter; now he stepped back and onto a hidden IED that had somehow been missed. He was from Port Talbot, and had celebrated his twenty-ninth birthday a couple of weeks earlier. He left behind a twin brother, Gareth, and a younger step-sister and step-brother. His father later told how 'The Duke' had been phoning home regularly to check on his fourteen-year-old brother's exam results, and to encourage him to revise. The only Welshman in a unit that recruits from the North East, he was 'one of the most loved guys in the regiment', said a comrade, and known for his muscles, his grin, and the Freddie Mercury moustache he'd once grown.

[17] Capt Ben 'B3' Babington-Browne, twenty-seven and from Maidstone, died with two Canadian soldiers in a helicopter crash. After starting his working life as a graphic designer, he had joined the Royal Engineers, and was a man with a bright future. He'd volunteered for Afghanistan, driven by a desire to challenge himself. His Troop Staff Sergeant, SSgt Richie Hines, said of him, 'He was not only the best Troop Commander I ever had the privilege to work with, but he was also a true friend. The nature of service on operations means that soldiers form a bond which is often stronger than that between blood relatives and I felt as though I knew Troopy, Ben, better than some of my own family, and I was proud to do so. As a friend he was supportive not only to myself but to my family. He had an ability to interact with any person, whether young or old, and would often entertain my children with his amazing sense of humour. He was the life and soul of any party and never failed to make an impact, whether with his hilarious dancing or by telling stories with his characteristic dry wit.'

Tpr 'Norm' Whiteside, twenty and from Blackpool, died in an IED blast. He had joined The Queen's Lancashire Regiment in 2005, but had been discharged after a year with a serious knee injury. As soon as it healed, he had rejoined the Army. Known as a quiet, thoughtful, and kind young man, he was a brilliant sniper spotter, 'uber fit', and an excellent fencer, who had every chance of making the GB team for the 2012 London Olympics. His sergeant, Keith Bell, said of him, 'Norm died on the battlefield doing what he loved, pushing forward, and taking it to the enemy with his mates beside him.'

[18] Cpl Carl Thomas, a Regimental Combat Medic in C Company, 2 Rifles, later talked about the moment the first bomb detonated. 'There was a bang and I saw a dust cloud over a compound which I knew a section led by Lt Horsfall

had moved into thirty seconds earlier,' he told *The Sunday Times*. 'I came around the corner and knew straight away there were mass casualties. The bomb had taken out the whole section. As the smoke cleared I saw bits of webbing, parts of weapons systems and casualties scattered around the place. One lad was killed outright. Mr Horsfall was lying against the wall and I could see straight away he was T1. He had lost a leg and badly injured his left arm. I applied tourniquets, a first field dressing and a HemCon haemostatic bandage. Mr Horsfall was not a good patient. He was fighting me, trying to hit me with his injured arm. I sorted him out.'

After getting Horsfall back to the FOB – and taking off his own body armour and putting down his rifle – the twenty-nine-year-old Liverpudlian heard the contact continuing, and ran back out to help his mates.

'In the confusion I couldn't find my body armour or helmet, and just ran out of the base back to the contact area,' he said. 'There were three enemy firing points in contact with the boys and I turned up, grabbed someone's rifle and started putting rounds down. At that point the colour sergeant gave me a massive bollocking to the effect of, "What the fuck are you doing? Get back to the base before you end up getting killed." Fair one, it wasn't my best moment. I got another bollocking off Sgt [Paul] McAleese when I got back to the base.'

McAleese, the son of former SAS trooper John McAleese MM, who took part in the famous Iranian Embassy operation in 1980 – was himself killed by a Taliban bomb along with another soldier five weeks later. Cpl Thomas was later credited with having saved the lives of thirty-five casualties during the tour, and was awarded the Queen's Gallantry Medal. Alex Horsfall later sent him a case of champagne for saving his life.

[19] Eleven did not come home from Herrick 7. The three 40 Cdo fatalities were Cpl Damian 'Big Dee' Mulvihill, Lt John 'JT' Thornton and Mne 'Crazy' Dave Marsh.

Cpl Mulvihill was a gentle giant of a man about whom no-one could say a bad word. Engaged to be married, he was thirty-two and from Plymouth. He was killed by an IED on February 20, 2008, while leading a section of men from Alpha Coy on patrol.

Lt Thornton and Mne Marsh were killed by another IED near Kajaki on March 30.

Lt Thornton was twenty-two and 'a hoofing bootneck officer' who had achieved fame partly for having worked out that a major survival exercise was taking place near his house. Using true Commando initiative, said fellow officers, he and a select few had managed to sneak off during the exercise for a shower and a barbecue! Lt Thornton kept a diary of his time in theatre; it later formed part of the book *Helmand: Diaries of Front-Line Soldiers* (Osprey).

Mne Marsh, twenty-three and from Sheffield, was married to Claire and the father of a little girl, Molly. In a tribute, Cpl Aaron 'Tiny' Winter said he was 'always smiling, whether in contact with the enemy, playing poker or smoking his pipe. The only time that his smile changed was when he spoke of his daughter, whereupon his smile would double in size and his face would beam with pride. He will be sorely missed by the Kajaki Pipe Smokers.'

[20] Cpl Stephen 'Whisky' Walker, an ex-Royal Navy chef turned Commando, had served twenty years in the Royal Marines. From Lisburn, Northern Ireland, he was married to Leona, with whom he had a daughter, Greer. He was also the proud father of a son, Samuel. Said to be the kindest of men, and an outstanding section leader, he was killed by an IED on May 21, 2010, aged forty-two.

With cruel irony, Sgt Steven 'Darbs' Darbyshire was one of those who had paid official tribute to that 'unselfish' warrior. Sgt Darbyshire was then himself shot dead on patrol in Sangin on June 23. He was thirty-five, a keen sportsman – from Wigan, he had represented the Corps at rugby league – and a great family man. WO1 Marty Pelling, 40 Cdo RSM, said of him, 'Darbs was a charismatic individual whose wonderfully dour Lancashire carapace belied a man of great humour, warmth, and camaraderie. He often spoke of his partner Kate and their two boys Ryan and Callum, and when he did so his voice was always full of pride and love.'

'He died a soldier's death,' said Alpha Coy OC Major Sean Brady, 'doing the job he loved, with the men he loved.'

Mne Adam 'Ads' Brown was the other Almas fatality. A veteran of Kajaki and Herrick 7, and the eldest of four children, he was regarded by many as the best marine at Almas, and was a constantly cheerful and positive man. He died in an IED blast on August 1, aged twenty-five. His wife and childhood sweetheart Amy said he was 'always a hero' in her eyes. 'I am so proud of you,' she said. 'I will treasure the perfect memories I have of our life together, always. You are a true inspiration to all who knew you and you made me the proudest woman in the world when I became your wife. I love you now, always and forever.'

[21] In 2010, responsibility for Sangin passed to American forces, specifically the 3rd Battalion, 7th US Marine Regiment. In that process, many of the smaller bases built up by the British during their long involvement in the town and wider area were destroyed to avoid their being used by the Taliban – Ezeray and Marshall's Post included. This did not go down well with the comrades of the 106 British soldiers and Royal Marines who had died trying to hold ground in and around the town since 2006, not least because they felt it disrespected the memory of the men like Mark Marshall after whom the bases had been named. In other cases, bases that were not destroyed

427

were renamed, causing further offence (for example, FOB Jackson, named after 3 Para Pte Damien Jackson, who died in Sangin in 2006, became FOB Sabit Qadam under the Americans). The Americans themselves finally left Sangin in 2014.

[22] Rgr Justin Cupples, a twenty-nine-year-old married man, of C (Ranger) Coy 1 R Irish, was killed in Sangin by an IED on September 4. Born in the USA, 'Cups' had served in the US Navy before moving to Ireland, where he met his wife and joined the Royal Irish. WO2 Frankie O'Connor, said of him, 'I have come to know Rgr Cupples very well over the past year. From the start I was very impressed with his polite and enthusiastic manner, coming across as a very intelligent person and a pleasure to talk to. Ranger Cupples was as strong as a horse and never let his comrades down in any situation. I will miss him greatly and I am proud to have been his Company Sergeant Major.'

[23] Royal Marine sergeant Barry 'Baz' 'Wets-on' Weston, forty, was the first. One of 42 Cdo's 'finest NCOs', originally from Reading, and married with three young daughters, he was killed on August 30, 2011, by an IED in Nahr-e Saraj. He was famous for his dry sense of humour and his love of Formula 1 racing and of pottering about in his garden shed, but most of all for his love of his family. Cpl Dearan Withall said in an official tribute, 'Baz would follow you around the checkpoint, even into the shower, and tell you how amazing his wife was, followed by some story about his girls. His devotion to them was amazing.'

Mne David Fairbrother also paid tribute to his 'hoofing Stripey'.

'His last words were spoken to me just before he died,' said Mne Fairbrother. 'And they couldn't sum up this hoofing bloke any better. He said, "Dave, nice one. Just keep those arcs to the south, push up a metre if you can't see the objective compounds."'

Tragically, Mne Fairbrother was himself killed on September 19, in a firefight in the same district, and was repatriated on the same flight as Jon McKinlay. The twenty-four year-old single marine from Blackburn had two sisters. His mother said he was 'a devoted, beautiful and giving son… I love you with all of my heart, Mum xxx.'

A graduate of Leeds University, he was known affectionately as 'ISTAR', and his deep tan and droopy moustache often led locals to take him for an interpreter, much to the amusement of his fellow marines. LCpl David Goodman summed him up as 'a legend [who] made me laugh daily.'

[24] Lt David Boyce and LCpl Richard Scanlon, both of The Queen's Dragoon Guards, died on November 17, 2011, when their Scimitar was hit by an IED in Yakchal, Nahr-e Saraj. Both men were crushed under the twenty tonne

vehicle when it was flipped onto its turret. Moments earlier, they had been 'just chatting away', said their driver, LCpl Christopher Donaldson. 'We were all in good spirits, cracking jokes. As we were going along there was just an almighty thud, followed by a loud bang. The next thing I remember, everything went black… and the next thing I knew I was upside down.'

Lt Boyce – a university friend of Lt Dan Clack – was twenty-five and from Bath. A keen skier and a member of the Army Offshore Racing Team who had sailed in the Rolex Sydney Hobart Race in 2010, he left behind his parents and a younger sister. A number of emotional tributes were paid by his men, who clearly loved him. One, Tpr Scott Halpin, said, 'He listened to his men and made sure the boys were happy. During my time in the Army he has been the best troop leader I have had. He will never be forgotten in my eyes, and he will be missed by us all. That is all I can say; he was one of a kind. You will be missed, boss.'

LCpl Scanlon, originally from Rhymney, Gwent, had celebrated his thirty-first birthday just three days earlier, and was on his second spell in the Army, having left after two tours of Iraq and then rejoined. He left his mother, step-father, father and two sisters. His many friends paid tribute to a man who was 'the life and soul of the weekend' but a highly-professional soldier when at work.

Pte Thomas Lake died three days later, when he was caught in an explosion on a reassurance patrol in Jamal Kowi, Nahr-e Saraj. 'One of the best soldiers in his platoon, liked by everyone', he was twenty-nine, from Watford, and left behind a loving mother, Carol. She said of him, 'Tom was a wonderful son, and I will miss him more than I can say. He had so many friends who will remember him as a loyal, fun-loving action man who was always the first to try anything new and usually excelled at it. Tom loved the Army and was so proud to be a soldier; he died doing something he loved and believed in. I will always be proud of my boy.'

PUBLISHER'S NOTE AND ACKNOWLEDGMENTS:

WE ARE VERY grateful to the families of those soldiers and Royal Marines who feature in this book for their support and assistance, and to many serving and former soldiers and marines for their help and encouragement.

The response from those families we contacted was overwhelmingly positive, which meant that we did not have to cast our net particularly widely.

It is an artefact of timing and chance that six of the chapters concern members of The Rifles, and three The Royal Marines, while many great and famous regiments which lost soldiers in Afghanistan are not represented, and neither is the Royal Air Force.

The story of The Rifles – the British Army's largest infantry regiment – is instructive. According to The Rifles' charity, Care for Casualties, since its formation in 2007 the regiment has lost more than sixty riflemen in action, and a further thirty have lost limbs. Two riflemen have been rendered completely blind; two are in neurological units where they will remain for the rest of their lives.

But other regiments suffered grievous losses in Afghanistan, and a number of RAF, RAF Regt and auxiliary personnel were also killed, including Senior Aircraftman Gary Thompson, who died in an explosion on April 13, 2008. SAC Thompson was a member of the Royal Auxiliary Air Force Regiment, a married father of five daughters, and, at fifty-one, the oldest Briton to die in the conflict. In the civilian world he was a successful businessman; that he should lose his life in volunteering to serve in a foreign land in the service of his country, and of the people of Afghanistan, is humbling.

We are grateful to the late Gp Capt Norman MacLeod OBE, RAF Retd, for his encouragement and assistance.

We are grateful also for the assistance of the Ministry of Defence, and in particular Charles Heath-Saunders and Lt Col Crispin Lockhart, in respect of certain chapters.

Where we use letters or emails sent home by soldiers or Royal Marines, we have replicated them exactly. Spelling and grammar can deteriorate when one has spent weeks under fire, on rations and with minimal sleep.

Interviews were recorded and transcribed. Where speech (and events) are reported, these are given to the best of the individual interviewee's recollection.

Distances and weights – except where given in speech by interviewees, in references to the Royal Marines Commando Tests, and in measurements of speed – are metric. (To help readers used to thinking in Imperial measurements, 10km is 6.2 miles; 10kg is 22lb, or 1.5st.)

Photographs in theatre are Crown Copyright.

The following charities were set up by or are supported by people featured in this book:

Care for Casualties
   Help Our Wounded Royal Marines and Supporting Arms
   The Invicta Foundation
   The William Aldridge Foundation
   The Mark Wright Project
   The Captain James Philippson Trust Fund
   Combat Stress
   Healing the Wounds
   Families' Activity Breaks (FAB)
The publisher and author will be making a donation to an appropriate charity out of the proceeds from sales.

AUTHOR'S ACKNOWLEDGMENTS

I am deeply grateful to the many people who agreed to be interviewed for this book. The following mothers, fathers, wives, husbands, siblings, children, friends and colleagues (listed here in no particular order) gave their time generously, never complaining about the often intrusive nature of my questions.

Carl Bryant
Maureen Feely
Des Feely
Krista Presch
Teresa Scully
Sue Stout
Rosaleen Reeve
Bob Reeve
Lisa McKinlay
Megan McKinlay
Valerie McKinlay
Sgt Gavin Sharrock
Cpl David Cartwright
Sgt Nick Howe
Susan Clack
Martin Clack
Cpl Hayley Reading
Helena Tym
Robin Thatcher
Becky Harrison
Gill Harrison
Martin Harrison
Russell Harrison
Cpl Terry Holland
Ann Chandler
Mike Chandler
Capt Johnny Mercer

Col Ian Bell
Lucy Aldridge
Cpt Alex Horsfall
Jenny Birdsall
Steven Birdsall
Matthew Baldwin
Nia Fortuna
Susan Fortuna
Rfn Dan Meally
Dave Hill
Angela Horn
Ian Sephton
LCpl Charlie Emina
Debby Morris
LCpl Paul Liddy
Deanna Collins
LCpl Duncan Milne
Jan Binnie
Allan Binnie
Karen Waspe
Dave Deering
Peter Waspe
Owen Atwell
Pte Scott Tombs
Maggie McCormick
Lesley McCormick
Rgr Ian McKergan

Rgr Vaughan White
Capt Neil Watson
Carol Horan
John Horan
Ann Horan
Kirsty Eustace
Margie Mooney
Danielle Mooney
Lesley Alderton
Daniel Salvage
Steve Daniels
Nicole Thangarajah
Sarah Alderton
Rosemary Day
Sgt Jodie Marling
Tony Philipson
Tricia Quinlan
David Philipson
Major Jonny Bristow
Bob Wright
Jem Wright
Tom Wright
Sgt Stuart Pearson
Sgt Stuart Hale
Al Reid

Thanks also to Grizelda Cockwell, Sheena Ross and Katrina Stephenson who transcribed some of the interviews.

Dan Collins conceived of this project and invited me to be part of it. Dan has been patient and encouraging, and, above all, he has worked hard to make it a reality.

My wife Nadia shared my view that the stories of the men and women who died in Afghanistan deserve to be more widely known. Nevertheless, she showed great patience and understanding when the work preoccupied me more than other important things in our lives. Thank you for your love and support.

Graham Bound